William Shakespeare:
A READER'S GUIDE

:

William Shakespeare:

A READER'S GUIDE

Alfred Harbage

:

OCTAGON BOOKS

A DIVISION OF HIPPOCRENE BOOKS, INC.

New York 1983

Reprinted 1971

Second Octagon printing 1978
Third Octagon printing 1980
Fourth Octagon printing 1983

OCTAGON BOOKS
A DIVISION OF HIPPOCRENE BOOKS, INC.

LIBRARY OF CONGRESS CATALOG CARD NUMBER: 74-184009
ISBN 0-88254-861-1

TO
Diana, Klara, Alfred & John

Contents

Introduction

:

M A N Y of us have observed in our travels that the best guides are often those who assert themselves least. They take us to the point where the view is best, step aside and let us look at it, assuming with a right sense of propriety that their forms are not essential to the landscape. They point out fine works in the galleries, and fine features of those works, but do not tell us how to respond. I am no huntsman, but I presume that huntsmen prefer guides who know where the game is but refrain from shooting it for them.

I aspire in this book to be a good guide, but I am not allowed to be taciturn. Making assertions is my only means of pointing, and if something strikes me as beautiful, I must say that it is so. The invitation to see may resemble an injunction to feel, the guiding may look like judging, but the intention is not to judge but only to bear witness. If the thing is not really beautiful, at least the possibility has been opened. Since discourse which is uniformly neutral is apt also to be unreadable, I must make my fallible assertions as persuasively as I can; impersonality is virtuous in a guide but dismal in a tone of voice. I believe that a guide may be warm in his testimony, providing he sticks to particulars. It is when he begins to generalize that he begins to abuse his function.

Generalization is for critics. Critics pronounce upon the nature and value of works as wholes, directly or by implication. They identify the significant, synthesize impressions, make statements designed to cover the combined effect of all particulars. Criticism is nobler than guidance but more hazardous to the reader. After a work has been discussed by many men through many generations, there exists in addition to the work, a lengthening shadow of it. This we may call its Criticism, with a capital C. It is composed of many documents, each shaped in part by the original work, in part by the other documents. It is proper that this should be so, since there would be no point in continuing the discussion if the speakers failed to listen to each other, and then to supplement and refine. From one point of view the discussion preserves the original work, keeping it in the mind's eye, proving that people still care about it. From another point of view it destroys the original work, burying it in its Criticism. Sometimes when we return to the words of the prophet after centuries of exegesis, we are a little abashed to find them so simple, lovely, and true.

My book owes much to Shakespearean criticism, and it seems churlish to say that it is intended in part to defend readers from that criticism. I am not thinking of the base simulacrum, in which great works are invaded by small minds and the coral of art turned to bone; this lives and dies in its own limbo where the fake is the rightful lord of the gulls. I am thinking of the true thing, the product of good minds, which the quite ungullible reader may defer to as possessing more insight and sensibility, more knowledge and wisdom than his own. It is from this true Criticism that he needs protection, or rather from its necessarily partial documents. The hazard lies in the fact that these are usually reticent about their supplementary character; often they appear to be isolating the essential when they are only altering emphasis. As a rough illustration, the critical spokesman may dwell at length on the 'flaws' of Prince Hamlet, without mentioning those of King Claudius. The late-coming listener may not realize that the latter are being subsumed, because of the prominence presumably given them when earlier critics held the floor; and he may suspect that in his own reading of *Hamlet* he has failed to identify the villain. Or he may gain the impression that the artistic distinction of the play lies in its delineation of 'flaws' and in their authenticity as neurotic 'symptoms.' It is inevitable that latter-day critical documents will emphasize the 'neglected' to the danger-point of distortion. It is inevitable, too, that an 'interpretive' tide will set in, transmuting values in the interest of modern times. Although this is often high-minded in intent, it can be damaging in effect, diverting the reader from values-pure, and sophisticating his response.

A good safeguard in reading Shakespearean criticism is to read it extensively, until one grows aware of its collaborative nature and of how extreme positions are canceled out. Better still, of course, is close knowledge of the works themselves, so that one can distinguish between critical opinions based on observation and those based on divination. One may view the latter with respect, but he will recognize them for what they are; he will meet the critics on sufficiently equal terms to accept stimulation without yielding to dictation. If the reader has noticed in the plays most of what is there to be noticed, he will not test the works by the criticism but the criticism by the works.

The object of my book is to induce a noticing mood, to encourage attentive reading, and to save the fundamental, the conspicuous, the important, from being dismissed as elementary. My commentary is 'pre-criticism'—analysis and appreciation rather than synthesis and interpretation. I wish to guide the reader but not direct him, to exhibit the plays but not expound them. I may not always have resisted the impulse to generalize, but I have been always aware that I should, and have returned rapidly to particulars. Since I am not free from the spirit of emulation, I have chosen a method of presentation which inhibits grandiloquence, the spinning of metaphysical webs, and the fashioning of Alexandrian mosaics with bright bits quarried from here and there in each play.

In the first section, after a glance at the difficulties confronting modern readers of Shakespeare, I have discussed in summary fashion the components of the plays—the diction, the metrical and non-metrical media, and the dramatic design as it emerges from a script. Technical terms are introduced, not that they have value in themselves, but because their definition and illustration may stimulate observation. Knowing the name of a thing often makes us more attentive to its nature and function. This preliminary section supplies criteria which the reader may apply for himself, and so test and supplement the guidance offered in the remainder of the book. This is divided into sections, preceded by brief surveys of Shakespeare's works chronologically grouped. The surveys are intended to supply a context for the plays treated at length, and the critical 'generalizations' in them need not be taken very seriously. I have selected for extended treatment great representative plays; thus *As You Like It* represents the middle romantic comedies, *Julius Caesar* the plays on Roman themes, *Measure for Measure* the so-called 'problem' plays. This means that other great plays are passed over with mere mention, but there was no alternative except a disastrous sketchiness. If there had been room for one more play, it would have been one of the three farces.

In the treatment of the chosen plays, I have provided an objective description of the action of each scene, followed by a commentary on details in the order in which they appear. The description of the action supplies a uniform frame supporting the commentary (which is uniform in neither kind nor quantity) and also supplies a constant reminder that we are dealing with a play. A play is a story acted out. It is fundamentally an *action,* its primary meaning conveyed by the concatenation of events, and to let these events slip out of sight, almost as an irrelevance as we concentrate on other things, is fatal to a balanced response. In the commentary I read along with the reader, not as his master but as one who has been over the ground before. It is assumed that he will have Shakespeare's text open before him, and my comments are cued to the line-numbering. The text I have used is the Pelican Shakespeare, of which I am general editor, but the line-numbering approximates that in all editions (cf. below, p. 37). In prose scenes where the numbering varies in various editions, I have quoted phrases that will help the reader 'find the place.'

The comments are upon the use of language, the versification, the prose style, the implied stage-business, the emerging traits of characters, significant juxtapositions, structural devices, and similar details of technique. I have aimed at variety rather than exhaustiveness since it would be intolerable as well as impossible to re-mark upon everything. Goldsmith once said that if angels wrote books they would not write folios, and I am inclined to believe that they would limit commentaries to duo-decimo. My method has been to comment fairly copiously on early scenes, while major characters and themes are being introduced, and to taper off as the reader gets *inside* the play and increasingly impatient of the guiding hand. Coleridge seems to have used this method in his lectures, and even if it was, as his detractors said, because he was too lazy to organize his remarks or too impervious to the warning of the clock, it strikes me as a good one. The opening scenes are the handle of a play. Coleridge and Granville-Barker, if I may dare to invoke such names, are actually my chief exemplars—not the Coleridge of the sonorous phrases and cosmic speculations, but the Coleridge who could illuminate a whole work by making us see a detail; and the Granville-Barker who never forgot that plays are plays.

My commentary has only the order and continuity imposed upon it by the play. The advantage of the method is that it lets the play retain its original shape, forestalling the creation of a rival construct; it lets the reader continuously check the commentary against the text, thus inducing caution; and finally it disciplines the commentator's pride, since his prose adorned only with reference-numbers is seen for what it is instead of what it might seem in the reflected glory of quoted passages. Although I have known what I wanted to do, I am aware of the truth of one of Portia's more oracular utterances: 'If to do were as easy as to know what were good to do, chapels had been churches, and poor men's cottages princes' palaces.' Great art is fashioned as direct communication from artist to receiver. A third party is an intruder, even though he tries to remain only a guide. I have always been torn between the impulse to talk about poetry (abetted by my calling) and the nagging suspicion that poetry ought not to be talked about. Hence this final caution. A reader is never relieved of the obligation to form his own judgments, and to cultivate his own mode of emotional, aesthetic, and moral response. This is a reader's guide. The reader's book is Shakespeare.

I

The Components

1

On Reading Shakespeare

:

MARK TWAIN'S remark, that a classic is something everybody wants to have read but nobody wants to read, does not quite apply to Shakespeare. Many want to read him, and some actually do. Nevertheless, the number of unread copies of his works is staggering. In moments of truth the owners concede that they have not read Shakespeare since school. Later starts have convinced them that this joy must be deferred; thereafter the book has sat 'like patience on a monument smiling at grief.' Shakespeare comes with dazzling credentials. Fragments echo in every mind—the unalterable phrase, the lovely line, the quip that has become proverbial. A reader expects in the reading an immediate huge return, matching the golden aura, and the pleasure afforded by familiar quotations. Perhaps he begins to look for these quotations, almost like a birdwatcher, peering into the enclosing thickets of blank verse. Then comes the murmur in the ear—is it honestly worthwhile? a whole evening of *A Midsummer Night's Dream* just to hear Puck say, 'What fools these mortals be!'

This may overstate the case, but truly many a person who likes to read, and feels justly proud of his taste, feels frustrated in reading the works of Shakespeare. Why should this be? Is one not quite up to them? Or does the inadequacy lie in the works themselves— have they really seen their day? The first alternative is probably not true, and the second certainly is not. The trouble, as in so many forms of frustration, lies in barriers to communion. The commonest barriers are formed by the exceptional nature of the experience: the reader is not used to reading plays, even modern plays; he is not used to reading poetry in massive units, even modern poetry; he is not used to reading works three-and-a-half centuries old; and he is not used to complex simplicity. This last baffling phrase will be explained after a few words about the first three 'barriers.'

Reading a play is not like reading a novel. In a novel a point of view is provided by the author's commentary on the characters and events. It requires little effort to detect the intention. We are given, so to speak, both the figures and the total at the foot of the column, besides periodic totings up. In drama the case is different. The characters and events are there, but not the author's reflections. We are given the figures but must do the adding ourselves; only then do we discover the point of view. Especially is this true with Shakespeare, whether read or seen in performance. In reading there is a further difficulty. The text of a novel is the whole work. The text of a play is not. Drama is not literature in the usual sense, but an art form with a literary component. A reader does not read the *play* but the *script* of the play, and his efforts of imagination must be constant if he is to encompass the whole work. The modern play is fairly easy to read because it has been influenced by the novel and has lost dramatic purity; also, it is provided with full stage directions intended for the reader. Shakespeare's plays were printed from scripts intended for actors with professional skill in visualization; the stage directions are sparse. The overall *action* is easy to follow, but interest depends largely on following piecemeal *actions*, the movement of the characters. After the reader acquires the knack, he finds pleasure in detecting the 'built-in' stage directions; he becomes his own producer.

Reading poetry is not like reading prose. The virtue of prose is to say what it has to say directly and explicitly, using words in a single sense. The meaning is easily grasped since it lies upon the surface, and the reading goes rapidly since the words function in blocks. Some readers can 'take in' a whole sentence at a glance, and a legendary few can 'take in' a whole paragraph. Poetry cannot be read in this way. The virtue of poetry is to say what it has to say beautifully and by the power of suggestion, initiating an emotional and creative response in the reader, so that it is able to convey more meaning more powerfully than prose. The words expand in the reader's mind. The greater rapidity with which we turn the pages of prose creates the illusion that we are covering more ground, but the ground covered should be measured by the amount of meaning absorbed, not by the number of words seen. A page of poetry may be equal to many pages of prose in what it conveys; we absorb it more slowly because there is more to absorb. Most readers are aware of this distinction, but they forget it when confronted by Shakespeare's abundance. They do not skim through an ode by Keats, or try to take in at a glance a quatrain by Emily Dickinson; the lines are few and they are given their time to operate. But the sheer number of lines in a Shakespearean play (often equalling the total output of a modern poet) may induce a prose-reading mood. If the reader expects to turn pages rapidly 'to get on with the story' he may feel that the play is 'slow' (even though dozens of characters live and die in it, and empires rise and fall) or that its people are 'talky.' Ten lines seem an absurdly large number for a character to use in saying 'yes' or 'no' if 'yes' or 'no' is all the reader is looking for—if he is reading the poetry as prose. But the lines may be invoking a lifetime's experience, or a whole ethical code, or a crisis of the human spirit. This 'yes' or 'no' may be knitting this moment to eternity. The poetry must be read as poetry.

Reading a work of the past is not like reading a work of the present, any more than traveling is like staying at home. If we want to be places, we must go to them; they will not come to us. And going means going wholly, not going in body and staying home in heart and mind. 'Place insularity' is not a bit more common than 'time insularity'—the inability to see the past except as it differs from the present to its own disgrace. A grammatical difference becomes a grammatical 'mistake.' If a word meant something different in the past from what it has come to mean in the present, so much the worse for the past. One continues to read it stalwartly in its present sense, a little like Mr. Podsnap, who assumed that Frenchmen would understand him if only he spoke English loud enough. Narrowness is an insuperable barrier to reading Shakespeare, but fortunately few who want to read him suffer from it in its acute form; they are willing to adjust themselves to the visible signs of antiquity, the double negative, the obsolete word, or the like. The more real danger is that intangible differences in values and sentiments, in moral, social, religious, and political attitudes, will set up an invisible barrier, blocking the reader's full sympathy. The gradual dissolving of this barrier, as one comes to take the past on its own terms, or rather to recognize basic kinship under the alien surface, is not the least of the rewards awaiting the reader of Shakespeare. One perceives the lasting values in the temporal symbols, and recognizes that the courageous warrior, the loyal subject, the loving daughter, are not endorsements of war, monarchial government, and parental domination, but of courage, loyalty, and love. No one ever became smaller by becoming a little Shakespearean.

And finally this barrier of 'complex simplicity.' A combination of words at war with each other is known in rhetoric as an 'oxymoron' and suggests an impossibility. Yet opposites can combine in a quite literal way—some things *are* bittersweet. Complexity and simplicity have combined in great human beings, like Abraham Lincoln, and in great human creations. The Parthenon impresses us with its perfect simplicity, and we learn with surprise of the complexity of the means by which this effect is achieved: the minutely calculated proportions, the apparently straight lines imperceptibly curved, and so on. One may almost say that complex simplicity is the hallmark of greatness. But the question here is, how can this quality form a 'barrier' to communion between the reader and Shakespeare? It can do so by putting the reader off-guard. Eastern politicians saw only the simplicity of Lincoln—no one was ever so under-rated until the error was recognized; they were right about the simplicity but wrong about its quality. The drama employs broad strokes habitually, and Shakespeare's strokes, especially his initial ones, can be very broad indeed. Iago's villainous intentions are stroked out like block lettering on a blackboard. That Lear's two elder daughters will prove faithless, his younger daughter faithful, is as transparent from the outset as any nursery fable. Accustomed to modern 'subtlety' the reader may be lulled into an unconsciously patronizing mood, only to awaken uneasily to the fact that he is not quite getting the point. Strangely enough, the point itself will be simple, but it will not always be the one he anticipated, nor will it be made by simple means.

These comments 'on reading Shakespeare' are a strange invitation to a feast. Some may feel that in view of all the 'barriers' they are lucky to have got anything from their reading; maybe they had better stop while still ahead. But to the extent that they *have* been getting something from their reading the barriers do not exist; the whole matter is relative, and the difficulties can be exaggerated. Others may feel that reading Shakespeare just does not sound like fun. Recalling the edited texts, with their introductions, footnotes, appendices, glossary, chronological tables, genealogical charts, bibliographies, and the rest, they may cry in renewed despair, 'I want to *enjoy* Shakespeare, not *study* him!' In this their instincts are right. We should not let ourselves be side-tracked. The study that fails to increase enjoyment should be avoided, provided that understanding is granted to be a factor in enjoyment. The apparatus included with texts is intended to be helpful, and it should be used only to the extent that it proves so. One can scarcely resent an introduction which puts the play in some kind of perspective, or notes telling what words mean. Those who argue for a page unsullied by notes are often self-deceivers, willing to float through their reading on a wave of delusion. We are not reading unless we understand the words, not just their general purport; the mere plot, after all, can be read in a synopsis. The notes can be ignored in the next reading— that is the consolation. A dramatic poem like a symphony deserves more than a single hearing. All great works of art make great demands upon us. To want to possess them without effort is human, but it is vain—like wanting to stand on the mountain peak without ascending the mountain. After all, the joy of standing on the peak and the joy of the ascent are indivisible.

If the above review of 'barriers' proves chilling, an antidote is available in the many fine testimonials to 'rewards.' Different in all other respects, the following books are alike in their infectious enthusiasm: Walter Raleigh, *Shakespeare* (1907); Logan Pearsall Smith, *On Reading Shakespeare,* 1933; Mark Van Doren, *Shakespeare* (1939); Harley Granville-Barker, *Prefaces to Shakespeare,* 2 vols. (1946-47). The commentary on Shakespeare up to the year 1700 is collected in *The Shakespere Allusion Book,* ed. John Munro, 2 vols. (1932). A vast body of later appreciation and analysis is inventoried by Augustus Ralli, *A History of Shakespearian Criticism,* 2 vols. (1932). A brief but invaluable anthology of the landmarks of early criticism (including tributes and essays by Jonson, Dryden, Johnson, Morgann, Lamb, Hazlitt, and others) is *Shakespeare Criticism,* ed. D.N. Smith (1932). The most influential critics of the Romantic era were A.W. Schlegel, (*Lectures on Dramatic Art and Literature,* trans. John Black, 2 vols. 1815) and Samuel Coleridge (*Coleridge's Shakespearean Criticism,* ed. T.M. Raysor, 2 vols. 1930; also in *Coleridge's Writings on Shakespeare,* ed. T. Hawkes, 1959). The most influential of the age last past were Edward Dowden (*Shakespere: A Critical Study of his Mind and Art,* 1889) and A.C. Bradley (*Shakespearean Tragedy,* 1904). Twentieth-century criticism is too diversified and controversial to be represented in brief, but the trends are illustrated and many of the prominent critics anthologized in *Shakespeare Criticism,* 1919-35, ed. Anne Ridler, (1936), and *Shakespeare: Modern Essays in Criticism,* ed. L.F. Dean (1957).

2

The Words

:

SHAKESPEARE in his life may have supplemented his scripts by suggesting gestures and inflections, perhaps 'directing' entire plays. At least he read them to his troupe; even non-acting dramatists sometimes read their scripts. It would be fine if we had recordings of his readings, films of the first productions, but we have only the written words. Modern actors, directors, critics, plain readers, all toe the same starting line. No one can claim authority for what he thinks, feels, says, or does about a Shakespearean play except the words on the page. There is no other authority.

1

With the words so all-important, they must naturally be understood. They should also be savored and loved. The first thing to be reckoned with is that they were written to be heard. The direct transfer of words from the page to the mind has been held up to us as an ideal in reading, but with Shakespeare this will not do. Lip-movement becomes a virtue; indeed the whole vocal apparatus should function, in fact or imagination. Hearing is indispensable, since the sound of poetry is pleasing in itself, and since it often illustrates or 'orchestrates' the meaning. On the night of Duncan's murder, Lady Macbeth 'heard the owl scream and the crickets cry.' The sound of the words is fittingly harsh and eerie. Prospero's island, 'is full of noises, sounds and sweet airs that give delight and hurt not.' The sound is fittingly harmonious. The word *noises* is no longer used for 'music' and it may offend the eye; it does not offend the ear.

Compare the following passages, reading them first silently and then aloud:

His [Antony's] captain's heart,
Which in the scuffles of great fights hath burst
The buckles on his breast, reneges all temper,
And is become the bellows and the fan
To cool a gypsy's lust.

How sweet the moonlight sleeps upon this bank!
Here will we sit and let the sounds of music
Creep in our ears; soft stillness and the night
Become the touches of sweet harmony.

Details of meaning may escape the reader in the first passage, as will be illustrated later, but the tone is unmistakable. It *sounds* like a soldier speaking angrily of a soldier, just as the second passage sounds like a lover in a moment of tenderness. It is not that the second is 'musical' and the first is 'unmusical.' There is music in both, but music in different keys. Poetry offers more than simple melody. If we are aware of the concordance of sound and meaning **(onomatopoeia)**, it is unessential to know how it is achieved, but the means can usually be analyzed. In the first passage there are many 'k' 't' and 'r' sounds. In the second there are recurrent vowel sounds **(assonance)**, as in *sweet, sleeps, creep, sweet.* In the first the initial consonant repeated **(alliteration)** is the plosive 'b' in *burst, buckles, breast, become, bellows.* In the second the initial consonant alliterated is the sibilant 's' in *sit, sounds, soft, stillness, sweet.* The term roughly descriptive of the first effect is **cacaphony** and of the second **euphony** but there is more to it than that; in the second passage we seem to hear the sighs of lovers although none are mentioned, and in the first the beat of drums.

The illustrative effect is often achieved by the speaking pace which the sounds enforce. Impatient for his wedding night, which must wait four days until the new moon, Theseus says 'how slow this old moon wanes!' The long vowels in five of the six words and the 'holding' quality of the consonants make it hard to speak otherwise than slowly. His bride-to-be replies that four days 'will quickly steep themselves in night.' The short vowels in four of the six words and the brisker consonants make it hard to speak otherwise than quickly. The lady (properly) is not so impatient. All such effects are lost unless we hear the words as well as see them.

It is comforting to know that the concordance of sound and meaning persists even though our pronunciation differs from Shakespeare's. The difference is less than was once supposed. He did not speak like a contemporary of Chaucer or like an Irishman with a brogue. His 'r' sounds were more prominent than the modern Englishman's, and some of his vowel sounds broader, but his accent was neither Irish nor American although similar in a few details to both. Neither was it a modern English 'public school' accent. If his lines sound better when spoken by English actors, it is because they speak with more precision and more respect for sound, and are more used to speaking verse, not because their accent is more 'authentic.' Fortunately the beauty of sound of Shakespeare's poetry, like the concordance of sound and meaning, may be regarded as a constant—in his day and ours, in England and America. The older pronunciation sometimes affects the riming and scansion of verse, as will be shown in the next chapter, and sometimes the play on words.

Comic **puns** and **malapropisms** are born of related sounds. A malapropism is an unconscious pun. Dogberry thinks 'comparisons are odorous' because he cannot read, and the sounds *odorous* and 'odious' have him confused. When Quince calls Bottom 'a very paramour for a sweet voice,' he is corrected by Flute—'You should say paragon. A paramour is (God bless us!) a thing of naught.' When Mistress Quickly calls Falstaff a 'honeysuckle villain' she seems to have 'homicidal' in mind. All of Shakespeare's word-manglers are illiterates whose ears have deceived them; they love words and have an enterprising spirit. Unless we hear Mistress Quickly's *honeysuckle,* we may think she is even more addlepated than she is.

When the Lord Chief Justice says to Falstaff, 'Your means are very slender and your waste great,' Falstaff replies, 'I would my means were greater and my waist slenderer.' The difference in spelling *waste-waist* points out the pun and gives us a stage-direction of Falstaff placing his hand on his great belly, but it was the identity of sound that set up the pun in the first place. Punning is for the ear. The spelling does not help when the words punned upon are alike in spelling as well as sound, as when Falstaff continues, 'I can get no *remedy* for this *consumption* of the purse,' and it can actually block us by fixing our attention on the spelled-out meaning, as when a cobbler says that he has a good conscience because he is 'a mender of bad soles.' It is because *soles* and 'souls' are identical in sound **(homonyms)** that our ear gets the point. Sometimes in Shakespeare's pronunciation words were homonymic that have ceased to be so. This has long been recognized with words like *room* and *Rome* in 'Now it is Rome indeed and room enough, When there is in it but one only man,' but recent phonetic research shows that there are more such puns than we have realized: 'whore' and *hour* were pronounced alike, and when Touchstone says 'from hour to hour we rot and rot,' the pun is unexpected, startling, but not uninstructive.

We may feel that some of the puns could be spared, or that some recur too often (*deer-dear, hart-heart, son-sun,* etc.), but the punning has other than comic uses. It deepens the sense of serious passages, in which case it is given the more honorable name of **wordplay.** The line between witticism and poetry is a fine one. The dying Mercutio says, 'Ask for me to-morrow, and you shall find me a grave man.' We may recoil at the idea of a man dying with a pun on his lips, but Mercutio's words are solemn. Behind them is the familiar old emblem of Death the Jester leading men to the end of what Raleigh called life's 'short comedy.' There is no jesting in the face of eternity; gravity becomes the grave. No one could say this more fittingly than the habitual jester Mercutio in a valedictory jest. Hamlet also puns while dying when he addresses the witnesses of the bloody end as 'audience to this act.' The play is upon *act* as 'action' and as 'theatre-spectacle' and has no comic intent, even though *this act* is literally as well as figuratively a theatre-spectacle. There is no joking in such wordplay as Angelo's 'I perceive your grace, like power divine, Hath looked upon my passes.' The *passes* are 'trespasses' and although *grace* is in one sense only the normal term of address for the Duke to whom Angelo speaks, it means also the instrument of Christian salvation; the Duke's intercession has saved Angelo's soul.

Hamlet the Prince is, among other things, a wit, and *Hamlet* the tragedy is full of wordplay serving many purposes. Here are two passages which raise vital points about how far we should go in detecting wordplay:

O that this too too sullied (solid) flesh would melt,
Thaw, and resolve itself into a dew.

And duller shouldst thou be than the fat weed
That roots (rots) itself in ease on Lethe wharf . . .

One early printing gives authority for using *sullied,* the other for using *solid,* one for *roots* the other for *rots,* so that editors are divided over which word to accept in modern editions. *Sullied* makes sense because Hamlet feels soiled by his mother's sensuality, and *solid* makes sense in association with *melt, thaw,* and *dew. Roots* makes sense because weed roots itself on banks or pilings, and *rots* makes sense because weed rots there too. The image of weed rooting and rotting, living and dying, in the wash of the waters of oblivion is a powerful symbol of lethargy, especially since *wharf* itself (whether used in the sense of 'bank' or 'dock') is an image of the stationary. The question is whether we must choose between the meanings in each case, or accept both in each case, yielding to the suggestion of the sounds, *sullied-solid, roots-rots*—fairly similar now, and even more similar in Shakespeare's time. A play on words based upon similarity rather than identity of sound is called **paronomasia** and Shakespeare certainly employs it at times. He is also sometimes governed by 'association of ideas' so that *sullied* might evoke in his mind the word *solid* and the latter the words for dissolving.

The question then rises whether we should let every sound convey every possible impression. Consider the following words addressed by Macbeth to his Lady as he plans his second murder:

Be innocent of the knowledge, dearest chuck,
Till thou applaud the deed. Come, seeling night,
Scarf up the tender eye of pitiful day,
And with thy bloody and invisible hand
Cancel and tear to pieces that great bond
Which keeps me pale.

Seeling is the falconry term for sewing up the eyelids of a hawk, and goes with *Scarf up,* meaning 'Blindfold.' Should *seeling* also suggest the word of identical sound 'sealing'? If so, it associates with a secondary meaning of *deed,* the primary meaning of *bond,* and a secondary meaning of *pale,* since the latter can mean both 'grow pale' and 'be paled in' by *deeds* and *bonds.* The play on the sound of *seeling* would thus link the two kinds of imagery which the passage indubitably contains, from falconry and from property-law. One may go further and say that *seeling* also suggests a truncation of 'concealing' ('cealing) applying to the darkness of night, and also 'ceiling' applying to its covering quality. But have we already gone too far?

The danger, of course, is that we will begin to convert the word-play into word-games, slight primary meanings, and get involved in the 'unconscious'—Shakespeare's, the type-setter's, or our own. The minds of readers respond in different ways, both to sounds and root meanings. The word 'carnation' contains the Latin root *caso, carnis* (flesh) as does the word 'carnal.' When Perdita says 'The fairest flowers o' th' season are our carnations,' one reader may detect a suggestion of 'carnality,' another of religious 'incarnation' while the poet himself was thinking only of fall flowers. He elsewhere hints at the meaning 'carnal' in so unexpected a word as *cardinal* (pronounced 'card'nal'), but the context makes the intention clear, and the idea of 'carnality' in Perdita's *carnations* may still be very far-fetched. Nevertheless, there can be no doubt that the doubly and triply suggestive power of many of the words adds dimensions to the poetry, and **connotation** (suggestive power) works in many ways. Perhaps the best solution is to let the sounds mean as much to us as possible, but to keep our more ingenious discoveries to ourselves.

2

After *hearing* the words, the reader's first obligation is to understand their primary meanings in the passage. Whatever difficulty we encounter is traceable mainly to **rhetorical conventions** and to **archaicism** in grammar and diction. In Shakespeare, parts of speech are interchangeable. Our adjectives 'false' and 'true' can be used as nouns: 'Say what you can, my false o'erweighs your true.' Our nouns 'word' and 'foot' can be used as verbs: Cleopatra says, 'He words me, girls, he words me'; and Shylock, '(you) foot me as you spurn a stranger cur.' Our adjective 'imminent' can be used as an adverb ('the imminent deadly breach'), and the pronoun 'she' as a noun: Rosalind is 'The fair, the chaste, the unexpressive she.' This freedom does not mean that the Elizabethans were ignorant of the difference in parts of speech; their rhetoricians had frighteningly technical terms for all such usages. One of the simplest is useful to know, because the usage it labels is sometimes confusing. When two words are joined by a conjunction although one modifies the other, we have **hendiadys.** Thus, 'This policy and reverence of age' means 'This policy of reverencing age,' the noun *reverence* appearing where we would expect an adjectival phrase. The difficulty lies in distinguishing such a combination from the much more common **double epithet,** where two words of identical or almost identical meaning are also joined by a conjunction. The double epithet is perhaps Shakespeare's favorite syntactical figure, and we shall hear more of it later on.

The linking parts of speech, such as conjunctions and prepositions, were also used more interchangeably than now: *on* for 'of' as in 'We are such stuff As dreams are made on'; *with* for 'on' as in 'I live with bread like you'; *and* for 'but' as in 'He has and a tiny little wit'; *but* for 'than' as in 'No more but e'en a woman.' One soon gets used to the plastic nature of the parts of speech, the survival of inflected grammatical forms (*thou shouldst* for 'you should'; *he doth* for 'he does'); and the absence of strict agreement in person, number, and case. Modern colloquial speech, especially slang, plays fairly free with parts of speech, and our conversational English would be somewhat hard to parse. We must remember that the language of the plays always represents people *speaking,* and its fusing of literary and colloquial forms is quite appropriate. The peculiarities which appear on every page are soon learned and accepted: double negatives, comparatives, and superlatives; royal plurals; *his* for 'its,' *and* or *an* for 'if,' *as* for 'as if,' *owes* for 'owns,' *moe* for 'more,' *still* for 'always,' and so on.

Words which are obviously **obsolete** give little trouble, since they are conspicuous and fairly few. Since the word *seeling* mentioned earlier is unrecognizable, a reader either looks it up or realizes he is proceeding blind; so also with *bankrout* (bankrupt), *meiny* (retinue), *paddock* (toad), *alarum* (call to arms), *nuncio* (messenger), and the like. The trouble comes from words which look simple and familiar but are used in an obsolete sense, *go* (walk), *sad* (serious), *let* (hinder), *head* (army), *will* (lust), *art* (learning), *free* (innocent), etc., especially since they are often used also in their present sense. The hazard is greatest when they yield some kind of meaning in the passage—the wrong meaning—as when King Henry IV is pictured as corpulent because he is called *portly* (grand), or when people sent on *bootless* (futile) *errands* are, as in the old joke, pictured as going barefoot. When a servant tells his mistress that he will go 'with all convenient speed,' he means that he will go speedily indeed, not that he will take his time about it.

But Shakespeare's language is itself a great instructor. Othello twice uses the word *hint* in telling of his wooing of Desdemona. Her father, he says, 'Still questioned me the story of my life,' and 'It was my hint to speak.' Clearly *hint* is here used in an old sense ('occasion' or 'opportunity'). This should alert us to the fact that, when he tells how Desdemona said that his story would woo her and 'upon this hint I spake,' Desdemona has not been furtive or coquettish. The word *hint* has only a trace of its present meaning as used this second time. Or take the word *questioned* in 'Still questioned me the story of my life.' Clearly it does not mean 'quizzed' or 'interrogated' but 'invited me to tell' or 'discourse upon.' When Hamlet says to the ghost,

Thou com'st in such a questionable shape
That I will speak to thee,

both the meter (question-àble) and the context show that the primary meaning of *questionable* is 'capable of discourse.' But there is here also a suggestion of one of the present meanings of the word, 'dubious,' since this Ghost is surely a dubious quantity. In these two examples, an attentive reader, without consulting notes or glossary, would learn the archaic meanings of *hint* and *question,* as well as something of their progress toward their present meanings.

This does not mean that one should do without notes and glossary. Self-instruction is slow, and the ideal is to understand as fully as possible on first reading. The primary meaning of some of the words is the reverse of what it has since become. When Bolingbroke *appeals* in *Richard II* he is accusing, not pleading. When Bernardo speaks of the *rivals* of his watch in *Hamlet,* he means 'co-sentinels,' his partners, not opponents. When Antony calls Octavius Caesar his *competitor,* the meaning again is 'partner,' not 'opponent.' A little Latin helps since Shakespeare had a fair amount and often used words in their root sense (here *cum*-together + *petere*-to seek). But we observe that Antony and Caesar are also 'competitors' in the present sense of the word. Similarly, when Horatio speaks of a ghost as 'Th' extravagant and erring spirit,' *extravagant* (*extra*-out + *vagari*-to wander) means 'wandering outside' (purgatory, not a budget), just as erring (*errare*-to go astray) means wandering. But *extravagant* also sometimes meant 'outlandish' or 'fantastic' as it sometimes does now, and *erring* sometimes meant 'confused.' These secondary meanings are also applicable in Horatio's address; the one thing that an 'extravagant and erring' spirit is *not* is a bungling spendthrift.

But the misapplication of present primary meanings in words like *competitor* and *extravagant* is none too likely even when such meanings make some kind of sense in the passage; an intelligent reader sees that it is not good sense. As in the case of *hint* and *question* compared with *seeling* and *paddock,* the hazard increases as the archaic quality becomes less obvious. A good many words have become weaker or more specialized since Shakespeare's time: our mild word 'naughty' then meant 'evil' or 'wicked': our nice word 'nice' then often meant something far from reputable, including 'lascivious.' When Othello speaks of his deeds as *unlucky* and himself as *perplexed,* he is not understating since the first often meant 'fatal' and the second 'mentally tortured.' Some words have become stronger, or at least more specialized. When the Ghost in *Hamlet* refers to his *crimes,* he means his 'venial sins,' and when Goneril refers to Lear's *crimes,* she means his annoying habits.

The trickiest words are those open to moral, especially sexual, misinterpretation. Shakespeare's wordplay often involves sexual innuendo, both comic and serious; *conceive* is several times used in the sense both of 'understand' and 'grow pregnant'; and a whole class of words including *know, lie, stand, tool, turn to, have,* and the like are used more than once with double intent. On the other hand, words are often more innocent than the suggestible reader supposes: thus, *possess me* means 'inform me'; *enforced chastity* means 'ravished (not compulsory) chastity'; and *virginaling* means (God bless us!) 'playing upon the spinet.' When Benedick says of his ideal woman, 'virtuous, or I'll not cheapen her,' he does not mean that he wishes to despoil virgins, but that he will accept only a virgin for a bride, *cheapen* meaning 'bargain for' not 'degrade.' It is in the area of sexual suggestion that the analyst of wordplay who considers the opportunities unlimited is most likely to get himself trapped.

All this sounds hard. A word of comfort may be timely. The vast majority of Shakespeare's words, counted by frequency of occurrence, are used in precisely their present primary sense, and in one sense only. He is the most monosyllabic of major English writers, and can write with great simplicity. Nothing could be plainer in expression than Othello's—

> Rude am I in my speech,
> And little blessed with the soft phrase of peace;
> For since these arms of mine had seven years' pith
> Till now some nine moons wasted, they have used
> Their dearest action in the tented field;
> And little of this great world can I speak
> More than pertains to feats of broil and battle;
> And therefore little shall I grace my cause
> In speaking for myself. Yet, by your gracious patience,
> I will a round unvarnished tale deliver
> Of my whole course of love.

Of these eighty-nine words, seventy-three are monosyllables, and we may ask ourselves whether we have ever written so simply even in barren prose. Yet this is poetry—giving us the spirit of the man, with hints of his pride and vulnerability. No one can fail to understand these words, and no one can fail to understand Lear's: 'You must bear with me. Pray you now, forget and forgive. I am old and foolish.'

Although basically Anglo-Saxon and monosyllabic, Shakespeare's vocabulary is, of course, the English vocabulary of the Renaissance, as enriched with Norman-French, French, Spanish, and Italian diction—all mainly Latin in origin. It contains also many new coinages directly from the ancient tongue, since Latin was the 'second language' of the realm, taught in all the grammar schools. Shakespeare was the master in fusing this German-Latin heritage. Horatio's last words to Hamlet, 'Good night, sweet prince, And flights of angels sing thee to thy rest!' shows the clarity and beauty of his use of Germanic monosyllables; but Hamlet's prior words to Horatio, 'Absent thee from felicity awhile,' are no less clear and beautiful in spite of their Latinity. A Latin and Germanic word in combination give us Cleopatra's wonderful, 'I have *immortal longings* in me,' and there are countless such combinations.

It is hard to find passages where Latin derivatives preponderate, but when they tend to do so, they are appropriate to a majestic or philosophical occasion. So in Hamlet's famous **apostrophe** (abstract address):

. . . this goodly frame the earth seems to me a sterile promontory; this most excellent canopy, the air, look you, this brave o'erhanging firmament, this majestical roof fretted with golden fire—why it appeareth nothing to me but a foul and pestilent congregation of vapors.

There follows Hamlet's equally Latinate apostrophe to Man, but its opening text is Germanic: 'What a piece of work is a man!' Nothing is commoner than the unexpected use of a short homespun word as a kind of catalytic in a passage: the landowner Osric is 'spacious in the possession of *dirt*': the spring daffodils *'take* the winds of March with beauty'; when Antony and Cleopatra are buried, 'No grave upon the earth shall *clip* in it A pair so famous'; and those who love Lear want him stretched out no longer on the rack of 'this *tough* world.' In Othello's cry of pain the word *aches* is as plain as it is inevitable,

> O thou weed,
> Who art so lovely fair, and smell'st so sweet
> That the sense *aches* at thee . . .

The term **double epithet** has previously been mentioned—the linking of two nouns, verbs, or modifiers of exactly, or nearly, similar meaning. So constantly does Shakespeare use the device that several examples have appeared among the brief quotations of the present discussion: *the bellows and the fan, thaw and resolve, cancel and tear, extravagant and erring, broil and battle, foul and pestilent.* Other typical ones are: 'the *files and musters* of the war,' '*knotted and combined* locks,'; '*book and volume* of the brain.' Dozens of examples appear in every play. The .general effect is plenitude, the particular purpose to give force and amplitude to ideas, but it may be noticed, in several of the above examples and many more, that a simple word defines or glosses a complex word, often in a Germanic-Latin pair. A notorious instance is where breath-borne gossip' is called '*exsufflicate and blown* surmises.' The effect can be both instructive and amazingly vivid. When Claudio is shuddering at the thought of death—'to lie in cold obstruction and to rot'—the Latinic *obstruction* (stagnation) gives the process, and Germanic *rot* the result. Macbeth's words,

Will all great Neptune's ocean wash this blood
Clean from my hand? No, this my hand will rather
The multitudinous seas incarnadine,
Making the green one red.

This is no longer a double epithet but its operation is similar. The poetic **hyperbole** of the last two lines draws its strength not from overstatement primarily, but from the way it translates abstract Latin into concrete Germanic terms. *Multitudinous seas* is grand, suggesting the vastness, variety, and wide distribution of all the oceans of the earth; then in the next line this is reduced to the single relevant characteristic in the monosyllabic *the green. Incarnadine* means 'redden' with an indication through the Latin root that the process is accomplished by blood; then the next line gives in monosyllables the huge result—*one red* (wholly and uniformly red!). Again we see how, if we read carefully, we may learn Shakespeare's language with only him as our teacher.

3

Thus far we have been looking mainly at single words. In looking **at** the words in groups, we must allow for the concentration and free arrangement of elements natural in poetry. Often the meaning becomes clear with a little filling out. Cleopatra's, 'What should I do I do not,' may puzzle for a moment; it means 'What should I do that I am not already doing.' Here again, reading aloud helps: read the line quickly and snappishly, and it becomes clear *without* filling out. In instances like the following we need only rearrange the word order,

There be some sports are painful (arduous), *and their labor*
Delight in them sets off.

That is, 'Delight in them offsets their labor,' with *and* meaning 'but.' Quite common is simple **transposition:** 'Gentle my lord' for 'My gentle lord.' There is **ellipsis** of every possible kind: 'I must (go) to Coventry'; 'If it were done (with) when 'tis done'; 'To die upon the bed my father died' (upon); (let) 'Fall not a tear.' The elliptical habit of poetry is something the reader must simply get used to; there is no way of classifying it. Each poet has his own shorthand; if it is impenetrable, the poet remains unread. Shakespeare's is easily penetrable after one begins to take for granted the omission of dispensable words. Rhetorical arrangement, like ellipsis, is a feature of poetic economy. Most of the patterns in which words were arbitrarily arranged by Renaissance poets (antithesis, parallelism, etc.) were devised, whatever we say of their 'artificiality,' to give maximum clarity and force. Some of the more common patterns will be illustrated in the chapter on versification.

Shakespeare learned his rhetoric and much of his poetic language from his immediate predecessors in the English Renaissance: the prose 'euphuists,' the Petrarchan sonneteers, the lyricists and romancers (among whom the chief were Spenser and Sidney), and earlier dramatists like Marlowe. The flowering of the new poetry was exactly synchronous with Shakespeare's boyhood and youth. If it had not come, he would not have come. The new poetry used an idealizing language of **metamorphosis** and **analogy.** It gave value to common things by emblematic devices, associating them with gold, silver, precious stones, silk and velvet, flowers, and all rich and lovely things. Hundreds of similes from the realm of plant and animal life began to pass current. Shakespeare absorbed this language, with its stock comparisons of lips to roses, breath to perfume, the new moon to a silver bow, etc. It is a mistake to suppose that he ever abandoned it; it remains in a measure his language to the end. What actually happened was that he so modified its terms, and supplemented them with his own imagination, that it is less *conspicuous* in his mature work. The reader of any English poetry older than that of the present generation will recognize the basic language; it is the twentieth century that has tried to liquidate it.

Naturally when we think of words in groups, we think less of formal arrangement than of intelligible phrases and sentences. In poetry these must have powers of suggestion, and this does not mean that they should simply be vaguely 'poetic.' The phrases and sentences associate with the furniture of our minds, as verbal reminiscence or concrete image. We feel the power whether or not we know how it is operating, but it is well to know something of the process. Let us consider **verbal reminiscence** first. The stock adornments do not persist in Shakespeare's style, at least in their stock form. What persists as a 'literary' influence is the ancient maxim— the traditional bit of wisdom in biblical, classical, or folk-proverbial form. Since we are more or less aware of the older versions, his version operates, so to speak, in both the front and back of our minds. In a single dictionary of proverbs, there are nearly 3000 citations from Shakespeare.

Take for instance the proverb, 'Thought is free.' It appears in exactly this form in *The Tempest,* but in *Measure for Measure* it appears as 'Thoughts are no subjects.' To recognize *no subjects* as meaning 'free' is at the same time to remember words already known. The old proverb 'Mordre wolde come oute' or 'Murdre abydith not hid' appears in various versions in the plays, from 'Murder cannot be hid' in *Merchant of Venice* to 'Foul deeds will rise' in *Hamlet*. In *Macbeth* it lies under the surface of the expression of the class of folk-lore associated with it;

. . . maggot pies and choughs and rooks brought forth
The secret'st man of blood.

Sometimes there is only an allusion; for instance the native proverb, 'The cat dothe love the fishe, but she will not wett her foote,' serves Lady Macbeth when she likens her hubsand, who wants the crown but hesitates to get it by murder, to 'the cat i' th' adage.'

Most of Shakespeare's aphorisms are traceable to native proverbs: to the Bible, which he knew thoroughly; and to classical and mediaeval authors, whom he knew chiefly in Latin quotations collected in school manuals, such as selections from Erasmus's *Adagia* (Adages) and Leonard Culman's *Sententiae Pueriles* (Sayings for Pupils). Now Shakespeare was reasonably well-read in English works of his own time, story collections, the chronicles, translations, and in the more popular Latin classics, such as Ovid and Plautus, which he probably read in the original. We know he read these works because he actually follows them closely when he uses them as the sources of his plots; nevertheless it is (with a few exceptions, such as North's translation of Plutarch) extremely hard to find verbal similarities, even when we study the play and the source side by side. However the proverbs, the Bible, and the maxims with which he was taught his Latin bit so deeply into his mind that their wording constantly emerges in recognizable form. One saying surely known to every reader appears as 'The tree is known by his fruit' in *Mathew,* 12:33; as 'De fructa arborem cognosco' in the *Adagia;* and as 'Arbor ex fructibus cognoscitur' in *Sententiae Pueriles.* The various wordings are echoed in various plays; in one we read, 'if then the tree may be known by the fruit'; in another 'The royal tree has left us royal fruit'; in another 'Truly the tree yields bad fruit.' Elsewhere the words are absorbed and transformed. In *Measure for Measure* we find the wonderful version, 'Spirits are not finely touched but to fine issues' (products). The context and an analysis of the words establishes this as essentially the same in thought as 'The tree is known by his fruit.' Angelo is being told that men are fine only to the extent that they do fine things. In the same speech, the words 'Heaven doth with us as we with candles do, Not light them for themselves,' have the same kind of suggestive richness through association with biblical texts and proverbs.

Reading the Bible is fine preparation for reading Shakespeare, both in its diction and in its formulations of gnomic wisdom. He himself read the Geneva version, but the Douay and King James versions, familiar to most readers, are near enough to it in wording to serve well as mental keyboard on which his language may play. Iago's celebrated aphorism—'Who steals my purse steals trash,

But he that filches from me my *good name*
Robs me of that which not enriches him
And makes me poor indeed.

places in a Iago-like context of theft the proverb of Solomon, 'A *good name* is rather to be chosen than great riches.' It would be interesting to count how often Shakespeare paraphrases parts of the Lord's Prayer. The last lines in his last play echo, 'Forgive us our trespasses as we forgive those that trespass against us'—

As you from crimes would pardoned be
Let your indulgence set me free.

The *crimes* (trespasses) for which he was asking forgiveness were his failures as a playwright!

In Shakespeare, then, literary allusiveness is no barrier to under-standing; quite the contrary. The allusiveness is not esoteric—not nearly so much so as in most modern poetry. The verbal frame of reference is our common heritage of wisdom literature, Native, Hebraic, Classical, as selected by Renaissance teachers. It is best to assume that his aphorisms are not abstruse, but reminders of truths already known, stored up in our minds in the words of the sages. We should not, however, reduce them to their primitive form, but take them as they are. They do not contradict traditional wisdom, but they often refine upon it, alter its emphasis, and give it new force and beauty.

4

The words also exercise their suggestive power through **images.** Images operate, as one might deduce, in the realm of the imagina-tion. They are the vehicle by which the poet's thoughts pass into the reader's mind as the reader's imagination responds to the poet's imagination:

And as imagination bodies forth
The forms of things unknown, the poet's pen
Turns them to shapes, and gives to airy nothing
A local habitation and a name.

Images exercise the imagination in two ways; first, by making us see things, and second, by making us interpret what we see. By making us see (and sometimes feel, hear, smell, and taste as well) verbal images give poetry the sensuous quality noted by Milton when he spoke of poetry as 'simple, sensuous, and passionate.' They can have this effect even in literal statements:

I know a bank where the wild thyme blows,
Where oxlips and the nodding violet grows,
Quite over-canopied with luscious woodbine,
With sweet musk-roses, and with eglantine.

The passage is not **figurative** although full of images. Its beauty derives from its sounds, and from the assembly of objects placed before the mind's eye. Shakespeare more often uses images in a figurative than in literal way, as we would expect of a dramatic rather than a descriptive poet, but there is more purely sensuous imagery in his lines than is sometimes conceded. He uses it for verbal scene-painting, to dress his bare platform stage. Beatrice's hiding place in the 'orchard' was, after all, only a rear-stage curtain or door, but in the lines it becomes 'the woodbine coverture'—

the pleachèd bower
Where honeysuckles, ripened by the sun,
Forbid the sun to enter.

The plays were performed in cold daylight, but 'lighting effects' were suggested verbally, of darkness and of dawn—

Look, love, what envious streaks
Do lace the severing clouds in yonder east.
Night's candles are burnt out, and jocund day
Stands tiptoe on the misty mountain tops.

The above in *Romeo and Juliet*—and in *Hamlet,*

But, look, the morn in russet mantle clad
Walks o'er the dew of yon high eastward hill,

and in *Julius Caesar,*

   Yon grey lines
That fret the clouds are messengers of day.

'Look,' say the characters, apparently to each other but actually to us. Once Shakespeare speaks to us directly: 'On your imaginary forces work'—

Think when we talk of horses, that you see them
Printing their proud hoofs i' th' receiving earth.

When we read of 'the bank where the wild thyme blows,' the greater the number of the flowers we actually know the more the passage will affect us. If reading the Bible is good preparation for reading Shakespeare, so also is looking at our world—the world of nature with its seas and skies, sunlight and rain, growing things, and animals that mate and kill; and the world of men—at work and play. Although the following is not a literal statement but an extended simile, its large descriptive element will work best with those who know the theatre:

As in a theatre the eyes of men,
After a well-graced actor leaves the stage,
Are idly bent on him that enters next,
Thinking his prattle to be tedious,
Even so, or with much more contempt, men's eyes
Did scowl on gentle Richard.

Most of the images make a double demand upon the imagination. In addition to making us see, they make us interpret. Images are, in poetry, the normal means of communication. When King Henry IV resolves that the soil of England no longer shall 'daub her lips with her own children's blood,' he is saying not only that civil war must cease but also that civil war is hideous, unnatural, cannibalistic. The image expresses the idea powerfully because it does so briefly and pictorially, and makes us participate in the expressive process by translating the concrete object into an abstract idea. The particular device used here is **personification** (Mother England as cannibal), of which more will be said later, but it belongs to the general class of figures of speech known as **metaphor.**

A few definitions will be helpful in indicating how metaphors work and what they require of the reader. When Hamlet tells a boy actor that he is nearer heaven by the 'altitude of a chopine,' he is not using a metaphor. A 'chopine' is a shoe with a sole several inches thick, and Hamlet is saying that the boy has grown several inches. This is literally true, not a figure of speech, with *chopine* used merely as concrete means of indicating the amount of growth. We may have to look the word up, but no interpretation was required of the original hearers. But when Hamlet continues, 'Pray God, your voice, like a piece of uncurrent gold, be not cracked within the ring,' he is using the metaphoric device known as 'simile' together with a pun. The boy's voice may have *cracked* (changed), and so may no longer 'ring true,' but in this respect only will it resemble a counterfeit coin (*uncurrent gold*). In all other respects it will not; we must extract the one similarity from the host of dissimilarities: we must *interpret*. The original hearers would have been precisely in our position. The badge of metaphoric language is that it must always be translated in the imagination. It is a symbol. It is never literally true.

A **simile,** like a literal comparison, usually employs the word 'like' or 'as,' but the things compared are not literally alike (as are the boy's inches of growth and the height of a *chopine*) but figuratively alike (as are his voice and a gold coin). The course of young true love,

Swift as a shadow, short as any dream,
Brief as the lightning in the collied night,

is, however brief, longer than the few seconds here stated. The simile, signaling as it does its comparative function, may be said to lie just over the threshold of metaphoric language. Certain other figures may also be said to lie just over the threshold; for instance **periphrasis,** where a descriptive phrase is substituted for a word: 'The *fringed curtains* (eye-lashes) of thine eye'; 'to see the fish Cut with her *golden oars* (fins) the silver sea.' Also superficially metaphoric are two figures of speech so nearly alike as to be scarcely worth differentiating, **synecdoche** and **metonymy.** In synecdoche a part is substituted for the whole or the whole for a part. Both kinds are illustrated in Theseus's statement that a lover 'Sees Helen's beauty in the brow of Egypt,' since *brow* stands for the whole face, and *Egypt* for a single Egyptian or Gypsy. (Helen was supposedly blonde and hence beautiful in contrast to swarthy Egyptians.) In metonymy the effect is substituted for the cause, 'none will *sweat* (work) but for promotion,' or the cause for the effect, 'I *eat the air* (am fed words) promise-crammed.' There are other varieties of both synecdoche and metonymy, but all are alike in that the reader is required only to make a simple connection. The words are *close* to literal fact.

It is a mistake to suppose that Shakespeare abandoned 'literal' and 'threshold' imagery as his style matured. All kinds of imagery appear in the writing of all periods. It is also a mistake to suppose that he tended to abandon the simile for the metaphor of direct statement, or that the latter is always superior to the former. The following passage makes consistent use of metaphor of direct statement rather than simile, yet is not distinguished:

But soft! What light through yonder window breaks?
It is the east, and Juliet is the sun!
Arise, fair sun, and kill the envious moon,
Who is already sick and pale with grief
That thou her maid art far more fair than she.

Why is it not distinguished? We may say that the imagery is ornamental rather than suggestive, or that it is too self-consciously worked out, but such terms as 'ornamental' and 'self-conscious' are hard to define, and Shakespeare's images at the height of his maturity are often equally ornamental and calculated. The real source of our dissatisfaction will be suggested later. When an image or

series of images is conspicuously logical or ingenious, it is referred
to as a **conceit,** but whether we use this term at all, or use it to express disapproval depends on whether we consider the image in
question successful or unsuccessful. Shakespeare's mature style is,
in one sense of the term, more full of 'conceits' than his immature
style.

In tracing the development of Shakespeare's style, we are likely
to make categorical statements about simile, metaphor, conceits,
etc. which wrongly imply the superiority of one class of imagery
over another, and are hard to justify when we actually examine the
'mature' as compared with the 'immature' style. Furthermore such
statements tend to belittle certain early plays, which, if they are
'immature,' are gloriously so. What actually happens is that as
Shakespeare's powers increase, the imagery of all kinds becomes
more closely integrated with the thought and more demanding upon
our imagination. We must constantly translate concrete symbols
into abstract ideas, usually aesthetic and moral values. To hear that
pity is 'like a naked new-born babe Striding the blast' is to realize
that pity is weak in present actuality but strong in potential. When
the terms of the image are abstract, the process is reversed and the
translation tends toward the concrete. To hear that a woman was
'as tender as infancy and grace' is to know that she lacked power
to harm but possessed power to heal. Often the product of the
image is a keener awareness of process. To hear that a certain king
cannot *weed* his land of rebels because 'His foes are so *enrooted*
with his friends' is truly to grasp his problem, especially if we ourselves have ever tried to weed an overgrown garden.

Often the metaphor is so absorbed into the language as to seem
to lie under it as an unspecified point of reference. The **submerged
metaphor** may appear early or late. In *A Midsummer Night's
Dream,* young love exists until 'The jaws of darkness do devour it
up.' No animal is mentioned, but one is there. In its extended form,
it is more apt to appear later, as in *Troilus and Cressida:*

> the *seeded* pride
> That hath to this *maturity blown up*
> In *rank* Achilles must or now be *cropped,*

Or, *shedding,* breed a *nursery* of like evil
To overbulk us all.

Here the sub-surface image seems to be a plantation of trees. Increasingly the images are more sustained and tend, by a process of association, to call up related images in clusters. Observe how the medical imagery here reappears after its apparent dismissal:

> If thou couldst, doctor, cast
> The water of my land, find her disease,
> And purge it to a sound and pristine health,
> I would applaud thee to the very echo,
> That should applaud again.
> (To one who is disarming him) Pull't off, I say—
> What rhubarb, senna, or what purgative drug
> Would scour these English hence?

As the imagery become increasingly functional and organic, it actually carries the thought and does so with visual aptness:

His [Antony's] legs bestrid the ocean; his reared arm
Crested the world; his voice was propertied
As all the tunèd spheres, and that to friends;
But when he meant to quail and shake the orb,
He was as rattling thunder. For his bounty,
There was no winter in't: an autumn 'twas
That grew the more by reaping: his delights
Were dolphin-like, they showed his back above
The element they lived in.

The vastness of the images (all metaphors) drawn from the spheres, the oceans, the seasons of the year, is fitting to a man of heroic dimensions. Now we see why we are somewhat dissatisfied with Romeo's tribute to Juliet quoted above (also all in metaphor); there was not the same correspondence of thought and imagery: the sun and moon are a little too big for Juliet, delightful though she is. In the same play the passage on the dawn, although equally 'ornamental,' is wholly successful.

By way of review we may look again at the first fairly extended passage quoted in this chapter. Its sounds alone communicated a sense of the speaker's anger. What is he angry about? The term *captain's heart* suggests the moral and physical qualities proper to a great soldier, with *heart* emblemizing moral courage and, by synecdoche, the whole physical endowment of heart, lungs, and muscle strained to the utmost in battle. *Buckles* by synecdoche suggests the coat of armor which hyperbolically *bursts* through the heaving of the *breast*. But this once-great leader now *reneges* (denies) *all temper* (resilient quality as in a 'tempered blade'), and that same magnificent physique and ardor suggested by *heart* becomes in a contemptuous double epithet, *bellows and fan* (suggesting heavy breathing), the mere instrument of sexual effort *to cool* by first bringing to a crisis of heat ('ellipsis') a *gypsy's* (the Egyptian Cleopatra's) lust. This is indelicate, but we must recognize that Shakespeare was a concrete thinker. The point is that the ideas painfully expressed in over a hundred words above are vitally pictorialized in the thirty-three words of the passage:

> His captain's heart,
> Which in the scuffles of great fights hath burst
> The buckles on his breast, reneges all temper,
> And is become the bellows and the fan
> To cool a gypsy's lust.

Yet this is, in Shakespeare, no extraordinary passage.

We may exercise ourselves on the following, a condemnation of abuse of power by any jack-in-office:

> man, proud man,
> Dressed in a little brief authority,
> Most ignorant of what he's most assured—
> His glassy essence—like an angry ape
> Plays such fantastic tricks before high heaven
> As makes the angels weep . . .

Dressed may suggest anything to us from a building superintendant's cap to a judge's robes, depending upon personal experience; *ignorant of what he's most assured* is highly elliptical for 'most misled by the thing which gives him most confidence in his authoritative wisdom.' But what of *glassy essence?* Is it the reflection of his imposing exterior, such as is shown in a glass (mirror), and therefore transient and, like the mirror itself, brittle? Such is what the image conveys to me, but there are other possibilities: we must not be dogmatic.

The reader must be pliable, willing to imagine and interpret, always open to appropriate suggestion. If metaphors are read literally or perversely, the effect is grotesque. Pelicans have long bills and necks, but Lear's 'Pelican daughters' do not look like Ubangis. Pelicans were reputed to live on the blood of their parents, and Lear's 'Pelican daughters' are blood-suckers. This is a metaphor within a metaphor, since they are not practicing vampires but are growing strong out of their father's weakness. The interpretation of a metaphor must go in the right direction, and so far and no farther. In *A Midsummer Night's Dream* a fairy describes Titania the fairy queen in verses containing the line, 'The cowslips tall her pensioners be.' The reader must 'look up' *pensioners* (the tall soldiers forming Queen Elizabeth's bodyguard), but he need not measure the height of an English cowslip. True, by this means and a little research he might get the precise height of Titania through an algebraic equation (average height of *pensioners* is to height of Queen Elizabeth, as height of *cowslip* is to height of *Titania,* i.e. about five and seven-eighths inches), but it is enough to know that Titania is quite small and, by association, dainty and flowerlike. Most of the sorrows of readers unaccustomed to poetry come from literal-mindedness: the metaphors must be read both imaginatively and with 'tact.'

5

The content of the metaphoric language should give little trouble. Shakespeare was able to assume some knowledge of classical mythology in his original auditors, but he did not overtax that knowledge. Like the verbal reminiscence, the imagery is usually the reverse of learned. Some of the metaphors come from Elizabethan law and institutions, obsolete medicine and general science, forgotten customs, sports no longer pursued, etc. (in which cases the reader must consult footnotes), but the great majority come from nature—earth and sky, weather and the elements, plants and animals; or from domestic life—food, clothing, the hearth, bodily action or bodily illness; or from social intercourse—buying and selling, tillage and craftsmanship, pastimes and worship. The average reader is not excluded; he need only exercise his powers of recognition.

The function of the **imagery** is highly varied. Besides its general concretizing and evocative function, it foreshadows events, lends atmosphere to particular occasions, helps to differentiate speakers, and underscores themes. Such functions cannot be discussed out of context, and illustration must wait until we begin going through actual plays. When Hamlet asks if it is better 'to take arms against a sea of troubles,' it is useless to speak of the 'mixed metaphor' if its very function justifies the mixture, if the very incongruity of attacking the ocean with a rapier suggests the futility of the proposed 'decisive' action—suicide, which decides nothing. One cannot justify every word in these plays; they are not perfect; there are lapses of artistry and taste. Still they are marvelously adept; their tendency is toward perfection, and it is best to give details the benefit of the doubt.

Sometimes the design of meaningful contradiction is obvious, as in the use of the **oxymoron**—

Death, death; O, amiable lovely death!
Thou odoriferous stench! sound rottenness!

We can easily see that memento mori may be repulsive to the senses but wholesome for the soul, and that death brings rest as well as decay; just as we can easily follow the logic of the gentler oxymoron —'Parting is such sweet sorrow!' But sometimes we are required to follow a similar logic of apparent contradiction in a cluster of antithetical metaphors, no one of which is technically an oxymoron. Shakespeare's imagination, as was seen long ago, is a reconciler of opposites and works toward 'unity in multeity.' But in particular instances there can be diversity in unity. A single metaphoric word may apply in one way to the speaker, in another to the one spoken to, and in a third to a future unknown to either. Expressions may be taken in either of several senses **(ambiguity)**, or suggest simultaneously attraction and repulsion **(ambivalence)**, or contain within themselves their own negation **(irony)**, and by any or all of these means draw the language taut by producing maximum effects with a minimum of words **(tension)**; but words like ambiguity, ambivalence, irony, and tension should not be used as vague critical counters. The means by which effects are achieved, and the usefulness of the effects on particular occasions, must be demonstrable. Such demonstration is possible only in the context of the occasion and the play as a whole.

So it is with **image patterns**—sometimes referred to as **leitmotiv** —where related metaphors run through a play as a unifying agency. The imagery truly functions in this way sometimes, but we must not look to patterns of imagery for the 'clue' to the meaning of the play. If the meaning is not otherwise apparent, it will not be revealed by the imagery. The whole play is the image—made up of other images, including the bodies of the actors and their actions, as well as the words spoken. Nothing can be isolated. Only as the verbal image or sequence of verbal images remains integral to the whole play has it any artistic significance. Perhaps Shakespeare's most characteristic mode of utterance is **diffused personification.** Of course there is much personification of an explicit kind, as when we hear that the end of hostilities is 'a time for frighted peace to pant' (catch her breath) and we feel as if *peace* should be spelled with a capital letter, but much more common—in fact pervasive, especially in the later plays—is the kind of personification which animates the inanimate. This is sometimes called 'pathetic fallacy,' a term which might profitably be discarded. When leaves are said to be weeping in the rain, the defect is one of logic, since rain is no reason for leaves to weep; the defect is not in the metaphor as such. All metaphors are 'fallacious.' As Shakespeare employs diffused personification, he constantly associates the human with the good ('the pitiful eye of tender day') and the sub-human with the evil ('The jaws of darkness do devour it up'). This is why there is so much 'animal imagery' in *King Lear*. In view of threat of evil in it, it could not be otherwise. The 'human imagery' is everywhere. It is what makes Shakespeare the most vital and humane of all poets. His words pulse with the blood of our kind.

Let us return to the single word. Here are eleven words, all monosyllables and all used in their simple primary sense, without a metaphor among them:

Keep up your bright swords or the dew will rust them. We would say 'Put up' or 'Sheath' rather than *Keep up,* but otherwise there is no archaism. These words have power. Why? Because of the nature of the speaker and his situation. The most operative words are *bright* and *dew.* They conjure up night in Venice with swords flashing under the moon, and they give us the character of the speaker. He is a great general, strong, proud, assured. He is flanked by two groups of excited men, mostly city-dwellers, who have drawn their swords in anger. Presumably these swords will be wetted with blood. But Othello's word *dew* coolly closes that possibility. He is saying in effect, I decree that there shall be no fighting, with such confidence in his military virtue that he can afford to say it obliquely, almost humorously, as if without making a move. His word *bright* hints that the swords of these gentlemen are only ornaments after all; their business with swords is to keep them nicely polished. At the end of the play he speaks of his own sword not as *bright* but *good.* Now the virtue has gone out of him, and he speaks in wonder of Montano who has disarmed him, 'But every puny whipster gets my sword.' Montano is no *puny whipster,* but he is a civilian governor, and the words sound a poignant echo to, 'Keep up your bright swords or the dew will rust them,' spoken when Othello could quell a rout of such men with a word.

Did Shakespeare consciously provide this verbal connection? He may have done so or he may not. What he did was to *imagine* Othello so thoroughly that Othello's words are consistently self-revealing. If we attend closely to the words, we know the Othello whom Shakespeare imagined. The knowing, in this instance wholly, and in most instances mainly, comes out of our imagination and sympathy rather than our learning. Learning is good, and the more we learn of the Elizabethans and their words the more chance the words have to exercise their power fully, providing imagination and sympathy continue to function. The initial premise of this chapter holds good: the words on the page are our sole authority. The rest is 'understanding,' full or partial, according to our capacity. The only 'inside information' is something inside the reader. We must trust our instincts and hope that they are good. They are apt to be best at the farthest range of our sympathy. The theme of *Othello* is not that 'Pride goes before a fall' just because of the detail reviewed. Othello's pride is not wholly bad any more than his innocence is wholly good. We must try not to islolate the elements in a play which teach the lessons we want to hear, thus grinding our own philosophical axes. Shakespeare is an artist, and artistry implores the open mind. Our eyes as we look at Othello must not be those of the sentimentalist, nor of a racist or hanging judge, but of a fellow human being. So, too, our eyes as we look at Iago until the words command us to disassociate ourselves.

It is possible to have a headful of knowledge and still be unable to establish contact with Shakespeare. It is possible for simple people to establish this contact. I recall a Shakespeare festival where an evening performance of *As You Like It* was preceded by an afternoon of scholarly discussion in which I helped to spread darkness; my spirits were revived and the evening saved by the tone in my landlady's voice when I told her what play I was seeing—'Ah, that's the *jolly* one!' In this play Orlando's reply when asked about Rosalind's height became a folk-saying among plain men similarly questioned—'Just as high as my heart.' Since their dear ones were bound to be of assorted sizes, this shows some grasp of metaphoric language. If one will leaf through the first work of reference listed below, he will find that certain nouns and verbs are used by Shakespeare more than a thousand times. They are all monosyllables, and their character is revealing. *Heart* is the most frequently mentioned part of the body, but *eye* and *head* run it a close race. *Love,* as we might have guessed, is Shakespeare's favorite word of all, but *see* and *know* occur with amazing frequency. These basic words are a signal that we cannot understand him with the intellect alone or with the emotions alone; we must see, and think, and feel. The last chapter ended with remarks on 'complex simplicity.' Again we can sum it up in an oxymoron: the best gift that we can bring to

Shakespeare's world of words, as to the world of men it images, is the understanding heart.

References have not been given for quotations, most of which are taken from plays treated in the present guide. The quickest way to locate a Shakespearean quotation is to choose the least common word in it, and turn to its alphabetical position in John Bartlett, *Concordance to the Works of Shakespeare* (1889 & later editions), where every line containing it will be listed and the reference given. This work is excellent for word-study since it lists every example of the use of every substantive word. Many editions of Shakespeare contain notes and glossary adequate for most readers, but the language is most fully glossed in the following editions: *The New Variorum,* ed. H.H. Furness and successors; *The Arden,* ed. W.J. Craig, R.H. Case, and others (now being revised); *The (New) Cambridge,* ed. J.D. Wilson; and *Sixteen Plays,* ed. G.L. Kittredge. The ultimate work in the study of the language is the thirteen volume *New Oxford Dictionary.* Standard reference works on Shakespeare's language are: A. Schmidt, *Shakespeare Lexicon,* 2 vols. (rev. 1923); C.T. Onions, *A Shakespeare Glossary* (1911); E.A. Abbott, *A Shakespearian Grammar* (1869 etc.); H. Kökeritz, *Shakespeare's Pronunciation* (1953); Sister Miriam Joseph, *Shakespeare's Use of the Arts of Language* (1947); Morris P. Tilley, *A Dictionary of Proverbs in the Sixteenth and Seventeenth Centuries* (1950); F.G. Stokes, *A Dictionary of the Characters & Proper Names in Shakespeare* (1924); C.F.E. Spurgeon, *Shakespeare's Imagery* (1935). The following are designed for general reading rather than as reference works: W.H. Clemen, *The Development of Shakespeare's Imagery* (1951); M.M. Mahood, 'The Fatal Cleopatra' in *Shakespeare's Wordplay* (1957); B.I. Evans, *The Language of Shakespeare's plays* (1952). Much modern criticism has concentrated on the language, especially the imagery; for a survey and list of works, see M.C. Bradbrook, 'Shakespeare's Style,' *Shakespeare Survey,* ed. A. Nicoll, Vol. 7 (1954).

3

The Lines

:

A C T O R S in the plays of Shakespeare used to be judged by how
well they 'read the lines.' It is a charming phrase, with the word
'read' quaintly used in the sense of 'studied.' Old prompt-books
show how lovingly some of the actors noted the pauses, stresses,
pace, and gestures written into the lines. Our pleasure is increased
immensely if we imitate a little of their zeal, and we are more apt
to do so if we recognize what 'reading the lines' implies.

1

In verse a **line** is precisely what the word suggests. In prose it
should logically be a corresponding structural or rhetoric unit, but
for convenience we identify it with the printer's line in the Globe
text of 1864, the first popular edition in which Shakespeare's lines
were numbered. Most works of reference use the line-numbering of
the Globe text. When lines are renumbered in modern editions, there
is close correspondence with the Globe numbering in scenes written
wholly in verse, but only approximate correspondence in scenes
containing prose; we usually find the cited line a little *ahead* of the
reference number given. In the Globe text the prose line was on
the average a few syllables longer than the verse line; hence the
28% total of prose lines account for about one-third the total discourse in the plays. The thirty-seven plays in collected editions
contain in round numbers 104,000 lines, an average of 2800 to a
play, about 28% of them in prose, 7% in rimed verse, and 65%
in blank verse. The proportion varies greatly from play to play:
Richard II is wholly in rimed and blank verse, *Love's Labor's Lost*

largely in rimed verse and prose, *Merry Wives of Windsor* almost wholly in prose, and *King John* almost wholly in blank verse. Most of the plays employ all three media, with blank verse predominating. Each medium has its special quality and special functions.

Initially, readers feel most at home with the **prose.** We are so used to thinking of Shakespeare as a poet that we forget that he wrote the best prose of his age as judged by modern standards. It employs every rhetoric and metaphoric device, yet remains clear, terse, colloquial. Shakespeare's most famous talkers, Falstaff and Hamlet, speak prose, the first always, and the second much of the time. Samples of their speech will let us test the general quality of the prose. Here is Hamlet's reproof of Guildenstern, who cannot play the simplest of musical instruments, yet thinks he can 'pump' a complex human being:

Why, look you now, how unworthy a thing you make of me! You would play upon me, you would seem to know my stops, you would pluck out the heart of my mystery, you would sound me from my lowest note to the top of my compass; and there is much music, excellent voice in this little organ, yet cannot you make it speak. 'Sblood, do you think I am easier to be played on than a pipe?

Here he is instructing the actors:

Be not too tame neither, but let your own discretion be your tutor. Suit the action to the word, the word to the action, with this special observance, that you o'erstep not the modesty of nature. For anything so overdone is from the purpose of playing; whose end, both at the first and now, was and is, to hold, as 'twere, the mirror up to nature, to show virtue her own feature, scorn her own image, and the very age and body of the time his form and pressure.

And here he is meditating upon the skull of the jester:

Alas, poor Yorick! I knew him, Horatio, a fellow of infinite jest, of most excellent fancy. He hath borne me on his back a thousand times. And now how abhorred to my imagination it is! My gorge rises at it. Here hung those lips that I have kissed I know not how oft. Where be your gibes now? Your gambols, your songs, your flashes of merriment that were wont to set the table on a roar? Not one now to mock your own grinning? Quite chapfall'n? Now get you to my lady's chamber, and tell her, let her paint an inch thick, to this favor she must come. Make her laugh at that.

Compare such passages, chosen at random, with the following, also chosen at random, sampling the prose spoken by Falstaff. Here is one of his comic casuistries:

Dost thou hear, Hal? Thou knowest in the state of innocency Adam fell, and what should poor Jack Falstaff do in the state of villainy? Thou seest I have more flesh than another man, and therefore more frailty.

Here is his comment when Prince Hal provides a tiny page to attend his vast person:

Men of all sorts take a pride to gird at me. The brain of this foolish compounded clay-man is not able to invent anything that intends to laughter more than I invent or is invented on me. I am not only witty in myself, but the cause that wit is in other men. I do walk before thee like a sow that hath overwhelmed all her litter but one.

And here are his meditations upon Justice Shallow:

Lord, lord, how subject we old-men are to this vice of lying! This same starved justice hath done nothing but prate to me of the wildness of his youth and the feats he hath done about Turnbull Street, and every third word a lie, duer paid to the hearer than the Turk's tribute. I do remember him at Clement's Inn like a man made after supper of a cheese-paring. When 'a was naked, he was, for all the world, like a forked radish, with a head fantastically carved upon it with a knife.

All six passages are equally expressive and vivid, but each of the speakers has his own idiom. There is contrast in both content and style. Hamlet is the generalizer, passing from specific instance to the wide application; Falstaff is the particularizer, passing from general instance to the specific application, usually himself. The style of Hamlet's prose is tense and galvanic, with short grammatical units crowding each other in passionate staccato. Falstaff's periods are longer, more relaxed, oddly enough more 'philosophical' in tone. His fat seems not to have impaired his wind, but only to have insulated his nerves.

The range of style in the prose is wide. There are passages so true to the tone of rustic speech that they might appear in a novel by Hardy. Here are carriers at an inn, preparing to set off with their pack-horses:

1 Carrier   Heigh-ho! an it be not four by the day, I'll be hanged. Charles' wain is over the new chimney, and yet our horse not packed. —What, Ostler!
Ostler   Anon, anon.
1 Carrier   I prithee, Tom, beat Cut's saddle; put a few flocks in the point. Poor jade is wrung in the withers out of all cess.
2 Carrier   Peas and beans are as dank here as a dog, and that is the next way to give poor jades the bots. This house is turned upside down since Robert Ostler died.
1 Carrier   Poor fellow never joyed since the price of oats rose. It was the death of him.
2 Carrier   I think this be the most villainous house in all London road for fleas. I am stung like a tench.

Here is the private soldier, Michael Williams, speaking his mind on the eve of Agincourt:

But if the cause be not good, the king himself hath a heavy reckoning to make when all those legs and arms and heads, chopped off in a battle, shall join together at the latter day and cry all, 'We died at such a place,' some swearing, some crying for a surgeon, some upon their wives left poor behind them, some upon the debts they owe, some upon their children rawly left. I am afeard there are few die well that die in a battle. . . .

The king in disguise is listening, and when Williams says that he may agree to take ransom after the throats of his followers are cut, we hear this:

King   If I live to see it, I will never trust his word after.
Williams   You pay him then! That's a perilous shot out of an elder-

gun that a poor and private displeasure can do against a monarch! You may as well go about to turn the sun to ice with fanning in his face with a peacock's feather. You'll never trust his word after! Come, 'tis a foolish saying.

The dialogue of the humbler characters is usually comic, but not in these instances. Such snatches of conversation, transcripts from life, are so good that we wish there were more of them.

At the opposite end of the prose spectrum are sententious speeches in the mannered style of the **Euphuists** (experimenters in ornamental prose), sometimes appearing as parody but sometimes also 'straight.' The following is a serious example:

If to do were as easy as to know what were good to do, chapels had been churches, and poor men's cottages princes' palaces. It is a good divine that follows his own instructions; I can easier teach twenty what were good to be done than to be one of the twenty to follow mine own teaching. The brain may devise laws for the blood, but a hot temper leaps o'er a cold decree; such a hare is madness the youth to skip o'er the meshes of good counsel the cripple. But this reasoning is not in the fashion to choose me a husband. O me, the word 'choose'! I may neither choose who I would nor refuse who I dislike, so is the will of a living daughter curbed by the will of a dead father. Is it not hard, Nerissa, that I cannot choose one, nor refuse none?

This in sharpened form is the style of the Euphuist-in-chief, John Lyly, with all the tricks of metaphor and rhetoric, including assonance, alliteration, rime, and the juxtaposition of old proverbs and new similitudes. There are also passages of stilted Arcadian grandiloquence, happily few:

But O, the noble combat that 'twixt joy and sorrow was fought in Paulina! She had one eye declined for the loss of her husband, another elevated that the oracle was fulfilled. She lifted the princess from the earth, and so locks her in embracing as if she would pin her to her heart that she might no more be in danger of losing.

All the passages quoted above, like all the prose in Shakespeare, whether euphuistic or otherwise, whether assigned to private soldier or prince, have three qualities in common: they make use of regular rhetorical patterns, they are rich in imagery, and they are rhythmic. The prose shares these three qualities with the rimed verse and the blank verse. It is because all three media are rhetorical, metaphoric, and rhythmic that they can be blended successfully, can be used in the same play without jarring incongruity. 'Rhythm' as distinct from 'meter' will be defined later. The point to be made here is that the reader must be just as attentive to the wordplay and imagery (discussed in the previous chapter) in the prose as in the verse—and just as susceptible to the rhetoric.

This is as good a place as any to discuss the patterned arrangement of words and sentence elements. **Rhetorical patterns** have two functions; to lend clarity and force to the expression of ideas, and to give us a pleasing sense of order and design. Like the great variety of puns, metaphors, and grammatical irregularities, the devices of rhetoric have been labeled with a host of alarmingly technical terms, but nearly all of them are subsumed under three heads: **repetition, parallelism,** and **balanced contrast.** (Actually assonance, alliteration, and rime are forms of repetition, and parallelism might be considered so too.) The ultimate values of repetition are logical emphasis and aesthetic concord. Parallelism and balanced contrast have the rational appeal of logic and the aesthetic appeal of symmetry. Frequently the same prose sentence or unit of verse will employ all three devices: repetition, parallelism, and balanced contrast.

When Hamlet says 'Suit the action to the word, the word to the action,' *action* and *word* are 'repeated' in inverted ('contrasted') order in 'parallel' grammatical units: noun plus prepositional phrase, noun plus prepositional phrase. In his speech to Guidenstern, the words *you would* are 'repeated' four times at the head of 'parallel' grammatic structures 'contrasting' in length, each one slightly longer than the preceding. Falstaff's *more flesh . . . more frailty* contains the 'repeated' adjective *more* with the alliterated *flesh* and *frailty* in 'parallel' phrases. His *I invent or is invented on me* contains a 'repeated' verb in 'contrasted' voices, active and passive. His *in myself . . . in other men* contains 'repetition' and 'parallelism.' The prose of the Carriers is, appropriately, the least rhetorical, but both rhetoric and imagery appear. The four clauses of the first Carrier's first speech are alternately balanced, with a reference to the time, then to the consequences, another to the time, then another to the consequences. The second Carrier's *dank here as a dog* and *stung like a tench* are both metaphoric, and the first is rhetoric as well. Michael Williams's words on the horrors of battle give us 'repetition' and 'parallelism' in *some swearing . . . some dying,* then continued repetition but varied parallelism in *some upon their wives . . . some upon the debts . . . some upon their children.* The rhetorical patterns in Portia's speech are too conspicuous to need comment; included is the very common device of **antithesis** (where opposites stand in 'balanced contrast'): '. . . so is the *will of a living daughter* curbed by the *will of a dead father,* with a punning 'repetition' of the word *will.* In extended passages the units of thought may be arranged to form a balanced logical syllogism; or a proposition followed by a parallel series of proofs; or a parallel series of items of evidence followed by a conclusion. The rules in the classical text-books on logic, argument, and persuasion stand behind the verbal patterns.

The identical patterns illustrated above from the prose occur repeatedly in both the rimed and the blank verse; for instance in the following typical examples of each:

His eyes do drop no tears, his prayers are in jest;
His words come from his mouth, ours from our breast.
He prays but faintly and would be denied;
We pray with heart and soul and all beside.
His weary joints would gladly rise, I know;
Our knees still kneel till to the ground they grow.
His prayers are full of false hypocrisy;
Ours of true zeal and deep integrity.
Our prayers do outpray his; then let them have
That mercy which true prayer ought to have.

The first line contains approximately parallel clauses; the second line antithesis; the second and third lines (and the next two pairs) stand in antithesis with each other. The whole is a series of parallel arguments, concluding in a plea. Identical words beginning lines or other parallel units, like the *his* in the first two lines, constitute **anaphora,** while such words recurring at intervals, sometimes alternating with other repeated words, like the *his* and *our* later in the passage, constitute **word-echo**—both fairly common devices.

Nothing could seem at first glance more dissimilar from all this than the following, yet it contains just as many identifiable rhetorical patterns:

> This supernatural soliciting
> Cannot be ill, cannot be good. If ill,
> Why hath it given me earnest of success,
> Commencing in a truth? I am Thane of Cawdor.
> If good, why do I yield to that suggestion
> Whose horrid image doth unfix my hair
> And make my seated heart knock at my ribs
> Against the use of nature? Present fears
> Are less than horrible imaginings.
> My thought, whose murder yet is but fantastical,
> Shakes so my single state of man that function
> Is smothered in surmise and nothing is
> But what is not.

The passage begins with anaphora and parallelism, and ends in antithesis. The parallel elliptical clauses *If ill . . . If good* introduce rhetorical questions. A sentence such as *Present fears are less than horrible imaginings* is balanced, with a modified noun appearing at both its beginning and end. The superiority of this second passage lies not in the abandonment of rhetoric, but in the more subtle and varied use of it. We observed this same phenomenon in the use of poetic language in the less mature and the more mature plays.

The point of all this is that the reader should realize that rhetoric language should be read rhetorically. He should observe the patterns and delight in them, giving the words the emphasis which the patterns suggest. When a word is repeated through a passage, often alternating with another word, while changes are rung upon the meaning of either or both, the appeal is not childish but often quite intellectual; the poet is building a structure of thought as well as a structure of words. Always we must enter into the spirit of the game, and be neither impervious to the rhetoric nor embarrassed by it, however 'artificial' it may seem. Art is by definition artificial. 'Naturalness' is not a virtue if it means mere formlessness; sometimes the discourse which we call 'natural' could more properly be called flabby. There is a moral as well as aesthetic value in *form;* without it man subsides to indistinguishable protoplasm and chaos is come again.

Another topic may be treated at this point since it also relates to all three media, prose, rimed verse, and blank verse: the **articulation** of the dialogue. The merit of dramatic dialogue, like the order of words, is not to be judged by its 'naturalness' in the loose sense of the term. In actual conversation we do not, of course, speak in rhetorical patterns, in verse, and at length. False starts and interruptions are the rule. However, a playwright may imitate the superficial characteristics of actual conversation and still write 'unnatural' dialogue—if the words seem to issue not from the characters but from himself as their manipulator. Dialogue is unnatural if it sounds like piece-meal monologue, an exercise in ventriloquism. Shakespeare's dialogue never does. However rhetorical the speeches, and however long, the dialogue is always *natural* in essentials; it sounds like individuals in communication; it is always truly dialectal.

This effect is achieved by the varying idiom of the speakers, reflecting their varying natures and points of view, and by the articulation of successive speeches. Units of any kind are said to be articulated when they are functionally connected, as are the bones and sinews of the body. In Shakespeare each speech is rooted in the preceding speech. It answers its question, explicit or otherwise, attacks its premises, or supplements its thought. There is always a question-and-answer, statement-and-rejoinder, give-and-take quality in the dialogue, except when one of the speakers is, by artistic design, portrayed as irrelevant or preoccupied. The organic connectedness is reinforced by mechanical means, as when a word near the end of one speech is repeated near the beginning of the next. Sometimes, especially in the early plays, Shakespeare tightens connections by riming the first line of a speech with the last line of the preceding speech; and sometimes, especially in the later plays, by splitting a line of blank verse between two speakers. All three devices are illustrated in the following bit of dialogue from *Romeo and Juliet:*

Capulet . . . Show a fair presence and put off these frowns,
An ill-beseeming semblance for a *feast.*
Tybalt It fits when such a villain is a *guest.*
I'll not *endure* him.
Capulet   He shall be *endured.*
What, goodman boy! I say he shall. Go to!

(*Feast* and *guest* were true rimes.) In *The Tempest* split lines are the rule:

Miranda . . . How beauteous mankind is! O brave *new* world
That has such people in't.
Prospero   'Tis *new* to thee.

Thus the 'artificiality' of the medium (verse) is canceled by the poet's control of it.

One oddly 'articulated' form of dialogue is known as **stichomythia,** where single-line speeches appear in succession and are tied together by their thrust-and-parry quality. It is only when there is some form of wit-capping, comic or serious, that the term should be used:

Romeo Thou chid'st me oft for loving Rosaline.
Friar For doting, not for loving, pupil mine.

The effect is more striking as the length of the dialogue increases:

Richard Should dying men flatter with those that live?
Gaunt No, no! men living flatter those that die.
King Thou, now a-dying, sayest thou flatterest me.
Gaunt O, no! thou diest, though I the sicker be.

Such single-line skirmishes can be fairly prolonged. Stichomythia was abundant in the plays of the Roman dramatist Seneca; it occurs commonly only in Shakespeare's early plays.

Although prose may now seem a more natural form of discourse than verse, Shakespeare's prose dialogue is neither more nor less natural than his verse dialogue. Prose is used less than verse because it was less suited to what Shakespeare was most often trying to do—catch the quality of human experience at highest pitch. The prose is used for limited specific purposes. Its **functions** will be listed here, but illustration must wait until we examine plays at length. It is used when verse would seem bizarre: in serious letters, in proclamations, and in the speeches of characters actually or fictitiously mad. Verse was considered too *orderly* for the expression of madness. Prose is used also for cynical commentary, like that of an Edmund or Thersites, although not invariably, and for the reduction of high-flown sentiment to commonsense terms. It is used when the rational is being contrasted with the emotional: Brutus's calm and logical oration to the Roman mob is in prose, while Antony's inflammatory oration is in verse. It is used for low-pitched expository, transitional, or introductory scenes or parts of scenes, especially when contrast seems desirable: *King Lear* and *The Winter's Tale* both begin with a crisis, and in both cases the verse is preceded by a brief dialogue in prose.

The remaining uses account for the bulk of the prose: in realistic scenes of everyday life, scenes of low comedy, and scenes of bantering courtship and social repartee. It is inaccurate to say that the lower classes speak prose, the upper classes verse. When the lower classes figure in serious or romantic situations (as, to be sure, they rarely do) they speak verse; for instance the gardeners in *Richard II*. Although prose is naturally spoken on the streets of middle-class Windsor, Ann Page is allowed verse in her love scenes with Master Fenton. The upper classes speak prose in low and relaxed surroundings; for instance Prince Hal and his retinue in the taverns of Eastcheap. The witty genteel lovers, Benedick and Beatrice, speak prose consistently, and Orlando and Rosalind do so in their witty scenes. As has been noted, Prince Hamlet is much given to prose—in interestingly contrasted circumstances, when he is being conspicuously rational and when he is being conspicuously irrational. The melancholy, tender, and impassioned Hamlet speaks verse. Caliban speaks verse by virtue of his supernatural connections, while his comic companions speak prose. Such are the rules of the game.

2

Of the verse lines only a small percentage are rimed, and versification in its technical aspects ('prosody') had best be discussed later
in connection with the unrimed verse. The variety and quality of
the **rimed verse** may be summarily treated, since this medium is
chiefly interesting for its functions. It appears in a wide variety of
measures, from doggerel to regular sonnets actually incorporated
in several plays. There are quatrains and six, eight, and twelve
syllable couplets used in the dialogue, and many stanzaic patterns
used in the songs. However, by far the major portions of the rimed
verse is in the form of **heroic couplets.** The term 'heroic couplet'
derives from the frequent use of the form in narrative poems, with
epic or 'heroic' themes, by Chaucer and other early poets. It consists
of ten-syllable lines riming in pairs, as in the following typical examples:

Your loss is great, so your regard should be;
My worth unknown, no loss is known in me.
Upon my death the French can little boast;
In yours they will, in you all hopes are lost.
Flight cannot stain the honor you have won,
But mine it will, that no exploit have done.

Troilus, farewell. One eye yet looks on thee,
But with my heart the other eye doth see.
Ah, poor our sex! this fault in us I find,
The error of our eye directs our mind.
What error leads must err. O, then conclude
Minds swayed by eyes are full of turpitude.

You nymphs, called Naiades, of the windring brooks,
With your sedged crowns and ever-harmless looks,
Leave your crisp channels, and on this green land
Answer your summons; Juno does command.
Come, temperate nymphs, and help to celebrate
A contract of true love: be not too late.

The passages illustrate several points, including the minor one that certain words which used to rime (*lost-boast*) no longer do so. Readers are used to the preservation of archaic rimes in modern poetry (*mind-wind, lane-again*), and can easily adjust to the **lost rimes** in Shakespeare: *best-feast, are-rare, blood-brood, give-relive, gone-alone, love-prove, wrong-tongue,* etc. The commonest involve the suffixes *y* and *ly*. Such words as *dignity* and *chastity* which now always rime with *see* could then be pronounced variably so as to rime sometimes with *see,* at other times with *die.* The fluctuating pronunciation of the *y* is worth noting since the rimes in question (*die-eye-sigh-company* and *see-thee-plea-company*) are among the most frequent in the verse.

More important to us is the fact that the passages quoted are pretty much alike in versification although the first was written in the beginning, the second in the middle, and the third at the end of Shakespeare's career. The last syllable in each line is strongly stressed, and there is usually a pronounced pause at the end of a line and a lesser pause within it. There is a slightly increasing tendency for the sense to run on from one line to the next, and a slightly decreasing tendency for the two lines of each couplet to present a self-contained unit of thought. The later couplets are richer in diction and more varied in the pattern of stress than the early ones. Nevertheless, the similarities outweigh the dissimilarities; it is often hard to tell the difference between late and early examples of Shakespeare's heroic couplets. In other words they proved a restrictive medium, admitting of little variety and development. In the three passages quoted, we could scarcely guess from the style that the first is spoken by the young warrior Talbot on the field of battle, the second by the maiden Cressida to her lover, and the third by the goddess Iris.

Its lack of adaptability made Shakespeare abandon the heroic couplet, like rime in general, except for very special uses. His early prose differs just as little from his late prose, but the distinction is this: the prose was not only good from the beginning but also highly adaptable to the tone of different characters; hence he continued to use it in extended scenes. In six plays only does he use rimed verse extensively: *Comedy of Errors, Love's Labor's Lost, Richard II,*

Dream, Romeo and Juliet, and *Pericles.* These contain more than half of the 7% total of rimed lines. Since *Pericles* is a late play, it is something of a freak in this respect and may contain verse from an earlier version. Four of the other plays were written in Shakespeare's so-called 'lyrical period,' the years 1594-96 when he seems to have written most of his sonnets and had recently written his narrative poems; presumably in these years he was interested in experimenting with rimed verse. The earlier plays, except one, contain as little rime as the later plays, and in that one, *The Comedy of Errors,* the rime is accounted for partly by the doggerel in comic scenes such as would later be written in prose.

In the cluster of plays where it is used extensively, the rimed verse has more varied functions than elsewhere, but it is not used at random. The experiments cannot be dismissed as failures. In *Love's Labor's Lost* we find almost an anthology of rimed verse forms, and the various measures give a properly stylized effect to the stylized situations. In *A Midsummer Night's Dream* prose is used for the comic dialogue of the Athenian artisans, rimed verse for the fairies and for the lovers while under fairy-enchantment, and blank verse elsewhere. The distribution is logical and highly successful. In *Richard II* and *Romeo and Juliet,* and occasionally elsewhere, rimed verse is used for ritualistic and choral effects, as in the parting of Richard and his Queen, and of Romeo and Juliet, as well as in highly lyrical or sententious passages.

In its more specialized uses rime is as common in the late plays as in the early ones. Those which contain the least rime are the three Roman plays, *Julius Caesar, Coriolanus,* and *Antony and Cleopatra.* (Possibly Shakespeare was deferring to the classical milieu: Roman poets composed in unrimed verse.) The conventional uses of rime are as follows: of course in the songs (the portion of the rimed verse we would least willingly sacrifice); in a few comic letters and examples of bad verse, as when a Hamlet or Orlando tries his hand as a poet; and in Prologues, Epilogues, and Choruses. It is used in masques and other plays-within-plays, for obvious reasons: the medium of this 'inserted' drama must be distinct from that of the drama as a whole as the latter is distinct from the medium of ordinary discourse. It is used for certain manifestations of the supernatural, as in the revelations of oracles and the incantations of witches, but not in the speeches of ghosts; the latter retain their human prerogative to speak blank verse. Rimed couplets are used for occasional 'asides' and sententious speeches. Since the blank verse is itself often sententious, the rime when it is used has the effect of pointing up the gnomic utterances almost like quotation marks. The Duke of Venice consoles Desdemona's father thus:

When remedies are past, the griefs are ended
By seeing the worst, which late on hopes depended.
To mourn a mischief that is past and gone
Is the next way to draw new mischief on.
What cannot be preserved when fortune takes,
Patience her injury a mock'ry makes.
The robbed that smiles steals something from the thief;
He robs himself that spends a bootless grief.

Brabantio's bitter reply, also in couplets, has almost the quality of parody:

So let the Turk of Cyprus us beguile:
We lose it not so long as we can smile . . .

Finally, and quite important, we have what may be called **capping couplets.** At the end of a scene, at the end of a speech, before the exit of a character, and, less frequently, before the entrance of a character, there will often be a pair of rimed lines and sometimes several pair. A theory once flourished that these were 'cue rimes'—signals for the actor who was to enter a progressing scene, or for the group of actors who were to begin the succeeding scene. Of course they do not function in this way, since they occur sporadically and are indistinguishable from other rimes; if actors depended upon such signals, there would be many untimely entrances and failures to enter. What these couplets actually do is lend concluding flourishes. They are forms of punctuation, marking with a note of climax the end of a speech, scene, or scenic grouping. At one time, any change of personnel on-stage was viewed as the ending of a 'scene,' and although Shakespeare did not split up his scripts on this principle, he was of course aware that an important entrance or exit spelled a new phase in the action. The capping couplet is a strong device and accounts for some memorable lines, like Hamlet's,

> The play's the thing
> Wherein to catch the conscience of a king.

and Macbeth's,

> Lay on, Macduff,
> And damned be him that first cries, 'Hold, enough!'

It can mark the end not of a scene but of the character himself, like Othello's,

> I kissed thee ere I killed thee. No way but this,
> Killing myself, to die upon a kiss.

Its very effectiveness makes it dangerous; too frequently used it would soon seem obvious and mechanical. Shakespeare was aware of the danger, and although he uses capping couplets throughout his career, he does so irregularly within each play, and in only a fraction of the possible places. He uses them scarcely at all in *The Winter's Tale* and *The Tempest*.

Now and then couplets seem to occur in blank verse passages unconsciously or accidentally; when the inevitable word was a riming word, Shakespeare saw no reason to avoid it. Nevertheless, in the great majority of cases, the couplets are used with shrewd calculation, like the rimed verse in general, and like the prose. The shifts in media are significant, and we should be alert to their intention.

3

By all odds the most important of the three media is the **blank verse.** In its perfected form it is used with such mastery that it has provoked the admiration and envy of everyone who has since tried to write poetic drama. With it Shakespeare was able to effect the perfect compromise between 'natural' and 'symbolic' speech. He was able to vary its music with each shade of passion and sentiment, and to catch the individual notes of many human voices. To read the plays with true appreciation, we must learn to read blank verse.

Since prose is our medium of everyday communication, and since it has become the normal medium of drama and fiction as well, one may ask why verse was ever used in the first place. It was used because works of literary art, such as dramas and epics, were formerly viewed less as reproductions of life than as symbols or parables of life—as fine distillations. The artist was inclined to sharpen rather than blur the distinction between art and actuality. Since he was presenting the extraordinary or super-ordinary rather than the ordinary, verse seemed more appropriate than prose—not only less *usual* but more valuable and memorable. Until about a decade before Shakespeare began to write, all popular English drama had been written not simply in verse but in rimed verse. The latter, for reasons we have noticed, proved insufficiently pliable when the aim of the drama became complex. Blank verse had recently been made available to English poets, and carried with it a certain prestige; Greek, Hebrew, Roman, and other great works of literature had been written in unrimed verse. The fact that Shakespeare's plays are written mainly in prose and blank verse is one token of many that he stood at the crossroads of yesterday and today. Certain things he could have done adequately in prose, he chose to do beautifully in blank verse.

It was noted earlier that good prose is **rhythmic.** This means that there is in it a distribution of stressed syllables, pauses, and changes of pace such as produces the pleasing effect of recurrence and alternation typical of all rhythmic things. Rhythm is a constant in our experience—in the heart-beats and breathing of our bodies, and in the cyclical nature of our day, month, and year. It is inevitable that it should please us. Un-rhythmic prose is never really pleasing. A perfect example is the newspaper headline, necessarily so since connectives are omitted and every word is stressed. Additional striking examples may be found in college catalogues, treatises on the nature of beauty, and all official forms. A perfect example of rhythmic prose is the Bible, but the style of all literary artists is rhythmic to some degree. The rhythm of prose is irregular, unmethodized, but it is apt to become increasingly regular as the emotional content increases. The fruit of this natural tendency is the regularized rhythm of verse.

Verse is distinguished from prose by its regular patterns of recurring pause **(measure)**, and its regular patterns of recurring stress **(meter)**. The following passages will illustrate the distinction between the irregular rhythm of prose and the regular rhythm of verse:

She disdained to set forward otherwise, but to take her barge in the river of Cydnus, the poop whereof was of gold, the sails of purple, and the oars of silver, which kept stroke in rowing after the sound of the music of flutes. . . .

The barge she sat in, like a burnished throne,
Burned on the water: the poop was beaten gold;
Purple the sails, and so perfumèd that
The winds were lovesick with them; the oars were silver,
Which to the tune of flutes kept stroke, and made
The water which they beat to follow faster,
As amorous of their strokes.

The prose is from North's rendering of Plutarch's Life of Mark Antony, the verse from Shakespeare's *Antony and Cleopatra*. The poet was here following the language of his source more closely than in any other instance, but the transformation is still remarkable. It is achieved in part by the use of metaphor, including the 'diffused personification' defined in the preceding chapter, but in equal part by the regularization of the rhythm. The passage is verse because of its measured pauses, indicated by the division into lines containing an almost equal number of syllables, and because of its measured stresses, the syllables in each line being unaccented and accented in regular alternation. It is 'blank' verse because the lines are unrimed.

Blank verse in England did not evolve directly from rhythmic prose but from the heroic couplet discussed above. We can best observe its basic characteristics in a sample written early in Shake-speare's career:

What stronger breastplate than a heart untainted!
Thrice is he armed that hath his quarrel just;
And he but naked though locked up in steel,
Whose conscience with injustice is corrupted.

The line is **decasyllabic;** that is it contains normally ten syllables as do the second and third, or eleven syllables, as do the first and fourth. A line ending in an unstressed eleventh syllable is said to have a **feminine ending** (evidently by analogy with woman's extra rib). About one-fourth of Shakespeare's lines have such endings, with considerably less than one-fourth in the early verse and considerably more in the late verse, so that in this respect the four lines above are untypical. At the end of each line there is a pause; in fact this is the whole point of the division into lines—to supply a **measured pause.** Within certain lines there is another, usually lesser pause, dictated by grammatic or rhetoric structure, and often although not always marked by punctuation. It usually occurs after the fourth, fifth, or sixth syllable and is called **medial caesura** or simply **caesura.** (If it occurs elsewhere, it is sometimes called **variant caesura.)** In the above passage a caesura appears after the fourth syllable in the second line, and after the fifth in the first and third lines; since the pauses, if any, in the fourth line are equal in length, it contains no caesura. These measured pauses punctuate units of thought. Each of the first two lines make a complete statement, and the third and fourth, although grammatically connected, each express a fairly complete idea. When there are such naturally stopping places at the end of lines, the lines are said to be **end-stopped.** In other words, the measured pauses coincide with **significant pauses.**

The passage on Cleopatra's barge shows considerable modification of this scheme. In the first four lines the significant pauses come sometimes at the end of lines, sometimes at caesuras, but they still coincide with measured pauses; however in the last three lines the measured and significant pauses, such as they are, do not coincide. Below are further examples of pause variation in the mature blank verse:

I have lived long enough. My way of life
Is fall'n into the sear, the yellow leaf,
And that which should accompany old age,
As honor, love, obedience, troops of friends,
I must not look to have; but, in their stead,
Curses not loud but deep, mouth-honor, breath,
Which the poor heart would fain deny, and dare not.

You do look, my son, in a moved sort,
As if you were dismayed: be cheerful, sir.
Our revels now are ended. These our actors,
As I foretold you, were all spirits and
Are melted into air, into thin air . . .

When meaning carries over without significant pause from one line to the next, as in *My way of life Is fall'n* and *These our actors, As I foretold you, were all spirits,* we speak of the **run-on** or **overflow** line, or use the more technical term **enjambment.** When the tenth syllable of a line is unstressed, like the *sir* and *and* of the second passage, we use the term **weak ending** as distinct from the feminine ending where there is an unstressed eleventh syllable (*actors*).

Now these run-on lines, weak endings, and feminine endings all tend to reduce the emphasis at the end of lines, and consequently the measured pause. Often there are full stops *within* lines (*I have lived long enough.—Our revels now are ended.*), which may or may not coincide with medial caesuras. Many lines, perhaps most of them, have no caesura at all, or at least no medial caesura. The general effect of the features listed above is to make us read the blank verse continuously, in paragraphs so to speak, instead of in single lines or pairs of lines. The significant pauses seem to be obliterating the measured pauses. However, and this is important, they never do so entirely. In a fair percentage of instances the measured pauses and significant pauses continue to coincide; moreover there is, or should be, a vestigial pause at the end of run-on lines; the reader is forced to hesitate, however imperceptibly, as his eye reverts to the first word of the next line, and a good actor will respect this arbitrary arrangement and not 'rush' the lines. There is a sense of *order* underlying the freedom.

The same thing holds true with stress. Measured stress survives even when significant stress seems almost to cancel it out. **Measured stress** is the patterned succession of unaccented and accented syllables. In the blank verse, as in the heroic couplets, the ten syllable line is divided into five feet of two syllables each. A **metrical foot** is a unit containing a fixed number of unaccented and accented syllables in a fixed order: the **trochee** has one accented and one unaccented syllable ('wonder'); the **iambus** has one unaccented and one accented syllable ('delay'). Other commonly mentioned feet are the **spondee** ('moon-beam'), the **dactyl** ('happiness'), and the **anapaest** ('indicate'), but the only ones truly useful in discussing Shakespeare's blank verse are the trochee and the iambus; in fact we can dispense with all but the last since the trochee may be viewed as an 'inverted' iambus.

The iambus is the most common of metrical feet in English verse because it derives from the natural rhythm of the language. With a basic monosyllabic vocabulary, and with grammatical relationships indicated by connective words rather than inflectional suffixes, English speech falls naturally into iambics: 'the morn, his beams, we see, my hall, to die, has gone,' etc. A two-syllable word accented on the first syllable, when used with an article or preposition, is an iambus plus the beginning of another iambus: 'in vel/vet cloak.' To speak in simple terms is to speak almost in iambic verse, and Robert Frost has said that he sees small point in using other measures in composing poetry in English. A blank verse line of ten syllables **(decasyllabic)** contains five iambic feet, and is called therefore an **iambic pentameter** line:

That light/we see/is shin/ing in/my hall;/
How far/that lit/tle can/dle throws/his beams!/

But look,/the morn/in rus/set man/tle clad/
Walks o'er/the dew/of yon/high east/ward hill./

The first foot in the last line is **inverted.** Such inversion is most apt to occur at the beginning of a line or after a medial caesura.

Several points must be noted at once. When we look up a word in a dictionary, we are informed that the **accent** falls on such and such a syllable. This means only that one of the syllables is stressed more than the others; *all* syllables are stressed somewhat or they would be 'silent' syllables. Accent is a relative thing, and the degree of accent in a succession of stressed and unstressed syllables varies greatly, according to the habit of the words containing them and to the use of the words in the line. Our symbols for **accented** (ˊ) and **unaccented** (˘) are crude compared with the distinctions they are supposed to indicate. The measured stresses vary in intensity, just as the measured pauses vary in duration, and we have no symbol to indicate pace. Hence a **scanned line,** when it is regular, looks mechanical even when it is far from being so. The lines scanned above are anything but 'sing-song' despite their regularity: the pattern is conspicuous but the meter is subtle because of different *degrees* of stress as well as the variations in pause and pace.

To read verse properly one must be attentive to the function of apostrophes, and be prepared to supplement this function by cultivating a 'good ear.' In order to compress words into a ten or eleven-syllable metrical line, all sorts of devices of **contraction** and **expansion** are employed. When a syllable is saved by suppressing an internal sound, the process is known as **syncope:** *sev'ral, bur'al* (burial), *mock'ry, con'frence, del'cate, pris'ner, ling'ring, char'ty* (charity), *court'sy, boist'rous, med'cine,* etc. Words can also be shortened by omission of internal consonants: *e'er* (ever), *o'er* (over), *e'il* (evil), *whe'r* (whether), etc. Words can be truncated by omission of first syllables (*'head* for behead, *'cess* for assess) or omission of last syllables (*sense* for senses, *hand* for handle, *execute* for executed). There is **elision** and **slurring** of all kinds: *'tis* (it is), *i' th'* (in the), *in't* (in it), *was't* (was it), *April's* (April is), *th'unworthy* (the unworthy), etc.

The commonest type of expansion involves the 'ion' and 'ed' endings. The 'ion' is sometimes pronounced as two syllables although in modern English we invariably slur it to one. The ending 'ed' used to be invariably pronounced whereas it is now invariably slurred except after 'd' or 't'. In Shakespeare's verse it is pronounced or slurred according to the needs of the meter. There are two ways in which the difference is indicated in modern editions: when the 'ed' is slurred, the words appear as *pleas'd, damn'd, interr'd,* etc., but when pronounced as a separate syllable as *pleased, damned, interred,* etc.; or, by the second method, the 'ed' is spelled out in all cases and is accented when full pronunciation is indicated, *pleased* or *pleasèd, interred* or *interrèd,* etc. In words like *condemned,* the original texts indicate two kinds of tri-syllabic pronunciation: *còndemned* (presumably pronounced 'condem-èd') and *condem'ned* (utilizing the 'n' sound, 'condem-ned'), and this distinction is preserved in some modern editions. Often an 'ed' ending is both fully pronounced and slurred in the same line: 'We are impressèd and engaged to fight.' A reversed arrangement, 'We are impressed and engagèd to fight,' would spoil the line.

Finally, and greatly influencing the pattern of measured stresses, an accent which now falls invariably upon a certain syllable of a word might in Shakespeare's time fall upon a different syllable, or might fall on one or the other syllable **(shifting accent)** according to the need of the meter. For instance the line, 'The pangs of despised love, the law's delay,' is perfectly iambic because despised is pronounced dèspised. The following are examples of quite common accentuations which may seem strange to modern readers: *àntique, èxtreme, sùpreme, charàcter, confìscate, commendàble* (there was usually such an accent in -ìble and -àble endings), *peremptòry, edìct, recòrd,* (noun), *aspèct, instìnct, àbsurd, sècure, rhèumatic, quìntessence revènue, canònize, obdùrate, sepùlchre;* there are many more.

Editors quite properly indicate the mode of accentuation only when it is indicated by the spelling and punctuation of the original texts. They do not wish to impose their own scansion of lines upon the reader. Original apostrophes are retained and additional ones are supplied in all words where the spelling indicates syncope or elision. However there is no help for the reader when the accent falls upon an unexpected syllable, or when expansion or contraction is present but is not indicated in the original texts. For instance such words as *speak, real, grow,* are sometimes obviously meant to be expanded to *spe-ak, re-al, gr-ow;* such words as *marriage* and *creatures* to *mar-ri-age* and *cre-atures* or *cr-eatures.* The 'r' sound was especially pliable. Sometimes monosyllables ending in vowels are elided with words beginning with vowels, with no signal given, *no impediment* becoming *no'mpediment, too unkind* becoming *t'unkind.* The elision may be with a preceding word, as when *succeeding his* is evidently pronounced *succeeding's.* The words *having* and *being* are often to be pronounced as monosyllables. Antony says 'I' th' East my fortune lies,' and the apostrophes in the original text makes the pronunciation unmistakable, but if the text had read, 'In the East my fortune lies,' the elision would probably be implied and the same pronunciation expected. One of the lines quoted above reads, 'Thou, now a-dying, sayest thou flatterest me,' but the intention was probably, 'Thou, now a-dying, say'st thou flatt'rest me.' The poet (or the copyist or the type-setter) has simply neglected to indicate the syncopated e in *sayest and flatterest.*

Fortunately most of the lines still read well even when the un-signalled expansions or contractions are disregarded. Some lines actually do have fewer than ten or more than eleven syllables, and since we do not wish these to be 'regularized,' we do not tamper with *sayest* and *flatterest* in editing texts although we may wish to syncopate them when 'reading' the lines. We should certainly not spoil lines by persisting in present-day accentuation in defiance of the meter; there is no special virtue in the pronunciation *antìque* as opposed to *àntique,* especially since, in Shakespearean usage, the word often means 'antic.' When a line sounds wrong to the reader, he should try it again, assuming that he is stressing a wrong syllable. There are some bad lines in Shakespeare—it could not be otherwise considering the vicissitudes of copying and printing—but they are remarkably few; he had himself a perfect 'ear.'

What follows may seem like odd advice, and yet it may bring with it a certain comfort. Having learned the system of measured stress in the blank verse, and the conventions of expansion, con-traction, and shifting accent which serve the system, the reader should not be too much concerned with the matter. A person may be able to scan lines perfectly, yet read them wretchedly. Another may know nothing of metrics, yet read the lines beautifully. The reason is that, although there is always the basis of measured stress, it is overlaid by a more obvious system of significant stress. **Significant stress** is the emphasis given words because of their literal meaning and emotional impact in the line. If we read the line with understanding and feeling, the stresses are bound to fall on the right syllables. The verse is, so to speak, self-scanning.

When we compare the same lines scanned for measured stress and then marked for significant stress, we observe a difference. The average line proves to have not five conspicuous stresses but only four and sometimes even fewer. We must remember that stress is relative, and that a strong stress will tend to obliterate a nearby weaker one even though the latter is theoretically present. There follow a few brief illustrations.

Measured stress:

What is't thou say'st? Her voice was ever soft,

Gentle and low—an excellent thing in woman.

Significant stress:

What is't thou say'st? Her voice was ever soft,

Gentle and low—an excellent thing in woman.

(*Excellent* was probably syncopated to *exc'lent,* but the point is immaterial.) In the above instance the significant stresses coincide with the measured stresses, but in typical fashion they tend to obliterate one in each lines.

Measured stress:

For God's sake, let us sit upon the ground

And tell sad stories of the death of kings!

Significant stress:

For God's sake, let us sit upon the ground

And tell sad stories of the death of kings.

Measured stress:

She lovéd me for the dángers I had pássed,
And I loved her that she did píty them.

Significant stress:

She lovéd mé for the dángers I had pássed,
And I loved her that she did píty them.

In the above instances the significant stresses work partly with and partly in independence of the measured stresses. (The system of measured stress in the first of the two quotations is repellent, since accents fall upon mere prepositions and fail to fall on more important words, but theoretically any monosyllable may be given an accent or denied one; the flaw itself is only theoretical since it is canceled by significant stress.)

Measured stress:

Miranda How beáuteous mánkind is! O bráve new wórld
    That has such péople in't.
Prospero   'Tis new to thée.

Significant stress:

Miranda How beáuteous mankind is! O bráve néw wórld
    That has such péople in't.
Prospero   'Tis new to thée.

In this last instance the most expressive way of reading the lines almost, but not quite, ignores the metrical pattern.

The placing of significant stress depends upon the taste and perspicacity of the reader, and of course there are permissible alternatives. The line conventionally scanned as 'To-mórrow ánd to-mórrow ánd to-mórrow' is usually read 'To-mórrow and to-mórrow and to-mórrow,' but endless monotony may equally well be suggested by To-morrow añd to-morrow añd to-morrow.' That stress can alter the whole meaning or emphasis of an utterance goes without saying. Coleridge's objection to the way ministers of his time read the third verse in the first chapter of *Genesis* is a perfect illustration. To read, 'And God said, "Let there be light," and there *was* light,' is to show a certain surprise that God was able to manage it, while to read, 'And God said, "Let there be light," and there was *light,*' is to acknowledge God's benign omnipotence. Thousands of lines in Shakespeare depend for their right meaning upon significant stress. When Macduff is receiving condolences after hearing that Macbeth has murdered his children, he says, 'He has no children.' If read 'He has no chíldren,' the line means that only a childless man like Malcolm would think he can be consoled, but if read 'Hé has no children,' it means that the only possible consolation would be to murder the children of the murderer. When Desdemona, after hearing Othello tell the story of his life, says that she wishes 'That heaven had made her such a man,' a stress must fall on *her,* since Desdemona is wishing that she too might have had adventures. If a stress falls instead on *such,* the line means that Desdemona wants Othello—as indeed she does, but not in so blatantly coarse a fashion. How truly we read a line depends on how truly we have read all the other lines. *Studying* the lines of Shakespeare for the proper placing of stress is one of the purest pleasures available to lovers of poetry.

The interplay of measured stress and significant stress, like the interplay of measured pause and significant pause, gives endless variety and flexibility to Shakespeare's blank verse. Even when the significant stresses seem to be distributed in lines almost at random, as sometimes in *The Tempest,* they coincide in a majority of instances with measured stresses; hence there is always the firm underpinning of iambic meter. Twice before in the present book the Shakespearean quality has been equated with the oxymoron—in the way simplicity and complexity are combined in the work as a whole, and in the way emotional and intellectual appeal are combined in the use of words. Shakespeare is the 'reconciler of opposites.' In his verse we see both order and freedom. The decline in emphasis at the end of lines does not mean that he became enamored of mere cadence. It was the verse of his successors which deteriorated to cadenced prose; the deterioration impelled the neo-classicists to reject blank verse and return to the most restricted kind of rimed 'heroics,' culminating in the 'closed couplets' of Pope. If one reads *The Tempest* and then one of the later plays of Fletcher, he realizes how firm the blank verse of Shakespeare remained even in its most free and subtle phase.

It is certainly true that the blank verse altered as the style in general matured; however there were abundant early intimations of later developments. The following passages represent the verse at five-year intervals. In each case the lines are quoted from the first considerable speech in blank verse in the play in question, and then from a speech in which a character is lamenting the death of a loved one. This arbitrary selection of samples provides us, so far as it can be provided, a 'controlled' comparison:

1590-91: *2 Henry VI*

As by your high imperial majesty
I had in charge at my depart for France,
As procurator to your excellence,
To marry Princess Margaret for your grace . . .

Fain would I go to chafe his paly lips
With twenty thousand kisses, and to drain
Upon his face an ocean of salt tears.
To tell my love unto his dumb deaf trunk,
And with my fingers feel his hand unfeeling . . .

1595-96: *Romeo and Juliet*

Rebellious subjects, enemies to peace,
Profaners of this neighbor-stainèd steel—
Will they not hear? What, ho! you men, you beasts,
That quench the fire of your pernicious rage
With purple fountains issuing from your veins!

Eyes, look your last!
Arms, take your last embrace! and, lips, O you

The doors of breath, seal with a righteous kiss
A dateless bargain to engrossing death.

1600-01: *Hamlet*

Horatio says 'tis but our fantasy,
And will not let belief take hold of him
Touching this dreaded sight twice seen of us.
Therefore I have entreated him along
With us to watch the minutes of this night . . .

       Lay her i' th' earth,
And from her fair and unpolluted flesh
May violets spring! I tell thee, churlish priest,
A minist' ring angel shall my sister be
When thou liest howling.

1605-06:*King Lear*

Meantime we shall express our darker purpose.
Give me the map there. Know that we have divided
In three our kingdom; and 'tis our fast intent
To shake all cares and business from our age,
Conferring them on younger strengths while we
Unburdened crawl toward death.

      . . . no, no, no, life?
Why should a dog, a horse, a rat, have life,
And thou no breath at all? Thou'lt come no more,
Never, never, never, never, never.

1610-12: *The Tempest*

If by your art, my dearest father, you have
Put the wild waters in this roar, allay them.
The sky, it seems, would pour down stinking pitch
But that the sea, mounting to th' welkin's cheek,
Dashes the fire out.

My son is lost; and, in my rate, she too,
Who is so far from Italy removed

I ne'er again shall see her. O thou mine heir
Of Naples and of Milan, what strange fish
Hath made his meal on thee?

The reader may exercise himself by studying the measured and significant pauses and stresses in these passages. He will find that, except in the very earliest period, all of Shakespeare's metrical resources were always available to him, and that the impassioned speeches have a great deal in common from 1595 onward. The idea of a gradual metrical development may be partly a statistical illusion. Perhaps what we mean is, that as the plays became more and more infused with authentic feeling, there was more and more call for the kind of blank verse we speak of as 'mature.'

Our final thought should be of its quality. With blank verse Shakespeare was able to do anything. He could even let us hear the voice of one speaker coming through the voice of another, as when Othello tells of Desdemona's response to the account of his hardships—

She gave me for my pains a world of sighs.
She swore, *i' faith, 'twas strange, 'twas passing strange;*
'Twas pitiful, 'twas wondrous pitiful.

or when Hotspur tells of the courtly fop who visits the battlefield and talks—

Of guns and drums and wounds—God save the mark!—
And telling me *the sovereignest thing on earth*
Was parmacity for an inward bruise,
And that it was great pity, so it was,
This villainous saltpetre should be digged
Out of the bowels of the harmless earth. . . .

The following brief snatches will illustrate the almost magical facility of this verse in catching the varying tones of speakers, indeed their whole characters:

Cleopatra   The messengers!
Antony   Let Rome in Tiber melt and the wide arch
  Of the ranged empire fall! Here is my space . . .

Glendower   I can call spirits from the vasty deep.
Hotspur   Why, so can I, or so can any man;
  But will they come when you do call for them?

Antonio   And what of him? Did he take interest?
Shylock   No, not take interest—not as you would say
  Directly int'rest. Mark what Jacob did . . .

Macbeth   How now, you secret, black, and midnight hags,
  What is't you do?
All.   A deed without a name.

In it we can even hear the tones of eternity:

      We are such stuff
As dreams are made on, and our little life
Is rounded with a sleep.

Good books on Shakespeare's prose and rimed verse are: M. Crane *Shakespeare's Prose* (1951); F.W. Ness, *The Use of Rhyme in Shakespeare's Plays* (1941). Standard discussions of the prosody appear in Jakob Schipper, *A History of English Versification* (1910) and in the *Shakespearian Grammar* by E.A. Abbott cited at the end of the preceding chapter. The works by H. Kökeritz and Sister Miriam Joseph also cited there remain relevant here. Tables on Shakespeare's meter appear in the indispensable reference work, E.K. Chambers, *William Shakespeare A Study of Facts and Problems*, 2 vols. (1930). Discussions of Shakespeare's blank verse have been over-complicated by the attempt to devise rules to cover all phenomena, and impaired by the failure to recognize the part played by unmarked syncopation and elision in his meter. I am not deeply read in the theory of prosody, and the pragmatic formulation I have given (measured *vs.* significant pause and stress) is, so far as I know, my own.

4

The Script

:

THE words 'how to read a book' strike us as whimsical because a book is rarely mistaken for anything else, and, allowing for differences in reading ability, the only way to read a book is to read it. The words 'how to read a script' may be used without whimsical intent. Even highly skilled readers are apt to disregard the special nature of this reading, and although they are getting a great deal from it, they could possibly get still more.

1

The **script** is that portion of a play available to readers—including those who will convert it into a play by playing it. It was called, in Shakespeare's time, 'the book of the play,' just as in our time texts are called 'librettos' rather than 'operas.' The script, when it left the playwright's hands, consisted of a sheaf of manuscript pages containing a continuous column of speeches, in verse and prose, with marginal indication of speakers **(speech-prefixes)** and inserted indication of entrances. Exits also were sometimes indicated, but they could often be treated as self-evident; for instance, if a speaker is assigned a farewell speech, his next move should be obvious. The script contained few stage directions, and no division into acts and scenes. When the play went into rehearsal, a few additional stage directions were added by the prompter, frequently ones related to sound-effects and hand-properties. There might also be some tidying up in the matter of entrances, exits, and speech-prefixes. A company's repertory was normally guarded from publication. When authorized publication of a particular play occurred, the printer simply reproduced the script, using Shakespeare's own draft, or a scrivener's fair copy, or the theatrical prompt copy. It is (or should be) this script as thus transmitted, with as little alteration as possible, that we read when we read Shakespeare. Modernized spelling and punctuation, and normalized mechanical details, are helpful, or at least unavoidable, but any other form of assistance should appear only in footnotes. Alterations in the script itself, even when apparently trivial, may do more harm than good.

Of course the script of a Shakespearan play was designed for use in an Elizabethan theatre by an Elizabethan company of actors. A reader needs only a general knowledge of Elizabethan theatrical methods, and the following sketch should suffice. A company was named after its nominal patron: Shakespeare's was called the 'Lord Chamberlain's Men' for some years prior to 1603 and the 'King's Men' thereafter. It consisted normally of ten highly skilled actors, who were partners in the enterprise and who played the principal roles. These employed six or eight additional actors who played minor roles, often 'doubling' in several small parts. Workers about the theatre could be used as supernumeraries, so that there was no lack of personnel for pageantry, mob scenes, and the like. Battles were usually represented by skirmishes or man-to-man combats on-stage, with the mass-fighting presumed to be occurring off-stage as suggested by alarm-bells, trumpets, drums, and peals of ordinance. Associated with the company, in what amounted to apprentice status, were boys who performed the parts of pages and other diminutive characters. The elder and more skilled of these, and they were very skilled indeed, played the parts of women. Since their number would be limited at any given time, the number of female characters in the plays had to be kept to a minimum; hence the playwrights portrayed an abnormally large number of widowed fathers.

A company rented, or, in the case of Shakespeare's after 1599, owned a theatre. This was a large three-tiered amphitheatre with a platform projecting from the shell into the center of its yard. The platform (forty-three feet wide by twenty-seven and a half feet deep in one known instance) was covered by a canopy supported by pillars, and was open to view from the sides as well as front. It had no proscenium arch, no 'scenery,' and no forward curtain—not because such things were unknown, but because the popular drama had its own traditions and had evolved its own techniques. This stage was **unlocalized**—meaning that the place of the action was left neutral, or was indicated when occasion required by the words and behavior of the actors. Exits and entrances were made through doors at the rear of the stage into the 'tiring-house,' that portion of the shell of the amphitheatre reserved for 'back-stage.' Between the stage doors of most theatres (although not of the one of which we have a contemporary sketch) was a recess covered by a curtain or tapestry, occasionally used for **discoveries** or other special effects. A trap-door in the platform was also occasionally used for special effects. There was a rear gallery looking down upon the stage. This seems sometimes to have been used for spectators, but when the play required, a portion of it could serve as the 'wall' of a beleagured city, the 'window' of an upper chamber, or the like. Access to this area would normally be from back-stage, but Romeo could descend from Juliet's chamber in sight of the audience by using his knotted cords.

The theatrical intermission seems to be a post-Elizabethan invention. In plays at the 'private' theatres, and perhaps occasionally at the popular ones, there were **intervals**—resting points in the performance filled with singing, dancing, and instrumental music. Probably there were four of these at the private theatres in deference to the five-act tradition, but this tradition did not prevail in the Shakespearean theatre. We simply do not know what was its practice, if any, in the matter of intervals. It is possible that the plays were performed without intervals, in the way of our motion pictures, although we should expect that, in the longer plays at least, one or two resting points would be necessary. The Globe theatre was a handsome structure, patronized by intelligent and receptive people. We need not regret the relative simplicity of the stage facilities. Since the plays were performed in the afternoon, darkness had to be simulated by the actor, groping his way or peering by the 'light' of his property-candle, link, or lantern. The play was created by the actors. The focus of attention was always upon them. They were lavishly costumed, and masters of their art.

2

It has been noted that the script when it left Shakespeare's hands consisted of a continuous column of speeches. It might seem, then, that in a discussion of 'components' such as the present, the logical progression would be from 'words' to 'lines' to 'speeches.' But this would be so only if Shakespeare had written 'closet drama' (plays originally designed to be read). Closet drama is composed of 'speeches,' which may be isolated and discussed without distortion as literary parts of a literary whole. With stage drama, however, we must reckon at once with 'speakers'—the real as distinct from the fictitious ones. Speaking the speeches is only part of what they do. Even if they did not 'act' in the usual sense, but only stood and recited, nevertheless they would *be* there, and their mere physical presence would alter the effect of the words. A speech on the lips of an actor is an aspect of impersonation. Viewed otherwise it is as dramatically meaningless as a costume without a wearer. Since the actor is in the presence of other actors, we are not listening to 'speeches' but witnessing **communication.** The communication is an action, which is part of a larger action, which is part of the play as a whole. The structural component is not the speech, but the relation of speech to speech—and to speaker, hearer, and occasion.

The point becomes clear when we recall how often 'Shakespeare' is quoted with relish and approval, and the lines quoted prove to be assigned in his play to a villain, madman, or fool. Jacques's 'All the world's a stage . . .' and Macbeth's 'Tomorrow and tomorrow and tomorrow . . .' function quite differently as they occur in the plays from what we might suppose when reading them as detached speeches. In the play Macbeth's words bear no resemblance to a rational philosophic conclusion; they symbolize a mood which might be succinctly labelled 'despair.' It may seem that the point is obvious, a mere matter of quoting 'out of context'—which is equally possible and indefensible in the case of closet dramas and other writings. The difference is this: the reader of the script of a stage drama may quote—and respond—out of context, because he is unaware of the **context.**

For instance, an evil character may be expressing righteous sentiments, and the unwary reader will view them merely as evidence of his hypocrisy, but the hypocrisy of this character may have been established long before, and the playwright's primary purpose is now to reveal the simplicity or goodness of the character who is listening to these sentiments with pleasure. The speech must be read in terms of this other person, who must be kept in our mind's eye even though he is standing silent. We may take as a crude illustration 'What fools these mortals be!' It sounds like an oracular utterance, and it may be true regardless of its function in the play. Observe, however, that the words could not be spoken by any *mortal,* including Shakespeare (who had not yet achieved immortality), since they would then have to read 'What fools we mortals be,' or 'What fools these mortals be, excepting myself!' As they stand, the words must be spoken by an *immortal,* and in the play they are—but by a goblin and not a god. The word 'mortals' is here a particularizing not a generalizing term, applied to the human (mortal) characters as distinct from the fairy (immortal) ones, in a situation where both mortals and immortals are behaving with equal folly. The speaker is not *wise*—but only partisan.

Sometimes observations which sound in themselves brilliantly rational are assigned to a speaker in circumstances where they demonstrate his aggressive stupidity; and sometimes beautiful utterances are shown as catastrophic in effect. The truth of the matter is present in the script for the reader who is alert and aware of the implied stage proceedings. If a speech suddenly changes its direction, or contains what appears to be an irrelevant interjection or injunction, it means that one or more of the actor listeners has made a silent but visible response. For instance when King Richard breaks into his pathetic and beautiful lamentations with 'Mock not my senseless conjuration, lords,' we must remember that his companions on the stage are men whose very lives depend upon his fortitude. We must be seeing their appalled faces as well as hearing his lovely lines.

True the **speeches** themselves often have perceptible structure, a studied relation of part to part. They range in length from a single word, perhaps an exclamation or oath, to several pages of text, and the longer ones, as noted earlier, may follow a regular text-book pattern for message, oration, indictment, argument and the like, affording pleasure through rhetorical design. They may even be 'framed' by the device of contrast, with, let us say, the nervous staccato style of one speech cast into relief by the slow bumbling style of the next. The contrasted styles will reflect the characters of the speakers, but it may be because he was after the contrast in styles that the playwright has let the second speaker speak at the moment he does. No matter what the style of a speech or succession of speeches, each will seem to have been brought into being by something in the immediate context. Each will be a *response,* expressing ideas or emotions apparently triggered by a preceding speech or action. For this reason, even though the speeches may be longer, more coherent, and less frequently interrupted than those of actual life, the dialogue always sounds like actual communication. This illusion of spontaneity is one mark of the true dramatist; his dialogue never sounds like monologue, snipped up and parcelled out to lay speakers.

Granting that the individual speech is a structural unit only in its relationships, are there any other identifiable units in the script which create structural relationships? When the plays were collected in the folio of 1623, a certain amount of editing was done, and a number of the texts were divided into 'acts,' which were sometimes subdivided into 'scenes.' This editorial process has continued, and now all the plays are divided into acts and scenes in our printed editions. So far as the **act-division** is concerned, the reader will find it harmless only so long as he realizes that it is meaningless. With very few exceptions, the act-division is a later and arbitrary imposition upon the original script. Classical playwrights had usually limited themselves to five episodes or actions in any single play, and their practice influenced the way of thinking of Elizabethan critics, learned playwrights, and editors when they wished to dignify the appearance of the printed text of a popular play. But there is no sign of act-division in the Shakespearean plays printed individually, and in the folio itself it is mechanical and often bad. In our modern editions, there are a few instances where the division is actually placed in the midst of an action, and many instances where it separates two closely integrated actions. The danger to the reader is that he will fail to see, because of the present intrusive act-division, the original effect of the juxtaposition of two actions when the first now appears at the end of one 'act' and the second at the beginning of the next 'act.' He may also expect the five acts to perform five perceptibly different functions, providing, let us say, 'exposition,' 'entanglement,' 'climax,' 'disentanglement,' and 'resolution,' or something of the kind. Any such relation of act-division to structure (and there is little) will be purely coincidental.

One might suppose that the act-division is roughly meaningful, say to the extent that the **exposition** does come in the first part of the play. But actually the exposition comes in all parts of the play. Certainly a **sub-plot** which only develops at the end will not have its exposition at the beginning. More important, however, is the fact (which should not be obscured) that exposition suffuses everything. We are constantly being 'filled in' on what has happened before the first action shown, and what is happening between the actions shown. And we are receiving additional data throughout the play on the character of the characters. One of Shakespeare's common devices, and a very effective one, is to show us something first and make us wait for the explanation.

The original script truly did contain another kind of division. At intervals, all the characters will have made exits, individually or in groups, so that the stage will be vacant. There will then be an entrance of characters, individually or in groups, so that the stage will be occupied and action resumed. The new action will usually be conceived of as taking place at a later time or in a different place or both. The divisional points were not numbered or otherwise labeled in the original script, but their presence is unarguable. Hence the play is blocked off into units which we may justifiably call **scenes.** The number of these varies greatly in the various plays—from eight in *A Midsummer Night's Dream* to thirty-nine in *Antony and Cleopatra.* The number of scenes depends not upon the length of the play but upon its nature, a most significant point: there are more scenes in the shortest of the tragedies, *Macbeth,* than in the longest, *Hamlet.* In the representative case of *The Merchant of Venice* there are nineteen scenes, and it is more accurate to say that it is a play 'in nineteen actions' than that it is a play 'in five acts.' The five-act division which the plays share alike in our modern editions suggests that there is a structural resemblance between *A Midsummer Night's Dream* and *Antony and Cleopatra* when there is no such resemblance at all.

The scenes are significant units because their relationship to each other can be perceived, but they vary enormously among themselves. In one scene the **action** may be a single episode, or even soliloquy, while in another it may be a whole chain of episodes, with different groups of characters present at beginning and end. The difference in the number and nature of the scenes makes for maximum flexibility, so that the structure of a play can be precisely what its subject and purpose demand. Sometimes we seem to detect a resemblance in structure in certain plays, for instance in those where almost the whole cast is assembled in a long and enthralling scene about three-fourths of the way through—as in the trial scene of *The Merchant of Venice* and the abdication scene in *Richard II.* In both these instances, the scene is followed by a striking new development—the ring plot in *The Merchant* and the Aumerle conspiracy in *Richard II.* But the structural resemblance is more apparent than real because the parallel units function quite differently. The ring plot focuses our attention on the marriage union of the various couples, the only remaining exploitable interest. The conspiracy plot, in contrast, *diverts* our attention from the ruthlessness of Richard's successor. There was plenty of significant action to round out the end of the play—nothing less than the virtual murder committed by Henry—but his act of aggression is juxtaposed with his act of clemency, the pardoning of Aumerle. It did not quite fit Shakespeare's book to focus our final attention too sharply upon Henry in the role of murderer.

Variation in structure does not mean lack of structure—quite the contrary. It does mean that any fixed conception of **structure** will fail to fit individual plays. The difficulty involved in buttoning a jacket on an eel does not mean that an eel lacks structure. Perhaps a happier analogy might be found, but structure in Shake-speare is truly organic and lithe. It is amusing to observe how often critics have busily buttoned it up in a ready-made garment, usually in the five-act style, without even noticing when they have finished that the play is not in it. But, one may ask, if Shakespearean dramatic structure is so evasive as to be virtually invisible, is it worth our contemplation? Indeed it is. We shall return to the point later on.

3

It will be useful now to consider a reader's position when he turns to the first scene in a script. **Characters** appear and begin to speak. Who are they, what are they like, and what is their relationship to each other? Where are they, where have they been, and where are they going when they leave? At this point the reader must display what Keats called 'negative capability'; he must be responsive 'without any irritable reaching after fact and reason.' The dialogue will answer any of the questions which are pertinent at the moment. When no answer is forthcoming, it means that the question is not pertinent, that the reader or spectator need not know. He should not fight against the artistic method by lusting after immediate certainty. So far as place is concerned, the reader is on equal terms with the original spectator since supplementary information was not provided by scenic backgrounds; and so far as people are concerned, the reader at least has a printed list of characters whereas the original spectator had no program. Early scenes employ various devices to identify characters: formal introductions of one to another, frequent use of names in direct address, sometimes even virtual roll-calls introduced on one pretext or another. It is interesting to observe the canny means by which the problem is solved.

Despite his printed list of characters, the reader is at a greater disadvantage at the beginning than at any other time. When the play is seen in performance, the process of identification is accelerated by the physical appearance of the impersonators. Old John of Gaunt *looks* old, and King Richard is regally attired. It is possible for a reader temporarily to mistake Richard himself as old because of the father-image implicit in the word 'king,' and because he is at the moment assuming an air of great gravity. The costumes and ornaments are an aid in indicating relative rank. It was probably apparent before either of the characters speak in the first scene of *Richard II* that Bolingbroke is of the blood royal and Mowbray is not. Especially in the history plays visual symbols would be helpful, because characters are numerous and are often addressed or alluded to by several **names:** a surname (Bolingbroke) a dukedom (Hereford), and a prospective dukedom (Lancaster); or a first name (Harry), a family name (Percy), and a sobriquet (Hotspur). Mortimer's sister is 'Lady Mortimer' to Prince Hal (Henry Plantagenet) even though he mentions her only in her role as Percy's wife.

But something may be lost as well as gained by this accelerated identification when the play is seen instead of read. The production may be a poor production, poorly cast, with the visual symbols inferior to the reader's imaginary ones. The visible symbols may reveal too much too soon, anticipating the reader's own discovery of villainy or folly by presenting at once the character with a vicious or vapid mien. In performances of *Hamlet,* Polonius is an utter fool from the beginning. In Shakespeare's script he *achieves* that status. It may not seem enough to the producer or actor to show that Richard is young; he must also show what he thinks he has learned about this character from the play as a whole, and Richard will appear as a sensitive martyr or a twittering effeminate in the very first scene. He is neither of these things, but even if he were, it would be tipping the playwright's hand to disclose the fact to the audience before the play itself does so. This error—and it is a common one in both Shakespearean production and criticism—is the 'error of omniscience.' It means that the play is being read backward instead of forward, and the poet's method of progressive revelation is being crudely cancelled out.

The **location** of the action is unimportant if unmentioned in the script, as is normally the case. Since the first scene of *Richard II* shows the King granting an audience, the place is the court. Where a king is, in his magisterial capacity, that place is the court. The court moves with the king from residence to residence, and it is pointless to ask in what particular royal residence, the actual historical audience took place. It was, in this case, Windsor, but if the playwright had considered the fact artistically relevant, he would have mentioned it. It is a bit of miscellaneous information such as some readers like to pick up, and may even feel insecure without, and there is no harm in garnering the item so long as it is recognized as having nothing to do with the artistic experience. The next scene mentions Plashy, the Duchess of Gloucester's residence, but Plashy is mentioned because a description of its desolation is atmospherically useful, not because the speakers are there; as a matter of fact we do not know where they are except that the place is private. This lesson the reader must quickly learn—to attend closely to what is present in the script, and never to vex himself with what is absent. If he craves additional facts, he is asking for information which at the moment would be irrelevant or premature.

When Shakespeare's plays began to be performed with scenic backgrounds, editors began to indicate places at the head of each scene, often playing a guessing-game. These **place-headings** survive in many modern editions, and are harmless if ignored. Such designations as 'Another Room in the Palace,' 'Another Part of the Forest,' 'Another Part of the Battlefield' are useless and often untrue. If the characters are battling, the place is obviously a battlefield, and the significant progress of the battle is from skirmish to skirmish, and not from one spot to 'another.' Even when the place is correctly labelled, the heading is supplying irrelevant information unless something is made of the locale in the lines themselves, in which case it is preempting their function. Awareness of locale when useful is communicated by the lines at the right time and at the right pace. Places are often indicated by **hand properties** rather than by furnishings, and the actors are usually standing: thus a few tankards passed about are enough to indicate a tavern setting, and waiters passing through with trenchers are enough to suggest a banquet. Sometimes, of course, there are **furnishings,** but a throne, a bed, a table, a few stools usually suffice. Given freedom by the unlocalized stage, Shakespeare supplies imposing **settings** when needed with poetic description appealing to the imagination, and 'jocund day stands tiptoe on the misty mountain tops' without need of stage sun, mist, or mountain tops. *A Midsummer Night's Dream* is flooded with moonlight, but it is not supplied by the material methods used by Bottom and his crew. A reader is as able as the original spectators, perhaps more able, to respond to the verbal stimulus and provide imaginary settings when invoked. Even the sketchy scenery on the current Shakespearean stage may be more of a distraction than anything else. When the script makes nothing whatever of locale, the reader is in a strategic position to leave the setting vague and to concentrate on the people. These are *always* important.

What the characters are *like* (that is, their **characterization)** is indicated by a wealth of data from which we may draw inferences. We are never *told* what they are like in direct statements issuing from the playwright himself. When one of the characters makes a statement on what another character is like, we have no guarantee of its reliability, but only a broadened base of inquiry; the question now becomes, what is the character who is making the statement like, and how far can his view be trusted? The exceptions to this rule are so few as to be scarcely worth considering. In the choral speeches in *Henry V* we seem to have extra-dramatic statements about the titular character; in one of these the adjectives 'royal,' 'modest,' 'fresh,' 'cheerful,' 'sweet,' 'liberal,' applied to a king who circulates among his soldiers, conferring 'a little touch of Harry in the night' seem to indicate Shakespeare's own appraisal, as does the exclamation, 'Praise and glory on his head!' But even this is not an absolutely clear case, since perhaps we should identify the choral speaker as the Spirit of England rather than the author 'in propria persona'; nevertheless it comes as near to 'authorial' comment as anything we get. In general we are given four categories of data upon which to base our inferences about what a character is like: what he does, what he says, the way he says it, and what others say about him. The relative importance of these categories varies immensely from instance to instance. If forced to generalize I should say that in the most usual order of importance they would be: what he does, the way he says things, what others say about him, what he says. The order is immaterial: it is the interplay of the factors which gives us our conception of the character.

We have been speaking of people and places as introduced in the script, and how the reader must adapt himself to the method of presentation. The reader must be equally adaptable to the method of treating **time.** He must get used, first of all, to what may strike him as violent interruptions in the early part of the script. A second scene may introduce a wholly new set of characters, apparently involved in a wholly different situation from that already introduced. The relationship will be suggested, and later made clear, but for the moment the reader must suspend and redirect his attention. This is easier for those accustomed to older forms of narration, such as the nineteenth-century novel, than for habitual readers of twentieth-century fiction, long or short, which tends to have a simple and unbroken 'story line.' The length of time intervening between the action is one scene and the action in the next will usually be unspecified. One must simply assume that it is 'later.' The chronological scheme is progressive. There are no 'flash-backs' except in an occasional dream, as when Richard III is haunted by his victims, or a special device like Hamlet's mouse-trap play, which allegorizes an action of the past. Past action is usually presented through allusion in the dialogue, sometimes in the form of extended descriptions.

There used to be considerable ingenuity exercised upon trying to work out **time-schemes** for the various plays—that is, the length of fictional time covered between successive episodes and by the play as a whole. It can be done in some plays exactly, in some approximately, in some not at all. The reason for the difficulty, if it is allowed to become a difficulty, is that time in these plays has an extremely elastic character. This is observable within scenes as well as between them. Someone will make an exit, and one brief speech by someone who remains onstage will suffice to cover the 'time' required for the absent character to transact considerable business offstage and then return. Such telescoping of time may mark the entire scene as well as any part of it: the first scene of *Hamlet* takes less than ten minutes to play, yet it begins at midnight and ends at dawn. The illusion is such that we never notice the discrepancy. All forms of art manipulate time and space; otherwise all paintings would be 'life-size' or, rather, there would be no paintings since two dimensions would not do for representing three. Shakespearean drama merely goes further in the manipulation of time than the art forms with which readers are more familiar. There is even **double time**—that is, the presentation of events in such a way that we would have to conclude, if we held a stop-watch on the proceedings, that time moves at a different pace for some of the characters than for others. In *Antony and Cleopatra* a scene portrays Cleopatra sending Alexas to get a description of Octavia from the Messenger who has just brought news of Antony's marriage to her. A later scene begins 'Enter the Messenger as before' and the description is given to Cleopatra's taste. A few minutes have apparently elapsed between these two scenes. Nevertheless, in scenes coming between them, we witness momentous and time-consuming changes in the Roman Empire, including Ventidius's defeat of the Parthians. Actually this is not so much double-time as 'zigzag-time.' In order that we shall keep Egypt and Cleopatra in mind, the playwright has split the Messenger episode in two, and inserted the halves among the Roman events. The 'timing' is literally absurd but artistically right. To begin working out literal time-schedules is to ask wrong questions and to peer at details intended to escape notice. What has been said above about place applies also to time. The reader should think about it only when his attention is called to it by words in the script.

4

The employment of elastic and double time is what is known as a **convention.** A convention is a customary and agreed-upon departure from literal probability in the interest of artistic economy. All art forms have their conventions, and these alter from age to age within each art form. Shakespearean drama shares many conventions with all forms of drama, from Greek tragedy to the motion pictures. These we scarcely notice. We notice those conventions which our present-day drama has, for better or worse, abandoned or almost abandoned. We must adapt ourselves to these, and not be disturbed or misled by them.

The **soliloquy** is the convention in Shakespearean drama that has most frequently attracted popular notice. In actual life a person 'talks to himself' only if he is old, eccentric, unbalanced, or emotionally disturbed. In Shakespearean drama this is not the case, but it is important to recognize that sometimes characters in the plays do 'talk to themselves' for precisely these reasons. In other words, not all of the soliloquies in the drama are conventional. The reader himself must be alert to the distinction, and recognize that there may be one. Even the 'conventional' soliloquies are not all alike, and the notion that they are always addressed directly to the audience is fallacious. In fact some of the speeches delivered by characters who are alone on the stage are not truly soliloquies. We do not call the present-day monologue of a 'stand-up' comedian a 'soliloquy,' and there are such **monologues** in Shakespeare's scripts. These would, of course, be addressed directly to the audience. Or there is the type of **expository speech,** partly choral in function, in which a character is conscripted by the playwright to convey information or interpretation quickly and explicitly. This information may be about the nature and motives of the character himself—a **self-characterizing speech**—and there is room for considerable difference of opinion about the manner in which it operates. May it be taken at full face value because the speaker is 'alone'? But he is scarcely 'alone'—he is addressing a thousand spectators. To what extent can his awareness of his own traits, and his willingness to expatiate upon them objectively (or brazenly), itself be considered a trait? The answer to such questions will vary considerably in various instances, and the reader must remain open-minded, taking each instance on its own merits. Much will depend upon the speaker and the occasion, and upon small signals within the speeches themselves. Finally there are the true soliloquies, in which a character (*not* speaking directly to the audience) is, for artistic convenience, speaking his thoughts aloud. It is interesting to note that such soliloquies are not given to characters who otherwise appear incapable of introspection. These true soliloquies are the most revealing, if not precisely of what the character is truly like, at least of what he truly supposes he is like.

The use of the **aside** shows the same variation. Some asides are actually snide remarks spoken from the corner of the mouth to other characters or to the audience. Some resemble the expository or choral 'soliloquy,' quickly putting the audience au courant with what is happening on the stage. Some, like true soliloquies, reveal the speaker's thoughts and emotions as he observes the action taking place. These may be as long as soliloquies, and are often spoken (as in famous scenes in *Love's Labor's Lost* and *Much Ado about Nothing*) by characters in concealment or in a removed position. They were not, of course, spoken in a hoarse whisper. Finally there is the type of aside which gives the most trouble because we are not always certain that it is an aside. Characters will be speaking to each other, while certain other characters, present in the scene, will not be hearing what they say. Often this is obvious, and the situation is rendered plausible by the grouping and spacing of characters. The reader can easily manage, in his own imaginary production, the necessary 'blocking.' But there are instances where a single character, who has just been or is about to be in communication with other characters, is spoken of as if he were not there. He may or may not be hearing what is said. Does Edmund in the first scene in *King Lear* hear his father Gloucester speaking jocularly about his bastardy? Some editors, considering the remarks indecorous, as indeed they are, insert 'asides.' Some critics, assuming that Edmund hears and resents them, treat the remarks as 'motivation' for Edmund's villainy. But in this case at least, as in most if not all similar ones, the script as a whole resolves the dilemma. Edmund, neither when they are made nor at any later point, shows any resentment about the remarks themselves. His grievance is not that he is a bastard but that he is 'uninheriting' (as he would be anyway as younger son, even if legitimate). It makes little difference whether he hears the remarks or not, and the text should not be tampered with. They are equally revealing of *Gloucester's* character in either case.

Mention was made above of characters speaking asides while in **concealment.** This does not mean that they are concealed from the audience, their voices issuing from hiding places. They are in 'con ventional' concealment from the other characters. We can see them, but their fellow characters supposedly cannot—unless the playwright doubles the convention, and lets those characters catch glimpses of the ones in 'hiding' who have been in plain view right along. The convention of concealment is related to the convention of **invisibility** and the convention of **disguise.** A character such as Prospero or Ariel is assumed to be visible or invisible as the occasion requires, his presumed condition depending upon his wearing or not wearing a certain garment, or upon whether the other characters seem able to see him, or upon his mere say-so. The identity of a character may be completely concealed from his nearest and dearest kinsman by the mere donning of a hat, a cloak, or a false beard. This disguise will prove penetrable only at the playwright's convenience. The convention of disguise had a wider utility than one might suppose. Of course it was useful as a means of complicating intrigue, or as comic mystification, but, more important, it permitted principals to act as their own agents. Kent could have looked after Lear from afar, and Duke Vincentio could have gathered his information about affairs in Vienna through a network of spies, but these 'realistic' methods would have been more cumbersome and less dramatic. Kent can respond at once and continuously to his master's falling state, and Duke Vincentio can hear with his own ears even himself traduced. The vital missions of such men, adumbrated by their 'disguises,' may be authentic and convincing enough.

We might add to such easily identifiable conventions as those discussed above the convention of **incidental entertainment.** At intervals the major movement of a drama may pause, or even come to a standstill, while we are regaled with a song, a dance, a masque, a playlet, or a bit of wrestling or duelling. Nearly always these divertissements have an organic function in the drama, but the function they perform could in most cases be performed otherwise and more economically, so that we must recognize them as being introduced largely for their own sake. Nevertheless, they are both delightful in themselves, and important in determining the overall character of a play. Some of the comedies would not sing to us as they do, were it not for their actual songs.

Sometimes Shakespeare's ends seem finely shaped, rough-hew

them how he will; he seems to excel by **serendipity,** achieving fine things by accident or petty necessity. He will capitalize upon a convention and convert it into a master stroke. In *As You Like It* somebody must say something to supply the time while Orlando leaves to fetch Adam, and so Jaques gets his speech on the seven ages of man: then when young Orlando returns with old Adam in his arms, we have a visual emblem of youth and age which takes all the conclusiveness out of Jaques's grim verbal vignette of youth and age. Real horses cannot be brought onto the stage, even in a highway-robbery scene, and so Poins and Prince Hal conceal Falstaff's horse —with inimitable comic results. A dead body must be got on or off the curtainless stage somehow, without having to walk, and the poet finds the artistically inevitable solution: 'Let four captains bear Hamlet like a soldier . . .'; 'Enter Lear, with Cordelia in his arms.' In art there is no such thing as serendipity: what appears like it in Shakespeare is, in fact, our best evidence of his complete mastery of his medium.

5

If the reader judges a script piecemeal, he may have many complaints: of lack of **motivation** or confused motivation; of abrupt moral deterioration or abrupt reform; of character inconsistency as when an intelligent person displays a convenient gullibility; or of characters suppressed midway in a play, either permanently or while their presence might expose the brittleness of some bit of intrigue; of loose ends in the conclusion, with quick matchmakings to swell betrothal processions or sudden deaths to augment funerals. The reader should remember Charles Lamb's injunction: 'Everything, in heaven and earth, in man and in story, in books and in fancy, acts by confederacy, by juxtaposition, by circumstance and place.' It is the 'sum total' of Shakespeare that effects us; the separate parts even of his 'princely pieces' look 'beggarly and bald' when divorced from 'connection and circumstance.' An evil action may be left unmotivated because to 'motivate' it would be, in effect, to excuse it. Some other action may be multiply motivated or confusingly motivated because, in similar circumstances in actual life, we never know precisely or fully the springs of human conduct. And so it goes. An inconsistency may seem so only because the reader has failed to notice something, or because he expects in literature a kind of consistency which he never finds in life. Sudden and inexplicable phenomena may occur, yet not where they do essential harm.

The reader must not be afflicted by belief in the **myth of perfection.** These plays are not perfect in the way of machines—a complex of precision-ground parts, the cogs exactly meshed and uniformly lubricated. They are works of poetic art, not precise and finite but suggestive and open-ended. And they *do* have imperfections, often considerable ones, even when measured by standards which are truly applicable. But these imperfections are miniscule when weighed against total value. It may seem that a reader who is told that he must read so as not to miss anything, and is told at the same time that there are details intended to escape notice, is put in a very peculiar position. He is, of course, but he is not being victimized by special pleading. We must remember what these plays are. They stand midway between **symbolic** and **realistic** drama. Behind them lies the kind of drama in which the peaks of biblical history from the creation of the world to the visions of doomsday might be played on a single Corpus Christi holiday. Only a few years before they were written, the conquests of Tamburlaine were compressed into two plays, as if, now, the whole Napoleonic Wars should be dramatized in a four-hour spectacle. Entire nations had to be symbolized by their kings. Ahead of Shakespearean drama lies the kind of play in which sweeping action disappears, while minutiae of human character and conduct are submitted to the microscope. Shakespearean drama combines many of the qualities of these earlier and later kinds. Its conventions had to be bold and eclectic. It has been foolishly said that Shakespeare's kind of drama did not adhere to its own conventions. What this seems to mean is that the critic prefers either wholly symbolic or wholly realistic drama. But the combination of the two in Shakespeare is itself a convention, to which he certainly adheres, with results that have never been matched in 'purer' forms of drama. Those things agreed upon as permissible are the 'conventions' of an age. The artists and lovers of art in that age are the only judges of whether these conventions were being 'adhered to.'

The reader of the script is obliged to transform it into a play by the operation of his intellect, and at the same time to respond emotionally to the play he is thus re-creating. He must read the script more than once, and yet retain the innocence of his vision during successive readings as if he were reading for the first time. He must be 'surprised' by what is familiar. It is less difficult than it sounds. Perhaps this is as good a place as any to mention the controversial issue of reading *versus* seeing Shakespeare. It is a false issue; first, because we are rarely offered the choice; and second, because it ignores the factor of quality. That theatres are wonderful places, that actors are life-givers to dramatic conceptions, that dramatic experience is richest when shared with an assembly of fellow human beings, and that Shakespeare properly produced in the right theatre by the right actors before the right audience is a grand artistic experience, are all so self-evident as to make argument superfluous. Nevertheless, just as lovers of classical music prefer silence to hearing their classics butchered, so a lover of drama has a right to prefer reading to seeing bad productions. We go to the theatre for an artistic experience, not to support a worthy 'cause.' Seeing bad productions may be preferable to bad reading, but the question then rises whether either is worth an argument. What we want is both better reading and better productions, and the two things are related. Readers of Shakespeare are apt to apply higher standards than non-readers. A producer may complain that they come with 'preconceptions.' They do to be sure—and should. One reads to form conceptions. A production is in no danger of an adverse response if it offers better conceptions. It will never amount to much if designed for those who are easy to please. It will amount to even less if designed for those who are hard to please—with Shakespeare—and who must be offered something to assuage their pain. The present guide is designed not to take business away from the Shakespearean theatre but to send it there. At present there would be no such theatre at all were it not for readers.

We must return in conclusion to the general subject of **structure.** In recent years there has been a tendency to interpret the plays in terms of the recurrent words and images in any given example. 'Iterative images' are cited, and are discovered to establish or emphasize themes. A perception of the relatedness of such verbal components is an excellent thing. Close reading is good. The difficulty lies in combining close reading with inclusive imagining, so as to retain perspective. A word or image, like anything else works by 'circumstance and place.' The risk is that the conscious extraction and grouping of words and images will slight context, and result in a rival construct, with the selector's juxtapositions substituted for the playwright's juxtapositions. A verbal image may be operating with other verbal images in other parts of the *script,* but it is also operating with visual images in its own part of the *play*.

One of the most sincerely offered and respectfully received of modern critical suggestions is that there is a pattern of 'divestiture images' in *King Lear*. Lear's words and actions having to do with clothing are brought together to codify his presumed shedding of corruption and progress to spiritual purity. But when Lear cries, 'Off, off, you lendings! Come unbutton here,' Edgar is standing by as Tom a Bedlam, 'naked and near to beast.' How will the juxtaposition of this visual image operate? Will Lear's words and action suggest a hunger for purity, or a hunger for degradation as he teeters on the brink of madness, or both? And earlier, when he refers to the gorgeous raiment which scarce keeps Regan warm, is he repudiating its superfluity, or defending her and his own right to 'more than nature needs'? Our eyes see her beautifully clad. Must we reject this beauty as a symbol of depravity because it is attached to Regan, or accept it as a symbol of the gains of civilization, without which 'man's life is poor as beast's'? Surely divestiture does not always signify purification: when we see Lear recovered from his madness, we see him *freshly clad*. And finally, in one of the greatest moments in Shakespeare, when Lear says at last, 'Pray you undo this button,' is the operative confederacy with earlier allusions to clothing, or to the wonderful words that follow: 'Thank you, sir'? Images are truly related to each other, but in this respect they differ little from other components in the play. Everything is related to everything.

Coleridge was a fine reader of Shakespeare, but he failed to see

the function of the Porter's speech in *Macbeth*. He considered it a
blemish, foisted into the script by another hand. De Quincy then
pointed out that the speech is far from a blemish; in its effect it is
the perfect structural underprop for the murder scene which precedes. Robert Bridges considered the total effect of *Macbeth* 'magnificent,' but he regretfully submitted the opinion that the effect
was produced by trickery, by what he called a 'dishonesty' of means.
But if a total effect is magnificent, the technical manipulation by
which the effect is achieved should also be deemed magnificent.
There is no such thing as 'dishonesty' in art which advances an
honest aim. Bridges in this case was reading badly. From the very
beginning Shakespeare intimates the kind of man Macbeth is behind his military heroism. The playwright does this partly by means
of a character we never even see. A dialogue about the treacherous
Thane of Cawdor, whose title has just been transferred in reward
to Macbeth, is thus concluded by King Duncan:

> There's no art
> To find the mind's construction in the face.
> He was a gentleman on whom I built
> An absolute trust.
> *Enter Macbeth, Banquo, Ross, and Angus.*
> O worthiest cousin. . . .

The entrance of Macbeth, the present Thane of Cawdor, upon such
a pronouncement about the past Thane of Cawdor lends the words
the quality of a conjuration. Past Cawdor, present Cawdor, cycle
recurring—again false face hides 'what the false heart doth know.'
A character whom we have never seen, but of whom we have
heard much, strangely compounded of good and evil, has been
functioning in these early scenes as a prefiguration of Macbeth
himself. Who can deny the artistic calculation in this particular
entrance of Macbeth at this particular time, the silent prompting by
the playwright, pointing us in an honest direction? This is Shakespearean structure.

As a convenience the verbal and rhythmical components have
been discussed separately, but the poetry resides not in words, or
images, or lines, but in the relationship of all. The poetry is part of

the structure. The whole play is a structure, and the structural principle cannot be isolated. It resides in those invisible junctures where every part impinges upon every other part. This is where Shakespeare himself resides, unseen but omnipresent. When we read well enough to perceive the structure, we are truly reading the man and can have no doubts about his intent. He is far from being that neutral, slippery, 'impersonal' artist of a critical legend which was brought into being by the process of reading scripts piecemeal and letting pieces 'cancel out.' Perhaps we have heard too much of Shakespeare's 'gentleness' and not enough of his honesty. It is beside the point that some of his plays are less good than others, and that even the best may contain occasional signs of careless improvisation: their affinity is with truth, and they always bear the stamp of their maker. No one who has learned to read him can be unaware of his presence, or mistake it for that of someone else.

The most comprehensive treatment of the nature of the scripts and their relation to early editions appears in the works of Sir Walter Greg, notably *Dramatic Documents from the Elizabethan Playhouses,* 2 vols. (1931), and *The Shakespeare First Folio* (1955). (On the moot question of act division, see W.F. Jewkes, *Act Division in Elizabethan and Jacobean Plays,* 1958.) Although there are good books on individual conventions, most of the older works on structure in general are obsolete because of their reliance upon inapplicable theoretical principles. Inductive studies are beginning to appear: see Hereward T. Price, *Construction in Shakespeare, Univ. of Michigan Contributions . . . ,* (1951); Madeleine Doran, *Endeavours of Art* (1954); Henry L. Snuggs, *Shakespeare and Five Acts* (1960); David Bevington, *From Mankind to Marlowe* (1962). For the general reader the most useful book on the Elizabethan type of theatre is the copiously illustrated *The Globe Restored,* by C. Walter Hodges (1956), and, on the methods of staging, *Shakespeare at the Globe,* by Bernard Beckerman (1962).

The standard collection of materials on Shakespeare's life and professional career is Sir Edmund Chambers, *William Shakespeare,* mentioned earlier. Recent biographies are Mark Eccles, *Shakespeare in Warwickshire,* 1961, (concentrating upon home, family, and friends); Marchette Chute, *Shakespeare of London,* 1949 (concentrating upon professional career); and Gerald E. Bentley, *Shakespeare: A Biograph-*

ical Handbook, 1961 (conveniently surveying the surviving records). Shakespeare lived before biographies were commonly written and before the memorabilia of poets were collected and preserved; hence, although we know more about his life than about those of most of the popular writers of his time, we know less than we would wish. This, and less ponderable factors, have led to the rise and fall of a succession of cults attributing his works to various 'true' authors ranging from Christopher Marlowe to Queen Elizabeth, with Lord Bacon running at the head of the pack in the last century and Lord Oxford in the present one. A sufficient answer to the peculiar books generated by these cults is a description of their contents; those interested may read such descriptions in W. & E. Friedman, *The Shakespeare Ciphers Examined* (1957); F.E. Halliday, *The Cult of Shakespeare* (1957); F.W. Wadsworth, *The Poacher from Stratford* (1958); R.C. Churchill, *Shakespeare and his Betters* (1959); H.N. Gibson, *The Shakespeare Claimants* (1962).

The brief bibliographies following these opening chapters are confined to a few unique reference works, and to the most recent and accessible specialized studies bearing upon the subjects treated. No attempt has been made to represent the vast body of scholarship upon Shakespeare's sources, times, ideas, contemporaries, audience, and the like. The omission implies no disregard. Many bibliographies and handbooks are available, one of the fullest by K.J. Holzknecht, *The Background of Shakespeare's Plays,* 1950. The best collection of the literary materials used by Shakespeare is *Narrative and Dramatic Sources of Shakespeare,* ed. Geoffrey Bullough, 4 vols., 1957-62 (as yet incomplete). Excellent periodicals devoted wholly to the author are *Shakespeare Quarterly,* ed. James McManaway, and *Shakespeare Survey,* ed. Allaradyce Nicoll.

II
Mastery Achieved

1

Works: c. 1587 to 1596

:

S H A K E S P E A R E was a native of Stratford-upon-Avon, born about April 23, 1564, married in 1583, and the father of three children by 1585 in his twenty-first year. In 1592, at twenty-eight, he was an actor-playwright in London and had scored at least one great hit, *1 Henry VI*. We do not know when he became an actor or when he began to write. As son of a burgess, he was eligible for a free education in the Stratford school. This education was primarily linguistic and literary, of a kind which sufficed most of the popular writers of the day. The acting profession, or 'quality' as it was then called, was open to talented members of his class from boyhood on. It was one of the 'literate crafts,' like the more restrictively organized crafts of the scrivener and printer. These proved a readier route to authorship than did university training; in fact a high proportion of the playwrights before and during Shakespeare's lifetime were actors. In addition to literacy and access to the acting profession, Shakespeare needed, in order to become a great dramatist, nothing more than genius. This, nature bestowed upon him in its socially indiscriminate way.

We have most of what he wrote in approximately the form in which he wrote it, a remarkable piece of luck considering the circumstances. Theatrical companies preferred to keep their plays out of print lest other companies steal them, so that a major portion of Elizabethan drama has perished. The plays which happened to get into print were considered not 'literature' but popular ephemera, chiefly useful as mementos of or substitutes for theatrical experience. They were issued in quarto-size books at sixpence each, and when the script was surreptitiously obtained, the version was often corrupt. Usually they bore no author's name on the title page, even when composed by so able a poet as Marlowe, but only the name of the acting company. Ben Jonson opposed this custom and supervised the printing of his plays; we owe much to his insistence that stage-plays, at least his, be taken seriously as art. We owe still more to Shakespeare's admirers, who decided, against the set of conventional opinion, that his plays were worth reading and preserving.

Midway in his writing career, printers began putting his name on the title pages of such of his plays as they could come by. In some cases they even adorned with his name the title pages of plays he had not written: *Sir John Oldcastle, The London Prodigal, A Yorkshire Tragedy*. Seven years after his death, several actors cooperated with a syndicate of London printers; and his plays were issued in collected form in a handsome folio (1623) complete with engraved portrait, dedication, commendatory verses, and epistles signed by the actors Hemming and Condell. These members of Shakespeare's company (whom he had remembered in his will) expressed the regret that he could not 'have set forth, and overseen his own writings,' but they themselves had done astonishingly well. Although the volume is flawed by the host of misprints often found in Elizabethan books, its contents are authentic. It reprints only the good quartos, and in the case of the plays which had not been printed at all (about half the total) it prints what appears to have been the best available manuscripts. It contains thirty-six plays, and not one has been successfully attacked as 'non-Shakespearean.' In fact the folio erred on the side of caution. Two plays, *Pericles* and

The Two Noble Kinsmen, were excluded, although the first certainly, and the second probably, are at least in part by Shakespeare, as evidenced both by their style and their quarto title pages.

The folio does not contain the non-dramatic poems. These are: *Venus and Adonis,* published in 1593 with Shakespeare's dedication to the Earl of Southampton; *Lucrece* published in 1594 and similarly dedicated; *The Phoenix and the Turtle,* a brief poem printed as Shakespeare's in a collection called *Love's Martyr* in 1601; and the *Sonnets,* published in 1609 without Shakespeare's permission but duly ascribed to him. These, then, are Shakespeare's works, the received canon: thirty-eight plays, and four non-dramatic works. They are known as his from both internal or stylistic evidence and external or objective evidence. Each of the forty-two works was ascribed to him by his contemporaries, who were in the best position to know, and in no case was a rival claim put forth. There are in addition a few brief poems and a few scenes in anonymous plays which have been attributed to him upon conjectural grounds which are fairly convincing. These miscellaneous pieces are interesting but need not concern us here—there is God's plenty without them.

What Shakespeare wrote is more of a certainty than when he wrote the individual items, but the situation is not hopeless. As an aid in dating the pieces, we have internal evidence such as style, allusions, and use of sources; the date of individual quartos (although normally later than the date of composition); occasional records of performances; and a tribute by one Francis Meres in his *Palladis Tamia,* 1598. Meres calls Shakespeare the best of English playwrights, and lists most of the plays and poems written by 1598, thus giving us a useful dividing point. Since the playwright's name had appeared thus far only on a few title pages, Meres must have gone to some little trouble; he seems to have missed only two titles.

For the time being we are interested only in the works written by 1596, by which year Shakespeare had attained mastery in each of the three categories of drama he essayed. In this period also came his two narrative poems and, in all probability, some of his sonnets. Meres mentions his authorship of sonnets, privately circulated, and versions of two of those in the collection of 1609 (numbers 138 and 144) were printed in a miscellany called *The Passionate Pil-grim* in 1599, but individual sonnets may have been written at any time in Shakespeare's career from the beginning until 1609. *Venus and Adonis* and *Lucrece* are retellings of the familiar classical stories indicated by the titles; they are fine poems, but few would be inclined to call them great ones. Any of the Sonnets written about the same time, 1593-94, were in all probability, although we cannot be sure of this, fine lyrics but not great ones. All of Shake-speare's one hundred and fifty-two Sonnets (two in the 1609 col-lection seem spurious) show his remarkable facility, but only a minority of them are great poems. These may have been written after 1594 or even after 1598, although a critical tradition places the bulk of the Sonnets in the mid-nineties.

We are primarily concerned with the plays. By 1596 Shakespeare had written, in all likelihood, thirteen of the thirty-eight plays in the received canon. Yet by the end of that year his name had not appeared on a single title page, and only one of his plays had been printed in a reliable version, *Titus Andronicus,* 1594. Two others had been printed in debased versions, *2 Henry VI* as 'The First Part of the Contention betwixt the Two Famous Houses of York and Lancaster' (1594), and *3 Henry VI* as 'The True Tragedy of Richard Duke of York' (1594). Two other play quartos, 'The Troublesome Reign of King John,' and 'The Taming of a Shrew' had appeared in 1591 and 1594 respectively; these are indubitably related to Shakespeare's *King John* and *The Taming of the Shrew,* and probably not simply as their sources, but what the relationship is still remains undetermined.

. For obvious reasons, then, the thirteen plays written by 1596 are the most difficult ones to date and arrange in a chronological order, especially since we have no record of Shakespeare's theatrical ac-tivities before 1590. One thing has become increasingly clear in recent years: not all of the thirteen plays in their entirety could have been written between 1590 and 1596. Their number is simply too great, a third of Shakespeare's total. Furthermore, the theatres were closed by the plague for considerable intrvals between 1590 and 1596, with theatrical activity often disorganized even when resumed. It used to be thought that Shakespeare began his career as a dramatist by revising the plays of earlier writers. All the supposed evidence for this theory has gradually eroded away, and we are left with the probability that all the early work is wholly his own. The most plausible explanation for the large number of plays seemingly clustered in 1590-96, and the curious unevenness and other anomalies that mark individual ones, is that Shakespeare began writing plays several years before 1590, then in 1590-96 revised, in whole or in part, some of these first plays, and also wrote some new ones.

A practicing playwright and actor would not be likely to revise extensively a play after it had been produced and become part of his company's repertory; but the company with which Shakespeare became permanently affiliated was not organized until 1594. Plays written before 1590 might have been designed for quite different kinds of companies and audiences, even those of the child professionals who acted in the so-called 'private' theatres, with scenery of sorts; and revision may have been necessary on other grounds than defective quality. This is not the place to review the evidence for the date, or the double date, of each individual play; we need only briefly survey the probable order of the five comedies, six histories, and two tragedies as their author progressed toward mastery.

It is likely that Shakespeare began as a writer of comedy, and that some of the following plays were written originally in the late fifteen-eighties: *The Comedy of Errors, Love's Labor's Lost, The Taming of the Shrew, Two Gentlemen of Verona,* and *A Midsummer Night's Dream.* The two which contain features most suggestive of an original date about 1587-89 are *The Comedy of Errors* and *Love's Labor's Lost.* The first is a farce adapted from Plautus's *Menaechmi,* embroiling two sets of twins in misadventures resulting from mistaken identity. It is brief, brisk, and amusing, but no one would call it profound. Its most original or 'Shakespearean' features are the elimination of some if not all of the Plautine hardness and coarseness, the attention paid the characters of a jealous wife and her more equable sister, and a sort of story 'frame' featuring a tender family reunion. One would guess that the play was first written about 1587-88 and revised about 1592-93.

The second, *Love's Labor's Lost,* is more interesting and unique.

It is a patterned extravaganza, in a variety of metrical forms, in which a set of villagers display their eccentricity, and a set of courtly ladies and gentlemen display their wit. An 'academy' formed by the King of Navarre and three companions is visited by a Princess of France and three ladies-in-waiting, with the result that the studious recluses forsake their solemn vows to avoid the companionship of women. The things of most value in this early experiment in 'comedy of manners' are the character portraits of sophisticated wit (Berowne), précieux Spaniard (Don Armado), village pedant (Holofernes) and his parasite (Curate Nathaniel), along with the remarkable display of verbal fireworks and the occasional fine lyricism, culminating in two matchless songs at the end. The play, like *The Comedy of Errors,* contains patches of doggerel, as well as structural and other oddities suggesting revision. One would guess that it was written about 1588-89 but extensively revised in 1596 or even a year later.

The Taming of the Shrew is 'all of a piece' to an extent to which *Love's Labor's Lost* is not, and it is possible that it was first written just as we have it, about 1593-94. Nevertheless there are hints that it, too, existed in a version before 1590. It improves certainly upon *The Comedy of Errors* as farce; and its perennially popular theme, its slap-stick business, and its colorful Petruchio and Kate have made it a favorite stage piece. It has its memorable lines, and it is highly skillful theatre in its burly sort of way.

An author like Shakespeare should improve steadily in each of the literary forms he cultivates, only lapsing temporarily as he shifts from one form to another. This is true, all things equal, but in the theatrical world of the sixteenth century all things were not always equal. There were pressures upon the writer, and the unevenness of his early work is not invariably explainable in terms of dating and revision. *The Two Gentlemen of Verona* and *A Midsummer Night's Dream* may offer a case in point. As we have them, they were probably written within a year of each other, the first about 1594-95, the second about 1595-96, but they are far apart in merit. We remember the first chiefly for its song 'Who is Silvia' in its touching dramatic setting, and for the wonderful clowning of Launce with his dog (II, iii; IV, iv). The play does not quite come off, even when taken on its own fanciful terms. We would prefer to think of it as an earlier play revised. And yet its affinites are with later plays, the romantic comedies, *As You Like It* and *Twelfth Night,* which succeed in producing the effect which *The Two Gentlemen of Verona* was intended to produce.

A Midsummer Night's Dream, in contrast, has affinites with the past, in content, structure, and *dramatis personae.* The parodic element in its main plot seems to stem from the English discovery of Italian pastoral drama with its love embroglios, and its abnôrmally large number of female and other parts for juvenile actors is puzzling. One can easily imagine its original as having been written for boy actors before 1590. As it stands, however, it is far more mature in its artistry than *The Two Gentlemen of Verona.* If it ever existed in an earlier form, the present version must represent such extensive revision as to amount to complete rewriting. Since *The Comedy of Errors* and *The Taming of the Shrew* are farces, while *A Midsummer Night's Dream* is a poetic and humorous fantasy, comparison is difficult. We might call it, too, a farce were it not so beautifully written; perhaps only its style makes us think of it as of a higher order of creative achievement. A better comparison is with *Love's Labor's Lost,* but its diverse parts come together in harmony in a way in which those of *Love's Labor's Lost* do not. It is Shakespeare's best comedy before 1597, indeed the best comedy in the English language before 1597. In it the playwright achieved mastery.

Dr. Johnson once remarked that writing comedy came naturally to Shakespeare, whereas his skill in the other dramatic modes had to be acquired by practice. It is doubtful if any kind of skill comes otherwise than by practice, but we can understand what Johnson meant. Shakespeare did one kind of thing as superbly well at the beginning of his career as at the end—depict the drollery of rustic and other 'low' comic characters, such as Launce, Bottom, Dogberry, First Gravedigger, Stephano, and the rest, scattered from beginning to end in his plays. The Jack Cade scenes in *2 Henry VI* are fine examples of this kind of thing, though written so early as 1590-91. They fortify one's impressions that Shakespeare was an experienced writer of comedy when he began writing history plays.

These history plays as a whole are too good to represent first experiments in play-writing. On the other hand, they are less good than Shakespeare's later histories, and so give us an excellent chance to watch a developing technique.

Anyone interested in the level of achievement reached by Shakespeare in a closely determinable early period would do well to turn to *1, 2, 3, Henry VI* and *Richard III.* The evidence is fairly conclusive that the four plays were written (and in the form in which we have them) between 1590 and 1592 or early 1593. *1 Henry VI,* oddly enough, may have been written after *2, 3 Henry VI,* but the time interval would have been short. The four plays are truly 'serial drama,' each of the *Henry VI* plays ending in *medias res* so as to require a sequel. *Richard III* provides the grand finale. The tetralogy might well be called 'The Wars of the Roses.'

The series begins with events just after the death of Henry V, and portrays the loss of the English dominions in France, the struggle for political power in England, and the wars for the crown itself as Yorkist claimants try to wrest it from the house of Lancaster. These middle and late fifteen-century civil wars, with the crown shifting back and forth, end when the Yorkist tyrant, Richard III, is slain on Bosworth field by Henry Tudor, grandfather of Queen Elizabeth. The turbulence is touched off by the fact that Henry VI is a child when he inherits the throne, grows into a 'holy' but weak and vacillating king, and possesses only the flawed title usurped by his Lancastrian grandfather Henry IV. The tetralogy is designed to instruct as well as entertain, portraying as it does the tragic consequences of royal weakness, a factious nobility, and a contested succession. Elizabeth, a childless monarch, was on the throne when it was written. Scattered through it are exemplary figures—secular martyrs who die brave and patriotic deaths.

It is unfortunate that the *Henry VI* plays are so monotonously titled, especially since Henry himself is never the dominant figure in them. The titles have reduced them to a sort of anonymity and helped to obscure their great interest. *1 Henry VI* might well be called 'Lord Talbot and Joan of Arc.' It treats of the machinations of the 'witch' Joan as leader of the French (a current historical distortion which some find hard to forgive), and the heroism of Lord

Talbot, 'the terror of the French,' whose death on the stage reduced thousands of Londoners to tears. Its most celebrated detail is the 'Temple Garden Scene' (II, iv), in which quarreling nobles pluck roses of different colors to indicate their allegiance, red for Lancaster, white for York, thus signaling the start of the great rift and providing its emblems. This scene and one or two others are of a higher literary quality than the rest, but it is no longer believed that they are the only ones which Shakespeare himself wrote.

2 Henry VI treats of the struggle between the good Duke Humphrey, Lord Protector of the realm and uncle of the King, and the evil Duke of Suffolk, who bids for power through his control of Margaret to whom he has married off the guileless Henry. Both perish, while the ambitious Yorkist pretender, Richard Plantagenet, promotes his own ends. One of his cat's-paws is Jack Cade with his rustic rebels, and we get the scenes previously mentioned (IV, ii, vi, vii) which are bad history but brilliant travesty.

3 Henry VI might well be titled 'Edward IV.' Richard Plantagenet does not survive, but his martial sons carry on the struggle for the crown, and Edward succeeds in procuring it. He and Henry reign in alternation until the final Yorkist triumph, which is brought about in part by the valor and ruthlessness of Edward's hunchback younger brother Richard. The horrors of civil war are epitomized in a famous scene (II, v) in which the hapless Henry delivers a touching threnody while we see the woes of a father who has slain his own son, a son who has slain his own father.

All three foregoing plays have been punctuated by atrocities, and the capping piece, *Richard III,* is dominated by the idea of political murder, past and present, underscored by the choral laments of mourning widows. Richard disposes of his brother Clarence, the children of his brother Edward (poor 'babes in the Tower'), and everyone else in his path, including his tool Buckingham, as he seizes the throne and exercises his tyrannous sway. A virtuoso in crime, witty and intelligent, he wears the blood on his hands with a difference, and fascinates while he horrifies. His dominance of the action gives the play a monolithic shape, which is complemented by other formal features, so that the piece is more unified in its structure, as well as more brilliant in its rhetoric, than any of its predecessors. Here Shakespeare learned the dramatic value of a towering central figure, or pair of figures opposed or allied, as we observe by his practice in all his subsequent serious plays. *Richard III* has always been a great theatrical success, and was so in its own day. It was often reprinted, and its second quarto, 1598, was the first playbook to bear Shakespeare's name on its title page.

Good as it is, *Richard III* is hard-surfaced and strident as compared with the history plays of three years later. *King John* in its present version and *Richard II* both probably came in 1595-96. The former may have existed in an earlier version, even anticipating the York-Lancaster tetralogy, but of this we are not sure. It turns to mediaeval history in order to treat another instance of the dire consequences of civil discord. In the breach between culpable nobles and culpable King stands the humorous patriot Faulconbridge, so that foreign conquest of England is averted. His concluding speech,

This England never did nor never shall
Lie at the proud foot of a conqueror . . .

has proved wonderfully useful to British statesmen in time of crisis.

Richard II is the first play of a new tetralogy, which includes *1, 2 Henry IV* and *Henry V*. These are not 'serial drama' to the same degree as the plays in the earlier tetralogy, but the playwright was certainly contemplating the writing of other plays in the series when he wrote the first. In them he turns to the reigns immediately preceding that of Henry VI, and the events, including the original usurpation, which laid the train for the Wars of the Roses. In characterization and philosophical interest *Richard II* excels its predecessors. If in *Richard III* he achieved theatrical mastery in the treating of history, here he achieved also poetic and dramatic mastery.

In tracing Shakespeare's progress in tragedy, it is unreasonable to confine our attention to the two plays of the early period which we now label 'tragedies.' Originally *Richard III* and other of the history plays were also called 'tragedies,' and we may say that Shakespeare learned to write tragedy by writing histories. Certainly there is little to be traced in the way of meaningful evolution between *Titus Andronicus* and *Romeo and Juliet,* the only early plays now viewed as tragedies. They are apparently closer together in date of composition than are *Richard III* and *Richard II,* but they are aeons apart in type and quality. There is record of a play called 'Titus and Ondronicus' as 'new' on January 24, 1594. If, as seems probable, this is Shakespeare's play (which was published in a good quarto in 1594), we have the most precise dating of any play in the canon. (A 'Harry the Sixth' was performed as 'new' on March 3, 1592, but we cannot be sure which of the *Henry VI* plays the record refers to.) It seems incredible that Shakespeare could write a play like *Titus Andronicus* in 1594 and one like *Romeo and Juliet* only a year or two later. Possibly the 'new' of the record means 'newly revised,' and *Titus Andronicus* represents merely the hasty salvaging of a piece written in the fifteen-eighties when the author could write comedy but could not yet write tragedy. In the case of *Romeo and Juliet,* although there had been earlier plays on the subject by other playwrights, Shakespeare's play was no doubt first written in 1595-96.

Even when all allowances are made for its revenge-play conventions, *Titus Andronicus* is a bad play—so bad that many still have understandable difficulty in believing that Shakespeare wrote it, despite the weight of internal and external evidence. It goes well enough when staged, in a Grand Guignol sort of way, but it is spectacularly lacking in artistic sagacity, the sanity, tact, and taste that we find even in the youthful Shakespeare. *Romeo and Juliet,* on the other hand, seems ahead of its time even in 1595-96. It is a remarkably original play, the first true 'love-tragedy' in the language, and if we exclude its later Shakespearean competitors, still the best. It had a tremendous impact upon the play-writing of its age.

A Midsummer Night's Dream, Richard II, and *Romeo and Juliet* are the plays in which Shakespeare achieved mastery in each of three discriminable dramatic modes. Linked with the extant versions of *Love's Labor's Lost* and *The Two Gentlemen of Verona* they are usually said to belong to Shakespeare's 'lyrical period.' We may take this to mean that the lyricism of the language is not quite so strictly disciplined to serve dramatic ends as it was later to become. All three of the plays came a year or two before 1597, and it is impossible to determine their order. They are presented below in the order in which the plays are presented in the folio: Comedies, Histories, Tragedies—which, I believe, also represents the order in which Shakespeare began his various dramatic endeavors.

2

A Midsummer Night's Dream

:

I, i

D U K E T H E S E U S and Queen Hippolyta are speaking long-ingly of their nuptials, which will be celebrated with pomp and merriment at the coming of the new moon, when Egeus enters to complain that his daughter Hermia rejects Demetrius, whom he has chosen for her husband, and persists in encouraging the courtship of Lysander. Theseus warns Hermia of the rigors of Athenian law: she must accept her father's choice, or suffer the penalty of death or lingering spinsterhood. Lysander argues his own eligibility, and charges Demetrius with jilting Hermia's friend Helena. When alone, the lovers lament their lot, and resolve to mend matters by eloping. They confide this plan to Helena, who decides to betray it to Demetrius.

1-19   Theseus does not seem to be the grim chieftain nor Hippolyta the doughty Amazonian of classical legend; they strike us rather as a gracious Renaissance prince and princess, young, imaginative, and in love. Their every word is felicitous. In place of the 'protracts' which we might expect, we find *lingers* (4) used as a transitive verb in the slow euphonious phrase *lingers my desires*. The word *wither-ing* (6) is multiply suggestive: the anticipated legacy is 'withering' away, the young heir is 'withering' as he waits, and the stepdame or dowager is out-'withering' both. (Tactfully the poet has refrained from associating the idea of inconvenient longevity with a widowed *mother*.) The movement of the verse alters with the shifting moods —the petulance of Theseus (3-6), the soothing composure of Hippolyta, and the elation of Theseus as her comfort takes effect. Hippolyta's lines, in graceful balance (7-8) seem to anesthetize (*dream away*) the pain of the waiting period, then (9-11) to give the longed-for wedding the imminence of the flight of an arrow from a taut bow. *Silver* and *heavens* are value-lending words. Moonlight and dreams are already beginning to suffuse the language, and unless Theseus's words deceive us (11-15) these hymeneal rites will spread universal joy.   **20-45**   How fortunate that Egeus is such a literal-minded man! As he designates Hermia unmistakably as his *child,* his *daughter* (23), and bids Demetrius *Stand forth* (24), then Lysander *Stand forth* (26), we are better served than by a program. No metaphors now, but flat statements, and nearly all of them made twice. Lysander's pernicious love-tokens are inventoried (33-34) like articles on a gift-shop shelf. The movement of the verse is harsh and hectoring. Egeus is a well-meaning man, but a heavy father, the world too much with him. Come to think of it, his tone somewhat resembles Shylock's. (Could it be that the latter is really an Athenian in disguise?)   **46-78** This is a cozy principality. Domestic problems are brought directly to the ruler, and he deals with them paternally. He warns but does not bully Hermia. Hermia might prove hard to bully. Her first words, *So is Lysander* (53), give a taste of her quality, as does her decorous but firm demand (58-64) to know the worst that can happen to her. This 'law' defined by Theseus is one of Shakespeare's handy fictions, but less preposterous than it sounds. It is a hyperbolic image of Elizabethan social facts: daughters of marriage age risked disaster (*the death*) as the only alternative to remaining single (*the cloister*) or coming to terms with their parents (unless, of course, their parents came to terms with them). The advice of Theseus to Hermia (65-78) is the finest passage in the scene. Paganism and Christianity are fused in the blended imagery: the votaress of Diana, moon-goddess of chastity, becomes a *nun,* no longer bearing bow and quiver as she hunts fleet-limbed in the sacred grove, but wearing the *livery* as she chants faint *hymns* while in *cloister mewed*. The *rose distilled* (76) is the woman ful-filled in the birth of a child. Cunningly, the rose undistilled is asso-ciated with the virgin *thorn* (77) as if her *earthlier happy* sisters bloomed on thornless branches. Although *single blessedness* emerges as a fate worse than death, these are charming lines, their sentiment hovering between humor and sobriety, didacticism and tenderness; they are life-embracing, yet delicate.   **79-127** Ly-sander's first words (93-94) like Hermia's are nimble and direct, as well as designed to raise a laugh. These lovers are well matched. Virtue, too, is on their side since Demetrius is tarred with incon-stancy. This puts the playwright in an awkward spot. Whatever the constitutional duties of the Athenian duke, he himself is a true lover and should not be aligned with Egeus and Demetrius. Observe his backing and filling (111-16, 123-26) as he shepherds the com-pany offstage—including Egeus, who makes no protest at leaving his daughter with the interloping Lysander. Theseus (or Shake-speare) is making heavy weather here. All this business to be transacted with Egeus and Demetrius! Obviously a dodge—we believe not a word of it.   **128-49** Now comes the most quoted line in the play, *The course of true love never did run smooth* (134), monosyllabic, as such lines are apt to be, then a plaintive litany of star-crossed love (135-40), and a fine capping passage of blank verse. As Lysander lists the woes of lovers, Hermia's inter-polated 'responses' suggest a ritual. As an aristocrat, her sympathies naturally attach themselves to the high-born member of the pair separated by social barriers (136), but why, since she is young, to the elder member of the pair separated as February and May? Is the idea of youth in love with age simply unimaginable in young Lysander's presence? It is her own kind of situation which touches her most: *O cross. . . . O spite. . . . O hell!* (140). Lysander's sad apostrophe to true young love (141-49)—a flash of light in enveloping darkness—combines images of a kind dispersed through *Romeo and Juliet* and might serve as its epigraph. Its last line is finely climactic and evocative, with young love expanded into a symbol of all bright things, precious and transitory.   **150-78** There is an oddity now. When Hermia reflects that they must patiently endure the universal cross of true lovers, Lysander agrees, and proposes that *Therefore* they incontinently elope (156). Is this what grammarians call a 'false transition,' or is something missing in the text, or is the playwright making a quiet joke on youth's conception of patient endurance? Hermia's vow (168-78) is also puzzling. Why such emphasis? True she refers to no casual 'date' but a final commitment, with, theoretically, a hazard of death, but it is hard to take it so seriously. And where is Lysander's matching vow? The verse has turned to rime. Perhaps this is our clue. We have stepped through the looking-glass, and had better stop asking logical questions about the conduct of these lovers. **179-251** The rime continues, and the new air of artificiality is heightened by Helena's extended 'conceit' on Hermia's superior luck and beauty (181-93), and by the rimed stychomythia following it (194-201). Irrationally, Lysander and Hermia tell the secret of their intended elopement to this first-comer, and, even more irrationally, Helena decides against her own best interests to betray the secret to Demetrius. We are tempted to say that the music-box has begun to chime and the figurines to dance, but this does not quite describe the effect. 'Natural touches' continue to appear, and keep the mood serio-comic. Hermia recalls her childhood exchanges of confidences with Helena (214-16) in the very wood where young dreams are now to be realized; Helena when alone seems not so convinced of Hermia's superior beauty as she was a moment ago; and, as for the folly of revealing the secret, has she not just said (236) *Nor hath Love's mind of any judgment taste . . . ?*

I, ii

Peter Quince, carpenter of Athens and dramatic impressario, meets with his star performer, Bottom the weaver, and four other craftsmen to distribute the parts of the play which they hope to perform at the wedding festivities of Theseus and Hippolyta: 'The most lamentable comedy and most cruel death of Pyramus and Thisby.' They plan to hold a rehearsal the following evening by moonlight in the same wood outside the city where Lysander and Hermia have agreed to meet.

1-20 Despite his native superiority, Bottom is patient with lesser men: he is willing to let one of his five companions make every other remark. We detect only a trace of intellectual arrogance in his first two speeches, as he brings his incisive logic and managerial skill to bear on the problem of who is present and why. (Again a roll-call serves in lieu of a program.) The legend of Pyramus and Thisby is the one from which *Romeo and Juliet* descends, and its theme may not seem strictly suitable to a wedding frolic, but no doubt Quince wishes to enhance its joys by artfully casting a contrasting shadow. Bottom has a good word to say for the literary efforts of Quince, whom he views almost as an equal. The other four are timid men, already suffering a twinge of stage-fright and huddling together protectively like amateur actors the world over. *Masters,* says Bottom, *spread yourselves.* (15).   **21-80** Like other actors to the manner born, Bottom has an affinity with downstage center. He is also a born teacher. After his bravura exhibition of the tyrant's vein, he explains that a lover's is different—it is (lovely word) more *condoling* (35). Naturally he wishes to play all the parts himself, since he could play them better, but he always graciously yields. It is touch and go whether he can bring himself to let an inferior performer render the lion's roar when his own roar would make theatrical history—or, alternately (he would have thought of this himself if given time), prudently soothe the ladies. Here Quince shows his mettle, as producer confronted with temperamental star: he makes the part of Pyramus seem enticing indeed—worthy of Bottom's manifold gifts (77-80).   **81-99** Most of Bottom's malapropisms almost mean something, and his *obscenely* (97) is challenging. But of course! A word with 'scene' in it must surely have something to do with the theatre. As the meeting adjourns, we can see even Starveling go off with shoulders back and chin uplifted at Bottom's call for high morale (99). Things would have gone more smoothly without him, but would have lacked salt and savor. What an ineffable ass this Bottom is, and how dearly Shakespeare loves him!

II, i

In moonlight in the Athenian wood Puck and a Fairy herald the approach of their masters, King Oberon and Queen Titania, rulers of Fairyland. This small but regal couple are drawn hither by the wedding of Theseus and Hippolyta, in whom they have a mutual interest, but they travel by separate moon-beams since they have been quarreling over possession of a child. When they confront each other with their separate retinues, Titania persists in her refusal to relinquish her adopted darling to serve as Oberon's page, even though their dissension is disturbing the balance of nature. Oberon resolves to bring her to terms by coercion, and sends Puck, who can circle the globe in forty minutes, to England for love-in-idleness, a flower whose magical juice dropped in Titania's eyes will make her fall in love with the first creature she sees, however frightful. Demetrius now passes through the glade to intercept the elopement of Hermia and Lysander, of which Helena has informed him. The latter is following him, and he harshly rebuffs her pitiful avowals of love. This arouses the chivalrous indignation of Oberon, who is standing by invisible, and when Puck returns with the magic flower, he is instructed to seek out a youth in Athenian clothes and anoint his eyes so that he will return the love of the pining lady.

1-17 The varying loveliness of the poetry in this scene would make the play a treasure even if it had nothing else to offer. Our ears have constantly been hearing the words *moon* and *wood,* and now we are in a wood drenched in moonlight and dew. It is undergoing enchantment. The opening verses have the sound of an incantation, the short rimed lines and trochaic meter reversing customary measures. Restricting time and place are annihilated (2-7) and common things are turned to jewels (8-15). The familiar and the wonderful become one; the *cowslips* with their *freckles* and pendant dew-drops are touched by the wand into gay-jerkined *pensioners,* miniature replicas of Queen Elizabeth's courtly guards, some of whom may actually have worn ear-ornaments of pearl.
18-59 Magic is domesticated in the figure of Puck. Juxtaposed

with the delicate world of Oberon and Titania and its delicate quarrels, stands the world of the folk-goblin and his boisterous pranks. Glimpses of cow-barns, milk-houses, country byways, and a pasture where a stud-horse feeds resolve into a bright genre picture of a rustic kitchen filled with noisy vitality. The cool mysterious moonlight bathing a haunted landscape is pierced by the glow of an English hearth. Puck and the Fairy have collaborated on this word-painting, both using heroic couplets and homespun diction, but Puck's speech (42-57) has a quality all its own—lent by the coarse monosyllables, and the wealth of 'b' and 'l' sounds which ripple like laughter through it. These fairyland heralds are quite partisan, and as their royal masters arrive, they bridle a bit at each other (58-59) in their concern for precedence.   **60-80** The dramatic vision makes no compromise with the stage image; the audience is required to imagine things in defiance of what it sees; the child-actors of the company must be seen through the large end of a telescope. The attendant elves are small enough to hide in *acorn-cups* (31), and Oberon and Titania tower over them only to the height of about half a foot (10). As they make their charges of mutual infidelity, the humor depends on our imaginative facility in visualizing the alleged love-affair of tiny Titania with Theseus, tiny Oberon with Hippolyta. The minor virtue of consistency is sacrificed; Hippolyta is, for the moment, not the perfect lady we have seen and shall see again, but the legendary Amazon, *bouncing* and *buskined* (70-71).   **81-117** Of course the quarrel of these nature-sprites has led to natural upheavals, including seasons of disastrous weather. A somber note sounds in Titania's description. England has been suffering, to the point of famine, such seasons as described, and her lines project across the centuries the vision of hungry holidays, grass-grown paths on village greens, mud-filled pockets in the meadows where children have ceased to play their games, the ox stretching his yoke in vain, the plough-man losing his *sweat*. No farmer would have been amused to hear of the wheat which has rotted before its youth *attained a beard* (95). In fact we do not care much for this witty metaphor ourselves, but poets must be daring. The same playful fertility which produced it produced also the inspired grotesquery of *old Hiems'* *thin and icy crown* decked with the *odorous chaplet of sweet summer buds* (109-10), and we would no more willingly part with this than with some perfectly wrought Silenus grinning in cathedral stone. There is much to be said for artistic ruthlessness. From the hideous plague of a few years earlier, Nashe had distilled the beauty of

> Queens have died young and fair,
> Dust hath closed Helen's eye;
> I am sick, I must die—
> *Lord, have mercy on us.*

The last line, the plague-cry of the stricken city, served him as his repeated refrain! The power of this poetry of a bygone age is a measure of the resilience of its people; the plague and famine years would have been no easier to bear if the poets had stood mute. **118-45** Titania's second description is the allegro of the pair, and is not for those who like their poetry cold and hard and dry. When she and her votaress amused themselves in the spiced evening air by the Indian sea, she and Oberon were at peace, and the winds and waters were benign. In this harmonious setting is placed a joyous fecundity image, appropriate in a marriage-play although Bowdler excised it as vulgar. The votaress of Titania has not withered on the virgin thorn; she sails *big-bellied,* her womb *rich* with child, and the universe smiles with delight. We regret that she died in childbirth, but Titania's way of putting it—this nymph, being mortal, *of that boy did die* (134)—makes us realize what uncommon things can be done with common words, at least by poets, and before language has congealed into customary patterns, such as 'died in childbirth.' **146-87** With a fine impartiality, tribute is now paid to a nymph of the more austere order of Diana. Once as he sat on a promontory by some other far-off sea, Oberon heard a mermaid on a dolphin's back shocking the chaste stars with her siren's song, but pleasing the libidinous waves. To crafty Cupid it seemed an auspicious moment, but the ever-watchful deity of the truly virginal thwarted his designs and saved a *fair vestal of the West.* In connection with this particular vestal there is no mention of faint hymns or confining cloister, no association of single blessedness with sterility. It is the poet's tribute to his unwedded queen, and even if there were no words like *throned* and *imperial* to provide a clue, we would associate the words with majesty because of the dignity of their music, their serenity and grace. Yet the touch is light—this imperial votaress walks in maiden meditation *fancy-free* (164). These successive passages—on the chaotic seasons, Titania's adoption of the mortal child, and the mythical creation of 'love-in-idleness'—must be placed with the finest examples of English descriptive poetry, and yet none seems a set piece. Each is evoked by the dramatic occasion, and is lent an air of spontaneity. We miss the sound of the deep inhalation of a writer about to produce a purple passage. The dramatic occasion is frivolous, and the passages appropriately fanciful; in the context, the verbal embroidery with which the realism of the first passage is mitigated appears as an artistic necessity. The fairy speakers are well disposed toward humanity, but they are not human themselves and, a little like Ariel's, their tone is disengaged. It is amusing to notice that the child over whom they are quarreling is not a *changeling* in the sinister folk-sense of the term, but has been charitably adopted; these fairies are not the kind who rob human cradles. Their benevolence, like their tiny size, is the poet's original contribution to fairy-lore, one which changed its whole subsequent history.

188-244 We might have expected the dialogue of Demetrius and Helena to be in the rimed verse of the end of the first scene, but the fairy King and Queen have been speaking in blank verse, and the medium of these human speakers must not be more artificial than theirs. The tone is right for the occasion. Oberon must be moved to intervene, but we must not be moved to hope for the success of his intervention. Helena's words are plaintive, but she is so ready with her elaborate similitudes that we begin to wonder if her grief is not a blessing in disguise, granting her an occasion to exercise her somewhat flaccid wits. Demetrius is harsh, but not wholly lacking in moral probity; he must remain reasonably respectable if he is to make up one in the final hymeneal procession. Their dialogue, although not arresting, contains a phrase which seems to have impressed Milton (*make a heaven of hell,* 243), and perhaps it was this play, especially this scene, which made him describe Shakespeare as 'Fancy's child' warbling his 'native wood-notes wild.' **245-68** Oberon's last speech, in couplets, begins as a descriptive lyric. The association of the fairies with flowers is climaxed by the rich lines on Titania's bower, the *bank where the wild thyme blows*. Of all the images of diminutiveness, the one picturing a snake's *enamelled skin* (255) as suitable for a fairy gown is the most vivid and surprising.

II, ii

Titania, having presided over the nightly stint of fairy revels, is sung to sleep with a choral lullaby. Oberon anoints her eyes with his magic drops as he repeats an appropriate spell. Hermia and Lysander, who have kept their tryst but lost their way in the wood, choose this glade as make-shift bedchamber, unaware that part of it has been preempted by fairy royalty. Hermia insists that they repose at a decorous distance from each other; and Puck, seeking the disdainful Athenian youth marked for enchantment by Oberon, misinterprets their separation and places the love-drops in Lysander's eyes. Demetrius crosses the glade, still followed by Helena. She pauses to catch her breath, sees Lysander, and upon awakening him, receives his fervid declarations of love. She is sure that these must be meant in mockery, and continues her pursuit of Demetrius. Lysander follows her, after a parting word of contempt for the sleeping Hermia. Hermia is awakened by a frightful dream, finds herself deserted, and goes off to seek her beloved Lysander or death.

1-156 Observe the antipathy of these dainty sprites for the more odious creatures of the night, such as rose-worms, owls, and bats, although the latter contribute to their domestic economy by supplying shoe-leather (4). Like all proper lullabies, this one promises shelter from harm—the harm here practically identified as outdoor pests. In reading we must not underestimate the contribution of such incidental music to the mood of the scene; the standards of vocal performance were high, and this lullaby would be rendered by well-trained child-singers—militant little soloist and chorus of fledgling nightingales warbling the abundant 'l' sounds

in the verses. The *sentinel* (26) proves not very effective, doubt-
less because of Oberon's knack for going invisible. The dialogue of
Lysander and Helena, opening with a quatrain and continuing in
couplets, is a self-contained little idyll (35-65), quite charming in
spite of the absurd situation. Like the rest of Shakespeare's young
lovers, these can be trusted anywhere without a chaperon. Helena's
estimate of Hermia's beauty (90-94) seems to rise with her desperation. The love-in-idleness drops must be quite potent, since
Lysander falls in love on the instant of awakening—in fact between
the two rimes of a couplet (102-03). What will be the dire fate of
the peacefully slumbering Titania? The *raven* and *dove* metaphors
(114) confirm our impression that Hermia is a brunette, Helena a
blonde. This dialogue (103-44) is less engaging than the other,
but it contains an astute remark on the ardor of converts (139-40).
Hermia's speech upon awakening is quite effective until we come
to its last pedestrian couplet. There is matter for an essay on
serpents-sleepers-betrayal, on Edens-dreams-death in Shakespeare
(146-47). His vile 'worms' seem somewhat more biblical than
Freudian, but who can say?

III, i

The craftsmen arrive in the wood to rehearse their play, and Quince
accepts Bottom's advice to mitigate its terrors. Puck eavesdrops
upon their council, and decides to exercise his magic during the
rehearsal. As a result Bottom returns after an exit with his head
changed to that of an ass. Unconscious of his transformation and
surprised when his fellow-actors scatter in fright, he shrewdly
guesses that they are trying to rattle him, and so displays his calm
by strolling about singing. Aroused by these angelic sounds, Titania
gazes at him in adoration. He accepts her devotion with aplomb,
gives gracious recognition to her small attendants, and makes a
stately exit with them in his retinue.

1-186 Bottom's suggested revision is not only judicious, doing
less injury to the plot than would Starveling's, but it also, incidentally, builds up his own part a bit. Only a man of the theatre

could have created this dedicated troupe. They wish to grip their audience but not harrow it. Their solution of the technical problems of staging advances somewhat from the symbolism of Shakespeare's theatre toward the literalness of ours: they are convinced that when objects are mentioned in the lines they ought to be represented on the stage. Could it be that the poet, under the cover of their high ideals, is subtly advocating a less cavalier attitude toward scenic effects? His company had probably failed to make the slightest effort to supply moonlight for the present play although it is constantly in demand. Bottom's complete lack of surprise when accosted by Titania (129) provides an insight into his character: to his unconventional mind one situation seems just as normal as another. The nature of his transformation may suggest his natural affinity with the ass, but Puck wrought better than he knew; Bottom is a very gentle fellow for all his seeming aggressiveness, and could not have been epitomized better than by a centaur-in-reverse. It is impossible to explain how our poet manages it (perhaps because he himself is less impressed than ordinary men by the distinction between credible and incredible) but he is able to give a casual air to the happenings in this scene. And he combines the uncombinable —slapstick and dainty fantasy. Natural magic and fairy cameo-cutting continue to enrich the lines (137-60), and this part of the 'dream' like the rest receives its fair portion of moonlight and dew.

III, ii (+ IV, i)

Oberon is pleased by Puck's report of Titania's infatuation, but when Demetrius enters in pursuit of Hermia rather than Helena, he deduces that Puck has bewitched the wrong youth. Obligingly, Demetrius pauses for a nap, giving Oberon a chance to proceed according to original plan. The correct eyes are anointed and the correct maiden sent for. But now when the four young people are assembled, both Demetrius and Lysander adore Helena whom they formerly despised, and despise Hermia whom they formerly adored. Helena is certain that all are mocking her. Hermia is certain that Helena must have slandered her, thus to alienate Lysander, and that the allusions to her small stature are intended as slurs. The two young men are divided between their anxiety to protect Helena from the attacks of Hermia and their desire to attack each other. They stalk off to combat, trailed after by the girls. Oberon issues the necessary orders, and Puck keeps the youths apart by imitating their voices in shouted challenges. Playing will-of-the-wisp is, after all, his specialty, and he misleads them in and out until both fall down in exhausted sleep. Hermia and Helena wander back and also fall asleep. Puck treats Lysander's eyes with a herbal antidote, so that the four lovers will be properly paired when they awake. (IV, i) There is still room in this sylvan dormitory for Titania and Bottom. Too engrossed with each other to notice the assortment of recumbent forms, they proceed to Titania's bower, and Bottom receives the tender ministrations of her fairy-in-waiting, Peaseblossom, and three elves-of-the-chamber, Cobweb, Moth, and Mustardseed. Bottom seems willing to be spiritualized by the delicate viands proposed by Titania, but feels a puzzling craving to make a meal of oats and hay and to have his head scratched. The attendants leave, and Titania and Bottom compose themselves to sleep. Oberon, who has been keeping a protective eye upon his queen, now tells Puck that she has yielded up the boy over whom they have been contending, so that he is ready to release her from the spell. He administers the antidote, and she awakes to tell of a strange dream—of falling in love with an ass! Bottom is displayed to her, lulled into a deeper sleep with music, and relieved of the ass's head. Oberon and Titania celebrate their renewed amity in a dance, and leave with Puck planning to bless the Athenian royal wedding. It is dawn by this time, and Theseus and Hippolyta enter with Egeus and other members of an early-morning hunting-party. When they see the sleeping lovers, Theseus charitably assumes that they have come to the wood a-maying and have dozed off while resting. They are awakened by a peal from the hunting horns. Lysander frankly admits that he and Hermia have tried to elope; and Demetrius (whose eyes, we must remember, retain the magic drops) announces that his old love of Helena has returned. With the four now so neatly coupled, Theseus decides to overrule the objections of Egeus (and the laws of Athens on parental authority) and invites the young people to join him and Hippolyta in a triple wedding. Dazed with this turn of fortune, and the odd sensation that they have been dreaming, the happy couples follow the hunting party back to Athens. Bottom now also awakes, and the scene ends with his sage reflections upon his own bottomless dream.

1-463, 1-216 Although split by a signal for an interval in the folio and subsequent texts, the action outlined above was originally continuous. It would be hard to find elsewhere in drama such a melange of unlikely matter so well kept under control. Oberon, with his factotum Puck, manages the events and lends them coherence until another 'power symbol' takes his place. The natural ruler Theseus consolidates the gains of his supernatural counterpart. The action has a logic of its own: if the characters wake and sleep by fits and starts—well that is the way of dreamers. All the named characters of the play appear in the scene at one time or another except Philostrate and Bottom's colleagues (who may have doubled as huntsmen and attendants), and there is always at least a modicum of plausibility in their entrances and exits. The action is as animated as it is complex, the quarrel and wild-goose chase of the lovers resembling at times a frenzied ballet. For us, the interest of the action is mainly farcical, but it must have had in its own day also a parodic appeal since pastoral fiction and drama often pictured quite solemnly love-entanglements almost as inextricable as those of this quartette. It would be too much to expect a sustained poetic distinction in so 'plotty' a scene, but there are several fine passages: Puck's description of the *rude mechanicals* (III, ii, 9-30); Helena's account of the *childhood innocence* (198-217) of herself and Hermia (the best of her habitual sentimental reveries); Puck and Oberon's evocation of the dawn (378-93) which seems bitter only to night-spirits of *another sort;* and, best of all, the sports-loving speeches of Theseus and Hippolyta (IV, i, 102-26). This is another of those wonderful fusions of ancient and modern: Hercules and Cadmus, Theseus and the Elizabethan gentry, are all connoisseurs of hounds, *Crook-kneed and dewlapped* and *matched in mouth like bells, Each under each.* In this verbal 'sporting-print' we can hear as well as see the noble pack of the Spartan kind. Much, too, may be said for the ruminative prose of

Bottom's concluding soliloquy, although he himself has more trust in immortalizing rime.

IV, ii

This is the great day of the royal nuptials—happy for everyone except the cast of 'Pyramus and Thisby' who realize that their show cannot go on without the star. Then picture their visions of fame and fortune when Bottom returns from the wood in the nick of time. He brings the joyful news that the weddings have been performed, that their play has been 'preferred' (placed on a stand-by basis by the Master of the Revels), and that he, Bottom, is ready to lead them to triumph.

1-40 We seem somehow to have gained on time. Theseus has spoken of four days of waiting in the first scene, but only two nights have elapsed. However, this one has contained enough action for four and a plentiful supply of moonlight instead of the glimmer we might expect from the *silver bow new-bent in heaven;* perhaps this whimsical behavior of the moon has been accepted by Theseus as a portent and he has moved up the date. Speculations upon another point are less acceptable, since the activities of Quince's troupe must be seen in an Elizabethan rather than a Greek context, despite the setting in ancient Athens. Although 'Pyramus and Thisby' is unified in time, place, and action, it shows few other formal characteristics in common with classical tragedy of the kind performed in the Theatre of Dionysus, and the idea that its author represents some sort of amalgam of Aeschylus, Sophocles, and Euripedes, perhaps critical in intent, must be dismissed as chimerical.

V, i

The remarkable events we think we have witnessed are coolly dismissed by Theseus as 'more strange than true'—such fictions as are conceived only in the seething brains of lovers, madmen, and poets. He selects 'Pyramus and Thisby' from the entertainments on tap, and assures Hippolyta that he intends no unkindness to its humble offerers. Their performance lives up to every expectation. Bottom is, of course, superb, and he as well as Wall, Moonshine, and Lion stand always ready to help the spectators grasp the subtleties of the piece. There is a dance to round off the tragedy, before the midnight bell signals bedtime for the happily-mated couples. Puck, Oberon, and Titania, with the fairy retinue now enter the deserted chamber, bringing moonlight and mystery back into the play. Titania leads a song and dance of the glimmering fairies, Oberon orders them to bless the bride-beds and the 'issue their create,' and Puck bids us goodnight.

1-427 Since the 'story' was really complete with the release of Titania and the lovers from enchantment, and the consequent reconciliations, we might expect little more here than a winding up of the formal business of the play. What we get is not a disentangling of strands but a weaving of all together, as if the play were made for this last scene alone. It offers graciousness, hilarity, and poetry in so pleasing a combination that the 'end crowns all.' What an imposing person this Theseus is! There is a lordly finality with which he disposes of *fairy toys* along with lovers, madmen, and poets (2-22) that leaves Hippolyta (and us) a little bemused. Who can argue against pronouncements so perfectly worded? Hippolyta appears at her womanly best in her two fine lines of compassionate insight (85-86), and Theseus at his manly best in his fine reply (89-105). These two are 'right royal' by nature as well as birth. But what of their later jibes at the amateur actors? Is the playwright ironically contrasting kindness in theory and cruelty in fact? Not at all. This audience is kind in practice by hearing the play out to the end. The mockery would seem cruel only if the performers were hurt; instead they are grandly impervious. If anything may be said against the jibes, it is that they are as broad and obvious as the occasion for them; actually they function less as sallies of wit than as expressions of delight, for in its own inimitable way 'Pyramus and Thisby' is a huge success. The play 'without' the play has a lovely close. The hall empties, the fire burns low, and enchantment returns. Fear reigns outside in the haunted night, but this house is warm, safe, *hallowed.* New life is being created, and death is held at bay. *Fairies* dance—proving that even the admirably rational Theseus is subject to human error. Puck in his Epilogue speaks with an unaccustomed gentleness.

3

King Richard the Second

:

I, i

I N A N audience before King Richard the Second, Henry Bolingbroke charges Mowbray Duke of Norfolk with embezzling war funds and plotting the death of the Duke of Gloucester. With equal venom, Mowbray brands Bolingbroke a liar and a traitor. Since neither the King nor the Duke of Lancaster can pacify the hostile pair, a day is appointed for a trial on the tilting field at Coventry. (The King's reputation and relationship with the other characters would be known to the original audience in advance. Son of the heroic 'Black Prince' and grandson of the great Edward III, he holds unblemished title to a crown inherited from a patriot line, but he is a luxury-loving monarch who has wasted his patrimony and failed to retain the English possessions in France. He will be deposed by his cousin Bolingbroke. The latter is the grandson of Edward III through the renowned Duke of Lancaster, John of Gaunt, one of the younger brothers of the Black Prince. His opponent Mowbray has been Richard's trusted associate, and has served as proxy in his marriage with the Princess of France.)

1-14   The inclusive direction *with other Nobles* . . . (1 s.d.) indicates the entrance of the full cast in an imposing scene of state. Richard will appear as young, and perhaps too lavishly attired, but there is nothing to suggest that he simpers or lolls on the shoulders of his favorites as he is often made to do on the modern stage. Actually he is on his best kingly behavior, playing with a great show of gravity the part of supreme magistrate. The slow sonorous line, *Old John of Gaunt, time-honored Lancaster* (1), lingers in our minds, predisposing us to accept this figure as symbol of the national ideal. The formally phrased questions and the terse replies have a properly legal flavor, but there is prejudice in the King's words for Bolingbroke's action, *bold* and *boist'rous* (3-4). It seems strange that the father, Gaunt, should know no more of his son's mind than he implies by *As near as I could sift him . . .* (12)   **15-24** Richard's orotund announcement, closed by a rimed couplet (18-19), resembles an induction to a show—which the royal showman anticipates with a certain relish. Mowbray caps Bolingbroke's greeting with a piety. Later the antagonists vie with each other in studding their vicious denunciations with religious oaths (not necessarily hypocritical).   **25-68** As accuser, and of the blood royal, Bolingbroke is given the initiative. Both his opening speech and Mowbray's begin at low pitch and rise in intensity, but the couplets into which Bolingbroke's falls seem to insulate the invective. Mowbray sounds the angrier, and proves more resourceful in insults; these have a grand eloquence and strike the heroic note (63-64).   **69-83** Now it is Bolingbroke who sounds the angrier. (Although the point cannot be pressed too far, the speakers in this play are apt to express particularities and deeply personal feelings in blank verse, social attitudes and moral sentiments in rimed couplets.)   **84-108** The King's question and Bolingbroke's reply, particularizing his charges, supply background information, but the expository function of the lines is absorbed by the high note of indignation. As Bolingbroke introduces biblical imagery with his reference to *blood, like sacrificing Abel's* (104) and concludes his fervid peroration, Richard's comment has the detached quality of a connoisseur of style: *How high a pitch his resolution soars!* (109)   **110-51** The scene is progressing in formally balanced units. Now we have the King's question and *Mowbray's* reply, also supplying background information with disguising emotionality. Richard's insistence upon his royal rectitude,

Th' unstooping firmness of my upright soul (121) savors of over-protestation. Observe that Bolingbroke, although second after Gaunt in the apparent line of succession, is obliquely rejected as his *kingdom's heir* (116). Mowbray's deprecatory admission of his plot to assassinate Gaunt discloses the rugged rules by which the political game is played.   **152-205** If resorted to by an older man, or if vindicated by success, Richard's playful cajolery would be less damaging to the royal image. As it is, his stature begins to dwindle. His command is at first indirect (162), then weakly iterative (164), and finally shifted from Mowbray to Bolingbroke (186). It is smothered by the moralizing couplets of his balky subjects, and his *Lions make leopards tame* (174) and *We were not born to sue, but to command* (196) underline its ineffectuality. (The unmotivated exit of Gaunt, 195 s.d., indicated in the folio text, is to provide the actor time for re-entrance, probably in a traveler's cloak, at the beginning of the following scene.) The formality of the concluding couplets (200-05) fits the ceremonial character of the scene as a whole, and the procession which clears the stage.

I, ii

The Duchess of Gloucester bewails the death of her husband and urges his brother to avenge it, but Gaunt replies that God's deputy the King has procured that death and God alone can hold him to account. The Duchess sends woeful greetings to Edmund Duke of York, the only survivor besides Gaunt of the seven sons of Edward III.

1-36 We now see that Gaunt was quite well aware of what lay behind his son's turbulence; and that Richard who figured as judge was actually chief offender. Thus this private occasion, where the truth may be spoken, serves as commentary upon the preceding public occasion, where it could not. The threnody of the widow does more than supply a conventional cry for blood vengeance. It postulates, though in partisan fashion, the conflict between personal and national loyalties with which the play will be concerned, and states (the tragic theme of repercussive evil, with wrong leading to further wrong.) **37-55** Gaunt's *God's is the quarrel . . .* (37-41) is a statement of religious and political orthodoxy: the King is God's anointed, and his sin of tyranny cannot be remedied by the sin of rebellion. When the Duchess is told that she can only pray (43), her prayer takes a savage form: may God in the trial by combat make the lance of Bolingbroke lethal; thus, although Bolingbroke's cause is identified with righteousness, the speaker's motives are not strictly righteous and the ethical issue is blurred. **56-74** The images are of ruins, waste, death, decay—epitomizing the effects of sin and civil discord, but also of inevitable mutability. Unrimed lines interrupt the couplets, giving a broken quality to the speech. The widow wishes to delay her brother-in-law, dreading to be alone. The interest is now purely human, in a grieving old woman and a kindly old man.

I, iii

After heraldic ceremonies, renewed accusations, and formal farewells to the King, Bolingbroke and Mowbray are about to battle in the lists when Richard throws his warder down. He confers with his lords, then banishes Bolingbroke for ten years and Mowbray for life. The two are required to swear to accept the decree and to make no common cause in exile. Richard seems unmoved by Mowbray's surprise and grief, but he reduces Bolingbroke's term to six years as a concession to the aged Gaunt. The latter remarks that his time on earth is too short to let him profit by the reduction, and laments that he has been forced by duty to concur in the royal decree. He tries to comfort his son, but Bolingbroke cannot be reconciled to banishment from the beloved homeland.

1-6 The opening lines set the scene and give the King a prepared entrance, with trumpet calls and pageantry. He is enthroned aloft upon a dais or in the rear stage gallery, flanked by his nobles (6 s.d.) so that his presence dominates the early portion of the scene as he both witnesses and directs proceedings. **7-45** This is ceremony for its own imposing sake, with two sets of speeches

(King, Marshal, Mowbray—King, Marshal, Bolingbroke) precisely balanced in length and purport preceding the formal admonition of the Marshal. Whether it is authentic we need not inquire— the cadences suggest ancient ritual.   **46-99** Suspense and human interest are provided by the farewells. The preceding scene has given us perspective to recognize the hypocrisy in the King's embrace of Bolingbroke. This is a show within a show. Bolingbroke's farewells to Richard and Aumerle have the virtue of honest brevity (63-64); his farewell to his father is in a different key, with blank verse replacing couplets. Gaunt's last words to Bolingbroke are frankly partisan (78-83), Richard's to Mowbray covertly so (97-98). In the latter's speech there is the note of chivalric gaiety before battle, such as will mark Hotspur's before Shrewsbury, Henry the Fifth's before Agincourt.   **100-17** Again comes the ritual of the tilt, with a renewal of tension until the discharge of the cannon. Presumably the combatants have mounted horses off-stage, and we shall next see the shock of their charge.   **118-43** Had the scene been less skillfully managed, the Marshal's *Stay! The king hath thrown his warder down* (118) would have come as disastrous anti-climax. It is the reverse, because the implied action is that of a monarch, who is stationed aloft and who has dominated the whole proceedings. Why does Richard halt the trial, and why does he do so at the last possible moment? The answer should not be sought in the actual event or the accounts of the chroniclers. The play provides no forewarning, or subsequent explanation. Richard gives reasons for his decision but not for its timing; and we may properly ask if he feels last-minute fears that Bolingbroke will prevail, or if he is a whimsical and unstable lover of histrionics, or if the dramatist himself considered the device good theatre regardless of Richard's character so long as it was not in open conflict with it. The style of Richard's explanation, with its succession of causal clauses leading to a *Therefore* (139), resembles that of a political debater; hence our impression that he is saying what serves his purpose rather than truly reveals it.   **144-207** Bolingbroke's response, *Your will be done* . . . (144-47), conceding Richard's status as God on earth, is both fulsome and perfunctory. There is a technical reason for this inadequacy; it is a stop-gap or holding speech; his emotional reaction will be expressed later. There are curious features in the exchange between the King and Mowbray. Both speakers show true emotion at the beginning, but since the King pronounces *with some unwillingness* (149) the sentence of perpetual exile (as indeed he should in view of Mowbray's 'covering' for him), why does he rub in its severity? Because he is callous? Or because he is merely being conscripted as the playwright's commentator? Mowbray's reply begins with restrained reproach and simple dignity—the sentence is *all unlooked for from your highness' mouth* (155)—but it deteriorates into fifteen lines of over-elaborated conceits. Then come a couplet each from Richard and the one he has betrayed (174-77) almost comically mechanical. It is as if the poet recognized the danger of making the episode seem Mowbray's tragedy and so applied a stylistic brake, but somewhat overdid it. (Or perhaps Homer simply nodded.) The oath administered the exiles reads like a contract (178-92), with the contingency it is designed to forestall reminding us of the shifting nature of political alliances. Bolingbroke's parting injunction to Mowbray serves the playwright's purpose of evoking Mowbray's ominous rejoinder (205-05), foreshadowing future events.   **208-309**   The scene concludes with debates and reflections, mostly in couplets, occasioned by the situation but contributing little to its development, or even to the individual as distinct from the generic character of the speakers. That the King commuted Bolingbroke's sentence is a fact of history, here utilized as a means of evoking Gaunt's poignant remarks upon the limits of kingly power. Richard's reminder to Gaunt of his consent to his son's exile occasions similarly poignant remarks upon the dilemma of a loving but judicious parent. The debate between Gaunt and Bolingbroke elaborates a recurrent theme in Shakespeare—the inadequacy of moral philosophy as relief to present pain. It is highly rhetorical, beginning with rimed stychomythia and ending in a set piece (294-303) in which striking images are artfully balanced in unrimed couplets, and given a general application in a rimed conclusion. Although thought and expression are here offered mainly for their own sake, the speeches suit the speakers—wise but futile father, patriotic but malcontent son. Both characters gain solidity through demonstrated kinship with common humanity.

I, iv

Lord Aumerle, another cousin of the King, facetiously rejoices over the exile of Bolingbroke, whom Richard himself describes as a popularity-seeker and aspirant to the throne. The King outlines plans to replenish his wasted treasury and finance an expedition against Ireland. When news is brought of John of Gaunt's sudden illness, he and his courtiers rejoice, and pray for a prompt death so that the Lancastrian estates may be confiscated.

1-36 Again a private occasion following a public one acts as a commentary upon it, as the King's inner circle delight in the hypocrisy of their show of regard for Bolingbroke. Richard's malicious portrait-painting of his cousin is quite at variance with his high-minded posing in the preceding scene, but the mimicry—*Off goes his bonnet to an oyster wench* . . . (31-34)—while perhaps unregal is not uningratiating.   **37-65** But if Bolingbroke is such a man, what is this King? He appears here at his worst, offending things held sacred by English subjects, their property rights and their sense of religious propriety. His plan to restore his treasury amounts to robbery; and in one short speech he twice (59, 64) prays God that Gaunt will die. Gaunt, we must remember, is his kinsman and a national hero. The choral *Amen* of his courtiers is comic, but its cynicism must alienate, at least for the moment, all sympathy from the King's party, here represented by the notorious Bushy, Bagot, and Green, as well as Aumerle.

II, i

John of Gaunt hopes that Richard will heed his dying counsels, but his brother York warns him that the King is too far corrupted by flatterers and too much in love with pleasure to be thus reclaimed. Gaunt extols the beauties of England and bewails its present state.

When Richard arrives with his Queen and court, the dying man is cruelly rebuffed, and, at the instant of his death, his estates are confiscated. York protests that the action is unworthy of their royal line, and that in depriving Bolingbroke of his hereditary rights, Richard is setting an evil precedent which may operate against himself. The King remains unmoved. He departs for his Irish expedition, leaving York as regent in England. The Lords Willoughby and Ross, with Northumberland, resolve to combat the corrupt reign by joining Bolingbroke, who is about to land an army on the northern shores in order to redress his own and the nation's grievances.

1-70 The poetry becomes more abundant and fine as the play progresses. York's harsh truths alternate with his brother's elegiac lyricism—*The setting sun, and music at the close* (12-14)—which reminds us of lovely lines in the Sonnets. The celebrated tribute to England (31-68) incorporates many value-giving images and ideas—of regal splendor, natural beauty, native prowess, familial loyalty, religious sanctions, and the security of the sacred hearth—all now tragically threatened from within. The structure of repeated words and parallel phrases, several times abandoned and then resumed, produces the effect of spontaneous improvisation, and of spurts of energy such as this subject alone could evoke in a dying man. The tone is both valedictory and ecstatic.   **71-93** Gaunt's extended punning upon his name, and his stichomythic wit-combat with Richard, proves offensive to some readers, and understandably so. It is unnecessary to rationalize into a virtue every detail in these plays, which, like Renaissance art in general, sometimes lapse into the bizarre. Still, it must be conceded that Richard's insults would be less endurable if uninsulated from Gaunt's great speech by these dubious passages in question, as well as by York's apology (69-70).   **94-223** Richard's conduct increases the hostility aroused in us in the preceding scene. Since the conduct was deliberately planned, it cannot be excused as the result of youthful pique. For the time being at least, we must be on Bolingbroke's side, and the extent to which we are required to modify our position later on is a central critical question posed by the play. The Queen, who makes her first appearance here, gains nothing by standing silent;

later, the pathos of her situation affects us, but she is never elevated into a heroine. York emerges as the character he will remain —querulously righteous, futile, confused—but he should not be stereotyped by the actor into a Polonius. He deserves the trust placed in him, never acting from self-interest, and always trying to pick the lesser of evils. His wit and his wits are those of an aged man, but it maims the play to distort him into a comic figure. **224-300** Northumberland, too, emerges as the character he will remain—the coldly efficient power politician and ruthless agent of Bolingbroke. Here he feels out the mood of the nobles, fans their resentment, and proceeds to decisive action. (Because the present episode is appended to that in which Richard appropriates the Lancastrian estates, we must not conclude that Bolingbroke has not had time to hear about the appropriation and so must later be using it only as pretext for his return to England. The convention of foreshortened time is being employed, and the long inventory of the nation's wrongs (238-269) tends to give the appropriation the immediate status of past history.)

II, ii

News is brought to the foreboding Queen that Henry Bolingbroke has landed at Ravenspurgh and the English lords are flocking to his banner. Old York takes measures to stem the rebellion, but laments his own weakness and the hopelessness of the King's cause. Richard's favorites, Bushy, Bagot, and Green, realize that their time is short as they go to join the royal forces.

1-149 The messages following each other in succession produce the effect of passing time, the gradual worsening of the situation, and approaching crisis. A bi-partisan balance begins to be restored. York assumes that rebellion is rebellion whatever the provocation; and, under threat, the King's favorites behave with dignity.

II, iii

Bolingbroke receives and returns the compliments of Northumberland, the latter's son Percy (the 'Hotspur' of *1 Henry IV*), Willoughby, and Ross; after which Lord Berkeley heralds the approach of York. Bolingbroke is upbraided by York as a rebel, but protests that his intentions are only to secure his right in the Dukedom of Lancaster. Powerless to resist him, York offers him repose at Berkeley Castle, and when he states his determination to seize the King's favorites and their 'accomplices' at Bristol Castle, agrees to accompany him as a neutral.

1-67 These may be merely the nervous civilities exchanged by men joined in a great risk, but there is at least a hint of the flatteries usually paid to a rising star, with thoughts of benefits to be given and received. **68-171** In this and in subsequent scenes, elements appear which prevent our accepting Bolingbroke's invasion as a patriotic crusade. That he is mindful of the nation's needs, and is more fitted to rule than Richard, is always apparent, but we are constantly reminded of the sanctity of anointed kings and the criminality of rebellion. An aura of duplicity surrounds Bolingbroke, because of the constant contrast between his compromising words and uncompromising actions, as here in his deference to York, yet assumption that he himself has the right to mete out summary punishment. The disparity between his stated and actual objectives becomes increasingly apparent.

II, iv

A Welsh Captain informs the Earl of Salisbury that Richard's forces have dispersed, owing to evil portents and the rumor that he is dead.

1-24 This brief scene will provide a point of reference, supporting the messages of catastrophe which will later be conveyed to Richard.

III, i

Having seized Bushy and Green, Bolingbroke accuses them of corrupting the King and being author of his misfortunes. They respond defiantly as he orders their execution. Bolingbroke sends courtly greetings to the Queen, and prepares to combat the King's Welsh allies whom he supposes are still in the field.

1-44 The indictment of the favorites has the effect of partially absolving Richard; it was customary to blame royal shortcomings upon courtly parasites. Bushy and Green themselves help to restore the King somewhat in our estimation by conceding nothing and facing death stoutly; in a more partisan play they would have cringed. If there is any suggestion of sexual deviation in Richard, it occurs here (11-15), but it is doubtful if homosexuality is implied; the more obvious implication is that the favorites have pandered to the King and encouraged him in adultery.

III, ii

Returned to England, Richard caresses his native soil and affirms his divine immunity. His followers try to hold him to a plane of practical resolution, but he keeps dipping from heights of visionary elation to depths of despair as he receives successively the news of the dispersal of his Welsh forces, the strength of the rebels, the execution of his favorites, and the failure of York to hold the northern castles. Neither Aumerle nor the Bishop of Carlisle can stem his pathetic laments, or alter his decision to succumb after he has heard Salisbury's and Scroop's ominous tidings.

1-218 In this great scene, the attractive and repellent qualities of Richard are subtly and fascinatingly balanced. His situation is so different from what it was at his last appearance, and its desperation is so cruelly driven home to him, that we are predisposed to pity him, but we are retarded by his seemingly limitless capacity to pity himself. His first words are touching, but there is a quick lapse into the excess which characterizes most of his later speeches. The implied stage business shows that his own followers recoil at the sight of his *senseless* (indeed childish) *conjuration* (23), and would prefer that the one who must provide them leadership would stand erect. His deportment throughout the scene is the reverse of that of the Shakespearean warriors whose fortitude is tested by cumulative ill tidings in similar scenes; here it is the followers, notably the Bishop of Carlisle, who recognize this as a moment for greatness. The excess of his responses appears in small ways, as in his reference to wandering in the *Antipodes* when he has only been to Ireland (49), and in large ones, as when he proclaims that for everyone of Bolingbroke's men *God for his Richard hath in heavenly pay A glorious angel* (60-61). His precipitous descents from elation are at times almost comic, in the fashion of Shylock's emotional gyrations when receiving the mixed budget of news from Tubal. Against all this stands the indubitable fact that his protests of royal sanctity adhere to the accepted doctrine of the times, and his descant upon *the hollow crown That rounds the mortal temples of a king* (155-77) is very beautiful. There is nothing in the play more perfect, and it is inconceivable that the playwright should have put such language into the mouth of one he wished us to despise. Richard is a poetic fantast, miscast as a king. The same counterbalancing of qualities appears in the next scene and, conspicuously, in the abdication episode of Act V. How we will respond will depend upon our own temperaments. We find authority in the play for viewing its titular character as a whining rogue and manic depressive, or as a gifted youth who has been victimized by his destiny and tragically misled—one whom a later character of Shakespeare describes as *that sweet lovely rose* (*1 Henry IV*, i, iii, 175).

III, iii

To the tune of York's reproaches, Bolingbroke arrives with his forces before Flint Castle and learns from Percy that it is occupied by Richard with a remnant of his followers. He bids Northumberland tell the King that he is ready to resume allegiance if his banishment is repealed and his estates are restored. Richard appears on the walls and rages at Northumberland, but he returns a soft reply to Bolingbroke's conciliatory message. Then he laments to Aumerle that he has debased himself, and falls again into a mood of renunciation and self-pity. At Bolingbroke's bidding, he descends into the 'base-court,' playing whimsically upon the appropriateness of the term, and allows himself to be escorted to London.

1-61 York's querulous wit and Bolingbroke's easy assurance serve as perfect foils for each other. The rebel's ambivalent oration to the *Noble lords* (31-61) is an adroit illustration of velvet glove worn upon iron fist; poetic imagination is not confined to Richard, but Bolingbroke's always serves purely practical ends. **62-199** Observe the continued counter-balancing; Richard appears at first as the sun and eagle—*like a king* (63-68)—but presently as a mere foolish talker—*like a frantic man* (185). We cannot be sure whether Aumerle weeps at the pathos in his words (160), or laughs at their excess (171), or whether Richard simply realizes that he might well do both. **200-09** Yet Richard is not lacking in a kind of dignity; there is royal magnanimity in his treatment of York, and something like humor in his final capitulation. The last spare lines (207-09) explode the bubble of Bolingbroke's pledge of allegiance on bended knee. There is no need of amplification of his *Yes, my good lord* (209)—obviously everyone present knows that the subject who lays hands on a king dare never relax his hold.

III, iv

The disconsolate Queen declines to engage in customary pastimes as she walks with her ladies in the royal gardens. The head Gardener appears with his assistants, and she eavesdrops upon their conversation. They speak of England as an ill-tended garden, ruined by the neglect of its royal caretaker. When they mention the deposition of Richard by Bolingbroke, the Queen steps forth and angrily challenges them. The old Gardener assures her that they speak the truth; and when she departs after cursing his art with sterility, he expresses his compassion for her and resolves to commemorate her tears with a bank of rue.

1-107   As the Queen devises allegorical glosses upon the proposals that they bowl, dance, tell tales, and so on (1-20), the way is paved for the extended allegory of the unweeded garden to which the scene is devoted. This allegory, so delicately and imaginatively expressed by these poetic gardeners, is a choral commentary upon the action of the play as a whole. Observe that the chief spokesman, although aware of Richard's culpability, expresses no approval of the one who has rebelled; his thoughts seem to be upon the ways of God, and he tolerates no recriminations against his King, who *Hath now himself met with the fall of leaf*. There is nothing in the slightest degree comic or base about this aged menial, whom the Queen addresses as *thou little better thing than earth* (78). His so-called *harsh rude tongue* (74) is the gentlest in the play.

IV, i

Bagot bears witness against Aumerle as an accomplice in the death of Gloucester and the exile of Bolingbroke. Fitzwater, Percy, and an unnamed Lord supplement the charges, and exchange challenges with the accused, while Surrey defends him and exchanges challenges with Fitzwater. When Aumerle claims that the banished Mowbray has belied him and offers to face Mowbray in trial by combat, Bolingbroke consents to his repeal, but learns from the Bishop of Carlisle that he has died abroad after valiant service in the crusades. Bolingbroke blesses the memory of his former foe, and assigns a day for the trial of Aumerle and his challengers. York enters with the announcement that Richard has abdicated, and Bolingbroke must ascend the throne as King Henry the Fourth. Carlisle vehemently protests, and is forthwith charged by Northumberland with treason. Richard is sent for to make public declaration of his willingness to abdicate. He does so with a long display of bitter grief, during which he likens his betrayal to Christ's, involves Bolingbroke in a symbolic charade with the crown, and finally dashes to pieces a mirror in which he has gazed at his 'brittle glory.' Bolingbroke orders him conveyed to the tower, and appoints a day for his own coronation. After his departure from the scene, the Abbot of Westminster enlists Aumerle and Carlisle in a plot to assassinate him.

1-113 The action is a reflection of that of the opening scene, and serves as reminder of the continuing and expanding propensities of civil strife. But Henry is not Richard. He displays maximum resolution with a minimum of words. He pays any tribute and makes any concession so long as it does not contravene his practical interests, combining lenience with firmness as a matter of both policy and inclination. **114-54** Carlisle's attack upon the 'de facto' ruler is heroic. Observe that the ruler leaves retaliation to his hatchet-man, Northumberland. Carlisle's speech borrows a prophetic quality from the speaker's episcopal robes and the audience's knowledge that the deposition of Richard will lead ultimately to the fatal Wars of the Roses. **155-318** These lines were omitted from editions of the play issued during Queen Elizabeth's lifetime; the matter seemed politically dangerous, evoking too vividly a precedent for forced abdication. Richard is wonderful in his métier in this scene, serving as both stage-manager and principal actor in his 'woeful pageant,' both feeling and exploiting his pain. In letting him liken himself to Christ, and proclaim that he has found not one man true to him (171), the playwright has not forgotten that Carlisle has just sacrificed himself in his cause. As Richard indulges his fantasies of persecution in matchlessly resourceful words and gestures, he is both poet and hysteric, creator and self-conscious critic of words, both pitiable and pitiful.

V, i

En route to the tower Richard is reproved by his Queen for base humility when he counsels resignation and a holy life. Northumberland comes with orders for his transfer to Pomfret Castle and the

Queen's exile to France. Richard predicts the day when Northumberland will turn upon the King he has helped to enthrone, then takes final leave of his wife.

1-102 He again lapses into self-dramatization (40-50), but in the main Richard's conduct is restrained. His prophecy (55-68) has the authority of the words of the doomed. Although his bearing to his wife is affectionate, it is too late in the day to present them as tragic lovers, and the rimed verse appropriately formalizes their parting.

V, ii

York describes for his wife Henry Bolingbroke's triumphant entrance into London, with Richard's humiliation. Despite his sympathy for the fallen star, he is resolved to be faithful to the present King. He now stands as surety for the impeached Aumerle, and insists upon reading a bond in the latter's possession. When it reveals complicity in a plot of assassination, he is enraged, and rides off to denounce his son for treason despite his wife's entreaties. The Duchess of York urges Aumerle to speed to Henry with a plea for mercy, and prepares to follow after.

1-117 York's moving description (7-36) is surely designed to contribute to our rising sympathy with Richard; at the same time, his display of loyalty to Richard's successor must be viewed as exemplary.

V, iii (+ V, iv)

King Henry is repining over the profligacy of his own son (the 'Prince Hal' of *1 & 2 Henry IV*) when the distracted Aumerle appears, pleads for a private audience, and locks himself in with the King preparatory to confessing his guilt. York arrives and shouts a warning, then breaks in and denounces Aumerle. The Duchess arrives and adds her pleas for mercy to her son's. King Henry grants a pardon to Aumerle, but declares that the remaining con-spirators must be destroyed. Sir Pierce of Exton tells his servant that the King has expressed a desire for the death of Richard, and that he himself is prepared to gratify that desire.

1-146, 1-11. Henry's allusion to his ne'er-do-well son provides a link to the next play in the Lancastrian cycle, which, although named for the present King, is chiefly concerned with the reclama-tion of his heir. The situation which arose in the preceding scene is immediately developed and concluded. The introduction of a new interest and minor crisis late in a play is not uncommon; it serves the purpose of sustaining attention during the denouement of the major action (see above, p. 75). The present episode seems to have been included, however, because it illustrates Henry's inclina-tion to clemency within the bounds of practicality. As in other in-stances in this play, rimed verse appears when it seems desirable to temper the emotional impact of an episode: it would have been inexpedient here to exploit fully the tragic implications of a father's sacrifice of his own son, especially since that son is destined to be saved. In these last scenes, both Richard and Henry are sympa-thetically presented, and the dramatist has had to cope with the problem of recording the lamentable death of the one, without completely alienating us from the other, who is responsible for it. Observe that Henry's opprobrius action is not only juxtaposed with his merciful one, but it is reported rather than portrayed. We do not actually hear his insinuations to Exton. This does not lessen the ethical gravity of the offense, but it lessens its emotional effect upon us.

V, v

In prison at Pomfret Castle, Richard peoples his solitary world with thoughts and fancies suggested by his fall. He is visited by a faithful groom, and learns that Henry has ridden his favorite horse, roan Barbary, on coronation day. When his keeper, acting on the orders of Exton, refuses to taste his food for poison, Richard abandons patience and beats him, whereupon the assassins come rushing in. Richard seizes a sword and dispatches two of them, but falls at the hand of Exton.

1-66 Playing for no audience but himself, Richard plays most honestly. His thoughts are weary thoughts, but such as could grow only in a fertile and perceptive mind. When he falls into his customary habit of embroidering language, he pulls himself up with an expression of self-revulsion (50-60).   **67-97** This is one of a number of instances in which Shakespeare, alleged disdainer of the multitude, is at pains to portray the fidelity of the lowly. Richard's patience begins to crack when he hears that the man who has taken his kingdom has also taken his favorite horse—a natural touch. **98-118** Richard makes a good end. If we do not think so, we should cease complaining about his earlier softness—we cannot have it against him both ways. As usual, the murderer expresses instantaneous remorse.

V, vi

King Henry receives news of the capture and death of the rebellious lords and of the conspirators who planned his assassination. Of the latter only the Bishop of Carlisle remains alive, and him the King magnanimously spares in recognition of his worth. Exton presents the coffin of Richard, but is rebuked instead of rewarded. The King confesses his guilt, expresses contrition, and resolves to seek absolution in a voyage to the Holy Lands.

1-52 In repudiating Exton while acknowledging his own responsibility for Exton's deed, Henry may seem illogical and unjust, but his action is symbolically acceptable—as the cutting off of a hand which has offended. Besides, Exton has established no claim upon our sentiments for fair treatment. Henry follows the course prescribed for all sinners—open confession, repentance of sin, and amendment of life. Since he retains the fruit of his sin, a firm seat upon the throne, his amendment is incomplete; but there is nothing in the play to suggest that his account with heaven is fully squared

The play ends at a moment of stability in the realm—now ruled by a good king with a bad conscience.

4

Romeo and Juliet

:

Prologue

A C h o r u s announces that the play is about two lovers of Verona, victimized by fate and the enmity of their families; then requests a patient hearing.

1-14 Delivered by a solitary speaker, probably in formal robes, this prologue is in the 'English' or 'Shakespearean' sonnet form, three quatrains and a couplet. It is unique (see above, p. 3) in that it gives the dramatist's own view of the overall significance of a tragic action. Two causes of the disaster are mentioned, concurrently and repeatedly—evil destiny (see *fatal, star-crossed, misadventured, death-marked*), and the *parents' rage* (5-11). The lovers are referred to, not as transgressing, but, twice (8, 11), as atoning for the transgression of others. Economical and adept, the lines serve also to indicate the locale (2), the approximate duration of the stage action (12), and the disarming modesty of the players (13-14). The tone is stately, as befits tragedy, conferring dignity upon the action as a whole though not necessarily upon the family feud which initiates it.

I, i

Clownish and truculent servants revive a standing feud between the houses of Montague and Capulet. Benvolio, a Montague of good will, tries to halt the fray, but Tybalt, a fire-eating Capulet, attacks him instead of joining his efforts. As citizens of Verona led in by an officer try to quell the rioters, the heads of the feuding families rush forth to join combat in spite of their protesting wives. The Prince of Verona restores order with his appearance and a stern reproof, then summons old Capulet to an immediate hearing, old Montague to a later one. Benvolio remains with the Montague couple to explain how the fight began. Their son Romeo was luckily absent. The three speak of the youth's recent melancholy and love of solitude. Benvolio promises to seek out the cause, as Romeo approaches and they withdraw. Romeo lets Benvolio know that he is hopelessly in love with a beautiful but coldly virtuous maiden, and rejects as useless his kinsman's advice to transfer his love to another.

1-36 Terms like *mutiny* and *civil blood* in the prologue, linked in our minds with grave issues and great conflicts, may have given us a wrong notion of the Montague-Capulet feud. It is here first projected as a ridiculous brawl, and no original cause is assigned it. How do Sampson and Gregory come to be wearing *swords and bucklers* (1 s.d.) since they seem to be neither gentlemen retainers nor hired bravoes of the house, but lower domestics and clowns absolute? Did they pilfer them in their cups from the household armory? Sampson's first line suggests that their conversation has been about some effront, real or fancied, offered by servants of the rival house, but the portion we hear is routine clowning, with Gregory as quipster and Sampson as stooge. (Sampson bears a champion's name, evidently for the playwright's own delectation since it is not spoken in the lines.) The dialogue, appropriately in prose, relies on the traditional comic potential of the hangman's noose (4), blustering cowardice (5-9, 34-36), and the ribald suggestiveness of such words as *head, feel, stand, tool, naked weapon* (22-32), all used as puns elsewhere in Shakespeare, to the death of sobriety whenever they appear.   **37-60** The Montague servants appear less clownish than the Capulet, but no more formidable. They too are equipped with swords, and we will have to accept the fact simply as an anomalous convenience. Additional stock humor is introduced, on keeping on the safe side of the law. The thumb-biting may be Italian local coloring, but the general atmosphere is English and even countrified. The increase in courage in the Capulet servants at the approach of a Capulet gentleman (Tybalt, not Benvolio, although the latter's entrance and speeches appear first in the text) is a touch of more subtle humor than any thus far. (Coleridge saw in these idiotic servants at least a pleasing 'ourish-ness,' presumably because they identify their honor with their masters' honor. It is a generous suggestion which we accept with some lack of conviction.)   **61-69** Benvolio, whose name de-scribes his nature, uses the correct word *fools,* then a phrase per-haps too much laden with religious connotation (62); however, it is a fitting cue for the speech by Tybalt, whose bearing is that of one of the personified seven deadly sins—Wrath.   **70-73** Thus a street-fight would be dealt with in London or Stratford, with a constable mustering the aid of artisans and apprentices. The fight-ing becomes tripartite, with the Montagues and Capulets combating each other and the citizens as well.   **74-78** If anything were needed to make this feud seem ridiculous, it would be the implied stage business with Lady Capulet's scolding remark on her hus-band's aged awkwardness (74) and Lady Montague's clinging to her husband's gown.   **79-101** Upon the entrance of Escalus and his train, the stage is filled and the play has opened with a fine hubbub. It requires several lines for the Prince to gain attention (79-80)—which does not improve his temper (81). There are a few decorative touches in his speech (83, 91-93) but in the main it is simple and downright, leaving a firm impression of a regulatory force in Verona which will have to be reckoned with.   **102-13** Now that old Montague has calmed down, he sounds a little rueful —and none too fond of his family feud. Benvolio's review will set anyone straight who has not quite followed the turbulent opening of the play; its bombastic conceit (109-10) has an honorable epic ancestry and is here fittingly associated with a swashbuckler; still, perhaps it could be spared.   **114-53** The shift in the substance of the scene from a street brawl to a youthful infatuation requires a swift transition in tone. It is effected by this series of lyrical speeches, resembling arias, assigned with little regard to the character of the speaker. The imagery is that of pastoral poetry, with a linking of contraries suggestive of blasted youth. Twice the freshness of dawn is associated not with birth and vitality but with gloom and solitude (116-23, 129-38), while the promise of bloom in the sun-lit bud is associated with both solitude and death by the *envious worm* (145-51). **154-236** This is an almost detachable eclogue in rime, with the stichomythic exchanges of wit and massed oxymora (174-79, 191-92; cf. above, p. 35) helping to create an impression of exploitable sentiment rather than deep emotion. The praise of the beloved is bookish (207-12), and the indictment of sterile coldness (213-18) is that of Shakespeare's most conventional sonnets. We can scarcely accept as authentic a love so artificially expatiated upon; still, if the Romeo of these postures proves real, he should be a fine responsive youth—capable of real love.

I, ii

Capulet considers his daughter still too young to marry, but gives Count Paris permission to try his luck as suitor. He is holding this evening a traditional family feast, and sends a servant to invite the Capulet clan and the youthful flower of Verona. The servant cannot read the list, and asks the aid of Romeo and Benvolio, who are still debating the latter's prescription for curing old love with new. The servant repays Romeo for his help by saying they may come to the feast providing they are not Montagues. Romeo decides to do so in spite of the barrier when Benvolio points out that the feast will offer a fine chance to compare his fair Rosaline with other beauties, but he insists that his purpose will be not to compare but to adore.

1-3 Old Capulet, too, seems to have had enough of feuding. **4-37** This is a pleasing colloquy. Capulet loves his only daughter and would like to keep her single a few years more, not for his sake but hers. The terms he offers Paris are fair-minded; and his sympathies, despite his years, are with April-youth against wintry age. **38-44** Each man to his trade, and that of a *clown* (cf. 1 s.d.) is mangling language, in this case mismating the halves of platitudes. **45-103** Although more playful now, the dialogue of Benvolio and

Romeo continues in the former ornamental style; here a speech by each even rimes ababcc, like the end-fragment of a sonnet (45-51, 90-95). But Romeo's dialogue with the servant is not Arcadian, and it helps a little to domesticate him in Verona. Is it Romeo's own ingenuity which converts the invitation list into verse (64-72) which hovers between the poetic and the comic? His Rosaline appears to be a Capulet (70) but no matter—a feud is no obstacle to worship from afar. The ominous name *Tybalt* appears in the list —and the oddly arresting name *Mercutio.*

I, iii

Lady Capulet orders a servant to summon her daughter Juliet. The servant, who is Juliet's former Nurse and present attendant, is allowed to stay for the conference, and she delays it materially with reminiscences of her charge's promising childhood. Lady Capulet tells Juliet that she is not too young for marriage, and extols the merits of Paris, who will be present at this evening's feast. Juliet's response is lukewarm but dutiful, as the arrival of the guests is announced.

1-10 Lady Capulet's initial lines are all curt and arbitrary, giving an immediate impression of peevish coldness. **11-57** Since she and the Nurse have presumably shaped Juliet's home environment, the poor girl seems perched between a crag and a bog. What a wonder of messy good nature and senile garrulity this Nurse proves to be! As recollection runs along the worn grooves of her mind into the cistern of gossip-eternal, her tones are as authentic as the gurgle of a drain. Everything reminds her of something else, but nothing deflects her from her central triviality, to which she always returns with an air of achievement. She is expert at coping with interruption; her technique is never to resist but to swerve and flow easily on. The drift of thought is circuitous and yet predictable: growing up means going to bed, and dying means going to God; the name of anyone departed (18-20, 39-40) draws praise and a pious aside. Nostalgically licorish, she still delights in the thought of the loss of her virginity at the age of twelve (2), is incorrigibly body-minded (53), and drools at the thought of a bridal. Still we cannot despise this Nurse. We must at least relish her relish, and marvel at its survival. Uncannily, too, she is our sister under the skin; if we followed our inclinations, we would all repeat our anecdotes thrice to make sure their delightfulness stuck. This poet has an incomparable ear for our voices.   **58-66** Juliet's words are few but they afford a glimpse at her sprightly (58) and charming (66) nature.   **67-99** Her mother's attitude contrasts remarkably with her father's. Lady Capulet seems anxious only to get the girl off her hands. The Nurse also exerts pressure in favor of marriage, but for more genial reasons. (The age of Juliet should not disturb us. She is young, but the play itself underlines the fact that marriage at fourteen, although exceptional, is not abnormal. The Capulets are not countenancing a child-marriage; their daughter is innocent and inexperienced, as the story requires, but is otherwise mature. In an era when seventeen or eighteen was a quite ripe marital age, a *youthful* bride had to be youthful indeed as judged by present standards.) In this scene, containing such 'natural' speeches, one is the exact reverse; Lady Capulet is not the person we would expect to elaborate the fancy of a lover as an unbound book (81-94). Intrinsically this extended metaphor is interesting, linking praise of the lover's beauty with the idea that marriage is a kind of confinement that confers completion. Since it is general in its application, it is transferable to Romeo; evidently it burgeoned in the poet's mind and was assigned to the only speaker available.   **100-03** Domestic confusion offers proof of the imminence of a party. **104-05** These lines have a reverse suggestiveness, like Romeo's positive assertion that he will look only at Rosaline. It seems unlikely that Juliet will land in the arms of Paris, toward whom she is so vigorously pushed.

I, iv

Romeo and Benvolio, with their friend Mercutio and other young gentlemen equipped as masqueraders and torchbearers, prepare to visit the Capulet feast. They agree to omit the old-fashioned speech of greeting, and simply perform their dance. Romeo prefers to be one of the torchbearers since he is in no mood for dancing; he is heavy-hearted and has had ominous dreams. The others try to jest him out of his mood, and Mercutio rehearses at length a dream of Queen Mab and the fairy-world. Despite his misgivings, Romeo enters the Capulet house with the maskers.

1-10 The visit of the young men to the Capulet feast is here demonstrated to be socially correct, not an intrusion. ('Masks' were originally impromptu and quite welcome visits during a festive occasion, by a costumed group consisting of those who performed a figure dance and those who lighted the performance with torches. It was understood that the maskers would later mingle and dance with those already present.)   **11-52** Romeo meets his social obligations by engaging in this wit-combat with his friends; in its course we become aware that his conventional love-melancholy is crossed by presentiments of a more grave and mysterious kind. Mercutio appears as a down-grader of love in general, a giber with a rough-shod wit. (This seems to have suggested his name; cf. 'The words of Mercury are harsh' at the conclusion of *Love's Labor's Lost* after gibing and 'glozing' have been renounced.)   **53-95** But he is also 'mercurial' in the modern sense—volatile and impulsive. This matchless exercise in verbal cameo-cutting and imaginative fooling, which with similar matter in *Midsummer Night's Dream* has created our present conception of the fairy-world, could more readily have been conceived by him than by the others, especially since its whole second half is distributive satire, of lovers, courtiers, lawyers, ladies, parsons, soldiers, and finally country maids. (Compare the 'seven ages of man' speech in *As You Like It* by the critical Jaques.) We must value more the earlier portion, with its vivid and delicately proportioned details. Granted that it is a set piece, too long for the dramatic occasion and introduced for itself rather than as a means of characterizing Mercutio, still we would not spare a line of it.   **96-114** The remarks of the others simply supply a lead-in for the portentous speech by Romeo. Earlier (48) he has said that they *mean well* but may be lacking in discretion. Now his forebodings, expressed in terms of destiny (107) and *untimely death* (111) are so strong that he must steel himself to proceed; his lines and the implied reckless gesture at their conclusion provide unmistakable tragic foreshadowing.

I, v

Old Capulet welcomes the maskers, spurs on the merriment, and chats with an elderly relative. Romeo sees Juliet and falls instantly in love. Tybalt recognizes him and is about to attack, but is scolded by old Capulet as a headstrong boy: Montague or not, Romeo is their guest and well-spoken-of in Verona. Romeo and Juliet talk briefly together and kiss. As the party breaks up, each inquires about the other. They learn to their dismay that they are sundered by the Montague-Capulet feud.

1 s.d. The stage direction in the original text, sometimes altered in modern editions, 'They march about the stage, and Servingmen come forth with napkins,' indicates that the action is continuous with that of the preceding scene. The entrance of the servants, then the Capulets and guests from the adjoining chamber where they have supped, creates a locale within the house which the maskers 'enter' simply by moving about the stage without the necessity of leaving it. **1-15** The bustle of clearing away, with the servants intent upon their personal grievances and on plans for a feast on the leavings, gives realistic dimension to the Capulet household. It does not seem oppressively aristocratic. **16-40** Lady Capulet says nothing, but her husband creates a party spirit as he welcomes the maskers and converts the occasion into a dance. After the maskers perform, the dancing becomes general; and the reference to the rising heat of the room, together with the snatches of reminiscence by the older generation, creates an illusion of the passage of time. **41-53** Why this *Servingman* does not know the young mistress of the house is the kind of question we should not ask. (Perhaps he is just extra help.) Romeo's knowledge of the identity of Juliet must come later. His first words about her, *O, she doth teach the torches to burn bright!* (44) monosyllabic, alliterative, with its series of open 'o' sounds succeeded by a series of 'r' and 'b' sounds, actually compel the speaker to begin open-mouthed and gradually compress the lips as in amazement. It is a fine full utterance, succeeded by a brilliant metaphor, but the language is not yet different in kind from that in which he expressed his love for Rosaline. However, he is now impelled to take action, and the dramatic function of the Rosaline episode becomes clear. Juliet's charms gain ascendancy in our imagination by their power to obliterate those of her rival. More important, Romeo's status as a true lover is implied by the contrast between his present and his past behavior; he is no longer the languishing amourist; the shadow has become substance. (Similar conversions are treated in *As You Like It* and *Twelfth Night*.)   **54-92**   The venom of the family feud is concentrated in Tybalt. The Montagues have all appeared as reasonable people, with no Tybalt among them. Old Capulet is a decent man. His tribute to Romeo (68) shows how approachable he might be in the matter of a reconciling marital alliance with the Montague clan. We love the way he ticks off his young relative, in splenetic colloquialisms. His is as truly the voice of a starchy old man as the Nurse's is the voice of a morally boneless old woman. **93-110**   In this first exchange of words between Romeo and Juliet, the lines form one complete sonnet and the beginning of another. The subliminal effect of this verse form, because of its association with love, is to place about the speakers a heart-shaped frame. The early stages of courtship are symbolized in the content of the speeches. Romeo is in the posture of attack, Juliet in the posture of defense, with the fencing that would normally fill many hours concentrated into a moment. They are Renaissance lovers, and they fence with a metaphor. At this juncture a truly passionate encounter would be untimely; the words and action are highly stylized, with Romeo *kissing by the book* as Juliet wittily remarks, but they do kiss—and kiss again. (The prompt and public nature of this kissing is not untrue to Elizabethan custom: it was usual for men and women to kiss—presumably once—upon meeting, and even upon being introduced.)   **111-45**   The Nurse, predestined to be a go-between, is the one who tells each who the other is. Observe the distinction between the masculine and the feminine approach. Romeo asks directly (112), Juliet deviously, by inquiring first about several others (128-31). Even before Juliet learns that

Romeo is a Montague, she couples the words *grave* and *wedding bed* (135).

II Chorus

The Chorus states that Rosaline is now forgotten, Romeo and Juliet in love but forced to meet secretly because *foes* by birth.

1-14 This choral speech, again in sonnet form, performs no vital function. The situation it recapitulates is already clear; and no gap is in need of filling, since little time elapses between preceding and succeeding action and no episode is omitted. Perhaps it can best be justified as punctuation—such as might otherwise be supplied by an intermission—separating the presentation of the situation from its swift and fatal development.

II, i (+ II, ii)

Romeo lingers on the Capulet grounds, hiding from Benvolio and the untimely jesting of Mercutio. He sees Juliet appear at a window, and overhears her profession of love. He greets her, and professes his own. She is torn between fears for his safety and the desire to have him remain, as they ardently exchange their vows. They are interrupted by calls for Juliet from within, and must make their plans in haste. Juliet offers to send him a messenger in the morning by whom he may return instructions on when and where they may marry. He tears himself away, to seek the aid of his father confessor.

1-42 Observe the contrast in behavior of Romeo's friends. When the courteous Benvolio is certain that Romeo wishes to be alone, he is all for drawing Mercutio off. Mercutio seems drunk with his wit. His speeches are among the bawdiest in Shakespeare; they become progressively more physiological, identifying love with the sexual organs. But just as he is mistaken in his belief that Romeo's passion is for Rosaline (17), he may be mistaken in other ways. Romeo is not in love with woman as woman, but with Juliet as Juliet; and Mercutio's estimate, though it has truth in it, is not quite true. It is expressed, however, in terms of remarkable vigor, vividness, and comic ingenuity. (There follows the so-called 'balcony' scene—although no balcony is mentioned in the text and none is required in the action—the most celebrated love-scene in literature. The love-making is at a physical remove, the powerful effect achieved wholly by the magic of language.)   **II, ii, 1-32**   By now we must have become conscious of the recurrence of light-imagery. Romeo was introduced in association with the light of dawn. His first words about Juliet proclaimed her brighter than torchlight. Here she is associated with sunlight, starlight, daylight, heaven-light. The language is ornate but not continuously so. Midway in Romeo's first speech are lines (10-14) which make the following extended metaphors seem to function almost as pretexts, filling his moments of hesitation before daring to speak to her.   **33-106** Juliet's language is plain from the beginning, moving and very lovely. The quality of Romeo's takes on increasingly the quality of hers as she expresses her solicitude and he his defiance of danger. There is a touch of the child (96-97, 103-05) in her admissions, rendering all the more poignant their candor.   **107-24**   She is beset from the very beginning by thoughts that their love may alter or end. Hers is both the natural fear that nothing so precious can stay, and the mysterious foreboding felt earlier by Romeo. The light-imagery alters in its nature. She compares their love to lightning (119), the kind of light, sudden and violent, which intensifies darkness. It is far different from the soft moonlight which suffuses *A Midsummer Night's Dream,* but the metaphor is anticipated in that play in the reference to young love, 'Brief as the lightning in the collied night.'   **125-59**   The calls from within, and Juliet's hasty withdrawals and returns create tension, and indicate by concrete example the general harassment of these lovers. Juliet's surrender, which has seemed so utterly complete, may not be quite so; she is the first to think of practicalities and her terms are marriage (126, 141-42)—not inappropriate if their love means truly a total commitment. There may be a hint that she could not hold to her terms, however much she might wish to (150-53), and that her honor depends wholly on the honor of the one to whom she has already given herself in spirit.   **160-91**   Their plans are laid, the lovers wrest sweetness even from their parting, and the music of this gracious scene closes with grace notes.

II, iii

Friar Laurence is out in the morning air gathering herbs, and philosophizing on their properties. When Romeo appears at so early an hour, he surmises correctly that he has been up all night and fears that he has seduced Rosaline. Astonished to learn that Romeo has transferred his affections to Juliet and wants to be married this very day, he chides the youth for his wavering but concedes that such a match might end the Montague-Capulet feud.

1-30 This rimed homily is light in touch, but its theme—the intermingling of good and evil in nature—is serious enough, and appropriate in a play on love and death. **31-94** The scene continues to the end in rime, and the artifice of its form is matched by the artifice of its functioning. The Friar is obviously a well-disposed and good-humored man, such as would like to see young lovers married and old enemies reconciled, and the episode canters by without raising the issue of whether he will suggest wise means to achieve these worthy ends. We are given no chance to think about it. The last line cannot be seen as ironical except in retrospect.

II, iv

Benvolio and Mercutio discuss Romeo's failure to return home after the Capulet feast and the probability that Tybalt has sent him a challenge. Mercutio lampoons Tybalt as a type of fashionable swaggerer; then, as Romeo appears, shifts his fire to the famous beauties of legend. The two engage in a duel of wits, until the Nurse makes a grand entrance followed by a groom, and becomes the butt of Mercutio's ribald jesting. When left alone with her, Romeo smooths her ruffled feathers and sends word to Juliet that she is to go that afternoon to confession at Friar Laurence's cell, where their marriage will be performed. Romeo's servant will give the Nurse a rope-ladder so that Juliet's chamber will be accessible for the consummation of the marriage. The Nurse seems completely mollified.

1-204   The bulk of this scene is comic interlude introduced purely for amusement, but its atmosphere is more suitable to the presentation of Romeo's practical arrangements than a poetic atmosphere would be. Tybalt seems to have acted upon his resolution at the feast to make trouble (6-8). Mercutio, the anti-romantic, is clearly serving as a foil to Romeo; yet he is not an unsympathetic character. He and Romeo insult each other with the freedom of confirmed friends; and beneath his bumptiousness and ribaldry we detect a hard vein of common sense as well as real concern for Romeo's welfare (83-85). Their slurring remarks about each other to third persons (10, 139-41) seem mere spillovers of their running contest in persiflage. New facets are revealed in that character-gem the Nurse; she shows a true cockney's elegance and hauteur, together with great pliability. Considering her errand and attitude, Mercutio's word *bawd* is not unperceptive; he is again skirting the truth. Observe that the scene is fittingly in prose, except Romeo's lines on his tryst with Juliet.

II, v

Juliet eagerly awaits the return of the Nurse from her embassy. When she arrives, she tantalizes her young mistress with long-winded complaints of her short-windedness and other occupational maladies, but finally imparts the good news of the plan for the marriage that afternoon and its consummation that night.

1-78   It seems incredible that so effective a scene could be composed of such contrasting materials—poetry and prose, romance and realism, pathos and comicality. The secret seems to be that, in their opposite ways, this lovely young girl and this deplorable old baggage are both so *natural*.

II, vi

Romeo waits with Friar Laurence for Juliet. She appears, and they withdraw for the marriage ceremony.

1-37 The gravity of the occasion is established by Romeo's brief speech (6-8) in the plain heroic style. The Friar's misgivings inspire another image of brilliant but destructive light (10). His last speech adds to earlier touches of the comic in his character, and perhaps hints at why he has not tried to effect a reconciliation between the families first and a marriage later as a wiser man might do. But we have not been encouraged to raise this question. Observe that his deliberations, if any, rest in limbo: when we last saw him he had not yet consented to perform the secret marriage, and when we now see him he has already consented to do so.

III, i

Benvolio scents Capulet-trouble in the air, but Mercutio refuses to take him seriously. Tybalt appears with several companions, spoiling for a fight, and Mercutio nullifies Benvolio's conciliatory attitude by contemptuously matching the youth's pugnacity. At the appearance of Romeo, Tybalt transfers his aggression to him and calls him villain. Fresh from his marriage with Juliet, Romeo refuses to be insulted, and professes good will to Tybalt and all other Capulets. Mercutio is chagrined by the attitude of his friend, which he mistakes for servility, and forces Tybalt into a duel with himself. In trying to stop it, Romeo comes between the two, and Tybalt is able to give Mercutio a deadly thrust under his arm. Mercutio's words are bitter as he is carried off. When news is brought of his death, Romeo feels both enraged and guilty, so that he can no longer refuse to fight when Tybalt returns, still on the prey. He slays Tybalt, is at once overwhelmed by the tragic implications of the act, and flies at Benvolio's urging. A crowd gathers, joined by the Prince of Verona and the heads of the houses of Montague and Capulet. Benvolio describes the whole episode; and although the

Prince recognizes that it was Tybalt who slew his kinsman Mercutio and instigated the fight, he holds the Montague-Capulet feud as ultimately responsible and banishes Romeo from Verona on pain of death.

1-195 Almost identical in length with the love-scene at Juliet's window, this 'hate-scene' matches it in being one of the most striking in English drama. Its vivid and vigorous action combines with subtle irony, its overall wantonness with internal inevitability. Mercutio is humorously paradoxical as he upbraids the mild Benvolio for quarrelsomeness (1-31), but the fault he humorously describes proves in large measure his own. We admire his stout partisanship for his friend, his concern for honor, and the sardonic courage with which he faces his end (89-106); but the fact remains that he has little right to call down a plague on both the *houses* into whose quarrel he has angrily and fatally intruded. Tybalt is the nemesis of the scene—and of the play. His sketchily motivated rancor is as near to a symbol of pure evil as it contains. Romeo is impaled on his hideous dilemma at the very moment of joy and triumph after his marriage with Juliet, when he is resolved upon loving-kindness toward the Capulets and all the world. The price he is asked to pay for peace is too high; as he draws his sword upon Tybalt, we must ask what else he could do. Observe that it is Benvolio to whom the dying Mercutio turns, not to Romeo (103), a reproof more painful than his words. There are many fascinating details. Lady Capulet is moved to a display of affection for a kinsman only when it can be combined with a shriek for vengeance (144-48). Yet her charge that Benvolio's account of the quarrel is weighted on the Montague side is not wholly without truth: it was Mercutio, not Tybalt, who first drew steel (cf. 72-83, 156-57). The interaction of ill-doing and ill-luck is so skillfully projected in this scene that such interaction must be recognized as basic in the design of the play as a whole. If we say that the play relies too much upon accident and coincidence, we fail to see this design. The complaint usually takes the form of a statement that the tragedy need not have occurred. From a logical viewpoint, of course it need not. Romeo and presumably the Montagues would be strong for a reconciliation with the Capulets. Old

Capulet himself is an approachable man, and Friar Laurence is an agent, possessed with all the facts, perfectly fitted to make the approach. The dramatist could easily have portrayed Capulet as an older Tybalt, and Friar Laurence as an utter fool (as is sometimes done in stage productions), thus rationalizing the events and making them seem more 'inevitable.' But he has been at pains from the beginning to stress their unnecessary, their *avoidable* character, thus emphasizing the role of fate. We are not, however, required to reconcile ourselves to the human folly through which fate is able to operate.

III, ii

As Juliet eagerly awaits her bridal night, the Nurse brings the rope-ladder and the dreadful news of the quarrel. She tells the tale in her usual maddening fashion so that Juliet first thinks that it is Romeo who has been slain. When she learns that he has slain Tybalt, she cries out against him, but quickly shifts to his defense when the Nurse chimes in. His banishment seems to her as terrible as death, and she welcomes the Nurse's proposal that he be summoned for a loving farewell. She sends him her ring as a token.

1-35 In this invocation to night and the physical consummation of love, the elaborate imagery dignifies but does not disguise the elemental emotion. Juliet is explicit to a degree which seems scarcely natural in one so young and inexperienced, but this soliloquy *by* her is primarily *about* her and should not be judged by narrowly realistic standards. Its truth resides in what is said rather than in how and by whom; still we are not troubled by a sense of unreality, both because Juliet is alone when she speaks, and because complete candor, complete lack of coyness, has always marked the expression of her feelings where Romeo is concerned.   **36-72** Although the Nurse as well as Juliet here speaks blank verse (in contrast with II, v), the tantalizing circumlocution remains comic. The remarkable effect is a sharpening rather than a blurring of the poignance of Juliet's outcries. This is comic accentuation rather than 'relief' or mitigation. To each successive speaker the dead

Tybalt seems dearer than the living Tybalt had seemed (61, 66), a phenomenon we can readily understand.   **73-85** Again massed oxymora (see I, i) appear in a passage where the emotion expressed derives from a false cause, so that there is self-contradiction in the passage as a whole as well as in its details.   **85-153** It is natural that condemnation by another should provoke Juliet's fierce defense of Romeo. She either knows instinctively of his essential innocence, or disregards his guilt; in either case we have eloquent proof that she has forsaken all others and clings only unto him. (We have further proof also of the Nurse's infinite tractability.)

III, iii

To Romeo as well as Juliet banishment seems as terrible as death. He rejects Friar Laurence's moral counsels, and is threatening to slay himself when the Nurse brings word of Juliet's distress. The Nurse prevents him, and the Friar delivers a lengthy homily of mingled reproach and comfort. Romeo is deeply moved at least by one portion of it, the proposal that he go to Juliet's chamber as planned, and he accepts with joy the token of the ring. The Friar warns him to be off by daybreak to Mantua, where he will be kept in touch with developments in Verona.

1-175 The idea of separation evokes even more passionate vehemence from Romeo than from Juliet. His imagination plays upon the idea with wonderful vividness (29-51), and the terms of his rejection of the comforts of philosophy (57-58) have the snap of a whip. The Friar is indubitably wise, but there always appears some detail, in this case the admiration of the Nurse (159-61), to undercut that wisdom and render it slightly absurd.

III, iv

Old Capulet tells Paris that he will persuade his daughter to marry him on Thursday next, then bids his lady break this news to Juliet.

1-36 Up to this point her father has shown no disposition to force

Juliet into marriage. He now becomes quite arbitrary, the dramatist 'motivating' this convenient behavior by what can only be described as a trick. The suddenness with which a wedding date is set is vaguely related with the suddenness of Tybalt's death.

III, v

The tender farewells of Romeo and Juliet after their bridal night are interrupted by the Nurse, who warns that Lady Capulet wishes to see her daughter. Juliet is told that she is to wed Paris within the week. She tearfully demurs, but is unable to explain that she is already the wife of the slayer of Tybalt. She is harshly rebuked by her father, coldly ordered to do what she is told by her mother, and, after these two have left, advised by the Nurse to find comfort in the arms of Paris now that Romeo is gone. She conceals her rage and disgust at this proposal, then resolves to seek the aid of Friar Laurence. If all else fails, she will evade this marriage by taking her own life.

1-144 There is a hushed and plaintive quality in the lyricism with which the scene opens (1-64), the language sounding an effective contrast to that which precedes and follows. The farewells are touchingly brief, harried, and pure, with a notable freedom from sensual suggestion. Juliet's premonition (54-57) is of a kind which has figured earlier, and now becomes increasingly abundant. In the interview with her father and mother, the clever ambiguity of Juliet's responses to the praise of Tybalt and blame of Romeo is ear-catching, but perhaps too suggestive of duplicity to be entirely congenial. Tybalt's death continues to be the convenient means of 'motivating' the Capulets' insistence upon an immediate marriage— with this resourceful refinement, that they now are assuming that such a marriage will help to assuage Juliet's presumed grief. Old Capulet's anger is depicted as that of one whose parental care is disregarded and whose generous gift is rejected. Great care has been taken with his language, which creates illusion through its finely authentic content and style, despite the dubious occasion for the indignation. The playwright is now isolating and rendering defenseless both Romeo and Juliet as they approach their **doom. Not** only are they separated from each other, but from others as well. Observe the effect of the father's anger, the mother's cold rejection (204-05), and the Nurse's lost status as confidante (214-37). This young girl is now alone, with no one to lean upon but Friar Laurence, who has never commanded our confidence. It will have been noticed that in recent scenes (as in all that follow) Romeo's **one** reliable friend, Benvolio, has been quietly expunged.

IV, i

Paris explains to Friar Laurence that he is to wed Juliet without formal courtship because of the effect of Tybalt's death. Juliet responds evasively to his affectionate greetings, and when left alone with the Friar, declares that she will take her own life if no other way be found to save her from this threatened union. Her willingness to face death encourages the Friar to propose a desperate remedy. He will provide a potion which will induce for forty-two hours the symptoms of death. There will follow a funeral rather than a wedding in the Capulet household. Romeo will be sent for, and he and the Friar will be present at the moment of her recovery to rescue her from the Capulet tomb.

1-47 The unreality of the stichomythic wit-duel in which Juliet engages with Paris distracts our attention from a more basic unreality. Paris being the well-disposed man he is, there is no logical reason why Juliet and the Friar should not appeal directly to **him** for release from this threat of a bigamous marriage. Again we **must** recognize, however, that the playwright has not striven for 'inevitability'—that is, a watertight articulation of cause and effect. He could easily have closed this avenue by making Paris a predatory bully, and most playwrights would have done so. He prefers to leave the avenue open, and slightly misdirect our attention. It may not have occurred to the reader that the resource of appealing to Paris was available to Juliet and the Friar. Let us say that it may not have occurred to them either, and let it go at that. It is a nice ironic touch that, among the inventory of desperate things **that**

Juliet says she is prepared to do, appears the very thing (81-85) she is required to do. The Friar's potion reminds us that we first met him as an herbalist, meditating on the good and evil properties of the materials he was gathering. Let us hope that he is able to distinguish between the two in making and prescribing his compound.

IV, ii

The Capulets learn to their pleasure that Juliet has withdrawn her objections to a marriage with Paris. The date for the wedding is advanced to the following morning, and preparations get busily under way.

1-47 Juliet's skill in deception steadily grows. Her falsehoods make small impact on our moral sense since they are employed to avert the greater evil of infidelity; however the general aura of trickery now associated with her and the Friar creates a sense of unease, to which Capulet's guileless description of the *reverend holy friar* subtly contributes.

IV, iii

Juliet requests her mother and the Nurse to let her spend this night alone; then, with fearful misgivings, bravely drinks the potion.

1-58 Juliet's imaginings are graphic to the limit of our endurance, but this is not horror for horror's sake; rather it is a means of underscoring the heroism of her act. Her last-minute expression of distrust of the Friar's motives (24-28) is unexpected, yet most natural.

IV, iv

At dawn the servants of the Capulet household are preparing the wedding feast under their master's happy direction; and the Nurse is sent to awaken Juliet.

1-28   Although Capulet is a nobleman, with a count for a prospective son-in-law, he all but ties on an apron himself in his anxiety that his guests be well served. The atmosphere in the Capulet household has been bourgeois throughout.

IV, v

The Nurse discovers that Juliet cannot be aroused. Paris, who arrives with the wedding musicians, joins in the general lamentations; and Friar Laurence preaches a sermon of comfort in time of death. Juliet's funeral is to follow at once, but the musicians engage in a comic dialogue with the servant Peter as if nothing very serious had occurred.

1-141   The original text makes it clear that the action is continuous with that immediately preceding (IV, iv) with no change in time or place. The present scene is the least successful in the play. The creative problem was a difficult one, and perhaps the best solution would have been to relegate the episode to a messenger's report. Since Juliet's true death will come later, orchestrated with true poetry, there seems to have been nothing to do here but match the spurious death with spurious, or at least spurious-sounding, words. Not only the Nurse, but Lord and Lady Capulet as well, sound somewhat like Bottom in the role of Pyramus lamenting the death of Thisby. The fact that the jests which follow are not very funny scarcely excuses them. They would not have appeared if Juliet were really dead; nevertheless, their effect remains grotesque.

V, i

In Mantua Romeo awakens from the kind of dreams that go by opposites. His servant Balthasar tells him that Juliet has died and has been buried in the Capulet tomb. He prepares to return to Verona at once, pausing only to buy from a needy apothecary a dram of deadly poison.

1-86   In portraying Romeo's response to the report of Juliet's death (the response in which we are primarily interested), the poet does not over-write as in the preceding scene. Romeo's words are spare, as of one for whom there is nothing left worth saying. The purchase of the poison might have been disposed of in a line, with a mere statement of intention, but the poet has given us out of his abundance a place, a person, a life history. The Apothecary's hunger-induced corruption and Romeo's savage contempt suddenly place the sad lot of the lovers in the context of a misery-ridden world.

V, ii

Friar John reports that he and his fellow messenger have been detained in a house visited by the plague, so that Friar Laurence's letter to Romeo informing him of the true facts about Juliet's 'death' still remains undelivered. Realizing that Juliet's time for awakening in the tomb is near at hand, Friar Laurence prepares to rescue her without Romeo's aid.

1-29 That the Friar's scheme had miscarried was evident in the preceding scene, and we are here given the reason why. That this particularly vital missive should have failed of delivery may seem to violate the law of averages, but the circumstances given are plausible in themselves, and there is the larger plausibility, that, at some point, such a scheme as the one in question was *bound* to miscarry.

V, iii

Paris comes to deck with flowers the place of Juliet's burial, and he bids his page to keep watch lest his mourning be disturbed. He receives the signal of someone's approach, and observes Romeo and Balthasar arrive with tools for opening the tomb. Balthasar suspects Romeo of designs against his own life, and lingers in the vicinity although ordered to be gone. As Romeo opens the tomb, Paris charges him with desecration. The two fight, and Paris is slain. Romeo recognizes the body of his antagonist and lays it respectfully in the tomb, then takes a last farewell of Juliet and drinks the poison dram. Friar Laurence now appears, prepared to release Juliet; he receives from Balthasar news of Romeo's presence and intimations of the fatal duel. As he exclaims over the bodies of Paris and Romeo in the tomb, Juliet awakens and receives the tragic tidings. She refuses to part from the body of Romeo, and Friar Laurence retreats in fear before the approach of the watch. Juliet kisses Romeo and slays herself with his dagger. The officers, the Prince of Verona, and the members of the Montague and Capulet households converge upon the tomb. Apprehended by the Watch, Friar Laurence recounts the whole tragic story and submits himself to judgment. The Prince declares that the death of these young lovers is a judgment upon them all. Capulet and Montague repent their strife, and each resolves to erect a golden monument to the memory of the other's child.

1-310 The principals in this scene and their underlings are adroitly marshaled by a skilled strategist so as to effect successively a crescendo of action, a predestined conclusion, and a moment of obituary calm while the lesson of the play is driven home. This lesson is spelled out in words by the Prince (291-95) which parallel those in the prologue. Despite all the theatrical bustle accompanying it, the death of the lovers has a true tragic impact because of the magic of their words; and the scene belongs, as of course it should, to Romeo and Juliet. Capulet speaks of them as *sacrifices* (304), and the suggestion of martyrdom is reinforced by the mention of golden monuments.

III

Infinite Variety

1

Works: 1597 to 1606

:

L I T E R A R Y historians have sometimes tried to link Shakespeare with the socially elite of his era by suggesting that he was the friend, protégé, or political adherent of one or another nobleman. Unconsciously inspired by this kind of effort are theories about some of his plays, to the effect that they were first created not for the regular theatres but for various private occasions. We know too little of his life to reject such possibilities dogmatically, but it must be remarked that the surviving evidence is against them.

Perhaps the most significant feature of his two dedications to the Earl of Southampton in 1593 and 1594 (see above, p. 96) is that they are his first and last. Thereafter he wrote nothing more like the two works dedicated, and the quartos of his plays, like those of others, were submitted to an anonymous reading public. The inference is that he had no patron apart from the nominal patrons of his acting company, and that he had, whether because of temperament or native shrewdness, resolved to remain purely professional, staking his fortunes upon his ability to write popular plays and to act in them. A man of his acumen should have been capable of this decision, in view of the frustrations and defeats suffered by the dedicating poets of his day. His rising prosperity, as indicated by Stratford and other records, is easily explained by his computable earning power as actor, writer, and part owner of the Globe theatre.

The Lord Chamberlain's Men (see above, p. 69), as organized early in 1594, was so well served by Richard Burbage as principal actor and by Shakespeare as principal author that it soon became chief of the London companies. In 1599 it moved into the newly built Globe, and thereafter, unlike the rival companies, owned the premises it used. After 1603, when all companies came under the nominal patronage of members of the new royal family, this one was signalized by being chosen as the King's Men. In the period with which we are now concerned, 1597-1606, both Shakespeare and his company were in their prime; indeed English Renaissance drama as a whole was in its prime. The public interest in drama was keen and audiences large, while a great number of playwrights and plays competed for approval. After 1599 two chorister-boy companies were reinstated, playing in so-called 'private theatres' and bidding for the patronage of select audiences by offering indoor comfort, musical intermezzi, and increasingly sophisticated plays at advanced admission rates. For a time they militantly invited comparison of their wares with those offered by the three popular companies, including Shakespeare's (see *Hamlet* below, p. 319). Fashions in drama were changing like everything else, and the plays of the period show an enormous range in variety as well as quality. Shakespeare, as the most versatile of the playwrights, himself offered infinite variety.

He forsook almost entirely the writing of non-dramatic poetry. Probably the bulk of the Sonnets were written by 1597, or at least by 1598 when Francis Meres mentioned the 'sugred Sonnets among his private friends,' but some may have been written later; a few of the finest show the same complexity, depth of feeling, and perfect union of thought and language observable in the major tragedies. Apart from the possibility offered by these, the only non-dramatic poem certainly his and certainly belonging within this period is *The Phoenix and the Turtle,* an allegorical elegy celebrating the union by immolation of a phoenix and a dove, symbolizing immortality and love. It is a striking poem of the 'metaphysical' kind, in which the beauty of the verbal music compensates for the obscurity of sense. It was written when Shakespeare and other poets, in fun or in earnest, contributed variations upon a theme to a quaint volume by one Robert Chester, *Love's Martyr or Rosaline's Complaint,* 1601.

To this middle span of ten years belong sixteen plays: seven comedies, three English history plays, and six tragedies (counting *Julius Caesar* as a tragedy, although it might also be described as a Roman history play, and *Troilus and Cressida* as a tragedy, although it is really unclassifiable). The trend is away from light comedies and history plays toward serious comedies and tragedies; but our knowledge of the order of the plays is too imprecise, as is our knowledge of the influence of dramatic fashions, to let us say with confidence that Shakespeare personally had a 'joyous period,' a 'tragic period,' or the like. What we know of the chronology fails to support this kind of autobiographical compartmentalizing, and all that we can justifiably say is that his writing in general through these years grows in complexity and power.

Although it had been anticipated by *The Two Gentlemen of Verona* in dealing with events potentially disastrous, *The Merchant of Venice,* 1596-97, is the first of Shakespeare's comedies to arouse in us serious interest in the psychology of its characters, notably Shylock, and in the moral significance of its conflicts; the theme of mercy-and-justice is one in which the playwright later shows recurrent interest. Arresting as are its serious elements, and exciting on the stage, they blend so naturally with the romantic love interest that we feel no inclination to label the work 'tragicomedy' or 'problem play.'

Much Ado About Nothing, 1598-9, may be paired with the play above because of its realistic setting and the threat of disaster in part of its action. And here too the serious is so deftly blended with lighter matter that we feel no hesitation in classifying the play simply as comedy. The serious plot, in which Claudio's affianced bride Hero is traduced by Don John and his accomplices so that she is rejected at the altar, and then restored to her disabused lover after having been reported dead, makes less impact upon us than the serious plot of *The Merchant of Venice* chiefly because Don John, Hero, and Claudio are not Shylock, Portia, and Bassanio. Still it has its fine moments, especially the scene at the altar. The way that the threatening action contrasts, without clash, with the 'low comedy' scenes involving Dogberry and the Watch, and the 'high comedy' scenes involving Beatrice and Benedick provides a remarkable demonstration in structural virtuosity. Dogberry is prototypical of all well-meaning but asinine constables, and Beatrice and Benedick of all fencing lovers; the bulk of the play is theirs, and the ruse by which they are made to admit their fondness to themselves and each other is the unique invention of Shakespeare.

As You Like It, 1599-1600, and *Twelfth Night, or What You Will* also form a pair. The elusiveness of their titles, like the transfer of locale from such real places as Venice and Messina to the mythical dukedoms of Arden and Illyria, is in harmony with their effervescent and otherworldly charm. They have as much in common with *A Midsummer Night's Dream* as with the comedies immediately preceding them, but in both there is a more subtle interpenetration of the worlds of human realities and of poetic sentiments than in the earlier dream. *As You Like It,* in spite of its heavy opening and extensive use of prose is a pure dramatic lyric. It is the most indescribable of Shakespeare's comedies, the most evasive of sober analysis, but a fondness for it is the best single test of a reader's compatibility with Shakespeare.

Twelfth Night, 1600-02, is suffused with the sunlight proper to its lost sector of the Mediterranean littoral, but much of this light seems to emanate from the dauntless Viola, who runs love-errands for Duke Orsino, whom she loves, to Countess Olivia, who loves her—under the misapprehension that she is really the handsome young squire she impersonates. The situation is sustained in precarious equilibrium between pathos and absurdity until Viola's twin brother Sebastian arrives in Illyria and the couples are sorted out according to the heart's desire. The life-below-stairs underplot which pins this fantasy to earth provides a fine gallery of comic portraits: Major-domo Malvolio the archetypal killjoy, Maid Maria his nemesis, Sir Toby Belch the bibulous poor relation, Sir Andrew

Aguecheek the inadequate lover, and Feste the sweet-voiced clown. It is worth remembering when we speak of Shakespeare's 'tragic period' with its 'mythical sorrows' or psychic disturbances that this happy play was written just before or just after *Hamlet*.

As different as *Twelfth Night* from *Hamlet* is *The Merry Wives of Windsor* from either, although it seems to have bustled into the world at pretty much the same time, 1599-1601. It is a hilarious farce, realistically set in an English provincial town among people like Shakespeare's own. Master and Mistress Ford, Master and Mistress Page, doddering Justice Shallow, the retarded 'rich boy' Slender, and sweet Ann Page might have walked the streets of Stratford in the playwright's own boyhood; as a matter of fact we hear one small 'Master Will' (with a different surname) being drilled in his 'hic haec hoc, horum harum horum.' Into this milieu, already richly peopled with eccentrics, steps Sir John Falstaff with his ragamuffin entourage, Pistol, Bardolph, and Nym; and the prince of the London wits and boozers gets badly bruised as he tries to breach the invincible virtue of the English middle classes. It is a marvelous play of its kind, even though it has disappointed the critics who have wanted Falstaff, the 'fat meat' of the *Henry IV* plays, served up in exactly the same way in Windsor that it had been in Eastcheap, London. Although there have been many theories about its genesis, including an early one that it was written to order for Queen Elizabeth who wished to see Falstaff 'in love,' the most plausible is that its author was keeping, in his own way, a promise to his fans in the theatre. At the end of *2 Henry IV* he had tentatively suggested that Falstaff would reappear in the next play of the historical cycle, *Henry V;* after deciding against this, for sound artistic reasons, he may have written *Merry Wives* as a compensation piece.

The two remaining comedies of this middle span were written concurrently with the major tragedies, and the prevailing gravity of their tone, and the debatable merit of the actions and ethical decisions of their principal characters, have led to their being called 'problem plays.' It has sometimes been argued, on very dubious grounds, that they reveal satirical or 'bitter' intentions. In *All's Well that Ends Well,* 1602-04, the theme is the common one among

English Renaissance humanists (and surely acceptable to us) that worth rather than birth confers true gentility. Since this position is endorsed by the most admirable characters in the play, the King of France, the Countess of Rousillon, and Lord Lafew, it is presumably being endorsed by the playwright; and his play 'ends well' with 'worth' triumphant, and 'birth' deferring to its claims. Nevertheless, the story of the worthy middle-class girl, Helena, who falls in love with the supercilious aristocrat Bertram, then takes the initiative in winning him (by royal edict), and finally consolidates her position as his wife by tricking him into consummating their marriage, has proved understandably unpalatable to modern tastes. Initially put off by Helena's coercive methods, readers miss certain nuances attending their application, including the fact that she is more concerned with saving Bertram from committing adultery than with achieving status for herself. Other times other moral ideals—modern readers tend to prefer adultery to constrained marital cohabitation, even though the latter proves to be to Bertram's practical as well as spiritual advantage. Response to the play is curious, often resulting in the critical stalemate that Bertram does not *deserve* Helena who does not *deserve* Bertram. The presence of two of Shakespeare's comic irregulars, Parolles the loquacious fake, and Lavatch the shopworn jester, has not sufficed to propitiate the average reader.

Measure for Measure, 1603-04, possesses, for moderns, some of the alienating features of *All's Well,* including the firm stand on the superiority of legal to emotional sanctions for sexual relations, with a recurrence of the 'bed-trick,' but parts of it are so powerfully written that it stimulates even those it repels. It is a disturbing play, canceling out the great ethical issues it raises, yet leaving them to haunt the mind. Clearly its purpose is not to shake our faith in the power of human beings to perform right actions and make right judgments, but such is the effect of parts of its greatest scenes. It presents artistic as well as other 'problems.'

Turning now to the English history plays, we find that the six plays spread through the period to 1596 are followed by three plays clustered into the early years of the period from 1597, after which the genre is abruptly abandoned. In one of the late scenes of

Richard II the newly crowned King Henry IV asks, 'Can no man tell me of my unthrifty son?' In *1 Henry IV*, 1597-98, Shakespeare proceeds to tell of this unthrifty son and the 'unrestrainèd loose companions' disconsolately mentioned by the father. Looming largest in every way among these is the inimitable Sir John Falstaff, with whom audiences became immediately entranced and have remained so ever since. A notable feature of the play is that the serious historical scenes, treating the rebellion of Hotspur and the northern lords against the king they had helped to make, are just as fascinating as the comic scenes in which Prince Hal and Falstaff doff the world aside in an Eastcheap tavern—until Hal is ready to turn to chivalry and wrest from Hotspur his life and honors on the battlefield of Shrewsbury. Among the history plays this has the most to offer, because of the unique combination of highly individualized characters, comedy, and exciting dramatic action.

It was probably Shakespeare's original intention to follow this play immediately with one showing Hal in his glorious conquest of France after ascending the throne as King Henry V, but the Falstaffian comedy of *1 Henry IV* proved so popular that he was impelled to do an intervening play, *2 Henry IV*, 1597-98, in which that comedy was continued. Some critics maintain that *2 Henry IV* was no afterthought, but part of the original design, and of course they may be right; nevertheless, this play comes nearer than anything else in the canon to resembling a 're-write' of another. In it Prince Hal has relapsed to the apparently unregenerate state in which he appeared to be at the beginning of *1 Henry IV*, and we witness a second regeneration, including a second climactic interview with his embittered father and a second emergence from the clouds. Except for the death scene of Henry IV, the serious historical matter is less striking than that in the earlier play, which had already rifled the most dramatic events of the realm. There is now only a remnant of rebellion to be mopped up, and the rebels have no Hotspur to lead them. The call to Prince Hal's conscience is less stirringly symbolized by the ingloriously righteous Lord Chief Justice than by the gloriously unrighteous Hotspur. On the other hand the Falstaff scenes, to which the major part of the play is devoted, are just as good as before. His involvements with his tawdry retinue, Bardolph, Peto, and Pistol, with Mistress Quickly and Doll Tearsheet, with his country conscripts, and above all with the ancient justices, Masters Shallow and Silence, offer a banquet of laughter. Falstaff's wit and humor deployed in his own defense as the epitome of erring humanity have an inverted moral appeal. It proves so seductive that his final (richly deserved) rejection by his royal companion has made countless readers mourn. They remember the ending not for Hal's march to his coronation but for Falstaff's march to jail.

The Epilogue of *2 Henry IV* indicates that Falstaff may reappear in the next play of the series, but in *Henry V*, 1599, his offstage death is reported. Humor is supplied by his survivors, Mistress Quickly, Nym, Bardolph, Pistol, who drop off in disgrace one by one, and by a comic figure of an opposite moral cast, the quaint but tenaciously dutiful Welsh Captain Fluellyn. We can understand the artistic necessity for this. Falstaff was a congenital scene-stealer, and his presence would have been inappropriate in a play celebrating the glories of Henry V, England's most religious and heroic king. It would be better to redeem the half-promise of the Epilogue by exhibiting Falstaff in Windsor (evidently in an excursion preceding his last illness) and to let Henry conquer France and the heart of Margaret the French princess without his embarrassing company. *Henry V* is unlike Shakespeare's other history plays in its militant patriotism and uncritical (or almost uncritical) treatment of the titular character. The ringing Choruses and the grand battle orations before Harfleur and Agincourt are wonderfully stirring, and Henry is a moving figure as he kneels in lonely prayer after mingling with his decimated troops, but we find it hard to admire him as much as the play requires us to do—partly, no doubt, because we are not sixteenth-century Englishmen convinced of the heavenly obligation to reduce France to a shambles.

With *Henry V* Shakespeare completed the Lancastrian tetralogy begun with *Richard II*. Since its story leads into the one previously dramatized in the Lancaster-Yorkist tetralogy (see above, p. 101) he had provided a histrionic chronicle of England from 1398 to 1485. There is an easy explanation of why he now suspended this kind of creative activity. The reign of the Tudors began in 1485, and the dramatic treatment of Tudor history was looked upon askance by Elizabeth Tudor's censor; hence subject matter that was fresh and politically vital was denied him. Moreover the best material of the times before 1398 had already been utilized by himself, in *King John,* and by other playwrights; and perhaps history plays as such were beginning to pall upon the taste of spectators at the Globe. It was natural that Shakespeare should now look back to the mythic or semi-mythic reigns in Danish, British, and Scottish chronicles, and select kingly figures whose legends could be freely shaped—such as Hamlet, Lear, Macbeth, and, later, Cymbeline.

The play which forms a bridge from Shakespeare's major histories to his major tragedies is *Julius Caesar,* 1599-1600. It is the first of four plays (cf. below, p. 435) levying upon Thomas North's translation of Amyot's versions of *Plutarch's Lives* (ed. 1595), which now took its place beside Raphael Holinshed's *Chronicles of England, Scotland, and Ireland* (ed. 1587) as the playwright's favorite hunting grounds for subject matter. *Julius Caesar* has long been a favorite of readers and playgoers for the best of reasons, that it is perfect in its kind. Although it retains most of the features of the history plays, it is disinterestedly conceived and its impact is philosophical; hence we can justly say that it crosses the vaguely defined boundry into the realm of tragedy.

There followed *Hamlet,* 1600-01, *Othello,* 1604-05, *Macbeth,* 1605-06, and *King Lear,* 1605-06. These plays, by the franchise of the ages, stand at the apex of Shakespeare's poetic and dramatic achievement. All are tragedies, yet each is sui generis, and so none can be passed by with mere mention in a book like the present. A brief note on their relationship will head the section where the analysis of them appears.

There remains to be mentioned only the provocative but baffling *Troilus and Cressida,* 1601-02. This play combines stories which have nothing in common except that both concern venal Greeks and Trojans: the ignominious slaying of Hector by Achilles after a period of politic jockeying among the Greeks besieging Troy, and the ignominious jilting of Troilus by Cressida after their liaison in the besieged city is interrupted and the maiden is placed in the enticing custody of the Greek Diomedes. The foul-mouthed Thersites among the Greeks and the sinuous Pandarus among the Trojans serve by their very presence to dispel any remnants of glamour associated with the famous war and the famous love affair. Like *Measure for Measure* the play presents a critical problem, and for essentially the same reasons. Some of the speeches of the Greek and Trojan leaders are magnificently written, and give particular episodes a sobriety and dignity scarcely in harmony with the mean motives of the speakers; and the treatment of the love affair hovers uneasily between the poetic and the satiric. The elements of the play fail to coalesce; part clashes with part, and, to a much greater degree than in *Measure for Measure,* the overall intention is unclear. In its own time, printers were undecided whether to call it 'history' or 'tragedy' and in our time it has been variously labeled, history, tragedy, and comedy. Something is to be said in favor of each alternative.

If we take a span of just two or three years at the turn of the century, we find that within it fall *Henry V, Merry Wives of Windsor, Julius Caesar, Twelfth Night, and Hamlet.* The excellence of these plays, each in its kind, is less amazing than their diversity. No other artist in the world, in a comparable span of years, has displayed at once such miraculous mastery and versatility. The reader of Shakespeare should try to match this wonder by versatility in response, approaching each individual play without preconceptions and taking it on its own terms. The worst one can do is to patronize *As You Like It* because it is not *Hamlet,* or *Julius Caesar* because it is not *Measure for Measure.* The nine plays treated below were spaced fairly evenly through the years 1597-1606, and an attempt has been made to select from the sixteen available plays the best of its kind. When, as in more instances than one, the 'best' is indeterminable, the more famous or complex has been chosen.

2

The Merchant of Venice

:

I, i

A N T O N I O cannot explain the melancholy mood into which he has recently fallen. Salerio and Solanio attribute it to worry about his fortune in merchandise scattered about the world, but he assures them that his ventures are too many and varied to involve any general risk. He also dismisses, emphatically, the suggestion that he may be pining in love. Bassanio, Lorenzo, and Gratiano join the conversation, the last waggishly suggesting that Antonio is assuming a taciturn pose to win a reputation for wisdom. Bassanio is distinguished by being the merchant's intimate friend, and when the two are alone, he speaks of the extravagances which have placed him in the other's debt. If Antonio will risk a further loan, Bassanio may be able to retrieve all by winning the hand of a beautiful heiress, Portia of Belmont, who has looked upon him with favor. Antonio is anxious to make the loan, but since his fortune is all invested in cargoes at sea, the cash will have to be obtained from another, with himself standing as security.

1-40   Antonio (not Shylock) is the 'merchant of Venice,' and his position as titular character makes us observe him with special interest. Although his age is not mentioned, his sobriety and extensive mercantile interests make us think of him as middle-aged. Like the other major characters, he bears no title, but the milieu in which he moves as 'merchant prince' seems fairly aristocratic. For Antonio's *sadne*ss (1-6) we should seek no cause other than he and the play supply. If he meets with misfortune, we will attribute it to premonition. Salerio and Solanio, who are indistinguishable, collaborate on a whimsical and sparkling montage of disasters at sea, in which images like that of the bolt of silk unwinding to *enrobe the roaring waters* (34) give color and motion. The argosies and their cargoes of Eastern luxuries belong both to wonderland and the estuary of the Thames; only an artist in a seafaring nation could have drawn them.   **41-46** We hope, superstitiously, that Antonio's confidence in his security will not tempt the gods, and that he does not assume himself to be as free from all human frailties as from love-sickness.   **47-118** Here is polite conversation among the socially-experienced Venetians. Gratiano is more aggressive in his pleasantries than Solanio. He appears to be a satirical wit, a minor Mercutio, acting as a foil to the gentle and romantic Bassanio. We discount at once, despite its intrinsic shrewdness, his discourse on owlish affectation of wisdom so far as any application to Antonio is concerned. The latter's *Is that anything now?* (113) sounds very natural, at once casual and lordly. Antonio has been referred to as Bassanio's kinsmen (57), and we are prepared for his avuncular concern for the youth if not his deep affection.   **119-85** The situation, crudely described, is one in which a spendthrift wishes to borrow more money from a friend, so that he can equip himself for fortune-hunting; but the nature of the speakers and the ideality of their speech counter the harsh appraisal. Bassanio acknowledges a debt of love as well as money (131-33), and his prodigality has not damaged his honor (136-37). His neatly turned illustration with *another arrow* (140-52) has a nostalgic appeal; we have all tried similar experiments in recovery—often to our cost. Antonio is not looking for a safe investment, and Bassanio is not thinking of Portia simply as a means of achieving solvency. His tribute to her virtue, beauty, and classic dignity dispels all sense of sordidness, and his use of the Jason analogy lends an air of high adventure to his designs. Portia's *sunny locks* and not her money are equated with the *golden fleece* (169-70).

I, ii

At Belmont, Portia herself complains of low spirits. Nerissa, her lady-in-waiting, reproves her for complaining, in view of her great wealth, but Portia has reason for dissatisfaction. By the terms of her father's will, she is forbidden from choosing freely among her many suitors, and must accept the one who makes the right selection among three caskets: one of lead, one of silver, and one of gold. They discuss the suitors who have been in attendance; and Portia satirizes successively the Neapolitan prince, the Palatine count, the French lord, the English baron, the Scots laird, and the German nephew of the Duke of Saxony. Fortunately all are departing, fearing to risk the penalty involved if the wrong casket is chosen. Portia would vastly prefer to any of them Bassanio the Venetian, who once visited Belmont; and she hears with distress of the arrival of a new suitor, the Prince of Morocco.

1-25 There is no compelling reason why this scene should be in prose; its matter is no more 'prosaic' than that of the preceding scene, and the speakers no lower in social station. However, the prose lends variety, and is of an interesting kind. Nerissa's speech is in the euphuistic style associated with moralizing, and Portia's rejoinder combats the moralizing and caps the style. It concentrates into its few sentences most of the euphuistic devices: balanced structure, antithesis, alliteration and rime, together with the use of proverbs, puns, and forced nature-metaphor (cf. the hare escaping the net). If this is parody, it is of a very subtle kind. **26-33** 'Exposition' is unobtrusively introduced; and we learn that winning in the lottery of the caskets will depend less upon luck than upon character. **34-91** In Portia's review of the suitors, the prose is not euphuistic; in these satirical vignettes we have a less ornate and more virile style, terse and pithy, reminding us of that of the Baconian essays and of later 'characters.' National defects are caricatured from an English point of view, with the enemy French and their Scots allies faring worst. The English defects selected for comment prove relatively venial. Why is no Spaniard

mentioned, when Spaniards were always fair English game? Per·
haps one will appear in person. (This character-sketching of characters who never appear, while not wholly unfunctional, is primarily
incidental diversion, such as the author is always willing to supply.)   **92-112** We return to the 'necessary business' of the
play. The lottery of the caskets involves an element of risk, but if
Bassanio chooses to take it and wins, he will obtain a far from reluctant prize. It is comforting to know that Portia's heart would, in
this case, go with her other good gifts.   **113-24** 'Four' foreign-
ers are mentioned as taking their departure. We thought we heard
Portia describe six, but never mind: four or six non-Bassanios—
it's all the same. In the person of the Moorish prince we are at least
approaching Spain. Portia has no taste for the dusky complexion,
but her remark is not contemptuous since it admits the possibility
of inner saintliness. Still, at this point in the play, we are more
convinced of her vigorous intelligence than of her amiability.

I, iii

Bassanio asks Shylock, the Jewish money-lender, for a loan of
three thousand ducats for three months, with Antonio offering security. Shylock wishes to speak to Antonio first, but declines an invitation to dinner since he will not eat with Christians. As Antonio
joins them, he reveals in an aside that he hates this merchant—as a
Christian, a lender of money gratis, and a despiser of himself and
his sacred nation. He then says that he will have to raise part of
the three thousand ducats by applying to Tubal, a wealthy member
of his sect. He tilts with Antonio about the latter's antagonism to
lending money at interest, and tells of the blessed Jacob who knew
how to increase his store. He reminds Antonio of his past insults to
himself and his kind, and asks if he should now fawningly return a
favor for the injuries he has received. When Antonio angrily rejoins
that the money should be lent not in friendship but in enmity, Shylock jovially disclaims hard feelings and offers to lend the money
interest free. Antonio needs only to agree, as a jest, to surrender a
pound of his flesh cut from any part of his body that Shylock designates, if the money is not repaid on time. Bassanio protests against

his friend's signing any such 'merry' bond, but Antonio is happy to do so. There is no danger: in less than three months his ships will be home, and he will have money in abundance.

1-8 Shylock's accent is not 'Jewish' but the universal accent of money-lenders. He is watchfully frugal of comment, echoing the applicant's words in brief installments, each stopped with a noncommittal *well*. It is Bassanio who is pressing, with his *Ay*, his *As I told you,* and his eager trio of questions (7-8).   **9-13** Tone of voice is written into these speeches. When Shylock, the despised, dares to pass a judgment upon Antonio, even a favorable one, Bassanio's words come with quick, tight-lipped anger, as we know from the other's exclamatory retreat.   **14-25** How well-informed Shylock is on Antonio's affairs! Observe the bare and explicit manner of speaking of this habitual dealer in hard facts. When he uses a metaphor (22), he explains it.   **26-35** A covert hostility lurks in his ironical agreement that he will be taking no risks, then shows openly as he stands on the sure ground of his religious superiority.   **36-56** At the beginning, middle, and end of Shylock's 'aside' come expressions of venomous hatred. The three reasons he gives are that Antonio is a Christian, lends money for nothing, and despises Jews. They are comically disparate but not unnatural: human motives are usually mixed. A fourth reason is implied; his description of Antonio as a *fawning publican* (37) betrays the resentment of the lonely and unpopular man. Slyness is painted thick in his pretense not to see Antonio, and in his demonstrative salutation.   **57-92** Antonio's application for a loan sounds suspiciously like a lecture. Shylock marks time for a moment, as he broods over the challenge to interest-taking and then launches into his biblical exemplum. The ruminative tone of this habitual reader of the scriptures as he digresses on Jacob's genealogy—*The third possessor; ay, he was the third* (70)—is typical of the inconspicuous touches by means of which Shakespeare creates third-dimensional illusion. The didactic streak in Shylock, his intentness upon being understood, prevails as he tells the story until he comes to the end. As he speaks the last two lines, he seems to forget the present occasion and to let his voice rise in exultation at

Jacob's god-given acumen. At Antonio's challenge, he wryly drops the subject as one this Christian could never understand. **93-101** Antonio's comment on Shylock, like Shylock's on him earlier, is probably an aside. We need not assume that Antonio would be too polite or too politic to make it; but Shylock's lines indicate that he does not hear it, and Antonio's next address to him (101) has the air of a fresh start. **102-25** No case could be put more powerfully than this. Whatever the status of the character, as Jew and as villain of the piece, the poet is now inside of him, speaking *his* thoughts in unanswerable words. **126-33** Antonio attempts no answer and reaffirms his enmity. Such moral superiority as the two Christians show in this scene resides only in their openness. It is hard to imagine anyone so courtly as Antonio spitting at Shylock, but he seems to admit the truth of the charge. We must remember that there is a vast difference between seeing such an act and hearing it reported; in the latter instance we tend to dismiss it as a metaphor. We never *see* Antonio offer indignities to Shylock (but then we never see any Shakespearean character spit at or kick another), and the Jew *is* invited to dine (but then the invitation may deserve only the rating that Shylock himself gives it; cf. below II, iv). Some very delicate balancing is going on. **134-38** And now Shylock actually does fawn! Partly this is play-acting, essential to the ruse he is contemplating; but it is also characteristic. Throughout the scene, we have observed him tentatively attack, hastily retreat, his manner betraying the habitually stifled aggressiveness of those who are denied normal means of retaliation. **139-77** Antonio and Bassanio may strike us as too credulous (as of course they are, in the interest of the plot), but the convention is skillfully managed. Bassanio *wants* to believe that the money will be painlessly obtained (139), and Antonio is too sure of his ability to repay to take much interest in penalties, real or fanciful. Presumably Shylock presents his *merry* terms with convincing joviality. It is ethically if not legally relevant that, in view of Shylock's verbal assurances, Antonio's signature is obtained by fraud. Bassanio shows up well (150-51) in his concern for his friend; Antonio not so well in his casual patronage of the Jew, and in his cocksureness —indeed he seems afflicted with a touch of 'hubris.'

II, i

The Prince of Morocco speaks proudly of his dark skin and his military prowess as he presents himself as a suitor. Portia receives him courteously but reminds him of the penalty if he fails. He must swear to remain single for life if he chooses a casket other than the one awarding Portia's hand. He is willing to accept this risk, and is conducted into dinner before making his choice.

1-12 The Moor is conscious that in a suit of love to a fair woman, he is placed at a disadvantage by his color, and he immediately speaks in its defense—with imagination and grandeur. The fine opening lines (1-3) would never have been given him if he were intended to appear as an absurd boaster; and his final concession (12) captures our sympathy.   **13-22** Portia responds with a courteous white lie, or, rather, in view of her low opinion of the previous 'comers' (21-22), with an equivocation.   **23-38** Even this we cannot regard as mere vainglory; this fighter wishes he could win the prize by fighting, and in such a case we would not care to place our bets against him: he seems noble, passionate, untamed.   **38-46** The Moor might have been introduced later, immediately before making his choice; the playwright has split the episode thus so as to keep Portia and the casket theme from languishing, while the other themes develop.

II, ii

Launcelot Gobbo's conscience bids him remain in the service of his master, Shylock, but the tempting 'fiend' bids him run away, and is winning the tug of war. Old Gobbo his father comes to visit him, and he diverts himself by at first giving bewildering directions to the house of the Jew and then reporting himself as dead. Having raised the waters of the old man's tears, he tells who he is and kneels for a blessing. He beseeches the old man to give the present he has brought for his master to Bassanio instead of Shylock, and to help him shift services. Bassanio has already been offered Launcelot by Shylock, and is able to interpret the confusing appeals of father and son. He accepts Old Gobbo's gift of doves, and orders a fancy livery for Launcelot since he is outfitting the retinue which will accompany him to Belmont. Gratiano wishes to make the journey also, and Bassanio consents on the condition that he will promise to curb his wild spirits and preserve a decorous demeanor. They promise themselves a merry night on this the eve of departure.

1-28 The dialogue between *conscience* and the *fiend* will be acted out, with Launcelot playing both roles, in alternating postures and alternately fiendish and angelic tones. The lines are neither subtle nor strikingly witty, but they offer great opportunity to the right clown; all depends on his magnetism and innate drollery. **29-94** Here too the 'business' must be visualized to gauge the stage effect, since it quickens to life the humor which seems lame and forced on the printed page. Nearly every speech contains an implied stage direction, requiring a specific action or gesture. The episode in general is a parody of 'recognition scenes' so dear to the drama, and it almost, but not quite, makes a mockery of familial love. To anyone whose sense of humanitarian propriety may be offended, it should be pointed out that the father is old and dim of sight, only *sand blind* not 'stone blind.' The quip about the *wise father that knows his own child* (70) is one of the most frequently quoted in the play, and the scene as a whole has considerable impact in performance. **95-143** The incidental effect is to downgrade Shylock, the parsimonious master. As the soul of jollity, Launcelot must naturally gravitate from his gloomy house to that of the magnanimous Christian. The best that can be said for the Jew-baiting is that it takes place in Shylock's absence. As the scene continues, it proves almost an anthology of comic routines —adding here a spate of malapropisms and the device of sense-converted-into-nonsense by the competitive eagerness of the speakers. **144-55** Launcelot is available for any kind of 'turn' that happens to be served up. He lacks the inner consistency of some of the other clowns; he wears his motley without a difference. **156-92** Why this stress upon the boisterous, even uncivil, aspect of Gratiano's character? Will it imperil the success of Bassanio's suit at Belmont? or have some other kind of dramatic usefulness?

II, iii

Shylock's daughter Jessica takes sad leave of Launcelot, who has lent their gloomy house its only sparkle, and gives him a letter to deliver to Lorenzo. She is determined, if Lorenzo keeps promise, to elope with him and turn Christian.

1-21 The bitter and repellent father has a sweet and attractive daughter, a not unusual anomaly in romantic fiction. Launcelot is inclined to attribute this fact to Christian intercession, but 'racism' is not otherwise invoked. It is her father's 'manners' not his blood that Jessica deplores. Her situation is remedial—by the simple process of conversion from the Jewish to the Christian faith.

II, iv

Lorenzo and his friends are planning to slip away from Bassanio's farewell supper, and to return as maskers accompanied by torch-bearers. Launcelot delivers the letter, informing Lorenzo that Jessica is prepared to flee her father's house disguised as a page and carrying a store of gold and jewels. Lorenzo tells Salerio and Solanio that he has now found his torch-bearer, and asks them to prepare for the mask and meet him at Gratiano's lodgings. Launcelot, who is bearing an invitation to Shylock to be a guest at Bassanio's supper, is instructed to tell Jessica that Lorenzo will come for her as planned. Gratiano is told of Lorenzo's intention to wed the lovely daughter of the hateful Jew.

1-39 When there is to be a festive supper, there may appropriately be a visiting 'mask' (see *Romeo and Juliet* above, p. 145); still the one projected here is an oddity in the plot. It might serve a practical purpose, if Jessica were lodged in the house where it is to be performed, as a cover for her escape; but, as it is, it merely lends a borrowed air of intrigue to the elopement, and a post facto appropriateness to Jessica's disguise as a page.

II, v

Shylock tells Launcelot that in Bassanio's house he will miss the ease and indulgence he has enjoyed here, then tells Jessica that he is accepting Bassanio's invitation to supper although it is not tendered in love. Something warns him he should not leave his home this evening, but he wishes to help eat up the borrowed riches of the young prodigal. As he orders his daughter to shut the house up tight against the vile music of the masks, and to keep all under lock and key, Launcelot cleverly conveys to her Lorenzo's message that he will come.

1-10 Shylock is evidently convinced that he has been a lavish master, though he measures abundance by his own peculiar scale. Again we notice the workings of his single-track mind, in the repetitions, in the intentness upon getting simple ideas across (1, 7). **11-18** In these lines, few as they are, the pathetic alternates with the ridiculous several times. **19-26** Shylock makes witty capital of Launcelot's malapropism (21), and Launcelot of Shylock's superstition about dreams. **27-38** The opening exclamation comes with hollow-voiced horror, at the thought of such impious frivolities as masks. Although Shylock has no music in his soul, he does have behind him a long tradition of puritanic solidity. Observe how he is again at pains to explain a metaphor (33; cf. above, I, iii, 22). **38-43** Jessica shows the facility in deception usual in Shakespeare's sweet young things. **44-55** Grudgingly though it may be, Shylock does say a good word for Launcelot. This villain is not all parsimony and spite, is not *all* villain. In this 'Shylock-at-home' scene he seems far from an ogre: he loves this home, which is his haven in an alien land, and he trusts his only child.

II, vi

Gratiano and Salerio, dressed in their masking costumes, take their stand outside Shylock's house, where Lorenzo joins them and calls to Jessica within. She hands down a casket and begs them to turn their eyes from her immodest disguise in boy's attire. Lorenzo reassures her, and pays tribute to her wisdom, beauty, and truth as she prepares to join him outside. The pair go off with Salerio, but Gratiano is intercepted by Antonio. There will be no mask tonight. The wind has come about, the ship is weighing anchor, and Bassanio is embarking for Belmont at once.

1 s.d. The entrance takes place immediately upon Jessica's exit, and there is no need to mark this a separate scene as is done in modern editions. **1-19** The ideal and romantic must not seem to win by default; hence the voice of skeptical realism (here Gratiano's) is usually given a hearing. **20-59** Jessica is charmingly shy and witty about her boy's attire, so that even Gratiano recognizes her to be as *gentle* as *gentile* (a common pun). Lorenzo attests fervently to her perfection of form and character. (Thus the poet presents her and thus we must accept her—or turn to some other play. To say that she is a traitor to her poor old father, and a thief as well, is simply to be perverse. We do not say that Juliet is a traitor to *her* father, or an apostate because she is ready to become a Montague, or that Celia in *As You Like It* should take sides with her usurping father. Such behavior must be read in its proper context, that of romantic love, in which revolt from the father is proper, indeed *de rigueur*. Since Lorenzo is the kind of handsome and sprightly youth which a Jessica should have, and since a dowry should be provided, we must be exhilarated not shocked when she wrests both from under the nose of the old curmudgeon her father. If we say that, as Jews, they should stick together, it is we who are raising the racial issue rather than the play. Drama has given us a vast number of curmudgeonly fathers outwitted by the young; surely Shylock should not be excluded from this club too. (A bit of business introduced in sentimentalized productions of the play in the nineteenth century is still sometimes seen. Shylock is given a re-entry at the end of the scene, and stands knocking at the door of his empty house as the curtain falls. This tugs at the heart-strings, but it is an odd sort of equity which would give Shylock a quart of tears to compensate for the loss of the pound of flesh.) **60-68** Now that it has served its equivocal purpose, the 'mask' is blown away in the shifting wind.

II, vii

The Prince of Morocco twice reads the inscriptions upon the caskets, and chooses the one of gold. It contains a death's head, and a scroll telling him he has lost his suit.

1-77 By the time Bassanio's turn comes to make his choice, we will be thoroughly conversant with the alternatives; Morocco reviews them again and again. We see him as no vain boaster; he is aware of his merits, but also of their limits (27-28). His error in choosing the casket of gold is a noble error, and our original conception of the nature of the man is confirmed as he suffers defeat. Like Othello he has an affinity with the vast open spaces, summoned up in the majestic images of his tribute to Portia (39-47). **78-79** We wish that she could have repaid him at least with a sympathetic phrase, but in her way Portia is as single-minded as Shylock. She simply does not care for the Moorish complexion; besides Morocco is not Bassanio; all Shakespeare's heroines are single-minded in the way they play the mating game.

II, viii

Salerio and Solanio speak of Shylock's enraged outcries in the street on the loss of his ducats and his daughter when he discovered the elopement of Jessica and Lorenzo. The two fled Venice in a gondola, not in Bassanio's ship as Shylock has alleged to the Duke; in any case, the Jew's animosity to Bassanio's friend Antonio is greater than ever. It will go hard with him if he falls into the toils of the Jew for non-payment of his debt, and it is reported that he has lost one of his ships in the English channel. In his affectionate farewell to Bassanio, he has told his friend to give no thought to the terms of the bond but to think only of winning his lady.

1-24 Salerio and Solanio, who remain indistinguishable, divide a 'messenger speech' between them. It puts us au courant with a number of developments, including Shylock's farcical conduct upon the discovery of his loss. The spectacle would have been sure-fire stuff if staged, and we must recognize that the dramatist is both pillorying the Jew and protecting him; it does not fit his book to divest the character of all human dignity as such a scene would do. **25-53** This part of the report is designed to remind us of Antonio's danger and to arouse our sympathy for him. The author is always more successful in portraying an emotion than in reporting one; there is a bit of 'pushing' here, a trace of sentimentality.

II, ix

Another suitor of Portia, the Prince of Arragon risks the lottery of the caskets, and chooses the one of silver. It contains a fool's-head, and a scroll branding him a loser and a fool. As he takes his sorry departure, a Messenger announces the arrival of a generous and handsome young Venetian. Nerissa hopes it will prove to be Bassanio.

1-83 Here is the Spaniard we missed in the inventory of Portia's suitors. He is not allowed to stand as high in our estimation as Morocco. This Spaniard is stiff-necked, conceited, and an ass, as the audience might have assumed, but the satire is fairly gentle. It would not have been tactful to use as a target of outright abuse, Spaniard or no Spaniard, one who is about to be afflicted in a practical way. Like a number of the author's fools, this one is given some very sage lines (38-48).   **84-100** We are now in a fine strategic position to observe Bassanio's choice. If we were in his place, we could not possibly lose.

III, i

The useful Solanio and Salerio lament over the report of the loss of another of Antonio's ships, in the treacherous Goodwins. Shylock enters and somberly accuses them of complicity in his daughter's flight. They respond with mockery, then ask if he has heard of Antonio's losses at sea. Shylock calls Antonio a bankrupt, and threatens to enforce the terms of the bond, worthless though a pound of flesh may be. Antonio has done him many injuries only because he is a Jew. A Jew is a man as all men are—and as ready as a Christian to exact revenge. Solanio and Salerio leave upon a summons by Antonio, as Tubal appears and brings news to his coreligionist. Shylock see-saws wildly between elation at Antonio's losses and despair at the way Jessica and Lorenzo are squandering the valuables they have taken from him. He commissions Tubal to procure an officer in advance, so that Antonio may be arrested immediately if he stands forfeit on the bond.

1-43 A vein of facetiousness runs through the remarks of Antonio's friends; his troubles are lamentable but stimulating. In Shylock's sullen rejoinders, we note his old trick of repetition (21-22), used with chilling effect when he begins to threaten. **44-64** The greatness of Shylock's speech lies not in its thought but in its feeling. Viewed objectively, the demonstration that a Jew is human is unnecessary, and the proofs offered are naïve. But this is the naïveté of the bared heart, and the mention of eyes, hands, hurting, healing, laughing, bleeding summons up in the most elemental way the whole idea of human sentience and frailty—feeling, hoping, suffering, dying. For a moment we see with a terrible clarity. In the very form of the words is the throb of pain, and we cannot repeat them without tears in our eyes. And yet the beginning of the speech is savage, and the ending is a devastating let-down. Nothing is distilled from the vision of human mutuality but authority for the inhumane. **65-115** Although glaringly striated in spiritual value, the speech we have been looking at is all of one piece in its emotional truth and seriousness. It is almost incredible that in this very next episode Shylock is *exhibited* as a comic character—is tickled and pricked to make him laugh and bleed. Tubal is conscripted by the playwright as exhibitor; if our attention were focused upon him (as of course it is not), we would decide that his way of alternating his items of good and bad news was malicious. It is merely convenient. Shylock whines in self-pity, whinnies in glee, and groans in horror. Amazingly, there is pathos even here. One three-line speech (106-08) illustrates the complexity of the conception, and the versatility required of the actor who would successfully project it. When Shylock hears that his daughter has traded his turquoise for a monkey, his *Thou torturest me!* delights us with its excess of chapfallen horror, like his *What, are there masks?* of II, v. But our laughter uneasily subsides when in plain and quiet words he says that the turquoise was the betrothal gift of Leah, his dead wife. Then immediately thereafter, in his myopic and materialistic way, he values it above a *wilderness of monkeys* as if thousands of pet monkeys, like thousands of pouched ducats, must be more precious than one. As the scene ends, observe how the approach of the crisis touches off almost explosively his habit of repetition, associated with his inner drive to make doubly and doubly and doubly sure.

III, ii

Portia confesses her love to Bassanio and begs him to postpone the decisive moment in the trial of the caskets, but he insists upon knowing his fate at once. A song is sung as he makes his choice and spurns the glitter of gold and banality of silver in favor of the casket of plain lead. It contains a picture of Portia, and a scroll awarding him her hand. As they joyfully exchange vows of devotion, Portia gives him a ring with which he must never part. There will be a double wedding, because Nerissa has promised Gratiano to become his bride if Bassanio wins her mistress. Salerio now arrives as a messenger from Venice, accompanied by Lorenzo and Jessica whom he has met along the way. Bassanio learns with dismay that Antonio's ships have all miscarried, and he is at the mercy of Shylock. Salerio and Jessica both testify that no intercession in Venice will have power to soften the Jew, who craves Antonio's life rather than the return of his money. Portia, even before hearing Antonio's own touching letter, insists that Bassanio leave for Venice the instant after their marriage ceremony, prepared to pay many times the sum of the loan to save his incomparable friend.

1-326 This love-scene, following the preceding hate-scene, is a linch-pin in the structure of the play. It contains the climax of the story of the caskets, announces the approaching climax of the story of the bond, and plants the seed (171-85) of the story of the rings. In all three, Portia is the key figure, and the play might well be called 'The Lady of Belmont.' She appears in more scenes and has many more lines than Antonio, the titular character, or than Shylock, with whom the play has come to be identified. In some productions, Portia is made to give Bassanio a hint of which casket to choose—a cute notion which effectively cancels the playwright's design. His ability to choose right is the proof of Bassanio's fine character, and cheating is unnecessary as well as offkey; it is the probity, the virtue of the lovers, as well as the truth and ardor of their love, that is stressed throughout. The moral excellence of the tie between Portia and Bassanio is stressed in juxtaposition with the moral excellence of the tie between Bassanio and Antonio, so that we are offered an emblem of ideal love and ideal friendship. We could spare Jessica's testimony about her father (284-90), but we should notice that it is offered when Shylock's power is ascendant, and that the playwright provides for the daughter's absence during the trial when the father will suffer defeat.

III, iii

Antonio, in the custody of a jailor, pleads for a hearing, but Shylock refuses to listen to him; he has been called a dog before there was cause, and now he will show fangs. Antonio gives Solanio a different view of the matter; he has often rescued debtors from this money-lender's clutches, and Shylock is exacting revenge. The

Duke of Venice can do nothing to prevent the fatal forfeit of the pound of flesh, because the city depends upon foreign trade and must retain its reputation for impartial administration of justice.

1-36 This scene is often omitted in modern productions, especially those sentimentalizing the role of Shylock, but it is essential to the balance of the play. As Antonio stands, probably in irons, pleading for a hearing from the man he has despised (3, 11), Shylock already is revenged in kind—humiliation for humiliation. To proceed against Antonio's life is to mete out a kind of punishment in excess of the kind of injuries received.

III, iv

Portia believes that no sacrifice is too great to save Antonio, since he is loved by her lord and therefore must be somewhat like him. She requests Lorenzo and Jessica to govern her house while she and Nerissa make a religious retreat to a nearby monastery until their husbands return. Actually she has other plans. She sends her servant Balthasar with a letter to Doctor Bellario, her learned cousin. Balthasar is to bring such notes and garments as he is given by Bellario to the ferry into Venice. Bassanio and Gratiano will be seeing their wives sooner than they expect, but in the saucy disguise of young men.

1-84 There has been some danger of Portia's solidifying into the image of a saint in alabaster: the ribald pleasantries she exchanges with Nerissa help to humanize her.

III, v

Launcelot jests with Jessica about her Hebrew line, and the economic consequences of conversion to Christianity. He is accused by Lorenzo of misconduct with a Moor, and uses this subject and the serving in of dinner as occasion for a discharge of puns. Jessica speaks to Lorenzo of the blessed character of Portia, and seems ready to qualify her husband's claim that he is an equally exemplary mate.

1-83 If we call this comic 'relief,' we must ask 'relief' from what? It is primarily incidental entertainment, getting Launcelot out on the stage for those who want more samples of his wares. So far as it has any organic function, this scene signals the passage of time while the travelers converge on Venice, and provides a pause in the action before the tremendous drive of the great trial scene that follows.

IV, i

At Antonio's trial, the Duke of Venice tells Shylock that all are expecting him to show mercy at the last moment. Shylock replies that he intends to exact the penalty of the pound of flesh regardless of the financial loss to himself, and that he is no more obliged to explain his antipathy to Antonio than to explain antipathies in general. He refuses Bassanio's offer of twice the value of the loan, and reminds these Christians of their own merciless insistence upon their legal property rights. Antonio intervenes to say that pleading is useless, and to request an immediate judgment. As Shylock whets his knife, and is execrated by Gratiano, Portia and Nerissa arrive disguised as young doctor of laws and clerk, bearing a letter of recommendation from the learned Bellario of Padua. Portia is designated by the Duke as the one who will hear evidence and render judgment. Since the terms of the bond are explicit and the law must be observed, she pleads with Shylock to show mercy, then to accept the return of his money multiplied. Shylock repeats that he will stick to the letter of the law and the terms of his bond; and when Portia bids Antonio to bare his breast for the knife, he hales the young doctor as a Daniel come to judgment. He refuses even a final plea that a surgeon be provided to attempt to save Antonio's life— it is not so nominated in the bond. Bassanio and Gratiano passionately aver that they would sacrifice their new and dearly beloved wives to save their friend—a declaration which draws wry comments from both Portia and Shylock. At the last moment the young doctor reviews the terms of the bond, and points out that it provides for no loss of blood. If Shylock spills a single drop, he will himself have violated the terms of the bond and must suffer grievous penalties. In consternation, he now wants to accept the money proffered, but is told that he has refused it in open court and may claim only the forfeit. Further, he stands guilty of conspiracy against a Venetian's life, so that his own life and goods are forfeit. With the tables thus turned, it is Gratiano who now calls the young doctor a Daniel come to judgment as he exults over the Jew. The Duke and Antonio intervene on his behalf. The state will spare his life and accept a fine in lieu of the half his goods it might claim, and Antonio will hold in trust for Lorenzo and Jessica the half which he himself might claim as intended victim. Shylock, however, must turn Christian and, upon his death, bequeath all his goods to Jessica and Lorenzo. Shylock has no choice but to accept these terms, and he leaves the court to the tune of Gratiano's taunts. Bassanio wishes to reward the learned doctor with the three thousand ducats due to Shylock, but payment is refused. He is asked instead to give his ring as a token of gratitude. Since it is the one he has promised his wife to retain forever, he clings to it desperately; however, when the stranger's sarcasms are followed by a request from Antonio himself, he sends the ring after the asker.

1-455 This is one of the most compelling trial scenes in drama. In such scenes the ritual of legal procedure lends portentousness and an air of objectivity, as in a controlled experiment; and the promise of a decision, a specific conclusion about an isolated specimen of human behavior, is a magnet to our attention. We are excited on several levels, by the events themselves, the element of uncertainty, and the hope that an ethical issue will be clarified. The present trial is not of the English type, with judge and jury and rival attorneys, but its methods are not fictitious. In a trial of this kind, the magistrate presides and administers the sentence, but he does not weigh the evidence or interpret the law. These functions are performed by a legal expert appointed by the court. This expert, standing in place of jury and both prosecuting and defending attorney, is in the most literal sense the 'judge.' Granted that Shylock's bond was drawn up by a bungler, who neglected to include some obviously necessary provisions, a correct judgment is rendered in the present case. So far as the larger ethical issue is concerned, it is nothing less than the claims of mercy as mediator between the strict letter of the law and true justice. The management of the scene is marvelously skilled as Shylock is given a series of chances to relent, in large ways or in small, but insists upon the enforcement of the letter of the law without mercy; and then is shown, by a parallel series of literal interpretations, that he himself stands in fearful danger and must hope for mercy. There is no point in arguing with the playwright about the sentence. We are dealing with a work of art and must accept its postulates. If the artist presents the sentence as merciful, it must be accepted as merciful. It was so indeed, if judged by what would have happened to Shylock under similar circumstances in an actual court of the time. To view his forced conversion as outrageous is to assume, as the play does not, that it is useless—a mere piece of persecution; but to *force* a man to escape eternal damnation would not have been construed as bullying in an age when damnation was taken seriously. Portia's speech (182-200) is beautiful and true; and to make a mockery of it by a parrot-like delivery, as has actually been done in at least one modern performance, is a piece of silly desecration. The performers who must thus *advertise* their aversion to anti-semitism must feel very shaky in their liberalism. It is a great misfortune that the playwright identified Shylock's defects as Jewish. He used the symbol of the wicked Jew appearing in the source story and viable in his time—a symbol, incidentally, which would do no one practical damage in the London for which the play was written, where the money-lenders were stalwart Christians. Shakespeare could have had small experience with Jews, and probably none with one who was also an extortionate money-lender. Shylock is given no physical racial characteristics, unless a beard and a mandatory gaberdine be considered such; and his Old Testament allusions are obviously atmospheric. What the author has done, by a remarkable exercise of the creative imagination, is to give Shylock characteristics which might well appear in a member of any persecuted minority. His proud spirit rankles at his having been falsely classified as inferior; he overvalues the only kind of power (that of money) that has been available to him; and he has retreated inward in defense against hostility. But he is basically as other men are, and his creator has given him great speeches of self-vindication, one of which appears in the present scene (90-103). These are as powerful as they are unexpected, raising in modern minds the whole question of racial and religious intolerance, and loading the play with a weight it was never constructed to bear. We should try to salvage its values. In the Shakespearean ethic, provocation is no excuse for evil-doing. Shylock has been ill-treated; but in the terms of the prayer of Desdemona, who has also been ill-treated, 'God me such uses send,/Not to pick bad from bad, but by bad mend!' He has responded to evil with greater evil, has become the incarnation of hatred. We should retain the right to rejoice in his defeat. We are not required to rejoice like Gratiano, earlier described as *too rude, and bold of voice* (II, ii, 167). The playwright has offered us other models in Antonio and Bassanio, who do not kick the enemy when he is down. The play is not suitable fare for children or others incapable of making distinctions. It is quite probable that, in the actual world, Jews have more often returned good for evil than Christians (as they have certainly been given more opportunities), but in the world of this play it is the Christians who do so (albeit somewhat sparingly), and who should command our sympathy. In reading the play we must discount the sectarianism, and concentrate upon the values in themselves. In the cognate stories it tells, mercy and love triumph over vindictiveness and hatred.

IV, ii

Portia bids Nerissa seek out Shylock's house and obtain his signature on the agreement assuring his daughter's welfare. Gratiano brings her Bassanio's ring and an invitation to dinner. She declines the invitation but accepts the ring. Nerissa promises to extract from Gratiano, while he conducts her to Shylock's house, the ring which she has given him with injunctions like those of Portia to Bassanio.

1-19   Now that the bond story, like the casket story, is fully re-solved, our attention is retained by the developing story of the rings.

V, i

As the moon shines on Belmont, Lorenzo and Jessica speak of lovers' vows, and tease each other about their own. A Messenger announces Portia's approach, and Launcelot announces Bassanio's. Music plays, and Lorenzo and Jessica are descanting upon its charms as Portia and Nerissa arrive. They enjoin secrecy about their absence from home; then, when their husbands and Antonio appear, offer welcome as if they had never left it. Unable to show Nerissa the ring she has given him, Gratiano swears it has gone to a lawyer's grubby little clerk, not to some woman as she charges. Portia reproves him for parting with so dear a token, and says that her own husband would never do so. Bassanio shamefacedly admits that his ring is also gone—to the lawyer who saved Antonio. The young wives pretend to suspect their husbands of infidelity, and threaten to retaliate in kind. Antonio enters a plea for them, and they are again given rings—the same ones as before. Portia then reveals that she and Nerissa were the lawyer and the clerk. Antonio learns that his ships have come safely to port, Lorenzo that he is Shylock's heir; and the play ends in jests and rejoicing.

1-307   This is one of Shakespeare's most charming endings. The soft moonlight, the background music, and the tender raillery of the runaway lovers provide the perfect setting. Lorenzo's lines on the music of the spheres (54-65) are so lovely as to seem true, in defiance of scientific cosmology, and Portia's quiet reflection on the *little candle* in the night (90-91) is fixed in our minds forever. The scene itself is a kind of music, poetic and profound, tender and jolly. The intrigue of the rings lends interest to the action right up to the merry finale. All threats are removed. All are fortunate. And the joys of marriage are yet to come. One can only envy an age with such faith in its institutions. No mate is provided **for**

Antonio, an oversight of the author, but the merchant regains his harem of ships. Destructive hate has been expunged, and creative love is free to go about its proper business.

3

King Henry the Fourth Part One

:

I, i

KING HENRY hopes that there will be no more civil strife, and that he may lead a force of united English to the Holy Lands. The Earl of Westmoreland reports that plans for the crusade have been postponed because of ill news from Wales: Mortimer has been captured by the wild Glendower and his men massacred. Moreover, a battle between the Scots under Douglas and the English under Percy has shaped up at Holmedon. The outcome of this latter battle is already known to the King through the hard-riding zeal of Sir Walter Blunt. Harry Percy has won a glorious victory and taken many prisoners. Henry wishes that his own truant son resembled this valiant son of Northumberland, even though he has arrogantly refused to turn over his prisoners. Westmoreland declares that the youth's malcontent uncle, the Earl of Worcester, has prompted his conduct; and the King calls a council to attend his inquiry into the matter.

1 s.d. The cast is split three ways, with the alienated groups usually moving in separate spheres, so that only the King's elder associates and his tractable younger son are available for this opening; however, enough actors can double from their main roles to make a fair showing of 'others' in a scene of state, justifying a royal oration. **1-33** This is, in fact, a public address—a fine piece of rhetoric, inviting the actor to make a right instrument of his voice in rendering its sonorous periods. These are artfully varied in length, long units alternating with short. In the four long units the pauses at the end of lines are so slight (or non-existent) as to produce the effect of majestic amplitude. The rich sounds harmonize with the rich and weighty metaphor—harsh images of war interspersed with glancing images of peace, the last and most extended evoking the moving figure of Christ. The *we* of the speaker shifts in meaning, designating sometimes the King himself using the royal plural, sometimes the company gathered on the present occasion, and sometimes the whole commonalty. We sense the power and self-control of this man beneath the somber, almost wistful, tones. (Some familiarity with the Chronicles, and Shakespeare's own *Richard II,* would have instructed the audience in advance that Henry is of direct descent in a great royal line, but has reason to feel morally and politically insecure. He has brought about the abdication and death of his legitimate predecessor, and been a fellow in rebellion with powerful lords who are now his subjects.) **34-61** Although England proper has been momentarily pacified since his coronation, unrest continues in Wales and on the Scottish border. Obviously he knew this, and his talk of a crusade could have expressed no more than a pious wish. Observe that he shows no regret over the capture of his officer Mortimer (who has a legal claim to his throne). **62-75** Blunt has ridden the length of the land without resting to change clothes; one imaginative descriptive touch (64-65) makes vivid the general sense of urgency and the zeal of the *friend.* Henry himself is a soldier, and his relish in Percy's feat makes him suddenly drop his stately idiom. **76-90** He is also a father and is quickly dashed by Westmoreland's mention of *prince.* The two Harrys, 'Hotspur' and 'Prince Hal,' with whom the play will be largely concerned are here promptly placed before us in apposition. The original spectators would delight in their sense of irony, knowing that this son whom Henry deems so unpromising will prove his greatest gift to England, the heroic Henry V. **91-108** We see, as the King must, thunderclouds on the horizon. Northumberland, Worcester, and Hotspur have all been mentioned in an ominous context. These are the 'Percys of the North,' who played a major role in seating him on his throne. It was predicted in *Richard II* that they would also play a major role in contesting his easy possession of it. Worcester did not appear in person in that play, but was mentioned as the Steward of the royal household who broke his staff of office and joined Henry after his defiant return from banishment.

I, ii

Instead of trading blows with encroaching Scots, the King's son and heir, Prince Hal, is trading jests with Sir John Falstaff—on the gamy subjects of sack-drinking, purse-natching, wenching, and the like, with which the knight seems highly conversant. Poins, another member of the Prince's tavern set, proposes a profitable escapade—a bit of highway robbery at Gad's Hill. Falstaff is all in favor of this enterprise, and hopes that Poins can win over the unregally hesitant Prince. When the two are alone, Poins suggests that it will be fine sport to let Falstaff, Peto, Bardolph, and Gadshill rob the travelers while they themselves hang back; they will then don buckram disguises and rob the robbers. The cream of the jest will be to listen to Falstaff's gross lies when they meet after the encounter. Hal consents to take part; then, in soliloquy, reflects that when he chooses to break from these shoddy companions he will shine with greater luster for once having mingled with them.

1-20 A knight would be the right companion for a prince if he were knightly—young, lean, trim, preoccupied with feats of arms. What if he is old, fat, unbuttoned, and preoccupied with the flesh pots? The visual stage image of Falstaff together with the Prince's inventory of his habits produce an early and instantaneous effect of travesty of knighthood. Appropriately its verbal component is threaded on the theme of disregard of time: those who 'doff the world aside' follow no fixed schedules. We get our first taste of Falstaff's mental agility when his vocative of majesty *thy grace* suggests the Christian quality of 'grace' and this suggests 'grace' (blessing) before meat and, with impeccable logic, the meager grace before meager meat (*egg and butter*) is used as the measure of the Prince's spiritual state.   **21-75** No lances are shivered, but this is jousting of a sort, with the old expert in frivolity exercising the clever neophyte. They cap similitudes, and they thrust, parry, and counterthrust with casual insults. Observe how conscious Falstaff is of Hal's status as heir of the kingdom; his brazen familiarity is a kind of toadying in reverse. He retires from the fray first, but he has not really extended himself; at this kind of combat he could handle the youth with his left hand (or brain-lobe), and he has never had to explain his slurs with an *I mean . . .* (61). The constant allusion to highway robbery before the Gad's Hill project is explicitly introduced would have puzzled no one: the robbery was one of the Prince's best-known legendary escapades.　**76-99** In his sanctimonious vein Falstaff becomes dodderingly repetitious. He is capitalizing on the way an old sinner like himself ought to feel but doesn't—or does he, just a little? He is a master at laying himself open with ludicrously vulnerable statements—as in his claim that he is the one who is being corrupted by the Prince. It is thus that he generously functions as the cause of wit in others. Obvious and subtle comic effects are oddly assorted: his obliging alacrity in falling from grace when invited to steal a purse is slap-stick, but his subsequent apology is profound: to suggest that thieves are obeying the biblical mandate by laboring in their *vocation* is to set teetering for a moment the whole structure of religious and social dogma.　**100-82** Poins, like Falstaff and unlike the slummy characters we shall presently meet, is indubitably upper-class, the typical younger son and hanger-on, boon companion of the Prince's own age. He is a convenient interlocutor and agent in the action, but distinctive characteristics seem drained away from him by the more colorful Falstaff on the one hand and Prince Hal on the other. He appears not too intelligent, a shadow of the Prince, echoing his blunter brand of witticisms. Falstaff's exit speech is a parody of the style of Puritan sermonizing, and the Prince's parting simile, *thou latter spring* (148), is his best. It is relevant to the time-honored discussion of whether Falstaff is or is not a coward that a distinction is made when the subject is first mentioned in the play (171-73): Bardolph and Peto are cowards born, Falstaff a coward on principle.　**183-205** There are several ways of taking the Prince's final soliloquy. The scene has progressed in racy colloquial prose, and this sudden transition to the dignity of formally-worded blank verse produces a choral effect. We may say that the Prince is making an explanatory statement about himself in the absence of any other available speaker, guiding and comforting the audience. However, even if we take the speech as a revelation of character, it is not damaging at this stage in the play. Coming as it does, before Falstaff has endeared himself to us, we do not view the speaker as an ingrate and a sneak. Actually Hal is refining on the methods of his father: just as King Henry husbanded from the multitude the display of his glorious person, as he will later virtuously point out, so Hal is husbanding the display of his virtues—in the manner, incidentally, most conducive to his (and our) enjoyment. The speech has its literary merits, as in the passage (192-95) *If all the year were playing holidays.* . . . The illustration reverses the present situation; the Prince is having his *playing holidays*—it will be his piece of *work* at Shrewsbury which will profit by comparison.

I, iii

Henry's warning that he intends to exercise his power draws from Worcester the reminder that the nobles he is threatening have placed him on the throne. Henry peremptorily orders him from his presence. Northumberland is more conciliatory, and says that his son has not actually refused to render up his prisoners. Hotspur himself explains that he gave his ambiguous reply only because he was weary, and annoyed by the pretentious fop who conveyed the King's demand. The King then charges that Hotspur is retaining the prisoners in order to bargain for a royal ransom for Mortimer, who has basely yielded to the Welsh and has wedded the enemy Glendower's daughter. He denies Hotspur's vehement claim that Mortimer fought bravely, orders immediate compliance in the matter of the prisoners, and abruptly ends the interview. Hotspur is furious, and when Worcester returns, is scarcely able to listen to the proposals of the elders of his house. However, when Worcester and Northumberland succeed in gaining his attention, he eagerly joins in a scheme of rebellion. He will make peace with Douglas, and ally himself with Glendower and with Mortimer, his wife's brother, who has a claim to the throne. Then the forces of the Welsh and the Scots, together with the Percy following in the North, will wage war on this usurper Henry.

1-22 It is hard to detect which side is the aggressor. Henry mentions *indignities*—presumably effronts from these haughty nobles, such as Hotspur's refusal to surrender his prisoners. But he also, in one striking line (9), shows his awareness of the expedience of acting every inch a king, and he may merely be forcing a showdown. How necessary this is is proved by the surly response of Worcester. Henry's reproof and dismissal of this lord comes as an interruption of a remark by Northumberland, Worcester's brother and a very powerful peer, so that his cool *You were about to speak* (22) with its implied 'And now have my permission to do so' is an imposing display of toughness.   **23-76** There is no tone of rebellion in Northumberland's speech—or even in Hotspur's, except that the courtly fop he describes so contemptuously must have been Henry's courier (though certainly not Sir Walter Blunt). It is a marvelous speech, vivid, nervous, virile. The battlefield with its reeking dead, the battle-weary leader, the fastidious popinjay from court are precisely sketched although ostensibly in effortless slapdash, the phrases tumbling out like extended interjections. This mettlesome young lord even lords it over the language. Blunt's slow, solemn, cautiously deliberative comment makes a perfect foil to the style.   **77-124** Henry's charge against Hotspur's brother-in-law is bound to have an explosive effect, and he at least takes the precaution of not addressing it directly to the young fire-brand. We now get two diametrically opposite accounts of Mortimer's conduct in Wales, and neither here nor elsewhere in the play are we told which one is true. However, intimations of the truth are written into the lines. Hotspur at least believes what he is saying as he describes Mortimer's efforts in epic terms, whereas Henry appears to be trying to convince himself as well as others. Observe how he keeps repeating himself, protests too much (113-17). In fact his last speech sounds suspiciously like bluster.   **125-210** Past history is reviewed and Hotspur's nature analyzed simultaneously, the processes absorbed in the latter's theatrically compelling gusts of passion. He is 'motivated' in complex ways. He seems first of all simply partisan, intensely loyal to his family and friends (such as Mortimer), to his *side* whoever is on it; and intensely antagonistic to anyone not on his *side* (such as Henry). But he also craves justification, and the facts suddenly take on a special elementary coloration, with good in absolute contrast with evil, the former friend Henry a *canker* and the former enemy Richard a *sweet lovely rose* (175-76). Finally he is simply spoiling for a fight, for victory, for *honor*—to which he is fanatically, almost mystically devoted. Although almost hysterical, in contrast with the calm purposefulness of his elders, his occasionally inspired language (201-08) and the sheer intensity of his feeling gives him supremacy over them in our imaginations, and we never question why he should be the leader of the combined forces rather than one of them. We must deplore his chivalric truculence, his lust to dominate without corrival, but we covertly admire his disdain for political maneuvering and conspiracy, the brakes applied by a *half-faced fellowship* (208). **211-56** This skillful and unpredictable interlude is very human, even comical. Hotspur's turbulent interruptions and his father's and uncle's wry comments upon them lead up to a point where he is scolded like a boy, such as in some respects he is, and almost tearfully responds like a boy (235-40). He is thrown off his stride, and his remaining outbursts are confused and sputtering until he obediently subsides. **257-99** It is Worcester, the archplotter, who maps out the practical moves. Observe that Northumberland's contribution is limited to two brief comments, neither of them enthusiastic. Hotspur, in contrast, who throughout has shown no sign of prior information about or reflection upon public affairs, uncritically approves of everything. We cannot be repelled by him. For all his defects, he seems unworldly, indeed curiously *pure*.

II, i

Two carriers complain of the accommodations of the inn as they set out at two in the morning to drive their pack-horses to London. Gadshill, a professional sharker, tries to pump them about the time of their arrival, and gets confirmation from his informer among the servants at the inn that a franklin carrying three hundred marks in gold will be in the train of travelers. He boasts that his neck will be safe on this occasion because he robs in the company of Sir John and even more exalted personages. The inn-servant will get his cut.

1-45 We have just seen the great lords of the land tightening their sinews for a renewal of the struggle for power. We now get a glimpse of a somewhat different stratum of society. The scene is not essential to the plot; we have already heard from Poins that the quarry has been spotted—the episode of the actual robbery might have followed at once. But this scene provides just the needed touch of homely realism to remind us that the lords are not ornamenting a pageant or exercising on a tilting field. The England they are struggling for is a place where people live. These carriers, in their unglamorous way, are pretty good fellows—up to work at dawn, concerned about the comfort of their *poor jades* (9), anxious to get their turkeys to market in prime condition. Their grousing about the food and sanitary arrangements at the inn is a sixteenth-century variation on a timeless theme. Still it is no sentimental picture of 'the people' in the abstract. Here are also Gadshill, the professional criminal (nicknamed after a notoriously dangerous stretch of the London road), and the crooked servant who serves as his spotter. The prose is a transcript of everyday English speech of the time, except that the picturesque Gadshill is given a more colorful idiom. His comment on the elevated company allied with him in the present adventure serves a double purpose: after just having parted from the Percy family with their hard-riding plans, we cannot confine to the Prince's tavern mates alone the application of Gadshill's sardonic allusion to those who *prey* on the Commonealth and *make her their boots* (76-79).

II, ii

Prince Hal and Poins marshal in the amateur highwaymen, Peto, Bardolph, and Falstaff, the last in a state of voluble discomfort because he has been deprived of his horse. Gadshill announces the approach of the travelers, and Poins and the Prince retire on the pretext of holding themselves in reserve. They don their disguises and set upon Falstaff and his mates when the travelers have been robbed and the spoils are being divided. Falstaff is only a little less nimble than the others in beating a retreat; and Poins and the Prince speak gleefully of his terror as they carry off the gold.

1-102 In the management of this scene the limitations of the bare platform stage are capitalized upon and a virtue made of necessity. Highwaymen and their victims would ordinarily be mounted, the latter accompanied by pack-horses, and the playwright has had to use his ingenuity to maneuver the animals to an imaginary position off-stage. Depriving Falstaff of his horse as a trick is at once a practical necessity and a comic opportunity, permitting the knight to expatiate, as he loves to do, on his physical disabilities. The scene is full of farcical action, hilariously exploiting the discomfiture of a fat man, but there is an additional kind of humor. Actually the butt himself is in top form and has some grand lines. His metaphors, as always, are resourcefully concrete; and his hatred of discomfort, which is real, inspires a string of paradoxes— on the inconvenience of robbing in *thieve's company* (10), on his seduction by evil companions, etc. We may infer that his reference to the twenty-two years during which he has hourly forsworn Poins's company (15) means that Poins is about twenty-two years old and has exercised his baleful influence from the cradle. Observe that when something especially preposterous occurs to Falstaff (as his having been bewitched into friendship by *medicines*), he savors it so much that he repeats it (17-19). There is paradox in his very presence: he is really too intelligent to be here, and his *Have you any levers to lift me up again?* (32) bears witness to his practical imagination, as does his *Zounds, will they not rob us?* (60). Paradoxical, too, is something we may call the alacrity of the slothful. Falstaff shows an endearing readiness for the business at hand, whatever it may be, a seemingly inexhaustible relish. When the time comes to go into action, he does so with fine ferocious battle-cries. True the enemy are sitting ducks, but how can we view as a bully this chastizer of opulent respectability? *Young men must live* (83).

II, iii

Hotspur reads, with indignant asides, a letter from a cautious lord, declining his invitation to join the rebellion. He suspects that his correspondent will now betray the plot to the King, and defies him in absence. Lady Percy asks about his recent abstraction and his day-and-night dreams of battle, but Hotspur is so intent upon ordering his mount that he pays her no attention. She suspects the truth, but is unable to extract from this cavalier husband anything but cavalier jests; however he promises that she will join him at his destination.

1-32 Hotspur's testy asides add touches to his characterization, review the present situation, and even intimate the fate of the conspiracy. An inexpert intriguer, he has let the cat out of the bag, and part of his irritation is owing to his awareness of the blunder. He reassures himself with a memorable metaphor (8-9) and burly expressions of confidence (15-18). Although he speaks in what may begin to appear as an habitual mode of contempt, he does not strike us as contemptuous-minded; with him approval—*an excellent plot, very good friends* (17)—is always as unqualified as is condemnation.   **33-71** His Lady's graphic speech is a set piece, describing the absorption of a warlike enthusiast on the eve of action. So far as the absorption is concerned, it is immediately illustrated by Hotspur's concern with his horse to the complete obliviousness of what his wife is saying.   **72-113** And yet their relations seem good. His rough humor and her readiness in abuse argue a basic confidence on the part of both in their mutual affection. Of course he does not really distrust her. There is irony in his refusal to reveal his plans because women talk too much, when he has just been proved guilty of this indiscretion himself. His final speech, with its echo of the book of *Ruth* (111), intimates the solidity of this union.

II, iv

Prince Hal tells Poins that he has won the dubious honor of being accepted in fellowship by the tavern apprentices; then teases one of them by holding him in bewildering conversation while Poins calls for his services. Falstaff enters and makes sorrowful allusions to the prevalence of cowardice in the land. He tells how valiantly he himself fought after being deserted by Prince Hal and Poins, exhibiting his hacked sword and pierced clothing, and describing the chameleon-like enemy with the aid of elastic statistics. After an exchange of epithets, the Prince gives the true account of the onset at Gad's Hill, but Falstaff is ready with an answer. A messenger from the King is announced, and while Falstaff goes to send him away, Bardolph and Peto tell how he has coached them to back up his story. Prince Hal seems more amused than impressed when Falstaff returns with news of the rebellion. Since he will have to face his father in an interview in the morning, they hold a rehearsal, with Falstaff and himself alternating in the principal roles. The merriment is interrupted by the arrival of the Sheriff and a Carrier, who have tracked Falstaff here. Sir John hides behind the arras while Hal turns the Sheriff away with promises that justice will be done. When the knight is discovered to have fallen asleep in his hiding place, his pockets are turned out. They contain little but a tavern bill for huge quantities of sack. The Prince resolves to afflict him with a commission as a captain of a company of foot-soldiers; he will see that the stolen money is returned, and will report to his father in the morning.

1-25 Since we have just seen Hotspur setting out on his perilous venture, the juxtaposed entrance of Hal in his idleness invites us to make comparisons. That this is a calculated effect is indicated by phrases introduced into Hal's long speech; he has *sounded the very bass-string of humility* (5-6) in his confederacy with the tapsters, and there is an ironic use of military terms in his remark that Poins has lost *honor* by being absent from this *action* (19). The note of disdain for the *good lads in Eastcheap* (13) who have proffered brotherhood and loyalty (as well as free sugar) is not engaging, nor is it necessarily intended to be. There would be little point in a story of reformation if there were no room for reform. We must remember that a Prince of Wales is speaking, and it is a matter of record that, in this imperfect world, princes show small fellowly feeling for tapsters. Although the speech seems only the casual chit-chat of an intelligent and bored idler, it has undertones of self-digust as well as arrogance.   **26-93** The tormenting of Frances plays well on the stage and is designed to raise a laugh— but not to honor Hal. It might be stuffy to call it cruel, but it is certainly wanton, and the playwright lets us ask with Poins, what is the point of it? (88) Hal's reply, which is irrefutable, is that he feels whimsical.   **94-106** This take-off of Hotspur is high comedy, and we love it as such, but it is also a glimpse into Hal's mind. The transition in thought is not abrupt, though it may appear so. The *industry* of the base *skinker* and the *work* of the glorious Hotspur offer a choice between the contemptible and the ridiculous. The Prince is *not yet of Percy's mind* (97), but he is uneasily pondering the nature of honor, and we may, if we wish, deduce that he might fight if he found something worth fighting for. Observe that the allusion to Hotspur's *roan* (102) utilizes a point of reference we have just been given—when we saw Hotspur and his Lady, though not quite as they appear to Hal.   **107-26** A naughty world this, bringing nothing but disillusionment to the simple, the true, the brave. Surely a weary old idealist deserves at least a few sips of unadulterated wine! Falstaff expresses himself with unaccustomed deliberation, as if he had rehearsed his lines— or is our suspicion unjust?   **127-48** The hint in the metaphors, that Hal is less courageous than a royal scion should be, evokes a challenge. Falstaff both meets it and does not. Instead of calling the Prince a coward directly, he asks a fair question. He does not directly call Poins a coward either—he defiantly refuses to do so— although his metaphors still carry implications. Who can censor his picayune inaccuracy about the number of his drinks? He has suffered greatly in spirit, and forgets that he has abandoned his customary abstemiousness.   **149-74** His opening of the Gad's Hill story is a bare statement of fact; no rhetoric is needed when feats speak for themselves. Still, why pretend that this one was less than magnificent? Epic action calls for epic terms. Gadshill and Peto simply are not reliable reporters; Falstaff himself must give the facts.   **175-219** The natural and the farcical are wonderfully commingled. Here are turns of speech we seem to have heard from every robust liar we have ever encountered: *'All?* I know not what you call all, but . . .' (175); *'Four, Hal.* I *told* thee four' (187); 'In *buckram?'* (93) As the attackers multiply, we cannot be sure if the wily old fraud is being patently outrageous in order to get a rise from his listeners, or if he is carried away by enthusiasm and really expects to be believed. Observe how the true facts peep through, as in the initial mention (181) of *two rogues in buckram suits* (Hal and Poins), and how the lines require accompanying heroic pantomime. When the Prince pours out his invective, Falstaff seems honestly taken aback.   **220-28** A tale so absurd of course needs no exposure, but Falstaff must be explicitly exposed so as to let us enjoy the effect. The playwright meets this problem by making Hal challenge the teller, not on the palpably false increase of assailants from two to eleven, but on the relatively minor inconsistency about recognizing colors in the dark, thus creating an illusion of detection. Falstaff will not explain the inconsistency on *compulsion* (224)—it would not be *honorable* to do so.   **229-35** As they pelt each other with similes, Hal is resourceful but Falstaff wins by a score of eight to four.   **236-65** Hal tells a plain unvarnished tale, such truth as shames the devil; then he, Poins, (and we) wait expectantly to see how the devil will dodge the shame. Falstaff does not disappoint us. In fact his moral vindication is so complete that it amazes even him, and calls for a celebration—that, and the fact that they have the money after all, since he never loses sight of tangibles. What a man! He may not be brave, but he is dauntless. It is not Falstaff's cleverness alone that seduces us. He has the appeal of the minor miracle—the old hulk that will not sink, the hollow trunk that always rides out one more storm. In fact, images of age and decay are inappropriate. This is a case of perpetual rejuvenation; Falstaff's sack seems dipped from the magic font, and his aged fat more durable than youthful muscle. Thoreau's hard pronouncement that most men past their youth live lives of quiet desperation is just true enough to make us rejoice in this one man, or dream of a man, who lives a life of noisy jubilation. **266-309** There is a knock on the door of cloud-cuckoo-land, and as Falstaff goes to hold sobriety at bay, the Prince's wit works minor mayhem upon a minor liar, who tries to emulate Falstaff's gift for transfiguring blemishes to beauties. **310-54** Harsh reality cannot be denied, and the murmur of war penetrates the taproom, just audible above the persiflage. Hal's lampoon of Hotspur was good, but Falstaff is able to do the other martial paragon in one quick stroke—*that sprightly Scot of Scots, Douglas, that runs a-horseback up a hill perpendicular* (325-27). It is formidable tidings, even as conveyed by Falstaff, and a real question lurks beneath his comic one. How *does* the Prince feel—*horrible afeard* (349) or *not a whit* (354)? **355-417** Falstaff is the born improvisor, and everything—chair, dagger, cushion, sack, hostess—yields its theatrical potential at his touch. Observe how he even conscripts his sound effects: the Hostess's giggle becomes a queenly sob (373). In the reference to *harlotry players* (377) Shakespeare the player is recording current slander but scarcely endorsing it (unless he is lurking in his play in the guise of the Hostess). Falstaff quickly changes his mind about doing his part in *King Cambyses' vein* (riming rant) and 'does it' in a perfect parody of Euphuistic prose, the style in which so much belle-lettristic moralizing had recently been written. He is, of course, complete opportunist as well as improvisor, and by some strange Falstaffian alchemy the King's reprimand of the Prince becomes a eulogy of himself. He is as pleased with his acting accomplishments as we are. **418-57** The Prince is pretty competent too, and he certainly throws himself into the performance, both in his epithets and his Euphuisms, but Falstaff deftly deflates him—*Whom means your grace?* (438)—leaving him merely flailing—*That villainous abominable . . . etc.* (439-40). This performance, too, by some mysterious process, becomes a eulogy of Falstaff—or rather an almost sincere and affecting apology. An interesting gesture is implied: since the word *plump* is reserved for the last sentence (456), Falstaff is 'directed' to caress lovingly his spherical belly as he reaches his climax *all the world* (456) Hal's response to the word *banish* sounds curiously flat: *I do. I will* (457). Does it sound ominous as well? Are Falstaff's prospects as royal favorite as good as he thinks they are? **458-523** For the present at least, Hal is willing to rescue him with a lie; and, always adaptable, Falstaff plucks from the nettle danger the flower of repose. There has been a flurry of excitement at the arrival of the Sheriff, but as the scene closes, a middle-of-the-night hush is in the tavern. All have faded from the picture except the Prince, Peto, and the recumbent knight. He speaks to us now only with his stertorous breathing, his empty pockets, and his tavern bill. Even Hal is shaken by this documentary evidence of the disparity between solid and liquid intake, and his plans for Falstaff's immediate future are somewhat lacking in benignity. The mood turns serious, and this matchless comic scene ends with good resolutions and sober good-nights.

III, i

Hotspur confers with Worcester, Glendower, and Mortimer on their plans to join forces with Northumberland at Shrewsbury and battle Henry for control of the kingdom. A map is produced, dividing the realm into three parts, with the North going to Hotspur, the West to Glendower, and the South to Mortimer. Hotspur derides Glendower's boast that his birth was attended by portentous upheavals in nature, and grows quarrelsome when the Welshman objects to his plan to alter the course of the river Trent so as to enlarge his share of the territory it bounds. But as soon as Glendower withdraws his objection, Hotspur yields the point; and when Worcester and Mortimer entreat him to be more conciliatory in his attitude toward their worthy host, he promises to try although Glendower's reminiscences of supernatural feats have been torturing him with boredom. Mortimer's wife is desolate because of her husband's imminent departure. They try to communicate although he speaks only English and she speaks only Welsh. She sings a Welsh song, to the accompaniment of music invoked by Glendower from the air. Hotspur is unable to coax his own wife to sing and contents himself with teasing her. This happy interlude is over, or will be after a few hours in bed: he is eager to sign the agreement of partition and be off to the wars.

1-69 Hotspur seems both sensible and foolish—sensible in his witty attacks on what strikes him as conceited and superstitious wool-gathering, and foolish in his cross-grained intolerance of his host and ally, whose literary and military distinctions are real, however eccentrically worn. The character of Owen Glendower is one of the treasures of the play although he appears in this scene alone. He appears in the Chronicles as a barbarous villain; he would have appeared in any serio-comic scene written by one of Shakespeare's rivals as a ludicrous butt; here, he is amusingly boastful and 'Welsh,' but also rather imposing—gently grave and even magnanimous.   **70-115** To have mislaid this map even momentarily, Hotspur must be unfitted indeed for 'paper-work.' It records nothing less than a plot to chop up England. Any admiration for Hotspur's gallantry in the original audience would have been considerably dampened by a reminder of these historical proceedings, as Shakespeare knew when he chose them for portrayal; yet he is not overtly critical of the conspirators. In fact Mortimer and Worcester, as they mediate between Hotspur and Glendower, are allowed to appear as temperate and fair-minded men. There is a fascinating ambiguity at this point. Who is Shakespeare gibing at during the debate on turning the river Trent? At Hotspur, Worcester, and Mortimer because they speak so breezily of reshaping the face of the country? Or at Glendower, whose bemused *Not wind? It shall, it must! You see it doth* (106) suggests that these others are only having fun with his gullibility?   **116-89** Hotspur is taking something or other seriously enough to quarrel about it. Only his vigor and downrightness, and his amazing articulateness, save him in our estimation during his philistine bridling at the cultivated Welshman. The latter strikes us as deserving Mortimer's tribute, as Hotspur deserves Worcester's rebuke. Still, we must withhold final judgment. Hotspur is generous enough when his 'honor' is not at stake (135), and he is able to listen to criticism, perhaps even to heed it a little (188). He may show up less badly when the action shifts from the council-table to the battlefield. We had best withhold final judgment. **190-210** The comic possibilities of the situation are so manifest that the lady can be entrusted with authoring her own Welsh or facsimile thereof: an ardent couple coping with the language barrier has proved sure-fire in many a later play. **211-63** In the preceding scene the entertainment-within-entertainment was histrionic; here it is musical. Since the words of the song are Welsh, we cannot too much lament its loss, but we should be aware of the nature of the tune. Obviously it is literally 'haunting'—melodious and tender in the fashion of a lullaby (214-15). It will be delightful in itself, and affecting as a prelude to departure for war. Surprisingly the instrumental accompaniment is magical, proving that Glendower's boasts were not empty. This is a rare intrusion of the supernatural into a Shakespearean history play, but it is so casual, and Hotspur is so unimpressed, that it has little impact as such. Although Hotspur sees merits in the singer, he is uncharmed by the song, his boisterousness reminding us of his previous attack on such concords of sweet sounds. If he wants his own Kate to sing, his impulse is mainly competitive. The relations between the two continue to please us. Hotspur is not uxorious, but neither is he cold, and his tyrannizing is not very tyrannical. The kind of tilting in which the two indulge suggests that whatever he is abroad, Hotspur is reasonably relaxed and human at home. (Although so vastly different in substance, this scene functions as a companion piece with the preceding, the two together demonstrating the craftsmanship with which the play as a whole is shaped. The play's beginning treats the brewing of civil war, and poses two questions: who will win? and how will Hotspur and Prince Hal figure in the upshot? Its ending will answer these questions, and provide exciting derring-do. In the present scenes the playwright triumphantly solves the problem of what to do with the middle. Since no 'thickening' is needed in this essentially simple 'plot,' the scenes have to be self-sustaining—and they prove so indeed. Either would be fine entertainment if performed as an independent playlet. The 'low' comedy of the one is succeeded by the 'high' comedy of the other, but 'low' and 'high' do not describe the relative level of intelligence of the participants. The scenes, of course, also serve a purpose in the general scheme of the drama, keeping the fact of civil war before us, and featuring first one and then the other of the young antagonists.)

III, ii

The King passionately reproves Prince Hal as unworthy of his line —less a dutiful son than a token of God's displeasure. No older than himself, the gallant Hotspur is leading armies in the field, making a bid for the kingdom even as Henry himself did at Hotspur's age while Hal behaves like the frivolous Richard. He is more likely to toady to the enemy than come to his father's aid. Stung by the reproof, Hal affirms his loyalty and swears that he will wrest away all of Hotspur's honors on a single field of battle. The King is overjoyed, and the Prince is promised supreme command of an army. Other armies, led by the King himself and by Westmoreland and Prince John, will join Hal's in the North.

1-180 This interview loses nothing by having been parodied in advance; if anything, it gains in impressiveness through the contrast it presents with the parody. Its blank verse is so brilliant, the King's tones so vibrant with passion, that even the long historical review is dramatic in effect. The conclusion of the interview provides the climax (in the sense of 'turning point') of the play. When the King gives up in despair and bitterly concedes the futility of talking to a son who is as likely as not to betray his father, and fawn on the enemy, the Prince, for the first time in the play, seems really reached, and the mask of debonair self-possession falls away. His *Do not think so. You shall not find it so* (129) sounds tight-lipped, and the rest of the speech as if it were delivered through clenched teeth. Whatever our preconceptions of the character, and whatever our reservations about the glory of war, we must be stirred by these lines, as by the King's cry of elation, *A hundred thousand rebels die in this!* (160) In this one instant, the disintegration of a family and the disintegration of a nation seem to have been simultaneously averted.

III, iii

Falstaff, who has just been inspired to new rhetorical flights by Bardolph's parboiled face, accuses the Hostess of loosing pickpockets upon him, and refuses to pay his bill for wine and miscellaneous services. If Prince Hal dares to back her claim that his pockets contained nothing of value, the Prince will simply have to be cudgelled. At this juncture the Prince appears, along with Poins, and Falstaff modifies his position with his usual dexterity. He engages in an altercation with the Hostess but magnanimously forgives her when the Prince reveals that it was he himself who supervised the turning out of the pockets. Falstaff receives with diminishing enthusiasm the news that Hal is reconciled with his father, that the money stolen at Gad's Hill has been returned, and that he himself will lead a company of foot-soldiers in the approaching battle.

1-197 If Falstaff's only function in the play was to serve as a symbol of the Prince's early lapse from grace, he should have melted out of it during the preceding scene, but here he is still larger than life in spite of his fears—*Do I not dwindle?* (2) His penitential moods are momentary, but sufficient to increase his pleasure in his relapses; and his visions of hell-fire are just vivid enough to brighten his conversational prose. The present impasse with the Hostess proves that he is not without military acumen; the best defense is an attack. The pantomime described in the exceptionally detailed stage direction (85 e.d.) illustrates that he is as quick as ever on the uptake. The Prince himself seems not especially changed since the interview with his father, and this raises an interesting point. Was there nothing to be changed? no reformation necessary? Was the early speech (I, ii), in which he described his slumming as a politic pose, literally true? If so, he must be posing now, on the eve of leading his army to Shrewsbury, and this seems scarcely likely; in fact he appears to be enjoying himself as he has done right along. We must reconcile ourselves to a little uncertainty in the matter, such as we feel in assessing the conduct of our actual acquaintances. Let us say that Hal is not now wholly 'reformed' as he was never wholly 'depraved' but the balances in his character are shifting. In the polarity symbolized by taproom and battlefield, we are prepared to accept the positive claims of the latter, but its superiority does strike us as so overwhelming as to render heinous another visit to the former, harboring though it does so vile a character as Falstaff. Perhaps 'vile' is not the mot juste. There must be good in a man who subscribes so literally to the Scriptures—*I have more flesh than another man, and therefore more frailty* (159-60)—and who so readily forgives the woman he is mulcting. The Hostess, like Bardolph, is a small planet orbiting about the luminous Falstaff, so that it is remarkable that we can detect her light at all. She does not yet shine forth in all her dim-witted but amiable sleaziness, but her character shows promise. (All these characters come to life again in the sequel: *Henry the Fourth Part Two.*)

IV, i

Hotspur, Douglas, and Worcester receive word that Northumberland is sick, and will not bring up his promised forces. Worcester is disturbed, but Hotspur and Douglas agree that Northumberland's men will serve as useful reserves. Hotspur persists in his optimism when Sir Richard Vernon reports on the strength of the armies approaching under command of members of the royal family. He feels a momentary qualm when he hears that even Prince Hal is at the head of a force, brilliantly equipped and high in morale; still, he welcomes the chance to meet this ne'erdowell youth in battle. Vernon's final item of news is the worst of all. Glendower cannot get his men into action for another fortnight, and the King's thirty thousand must be faced by their present remnant. Hotspur cheers his comrades with desperate bravado.

1-136 The valor displayed by Hotspur as the bad news pours in is different in quality from that displayed by Douglas; it is more than high-mettled recklessness. He is the responsible leader, fully aware of the lengthening odds, but he dare not display uncertainty before his lieutenants. He momentarily quails upon hearing each item, then recovers and displays reassuring confidence. From one quarter at least he thought he had nothing to fear, and Vernon's dazed and dazzling account of Prince Hal and his prancing company (97-110) catches him unawares. It is a brilliant description, rich, hard, scintillating, like stained glass transfused by sunlight. When Hotspur is at the height of his rebound from this ominous piece of news, he gets the last and worst. Observe that even Douglas recognizes its gravity (127), and Worcester's brief *that bears a frosty sound* (128) is more expressive than his lengthy lament about Northumberland's absence. Hotspur makes no comment at all, but asks for the total number of the enemy. He does no repining, although his last line indicates that, in his mind, the figures add up to death. (The play offers no explanation for Northumberland's conduct, which must appear strange whether he be sick or only malingering. Its strangeness lies less in his failure to appear than in his willingness to let his son fight anyway (36-37). Of course he does not know that the troops from Wales will also fail to materialize, and that he is issuing a virtual death-warrant.)

IV, ii

Falstaff orders Bardolph to replenish his stock of sack at Coventry. He is reluctant to march through the town with his rag-tag company, which consists only of those too beggarly to pay him for release from the draft. Prince Hal and Westmoreland overtake him on the road and remark on the strange condition of his troops. Falstaff is able to counter the criticism, and the Prince seems more amused than indignant. All will meet on the field where the King is already encamped.

1-76 Does Falstaff rise to the new occasion? He does indeed— to all its opportunities for plunder. His great description of the results of his wholesale abuse of his commission (11-45) is too macabre to be wholly amusing. Compare it with Vernon's description of the noble cavalry: here no golden coats glitter in the sun, no ostrich feathers wave in the breeze. To these *pitiful rascals* (61) war offers no chance to bid for glory, and Falstaff's apology (62-64) has in it a disturbing element of truth.

IV, iii

Worcester and Vernon counsel delay, but Hotspur and Douglas favor an immediate engagement. A parley is sounded from the opposing camp, and Sir Walter Blunt brings an offer from the King to arbitrate the dispute. Hotspur rehearses the story of how Henry received aid from Northumberland, Worcester, and himself upon his return to England, how he subsequently usurped the throne, and how he now slights his benefactors and ignores the rightful claims of Mortimer. Blunt asks if this is his final answer, and Hotspur replies that it is not: he will send Worcester in the morning to hear the King's terms.

1-113 Hotspur rises in stature. His aims are not solely personal glory, and his instincts are not suicidal. In the crisis he proves capable of compromise: facing almost certain defeat, he will negotiate and yield to honorable terms. The last three speeches in the scene are poignant—in their unexpectedness, their brevity, their muted ring of hope.

IV, iv

The Archbishop of York sends Sir Michael with instructions to such of his relatives and friends as have any power. He knows that Hotspur must fight without the aid of Northumberland, Glendower, and Mortimer. He will probably be defeated, and the King will bring an army hither to punish the Archbishop for encouraging the conspiracy.

1-41 It is true that if this scene had been accidentally omitted from the printed text, we could not detect the lacuna; hence, it may be called 'unessential,' and it has in fact often been viewed as a linking scene, offering with its unfinished business the promise of a sequel—either *Henry the Fourth Part Two,* or, if that was unpremeditated at the time, then *Henry the Fifth*. It may serve such a purpose, but it justifies itself in other ways: it recapitulates the present state of affairs, reinforces the earlier intimations of Hotspur's defeat, and enlarges the dimensions of the arena of struggle by suggesting repercussions. If we deny the utility of such contributions, we would also have to call the inn-yard scene (II, i) or the foot-soldiers scene (IV, ii) 'unessential.'

V, i

At daybreak Worcester and Vernon appear as emissaries in the King's camp. Worcester speaks in the same vein as Hotspur, but Henry dismisses the bill of grievances as mere pretext for insurrection. He refuses to entertain Prince Hal's proposal that he and Hotspur settle the dispute in single combat, but offers the rebels free pardon if they will lay down their arms. The Prince predicts that Hotspur and Douglas will refuse these terms because of their relish for battle. Falstaff displays no such relish. He requests the Prince to look out for him in the pinches, and soliloquizes sardonically on the value of 'honor.'

1-82 Again the rebel side is given its say, and instead of meeting the argument Henry begs the question (72-82). He might have pointed out that the solicitude for Richard displayed by the Percys appears a little tardy, since Northumberland was the most active agent in removing him from the throne. Worcester evidently believes what he is saying, but there are details in his speech betraying the envy that has, at least in part, motivated him (38). The play is politically impartial, in the sense that it recognizes the impulse on both sides to find ethical sanctions for what is basically self-interest. **83-126** Henry may give the impression of being unprincipled; another way to look at it is to say that he is efficiently pragmatic— using the most economical means of getting what he knows he must have in order to survive. If he *dares* to risk Prince Hal in single combat with Hotspur (101-03), why does he not do so? What are the *considerations infinite* that restrain him? The answer is that he does *not* dare, and he has the larger army. Prince Hal speaks well of Hotspur, whereas Hotspur in these latter scenes never speaks well of him. In his handsome tribute and his offer to save lives by facing the doughty enemy in single combat, the Prince emerges as the perfect pattern of chivalry. Nothing in the scene suggests that we are intended to take his words at less than face value. Here is the hero—the future Henry V.   **127-39** Falstaff's famous piece of 'debunking' is directed not at Hal, or even Worcester and Hotspur, but at honor itself. We cannot say that mere military prowess, and not true honor, suffers detraction in this speech, because, under the circumstances, the two things are one. As usual the speaker's ingenuity and concreteness are devastating: *Who hath it? He that died a Wednesday* (134). Here again is the paradoxical mingling of the comical—and the what? The truth?—or the half-truth?

V, ii

Worcester decides, with Vernon's reluctant consent, to say nothing of the King's offer; the young and impulsive Hotspur may actually win pardon, but not themselves, the elder principals in the rebellion. They tell Hotspur and Douglas to prepare for battle, and Vernon speaks with admiration of Prince Hal's willingness to fight alone. Hotspur's response reminds us of his earlier skepticism about miracles. He briefly exhorts his comrades to fight nobly, and embraces them in farewell as the trumpets sound the beginning of battle.

1-100 This act of betrayal, the most dishonorable behavior portrayed in the play, follows hard upon Falstaff's exit, so that his soliloquy on honor serves just as definitely as prologue to the episode as it serves as epilogue to the last. Understandable though their motives may be, this pair sacrifice Hotspur for what they deem their own welfare, and Vernon's compliance is reminiscent of Pilate's. Their act does not save them, and perhaps we are being quietly invited to reappraise Falstaff's sentiments. 'Who has *dishonor?* He that died a Wednesday.' Even from a practical point of view the Falstaffian philosophy appears vulnerable, and our enthusiasm is diluted. Observe the progressive building up of Prince Hal in the tribute from one of the enemy (51-68), but this is not entirely at the expense of Hotspur, who, in the way most fitting for his kind, is assuming larger dimensions. We must love his rejection of baseness, and the beauty of its expression (81-84), even though we see no value in treading on kings. We must be moved, too, by his brief battle oration, and the parting embrace of the doomed. Inevitably our sympathies go to the outnumbered brave.

V, iii

Douglas slays Sir Walter Blunt in the likeness of King Henry, as he has already slain Lord Stafford. Hotspur tells him that many on the field are disguised as the King, and Douglas resolves to slay them all. Falstaff, separated from his riddled foot-soldiers, gazes with consternation at the body of Blunt. Prince Hal tries to borrow his sword, but he clings to it in fear of Hotspur. He offers to lend his pistol, but his holster contains only a bottle of sack. Prince Hal throws it at him, and leaves him to speculate on his chance for survival.

1-60   The early episodes in the battle (the death of Blunt, Douglas's other victories as here reported, and the unimposing performance of Falstaff's foot-soldiers) help to obscure the fact of the King's numerical superiority, and place Prince Hal's later feats in a better perspective, making them seem important when they come. The mere presence of Falstaff in the battle scenes is an incredibly daring bit of grotesquerie, but it *works,* channeling off our risibility. If he were not present, the serious heroics themselves might have seemed ludicrous.

V, iv

The King bids his sons rest from battle. Both refuse, and the wounded Prince Hal praises the valor of his brother John, then rescues his father from the onslaught of Douglas. At last he and Hotspur meet face to face. Falstaff is content with the role of spectator, and plays dead when attacked by Douglas. Hotspur is vanquished, and dies lamenting the extinction of his glories. Prince Hal pays tribute to his noble adversary, and speaks a word of farewell to the prone body of Falstaff. As soon as he has left, Falstaff rises in a mood of nervous self-congratulation. He gives the body of Hotspur some additional wounds and hoists it onto his back. When the Prince returns with his brother, Falstaff explains that both he and Hotspur were only winded, and fiercely renewed the fight after Hal had left. The Prince decides to let him claim the honor of slaying Hotspur, and Falstaff resolves to live cleanly after he has been rewarded with a peerage.

1-161 The disposition of the episodes in the battle continues to serve the purpose of enhancing Prince Hal—his refusal to nurse his wounds or to rest, his generous praise of his brother, and his rescue of the King. It sounds strange to our ears to hear him praised for not letting his father be killed; but one of the slanders which legend attached to the Prince was that he wished to accelerate the day of his inheritance. The climactic episode in the battle, this non-historical hand-to-hand conflict of Hal and Hotspur, conveys the impression that the issue was after all decided in single combat. There is true pathos in Hotspur's last words. Dying, he displays a reflective capacity he never displayed while living (80-82). The Prince's words and actions as he stands over his dead rival are magnanimous, as is everything he now does. The ambiguity previously noted in his relations with Falstaff is epitomized in his address to the supposedly dead body. His *I could have better spared a better man* (103) scarcely sounds as if he had been using this companion as a mere means to an ambitious end: he grieves—and yet to grieve more would be to be *in love with vanity* (105). The playwright's creative ruthlessness is demonstrated by the way Hotspur's body (which, of course, had to be got off the stage somehow) is used as a comic prop, just after his spirit has been allowed to glow with a final brightness and flicker out with somber dignity. Falstaff's hope of high reward is implied in his words *as a nobleman should do* (161).

V, v

In the aftermath of the victory, King Henry orders the execution of Worcester and Vernon. Prince Hal reports the capture of Douglas and wins the King's consent to dispose of him. He gives Prince John the honor of setting the brave Scot free without ransom. The King now divides their forces, so that they may march upon the remaining centers of opposition and clear the land of rebellion.

1-44 In the previous scene Prince Hal seemed willing to let Falstaff steal the honor of defeating Hotspur, and now he gives his brother the honor of liberating Douglas. There can be no question that these concluding scenes have marched steadfastly in the direction of glorifying Prince Hal; so that we might say that the play is a mere prelude to the further glorification of this national hero in *Henry V*. In this case, we should value it chiefly for its language, its theatrical effectiveness, and its excrescences, such as Falstaff (all worth valuing), but actually the play as a whole does more than record the reform and apotheosis of a Prince. It intimates truly the mixed nature of human responses and motives, and the influence of personalities in shaping the course of history. Like all works of art it is more than the sum of its parts.

4

As You Like It

:

I, i

T o A D A M, an old family servant, Orlando de Boys complains that his elder brother Oliver is disregarding the will of their deceased father and is rearing him as an oaf. He repeats this complaint to

Oliver and is rewarded with a blow, whereupon he lays hold of his surly guardian and demands the legacy due him so that he may make his own way in the world. Oliver half promises to meet the terms but has no intention of doing so. When Charles, the champion wrestler, comes with a warning that Orlando is apt to be injured if he persists in his plan to enter the matches about to be held at court, Oliver traduces the youth and incites Charles to do his worst. Secretly he hopes that the bouts will prove fatal to Orlando, whose natural graces have been putting his own merits in the shade. In the course of his conversation with the wrestler, we have learned of the situation at court. The rightful Duke has been forced to retreat to the Forest of Arden where he lives a Robinhood sort of life with some faithful comrades, while power at home resides in the hand of Duke Frederick, his usurping younger brother. The banished Duke's daughter Rosalind remains at court as companion to Frederick's daughter Celia.

1-22 This is a somber opening for a play with so beckoning a title. A recital of grievances can never be truly engaging, but the note of aspiration in Orlando's voice offsets the petulant tone. He craves the education, the *gentility,* proper to his birth. As he invokes the spirit of his honored father, he seems less concerned with personal status than with the honor of his line. The speech, evidently continuing a conversation with Adam (*as thou say'st*), but with something of the air of an expository soliloquy (*As I remember*) comes out as a compromise between the two. It has the virtue of indicating at once the domestic situation and the nature of this ménage, a considerable manor, with home-farm, horse-trainers, *hinds;* the names *Oliver, Rowland, Jaques, Dennis* make it sufficiently 'French.'
23-78 The ethical basis of Orlando's rejoinders save them from seeming impudent. He gains greatly in contrast with his snarling brother, indeed seems the more mature and restrained of the two. His physical prowess is impressive: obviously he is able to subdue Oliver without much personal agitation or expenditure of energy. This physical conflict of brothers, one of whom stands in place of a parent, is an ominous sign of decay, as witness Adam's distress (58-59) and Orlando's own apologetic words at its conclusion. It

is evidently no casual thing, but the first overt act of rebellion against long oppression. When Oliver's spleen is vented on Adam— *you old dog* (75)—the latter's remark makes clear which of these brothers is truly the family renegade. There is an iron-age atmosphere now; things were different in the days of the good Sir Rowland.   **79-111** Charles's *old news* (92) is so obviously old that there is no reason why it should be conveyed except to post the audience. Shakespeare's expository devices are usually less flat-footed than this question-and-answer sequence, yet it contains the most memorable speech in the scene—on the merry men in the Forest of Arden who *fleet the time carelessly as they did in the golden world* (110-11). It is relieving to hear, in this gloomy establishment, that something *merry* and *golden* survives at least somewhere. (Charles, incidentally, is more articulate than most wrestlers we have known.)   **112-49** And he is not ill-disposed. Actually he has come on a mission of good-will, and Oliver bends him to his purpose by deceiving him, in fact by appealing to his moral sense. Oliver's *brotherly* characterization of Orlando functions like a photographic negative: we deduce that the youth is the opposite of what he is here said to be.   **150-59** The 'positive' of the portrait follows, furnished by the same villainous speaker but when no one is present to hear. This is one of many instances in Shakespeare where virtue receives tribute from vice. Oliver's rancor reminds us of Iago's remark about Cassio: 'He hath a daily beauty in his life That makes me ugly.'

I, ii

Troubled by the absence of her banished father, Rosalind is rallied by her cousin Celia. The two amuse themselves with remarks about the vagaries of Dame Fortune and Lady Nature in bestowing their gifts upon women. With the appearance of the court-jester Touchstone, the conversation erratically swerves to the subjects of wisdom, folly, and empty oaths. The courtier Le Beau brings news that Charles the wrestler has just maimed three challengers and is about to take on a fourth. If they remain in this place, they will see the 'sport.' Touchstone is dubious about the appeal of bone-crushing as an entertainment for ladies, but Rosalind and Celia decide to stay when they see the young and handsome challenger. They add their pleas to Duke Frederick's to dissuade Orlando from the unequal match, but he is resolved to risk everything in this chance to distinguish himself. The girls lend him ardent support, and he easily defeats the champion, but Duke Frederick sourly withholds his favor upon learning that the young victor is a son of a former enemy. Celia deplores her father's ungraciousness, and Rosalind, who remembers old Sir Rowland as a supporter of her father, rewards Orlando with a guerdon. She gives him ample chance to improve the acquaintance, but he can only gaze at her in awe. Le Beau, who has departed with the Duke and his retinue, returns with a warning that Orlando stands in danger of the Duke's active displeasure, as does also the exile's daughter upon whom he has just been gazing. Orlando realizes that he is in worse plight than before, but consoles himself with thoughts of *heavenly Rosalind!* (270)

1-21 Our knowledge of the political situation is here reinforced, and we see the children of the enemy-brothers behaving as loving foster-sisters. Since Celia intends to right the wrong done by her usurping father, the future as well as the past is tinged with gold. **22-49** Rosalind's conversational gambit on *falling in love* (22) is dramatic 'foreshadowing.' Observe how swiftly the subject is switched off by Celia's moralistic reply. Shakespeare's heroines are not permitted to fall in love in the abstract; ripeness is not all in this area: there must be single and worthy objects. The logic-chopping about Nature and Fortune will do as a sample of small talk between lively and cultivated girls, but it seems to come from the top of their heads. **50-85** Touchstone will do better, too, when the occasion improves. The words *dullness of the fool* (51) promises no scintillating performance, indeed no more than the routine clowning we get. The 'demonstration' (about invalid oaths sworn on non-existent beards) is of the tried-and-true order of comic business such as would be part of any jester's repertory, but observe that aspersions are slyly cast upon the usurper, as his daughter notices (76-79): Touchstone's knight without honor is one whom Duke Frederick *loves*.   **86-111** Le Beau is a tame courtier, in contrast with the *merry men* who have followed the elder Duke; he is a gossip and perhaps a fop, but his officiousness is good-natured, and there is nothing in his lines and actions to suggest the effeminacy that is often projected ad nauseam in modern productions; a slightly vapid timidity should do. The merriment of Rosalind and Celia is determinedly sophisticated. For the moment they appear as a pair of smart little minxes.   **112-203** The impression does not endure. They grow tender when they hear of the injured wrestlers, more tender still when they see Orlando. Now they are sketched with swift contrasting strokes. They address the youth with a studied grown-up gravity, but when the match is on, show the delightfully uninhibited partisanship of children. Celia's impulses are especially fetching (193-94). Charles's boastfulness is just enough to set off the quiet modesty of Orlando, who is remarkably successful in concealing his uncouth rearing; in his plaintive and courtly address to the girls he proves quite the rhetorician. Again his physical prowess is impressive: he is Shakespeare's most muscular lover.   **204-41** Duke Frederick has appeared anything but villainous thus far—trying to spare Orlando, limiting the bout to one fall, even making an inquiry (as the girls do not) about the condition of the loser. There is a hint of regret in his manner as he turns upon Orlando, so that the action seems prompted more by a bad conscience than by evil nature. Celia sides against her father in his churlishness (as does Jessica) without forfeiting our esteem. With the Duke's display of passion, the medium shifts to blank verse, and naturally remains so; it would not do for Orlando and Rosalind to fall in love in prose. As usual in these plays, it is the lady who makes the first practical overtures. Rosalind's four-line speech (233-36) illustrates the suppleness which the playwright required of his principal actors, as she lets a wish be father to a thought (*He calls me back*), speaks to herself in an aside (*My pride fell with my fortunes*), addresses a face-saving remark to Celia (*I'll ask him what he would*), and then almost proposes to Orlando. A fine bit of business is implied here, as she hovers invitingly before him while he stands too dumfounded to speak. How he *should* have responded, of course he realizes later with chagrin.

242-70 Frederick's villainy is carefully kept within bounds. Le Beau speaks of his *condition,* his *manners,* his *humorous* state, rather than of inveterate malice. Perhaps he will not prove obdurate in evil, and this iron age will pass. Again the idea of a *better world than this* (265) is obtruded on our attention. To Frederick as to Oliver, it is someone's virtue (260-62) which seem to constitute a threat.

I, iii

Rosalind replies to Celia's questioning by confessing that she has a new reason to be pensive: she has fallen in love with Orlando. Duke Frederick breaks in on their council with an order that Rosalind leave the court within ten days on pain of death. Both she and Celia staunchly protest, but the Duke distrusts Rosalind as the daughter of his banished brother and the object of his subjects' love. Celia resolves to share Rosalind's exile; they will disguise themselves and seek out the elder Duke in the Forest of Arden. Rosalind will don male attire and swagger it out as 'Ganymede' while Celia will pose as 'Aliena.' Touchstone will be persuaded to go along.

1-35 The repartee of the girls has improved now that they have worthy matter to work on. Rosalind is no longer pensive about her father but about her *child's father* (11). How swiftly and implacably her thoughts have fixed upon ultimate objectives! **36-85** Again the shift is from prose to blank verse, with the shift from wit and whimsey to passion. Duke Frederick's anger seems a kind of seizure, like that of Leontes in *The Winter's Tale*. Rosalind and Celia are armed only with honesty, but their plain-speaking is so formidable that we almost pity the Duke. Twice he calls Celia a *fool* (76, 83) because, blinded by love, she fails to see that Rosalind's virtues make her a serious rival. The playwright loves these ironic collisions, where hatred and moral defect must, in self-defense, attack love and virtue as dangerous. The Duke is convinced that his appraisal of the situation is quite rational. **86-134** So resolute a moment before, Rosalind and Celia now sound defenseless and forlorn—but not for long. Cheerfulness seeps rapidly into their voices, so that by the end of the brief dialogue they sound less like refugees than like schoolgirls planning a Halloween junket. Epecially captivating is Rosalind's eagerness to wear a *gallant curtle-axe* and to cloak her timidity in a *swashing and martial outside* (110-18). The two seem truly standing in half-water between childhood and womanhood. Of course Touchstone will go along; Shakespeare's fools all adhere to the right side.

II, i

In the Forest of Arden, Duke Senior extols the simple life and the sweet uses of adversity. His comrades share his content, if not his solicitude for the dappled deer whose dominion they have invaded. They tell of how one of their number, the melancholy Jaques, lies sighing by a brook, moralizing the fate of a wounded stag into an allegory of corrupt society. The Duke goes to seek Jaques out, since he loves to 'cope him' in his 'sullen fits.'

1 s.d. The direction *like Foresters* (later *like Outlaws*) indicates the Kendal green attire of the little band, in contrast with the courtly finery of Frederick and his retinue. We are in the Forest of Arden. After the somewhat asphyxiating atmosphere of Oliver's manor and Frederick's court, the air seems cleansed and cool. The effect is achieved by the relaxed words and conduct, as well as the Robinhood attire of the actors.   **1-20**   The rightful Duke is not even equipped with a proper name, but he has the composure and graciousness of the natural leader, like Theseus. Although his opening lines are filled with allusion to what is *painted* and *envious* in society, to what is *churlish* in nature, the tone is serene and the verse is limpid, in harmony with the theme of peace-of-mind. Amiens describes truly what the speaker does, *translate,* and the style in which he does it, *so quiet and so sweet* (20). The image of the ugly toad wearing in its head the precious jewel (13-14) lends just the touch of strangeness needed to set off the easy simplicity of the rest. His last two lines, with their artfully varied parallelism rising to a climax, *good in everything* (17), have a peculiar significance, as the first generalization we hear in the Forest of Arden spoken by its tutelary spirit. The Duke is not a Pangloss, since, in his pronouncement, that which is not *good* is absorbed and neutralized rather than ignored, and happiness is something earned. The Forest is not an earthly paradise, for here the *fang* of winter *bites* even though it bites to man's advantage; Arden seems to symbolize a process rather than a place.   **21-69**   The Duke's next brief speech contains the text of the two long speeches following. The suggestion of pathos in the fate of the hunted deer, and the idea of their being the *native burghers* (23) of this sylvan city, are imaginatively expanded. The picture of the brook which *brawls* past the gnarled oak-roots, the stag which stretches with groans its *leathern coat* (31-38), is painted from nature sharply observed, but the painting is stylized—decorative and consciously artificial rather than realistic, as is the treatment of the Forest as a whole, in harmony with the symbolic use to which it is being put. The 'moralization' of the picture attributed to Jaques is remarkable for its ingenuity and neat devices of condensation, but its excesses create the impression that the orator was enjoying himself, and we feel a little skeptical about his *weeping* (66). Perhaps he can weep at will.

II, ii

The absence of Celia and Touchstone as well as Rosalind leads Duke Frederick to suspect connivance on the part of Orlando. He orders the youth brought to court for questioning. If he is missing, his brother Oliver must answer for him.

1-21   The birds have flown as we knew they would, and Frederick scents treason as he was bound to do. However one new detail is introduced, the eavesdropping of *Hisperia,* which directs the Duke's attention to the de Boys household. Presumably this will have importance in the economy of the plot; at least we are pleased to hear that Oliver will have to answer for something.

II, iii

Old Adam warns Orlando that the praise he has won for his wrestling victory has inflamed his brother's rancor, so that if he tarries at home he is apt to be burned in his lodgings. Adam puts at Orlando's disposal his life's-savings of five hundred crowns, and the two set forth to seek in the world some 'settled low content.'

1-30 The virtues of Orlando and the danger to which they have exposed him are described in an excessively exclamatory style, but Adam is an octogenarian and we must give the aged leave to wail. **31-76** What follows, in addition to getting Orlando off on his journey, is a moral exemplum in its own right. First Orlando chooses, in exemplary fashion, the lesser evil, personal danger, to outlawry and vagrancy. Then Adam (surely the 'Adam before the fall') performs an act of charity in a spirit of Christian faith, explicitly expressed (43-45). Then comes an oblique lecture on good moral habits, with Adam's hale old age offered in evidence. All this is too well written to be dismissed as perfunctory padding. There is feeling in the reference to old and cashiered servants—*unregarded age in corners thrown* (42). Finally Orlando, using Adam for his text, reproves the world where men work only for *meed* and not for love and duty. The present is compared again to its disadvantage with a golden past. The weighty moral content of the scene suggests that regeneration is in order, and the direction the comedy will take. It would not have been surprising if it had been written throughout in couplets, such as appear in the last speech and sporadically just before it. There is pathos in Adam's rueful words about taking to the road at *fourscore,* and performers should defer to the playwright's obvious regard for this *good old man* (56). To portray him as ludicrously senile, on the principle that every play must have its Polonius, is a detestable piece of blotting. (A tradition, none too reliable, maintains that Shakespeare played this part himself.)

II, iv

Rosalind as 'Ganymede,' Celia as 'Aliena,' and Touchstone as himself arrive weary at Arden, where there appear to be pasturelands as well as trees. They overhear the young shepherd Silvius tell the old shepherd Corin of his love for disdainful Phebe; and Rosalind is put in mind of her own love-longings for Orlando. They ask Corin if he can supply them food and shelter, and learn that he is only the hireling of another man, whose cottage, flocks, and pastures are up for sale. When they offer to make the purchase themselves and retain Corin as their shepherd, they are led off to view the holding.

1-16 The runaways have made it, a little the worse for wear, so that Rosalind must look out for their morale. She speaks partly for herself, partly for 'Ganymede,' whose masculine courage she must emulate. Each of her companions is given a speech or two in character (and in prose) before natives step into view. **17-58** They step out of the literary pastoral-tradition, where shepherds are chronically in love, of exquisite sensibility, and speak a dialect as poetic as their names. Observe the patterned speech of Silvius, the three unrimed couplets, each followed by a half-line, *Thou hast not loved* (31-39), the last patly illustrated by his *passionate* exit. Rosalind and Touchstone, each after kind, is touched, so that *love* sounds a three-note chime. Touchstone's *Jane Smile,* with her chapped hands, is a less ethereal example of rural mistress than Silvius's Phebe, and there is more than a hint in the language that Touchstone's designs upon her were not ethereal either. Rosalind's love must be more in the ideal fashion of Silvius's, but it is odd, if the issue were clear, that she should say so in a jingle (55-56). **59-65** There is something strange about this Forest of Arden. In the scenes back in 'civilization' there was a reasonably plausible consistency in the treatment of character and event. Here, experience has an amiably schizoid quality, with plausible and implausible consorting comfortably together. Touchstone's arrogant hail to one whom he deems even lower in the social scale than himself, and Rosalind's engaging embarrassment over his rude snobbery, are as natural as can be. But Corin, who a moment before was a conventional pastoral shepherd (whom love ere now had drawn into a *thousand* acts ridiculous) suddenly changes into an authentic old countryman, humble and kindly, who speaks with a lovely simplicity (70-95). Like the wood outside Athens, this one seems enchanted too, but the dreams are the dreams of daytime.

II, v

Amiens sings 'Under the greenwood tree' and, for reasons of his own, Jaques asks for more. As they spread for the Duke's evening banquet, Amiens sings again, with all joining in the chorus. Jaques produces a parody of the song, and Amiens sings this too, before going to summon the Duke.

1-7, 33-39 We are grateful to Jaques, whatever his motives, for persuading Amiens to give us the second *stanzo*. It is a festive song, just right for a woodland feast, and we are reminded of the line of light operas sired by this play. Fine solo and choral singing in a comradely atmosphere has its own undeniable appeal, and the scene would justify itself simply as a musical interlude. But it also adds a dimension to this forest world. Observe that the words of the song repeat, in their own way, the message of the Duke (II, i, 1-17), so that we have been twice greeted in Arden by the idea of triumphant contentment, but now the idea is challenged.   **8-55** The Jaques we met 'in absentia,' sobbing over the fate of the stag and the inhumanity of man, struck us as a doleful sentimentalist. Either we were mistaken, or he himself has changed. Here he seems truculent and carping, a determined cynic—Diogenes with a parody up his sleeve. A moment ago we heard Touchstone say *now am I in Arden, the more fool I* (II, iv, 14). Now it is Jaques who says the same thing, in express opposition to the official sentiment of the place. The fool and the eccentric see eye to eye, and see what common sense tells us is true—that the efficacy of retreat into the great open spaces is a lot of sentimental nonsense. At least our common sense would tell us so if the issue came to debate. But there is no debating here. No one contradicted Touchstone, and no one contradicts Jaques. Instead, the same singer who sang of the joys of the forest-life happily sings the parody. This has the odd effect of keeping the issue open. Either the Duke and his followers are aware of some truth denied the dissenters, or they know the value of pretense. Perhaps this is the secret wisdom of Arden, a stronghold of passive resistance to disillusion.

II, vi

Adam, faint with hunger and fatigue, tells Orlando to go on alone. Orlando speaks words of cheer, and promises to find food somewhere in this forest to which they have wandered. He bears the old man to shelter before leaving for his search.

1-16 There is no condescension in Orlando's speech, but such eager assurances as are designed to put heart into the old and ill. Toward its end, the broken continuity indicates the pauses for action as he ministers to his servant. His actions must not be viewed casually. A young aristocrat carrying an old servitor to shelter is a symbol which would have had a strong ethical and emotional impact.

II, vii

At the woodland repast of the Duke and his following, Jaques describes with high glee his meeting with a fool in the forest, and he begs for a motley coat so that he may rail upon the times. When the Duke questions his motives, he defends the satiric mode. Orlando breaks in upon them with drawn sword, demanding a share of the food, but he relaxes his posture when the Duke addresses him kindly. He goes to bring Adam to the feast, and returns with the old man in his arms just as Jaques is concluding a survey of the seven ages of man. All sit to the repast, and Amiens sings another song. The scene ends with the Duke proffering permanent refuge to this young son and this former servant of his onetime friend, Sir Rowland de Boys.

1-11 For one alluded to in such terms—*nowhere . . . like a man* and *compact of jars* (2-5)—Jacques seems to have a strange fascination for the Duke. **12-43** The Touchstone whom Jaques describes bears small resemblance to the Touchstone we have met; he has undergone a Forest-change and gained a languid elegance as he poses for this brilliantly comic picture of utter boredom and futility. Jaques himself, now almost hysterically elated, keeps changing before our eyes. When we first heard of him, he was anguished, and when we first saw him, he was bitter. His moods are as motley as Touchstone's coat, and he has been virtually functioning as the Duke's jester before he requests the role. There is a chameleon quality about Jaques and Touchstone, their coloration exchangeable, so that it is hard to decide which if either is the 'touchstone' of what. The season in Arden appears to be a mixture of autumn, winter, spring, summer; and between them Touchstone and Jaques manage to mix up the spirit of the boxing days with the spirit of lent. **44-87** In two lengthy and nicely-turned speeches Jaques defends the integrity of satire. The burden of his discourses—'If the shoe fits, wear it'—is the standard apology of the satirists of the day. Between his speeches comes the Duke's 'ad hominem' charge that the satirist is a warped and corrupted man, with an affinity for the vices he castigates. The issue is not resolved. The Duke is an important and incisive speaker, but Jaques is permitted to speak longest and last. **88-109** If the question is the relative powers of persuasion of vinegar and honey, the latter wins the palm in the action. As Orlando, always the tall-man-of-his-hands, bursts pugnaciously upon them, it is the Duke's mild courtesy which disarms him, not Jaques' witty sarcasms. **109-26** Orlando's inventory of those influences which account for humane action—gratitude for one's own well-being, religious teaching, good example—is repeated by the Duke so as to receive a ceremonial endorsement. The 'conventional' morality here has been used as a butt of Shavian wit, but there is nothing logically wrong with the liturgy. Orlando thinks that *all things had been savage here* (107), and he recognizes that things cease to be savage because of civilizing influences; he is mindful of the ultimate reasons why he will be eating instead of eaten. **127-66** The Duke's comment, as

Orlando goes off to fetch Adam is cheerful in intent; he is telling
the company that relatively they are not *unhappy* (unlucky). Jaques' extension of his metaphor of the theatre into *All the world's a
stage* . . . (139-66) is different in spirit. It contains seven miniature portraits, sharp, animated, credible, the amount of detail increasing from one to the next, but all miracles of condensation. The
data is highly selective: the babe is *mewling* and *puking* (not smiling), the child *creeping* to school (not running to play), and at no
point is man seen to advantage. Although in the first five ages, he
grows a little more imposing, in the last two, after the deft punctuating clause *And so he plays his part,* he suffers a devastating
fall. Like the scorpion, Jaques' summation bears its sting in its tail:
the crown of life is—senility! And yet generations of youngsters
speaking their 'memory pieces' have cheerfully chirped out *Sans
teeth, sans eyes, sans taste, sans everything;* and, in productions, the
lines are often spoken like a benediction. How can we account for
this oddity? In its substance the speech denigrates life, in spite of
the few relieving touches, like the schoolboy's *shining* (fresh-
scrubbed) *morning face,* but the tone of the speaker is not that of
the malicious debunker; rather it is sympathetic, regretful, a little
nostalgic. The words say one thing, the 'tune' something a trifle
different, and as an act of faith we attend to the tune. The speech
is a wonderful literary feat.   **167-200** Although we should
feel grateful for it, we should also feel grateful for the stage direction following: *Enter Orlando, with Adam.* Orlando will soon be
composing sonnets to his mistress's eyebrow, and Adam is approaching Jaques' seventh age; indeed at the moment his life has
come full cycle for he is resting in another's arms as at the beginning. But Orlando and Adam together are something different from
Orlando and Adam apart, and different as individuals than as types.
And which of Jaques' capsulated 'ages' fits this gentle and generous
Duke? The tableau formed by these three is a silent commentary
upon the preceding speech, for the nuances in Shakespearean drama
are not confined to the words. For a moment we thought we were
hearing something bravely definitive about the vanity of human
life, but now we are less sure. There is ambiguity even in the
concluding song—a wintry companion to the one sung before the

banquet began. After Orlando, Adam, and the Duke have begun acting as if gratitude, friendship, and love are potent realities, the song voices serious doubts. Or does it? *Most friendship is faining, most loving mere folly* (181); but 'Most' is not 'all,' as Celia would say, and little candles throw their lights far. Never have such melancholy verses been followed by such rollicking choruses.

III, i

Duke Frederick orders Oliver to set out and seek his brother while his house and lands are held in bail. If Orlando is not produced within a year, Oliver will lose everything.

1-18   We glimpse the court again, like a receding coastal point. The episode might easily have been included in II, ii, but it is split off for structural reasons (see above, p. 81): we are reminded that there is such a place as the court, that the exodus of characters has been noticed, and that something is being done about it. (This is anticipating, but observe that preparation is made for Oliver's appearance in Arden, but not for the Duke's warlike approach. Threat of invasion would not suit the atmosphere of the place.)

III, ii

Orlando adorns the trees with verses in praise of Rosalind. Touchstone and Corin debate the rival claims of court and country life. When Rosalind reads aloud a sample of the poetry, Touchstone extemporizes a parody. Celia reads another sample, and after impish delay, tells Rosalind that the poet is her Orlando. The two step back to witness an encounter between him and Jaques, demonstrating the antipathy of a person-in-love and a person-out-of-love. Rosalind, retaining her identity as 'Ganymede,' engages Orlando in conversation, and offers to cure him of love by posing as his loved-one and tormenting him with a woman's whims. He has no wish to be cured, but welcomes the chance to unburden his heart by addressing this youth as 'Rosalind.'

1-10 Orlando's speech is a sonnet lacking the first quatrain (no doubt spoken before his entrance) and a better lyric than any he is able to get on paper; perhaps he should dictate his poetry. He has seen so little of Rosalind that the second of the qualities he attributes to her, *The fair, the chaste, and unexpressive she* (10) must be known to him through pure intuition. We soon learn that he is now outfitted neatly as one of the Duke's foresters, so that we must visualize him as an amalgam of Petrarchan love-lyricist and husky youth in Kendal green. At least one of the trees upon which he pins his verses is a palm (167), which here seems able to survive the *icy fang* of winter as readily as the *gnarled oak*. Since in Arden the glades of Arcadia are superimposed upon Sherwood Forest, and tropical flora and fauna (presently we shall hear of a *lioness*) flourish in France, Orlando can be two selves with perfect propriety.

11-82 There is an Alice-in-Wonderland inconclusiveness about this debate. After it is over, Corin might justly feel like a Kafka victim, wondering just what kind of guilt he has incurred, but luckily his nerves are sound. In one of his Sonnets Shakespeare speaks sadly of 'simple truth miscalled simplicity,' but the miscalling proves a jolly business when done by a professional simpleton. Frivolousness is Touchstone's métier, and his air of tolerant superiority is as engaging as Corin's innocence. Although handicapped by his sincerity, as any *natural philosopher* (30) is bound to be in a skirmish with a wit and a punster, Corin manages to get his view of life on record, unforgettably so (69-73), and Touchstone's persiflage sounds no more damaging than the crackling of thorns under a pot.

83-117 Once having found his rime, Orlando has stuck to it, and to his jog-trot meter (*the right butterwomen's rank to market*). Touchstone is right in his critical judgment, but his parody, reducing love to lust and Rosalind to a trollop, turns Orlando's idealism inside out, and merits Rosalind's rebuke. But, as usual in this least cynical of all plays, the cynic is given the last word.   **118-239** This second poem, achieving a quite respectable mediocrity, must have been composed after Orlando had acquired the knack of it. Perhaps Rosalind would like it better if she had not already been *berymed* like an *Irish rat* (169), or if she knew who the author

was. When she is told, her first words are *Alas the day! What shall
I do with my doublet and hose?* (208) What she does is keep them
on, thus remaining incognito both to the lover she has been longing
for and the father she has come to Arden to seek. Fortunately there
is no attempt to rationalize this irrational behavior. To do so would
be like trying to explain why palm trees are growing in this forest,
or who is tending to Silvius's and Phebe's sheep. The clock has been
stopped, the laws of logic suspended, and the dwellers in Arden
freed from the obligation to do anything but what is enjoyable.
Still, and this makes it unique, the play never labels itself 'fantasy,'
thus apologizing for its devices, and its characters never become
marionettes—but only pose as marionettes. One of the minor triumphs among them is Celia. In the constant presence of the witty,
ardent, and magnetic Rosalind, she might have easily lost identity
and dwindled to a cipher. Instead she remains quite distinct, alternately teasing and lecturing the friend in whose love-affair she
is so whole-heartedly interested. Since there is no malice or envy
in this interest, she can be as outspoken as she pleases. Her remark
that she has found Orlando under a tree *like a dropped acorn* (224)
is a sample of her piquant conversational style.   **240-81** A
moment ago Goodman Kersey-woolen encountered Sir Taffeta, and
now *Signior Love* encounters *Monsieur Melancholy*. Orlando is the
more hostile of the two, shying away as if he feared Jaques' malady
to be catching. The dialogue lacks the 'articulated' style of real
communication (see above, p. 45) since the incompatibility of this
pair is absolute; their speeches are pot-shots exchanged across a
chasm. These interpolated encounters (Corin-Touchstone, Jaques-
Orlando) provide time for Orlando's poems to be found, identified
with their author, and serve as a means of bringing the lovers face
to face, but they are rounded off as self-sufficient 'skits.' Through
the remainder of the play similar encounters between substance and
shadow (not always easily distinguishable) provide the true center
of interest, with the plot-action slipped into the interstices. This
fragmented dramatic technique resembles impressionistic painting,
and renders commentary upon separate details somewhat irrelevant. The succession of impromptu charades, comic eclogues, musical interludes, wit-skirmishes, suggests an extemporal allegory, a

parade of the seven-or-so-not-so-deadly-attitudes, a whimsical dance of love and life. Its proper lighting is dappled sunlight, and it could be set nowhere in the world but the Forest of Arden. **282-408** Rosalind's disguise as a *saucy lackey* (282) lets her express the misgivings about love and marriage which she is intelligent enough to have but healthy-spirited enough to disregard. Her mind says one thing, her heart another, and like the play as a whole, she is unromantically romantic. Orlando is reduced to the role of 'straight man' as he converses with this volatile youth who dwells on the skirts of Arden *like fringe upon a petticoat* (319), but he is passing a kind of test. His dogged refusal to escape the pangs of love—*I would not be cured, youth* (398)—although addressed to 'Ganymede' must sound sweet in the ears of Rosalind.

III, iii

Touchstone pays court to the country-maid Audrey while Jaques stands gloomily by. A forest wedding is about to take place, with Sir Oliver Mar-text officiating. Jaques steps forth to give the bride away, then persuades Touchstone to postpone the ceremony until it can be more properly performed.

1-94 The courtship of ideal lovers now in process casts this antic shadow—a travesty in action, like Touchstone's travesty of Orlando's love-lyric. Audrey is available and willing; and Touchstone, who *hath his desires* (70), is resigned. Any action involving Touchstone is bound to be subversive, and his remarks upon compatibility, poetry, chastity (*honesty*), fidelity, and the ultimate sanctions of marriage (69-71) are saturnalian in spirit. In contrast Jaques' spirit is saturnine; he here appears as primly censorious, and a stickler for propriety. Audrey, whose wit and beauty may leave something to be desired, lays stress on moral character: her question about poetry—*Is it honest in deed and word? Is it a true thing?* (14)—is as priceless as Touchstone's reply (16-17). Arden, we observe, is suddenly provided with a nearby village and *vicar*. Are his services rejected because of some Puritan taint? or because marriages in comedy should be reserved for the last scene? Poor proud Oliver

Mar-text—we remember him always, although he is only given three speeches and then elbowed into oblivion.

III, iv

To Rosalind's distress, Orlando has failed to keep an appointment, and she and Celia discuss his truancy. Corin comes to invite them to witness a meeting between Silvius and the scornful Phebe.

1-54 In tantalizing Rosalind, Celia displays her usual deftness in the use of metaphor. The prose dialogue of this play sparkles with splintered poetry. Observe that Corin reverts to his 'pastoral' role whenever he is associated with Silvius and Phebe: his terms are not countrified as he invites the girls to see *the pageant truly played* (47).

III, v

As Silvius pleads for gentler treatment, Phebe makes mock of his devotion. Rosalind steps forth and indignantly upbraids her, giving short shrift to her alleged beauty and charm. The tirade succeeds only in arousing Phebe's interest in the one who utters it, and when Rosalind and Celia have left, she employs Silvius to convey a 'taunting' letter to the scolding 'Ganymede.'

1-138 Phebe's manner is wanton and irritating as she pecks away at Silvius's metaphors, ignoring the spirit in her literal interpretation (8-27). It is a small offense, but it will serve. Since Silvius is in love, and is the only eligible shepherd in view, Phebe seems to personify coy fastidiousness; and all male hearts respond as Rosalind pitches into her (8-27). A woman should indeed *thank heaven fasting for a good man's love;* it is a regular manifesto.

IV, i

Jaques defines the nature of his melancholy to Rosalind—who is unimpressed. She chides Orlando for coming late, then plays the part of skeptical mistress, subjecting his sentiments to stiff strokes of common sense. However, she acts out a marriage ceremony with him with Celia serving as 'priest,' and when he has left to attend upon the Duke, she admits how 'many fathom deep' she is in love.

1-201 Rosalind proves as hostile to Jaques as did Orlando—they are young growth resistant to frost. Our impression that Jaques alters in mood from scene to scene is confirmed by his own diagnosis: his is an eclectic melancholy, *compounded of many simples, extracted from many objects* (15). What follows is a strange love-scene, with its haunting, *Men have died from time to time, and worms have eaten them, but not for love* (96-98). More critics have fallen in love with Rosalind than with any other of Shakespeare's heroines, and the reason is fairly clear. She is witty, warm, and presumably beautiful, but, further than that, she seems the perfect risk as a wife, since her capacity for love is so great that it has survived disillusionment in advance. In spite of the preposterous masquerade, Orlando and Rosalind remain convincing as lovers in the scenes where the masquerade is maintained—he a little subdued, hang-dog, put-upon, as young lovers are bound to be; she a little desperate, for all her high-larking spirits, as one who can only pretend that her soul remains her own.

IV, ii

The 'foresters' have killed a deer, and at Jaques' suggestion march off to present it to the Duke, singing a song of the 'lusty horn.'

1-18 We have not had foresters or a song for some time, and the scene needs no further justification. With horned beasts on the premises, and marriages in the making, a cuckoldry song was inevitable. It does not reflect upon the characters of Rosalind, Celia, Phebe, or even Audrey.

IV, iii

Apologetically, Silvius delivers Phebe's letter, supposing it to consist of insults. When it proves to be a protestation of love for

'Ganymede,' the receiver rebukes Silvius for his infatuation, and returns an answer to Phebe that her love will be reciprocated only when Silvius consents to act as her intercessor. Oliver now appears bearing a blood-stained handkerchief and a message from Orlando. The latter has been wounded by a lioness in rescuing Oliver from death, thus returning good for his brother's evil. Oliver is now penitent, and he and Celia minister to Rosalind, who has fainted upon hearing of Orlando's own narrow escape. They conduct her home, her jauntiness all wilted away.

1-181 Silvius has been too tame a lover. Phebe's emotions have been thawed by 'Ganymede's' fire, and need only the proper channeling. The idea of love-congealed, of frozen immobility awaiting a spring thaw, reminds us of Romeo and Rosaline, of Orsino and Olivia (*Twelfth Night*). (In all three plays the thawing agent is an ardent young girl.) An air of the miraculous attends Oliver's sudden appearance as a completely reformed man. His reformation borrows a semi-mystical character from the description of the circumstances (99-121, 128-33). He has been awakened from *miserable slumber* after Orlando has resisted the temptation to return evil for evil. The brightly-enameled image of the *green and gilded snake* which retreats at Orlando's approach, and of the *sucked and hungry lioness* which dies at Orlando's hands, suggest the allegorical illumination of ancient manuscripts. If anything were needed to endear Rosalind to us, it would be the collapse of her bravado when she sees Orlando's blood: *I would I were at home* (162).

V, i

Touchstone comforts Audrey, who sees no reason why their nuptials should have been interrupted. He then deals with William, her erstwhile suitor, treating the country swain to a display of courtly patronage and courtly swashbuckling.

1-60 William is an inoffensive youth although, like Silvius, a little wanting in fire. Still, better men than he might quail before Touchstone's invincible superciliousness. This jester, among other things, is a kind of 'fetch.' He is a living parody of the mannerisms which prevail in the effete courtly circles he loves to flout.

V, ii

Orlando learns that his brother Oliver has fallen in love with the shepherdess 'Aliena' (Celia), and the two wish to marry at once. Oliver will share her humble lot, and Orlando may take possession of the de Boys estates. Rosalind promises Orlando that he himself may marry on the morrow, not in another mock-ceremony but in a true one with his actual mistress, who will be brought hither by magical aids. Silvius and Phebe are also promised a resolution of their problem: 'Ganymede' will marry Phebe or never marry any woman, and yet Silvius will be satisfied. The principals in these crossed love-affairs chant out a litany of love, which Rosalind abruptly terminates with a repetition of assurances that all will be properly paired off.

1-117 *Is't possible . . . ?* asks Orlando. It must be, since it has happened. What would be *impossible* would be for the eminently marriageable Celia to finish the course unclaimed. The scene contains another and more elaborate passage of schematized repetition (see above, II, viii, 109-26), this time a lovers' creed and testament, both poetic and absurd. It dissolves in Rosalind's laughter, so that the effect, like so much else in this play, is spicy-sweet, not cloying.

V, iii

Touchstone gives Audrey the joyous tidings that they, too, will be married on the morrow; then sits between two pages of the Duke and joins them in singing 'It was a lover and his lass.'

1-40 As the two little boys appear from nowhere, and perch on either side of this antic figure (who surely must be long and lean), and as the three voices join in this golden catch, we have a sense

of the 'rightness' of the whole design—an unpremeditated rightness, as hard to describe as a peal of bells or the fragrance of a
garden.

V, iv

Duke Senior will willingly accept Orlando as his son-in-law if
'Ganymede' is able to produce Rosalind as promised. Still posing
as this masterful youth, Rosalind repeats her assurances, and makes
certain that Phebe will accept Silvius if she decides not to wed
'Ganymede.' She and Celia retire, and Touchstone leads in Audrey
to make up another couple in the impending nuptials. Prompted by
Jaques, Touchstone expatiates upon the 'seventh cause' in the code
of the duello. Rosalind and Celia return in their own proper forms,
and to tne sound of soft music, and an Epithalamion by Hymen,
the four couples link hands, all mysteries resolved and all obtacles
removed. Even Phebe seems contented—Silvius will do, now that
'Ganymede' is no more. At this juncture another brother of Orlando
and Oliver appears on the scene, with news that Duke Frederick
has abandoned plans to invade the Forest of Arden; instead he has
been converted to the religious life and has abdicated the Dukedom
in favor of its rightful ruler. All may now return to their inherit-
ances. Jaques pronounces a benediction upon the fortunate ones,
but withdraws from the celebration; he will join Duke Frederick
and commune with the convertite. Duke Senior leads off the couples
in a dance, and Rosalind speaks the Epilogue.

1-192 Despite the somewhat offhand methods used in the tying
of it, a quite respectable knot is available for untying in this conclusion, and we have a comforting sense of accomplishment.
Everyone is enlightened, united, reformed, reinstated, and, so far
as possible, married. True to themselves, Touchstone, after pressing in with the *country copulatives* (53), gives a fine display of
jesting virtuosity, and Jaques retires to enjoy his melancholy in
peace. Hymen's hymn to that *blessed bond of board and bed* which
peoples every town (135-40) is the properly decorous sequel to
Touchstone's song of the *lover and his lass* in the vernal fields of

rye (V, iii, 15-32). Thus ends a play which leaves the critical commentator always an awkward step in the rear. Its moods, sentiments, mockeries, perceptions form patterns as bright, translucent, shifting, and apparently accidental as those in a kaleidoscope. In the Epilogue Rosalind proceeds unscrupulously to coerce a display of audience approval with her charm. The play as a whole coerces us with its charm. What appears to be a medley, a structure of spontaneous improvisation, cannot be evaluated by objective standards, and we may well speak of the artistic level of this play as Orlando speaks of Rosalind's stature—*just as high as my heart* (III, ii, 258). One may say with Jaques that this is but a *pretty answer,* or, indeed, that *As You Like It* is but a pretty play. However, it does something which mere prettiness could never do. It makes the world seem young. It sweetens the imagination.

5

Julius Caesar

:

I, i

F L A V I U S and Marullus, custodians of popular rights, challenge a cluster of Roman artisans for idling on a working-day. Their Cobbler leader frivolously replies and says that they are out to celebrate Caesar's triumph. When Marullus upbraids them for honoring the slayer of Pompey, their former idol, and Flavius bids them mourn, they shamefacedly disperse. The two tribunes go to strip Caesar's trophies from the statues which have been decked for the Feast of the Lupercal. They must work upon the people to check Caesar's rise to absolute power.

1-9 The peremptory tones of their own officers reduce these *commoners* to the rank of menials. **10-31** Their spokesman is amiably clownish in his verbose first speech and subsequent pun-

ning (*sole*-soul, *out*-out-worn, *awl-*'ole-hole, *withal*-with 'ole),
which is comical but impudent and untimely. He is not all-clown, a
vein of shrewdness and craft-pride mingling with his facetiousness,
but we are bound to look patronizingly upon this representative of
the 'people.'   **32-55**   Marullus is a Roman office-holder, hence
a master of reverberating oratory. Three rhetorical questions,
graduated in length, open his speech, followed by five abusive
epithets in a parallel series (*You . . . you . . . you . . . you
. . . you . . .*). His whole tirade is rhetorically adroit. The name
Pompey is thrice repeated, the name *Caesar* not dignified with mention. In the description of the triumphs of Pompey, the periods are
long and rolling, the imagery epic; in the allusion to the present
occasion, they are short, the phrasing contemptuously mundane,
with the *And do you now . . . ?* repeated like a rhythmic whip-
lash. At the same time that the speech is subduing the craftsmen, it
is summoning up Rome for us, with such words as *conquest, tribu-
taries, chariot wheels, Tiber* with *concave shores*. (The *chimney-
pots* have strayed hither from a more northerly capital.)   **56-62**
Flavius shifts the key as he substitutes *good countrymen* for *You
blocks, you stones . . .* , and invites them to shed their tears. It is
when he speaks thus that they visibly respond, moving off in silent
dejection. There is a trace of smugness in his comment that *basest
mettle* can be *moved* (61). Will he one day wish that popular emotions were less easy to manipulate?   **63-75**   The speech of
the tribunes ceases to be oratorical when they address each other,
but it remains incisive, masculine, 'Roman'—the style simple and
open. There may be a slight suggestion of ill-omened sacrilege in
the decision to undeck the images. (*May we do so?*) The concluding lines state the political issue in moderate terms—Roman liber-
ties will survive if Caesar flies *an ordinary pitch*—but the metaphor
of the *growing feathers* plucked from the *wing* suggest inevitably
the fall of an Icarus to his death.

I, ii

Music sounds as a procession moves toward the games of the
Lupercal, with Caesar at its head, the tribunes to the rear. Antony,

who is dressed to run the ceremonial course, is reminded by Caesar to touch his wife Calphurnia in the fashion prescribed by the elders as a cure for sterility. When the shrill cry of a Soothsayer bids him beware the ides of March, he calls the man a 'dreamer,' and moves on. Brutus and Cassius remain behind speaking of Caesar as shouts echo back from the multitude. Cassius attacks Caesar bitterly, and plays upon Brutus's patriotism and pride in an attempt to enlist him in a plot of resistance. The procession returns, its members visibly perturbed, and Caesar pauses to voice suspicion of Cassius and his kind. In response to a question from Brutus, Casca disdainfully describes what has occurred. The people have expressed approval of Caesar's refusal of a crown, thrice offered him by Antony, and in chagrin the mighty man has collapsed in a fit of the falling sickness, then made a histrionic bid for sympathy. Casca accepts Cassius's invitation to dinner, and Brutus proposes that he and Cassius confer again. When alone, Cassius exults. Brutus can be worked upon, in spite of his aloof nobility. Forged letters will be strewn in his way, glancing at Caesar's 'ambition' and his own high standing in Rome.

1-24 (Caesar's was the most imposing name in history. For centuries it had moved the imagination of men—in its association with power and glory, and also with tragic disaster and the vanity of human wishes. One would suppose that a paralyzing self-consciousness would afflict anyone introducing this character in his play. Who can create Caesar? But Elizabethan playwrights seem to have felt at ease among the illustrious, and Shakespeare creates his Caesar without the slightest sign of strain, as if he was saying to himself, 'One need only set things down the way they must have been.' The small pomp in the scene is Roman pomp, not Shakespearean. A moment before he had depicted a Roman Cobbler in twenty-four lines. He now depicts a Roman conqueror in precisely the same number—and the figure is fixed indelibly in our minds.) The lines contain not a single metaphor, and their diction is predominately monosyllabic. There are twenty-one brief speeches, eleven of them including the first and last Caesar's, the other ten divided among five speakers. By such measurable devices is the dictatorial impression conveyed. He says one word, *Calphurnia*. Then comes *Peace, ho! Caesar speaks,* and the music stops. (Twice the voice of Caesar stops the music.) He repeats, *Calphurnia*. Then comes *Here, my lord,* as if a subaltern were snapping to attention. Each of his speeches gets this kind of 'over-response.' Note Antony's *When Caesar says 'Do this,' it is performed* (10). Nearly all his remarks are demands for information or action, as lacking in social amenity as military commands; he uses ten verbs in the imperative mode. But the impression of power is subtly undercut by the very excess of the evidence, and by the taint of sycophancy in the air. Caesar is too intent upon his own ascendancy (speaking of himself in the third person), too unrelaxed and wary (instantly attentive to an off-pitch voice in the throng), and too evidently the captive of his own wishes (deferring to what the *elders say* about cures for sterility, but dismissing the foreboding soothsayer as a mere *dreamer*). He is imposing enough, but the laughter of the gods is faintly audible. Simple though they are, the lines are dramatic poetry of the highest order, a superb example of imaginative writing.   **25-89** Unlike Casca, Antony, and even Cassius, Brutus has not been heard as one of the strings vibrating at Caesar's touch, and his withdrawal from the procession is a significant act. He has no taste for this occasion, and although he avoids political reference as he contrasts himself with Antony, and speaks of being *with himself at war* (46), it becomes clear that the abstraction he describes stems from concern over Caesar's dominance. Observe that he withdraws voluntarily, not at Cassius's instigation, and that it is the shouting off-stage that pierces his reserve, not Cassius's slighting allusions to *immortal Caesar* and the *age's yoke*. The way Cassius seizes upon his remark that he *fears* the people are making Caesar king underscores its inadvertence and hence the cast of his private meditations. Brutus is presented to us as a courteous, reticent, perhaps cautious man, devoted to personal *honor* and the *general good* (85), feeling no animus to Caesar—*yet I love him well* (82)—but disturbed by the threat of monarchy.   **90-177** We are attracted by the graphic vitality of Cassius's words, their frank vehemence, but they obviously express a grudge—arising from a sense of rivalry and injured self-love. He seems to feel that greatness is measurable in terms of physical stamina, since he mentions no other quality. He is a pure empiricist, denying any role to destiny (140-41), and his incredulous exclamations— *Upon what meat doth this our Caesar feed . . . ?* (149)—although effective, are nevertheless obtuse. He assumes that Brutus's attitudes are like his own, and, addressing a man of principle, never mentions ethical principles. How well does he know this man? How well does he know himself? Brutus's response (162-75) is almost a rebuke, proclaiming his own commitment to rational deliberation. The excessively categorical style and the self-righteousness of tone are not engaging, and we begin to suspect that the speaker's very judiciousness is slightly alloyed with pride.   **178-214** As the procession returns, Brutus's descriptive speech refines upon and supplements such visible signs of unease as the actors would be able to project. He does not speak well of Cicero (a rival in moral prestige?) although we would expect him to be well-disposed to such a man. Antony's few words, in contrast, are engagingly hearty and free from gall, confirming the allusions to him as a cheer-loving extrovert. Caesar's analysis of Cassius, of the *lean and hungry look* (194-210), serves both as dramatic foreshadowing and evidence of the speaker's present irritation and general shrewdness. Its accuracy has been demonstrated in advance, but its method is almost comically pragmatic, the equation of fat men with safety and thin men with danger reminding us of Cassius's equation of swimming ability with greatness..Caesar continues to over-project, and the juxtaposition of his godlike *for always I am Caesar* (212) with *Come on my right hand, for this ear is deaf* (213) is the most overtly deflationary touch thus far.   **215-84** The description of the demonstration is deflationary to a degree. Observe that the medium shifts to prose as the note of cynicism begins to sound, and that the speaker Casca is converted for the occasion into a *blunt fellow* (292). The proceedings were a hollow show staged to test the temper of the populace, with Antony as stage-manager and Caesar cast in the principal role, improvising his part as circumstances required. Casca's tone of disgust, despite his pose of indifference, represents for us the revulsion of feeling of the natural man against the hypocrisies of public life. Yet this very Casca is caught in the web; we first met him behaving as Caesar's lackey. Note the prophetic quality of his impulse to accept Caesar's offer of his breast to the assassin's knife (264). No one has appeared in a good light. The anti-monarchical demonstration of the populace was, we know, artificially induced (see I, i), and the emotional response to Caesar's ignominious bid for sympathy was maudlin (as represented by the *Alas, good soul!* (270) of the blubbering wenches).   **285-319**   This intimates that Brutus may make common cause with Cassius, whose final remarks, if taken at face value, expose the baseness of his motives. Cassius is saying in effect (307-12) that he would ride in Caesar's band-wagon if he could, and that the guileless Brutus is letting himself be *seduced* into abandoning his own best interests. We have a choice of interpretations. Is the playwright putting his own assessment of the situation in Cassius's mouth? Or, since we are far from sure that Brutus is under his sway, is Cassius being shown as duped by his own cleverness? To a remarkable degree the scene has prefigured the whole play, suggesting the nature of the persons and social forces involved, and establishing an objective viewpoint. There is civil unrest in Rome. The populace will exercise no initiative since it has already lost its spokesmen with the checking of Flavius and Marullus after their momentary success; the latter were themselves less spokesman than watchdogs of the flock. The instincts of the populace are not evil, and may even be good-natured, but this populace is so emotional, ignorant, and malleable as to be fair game for any demagogue. Among the patricians there is a recognized leader (Caesar), but although he shares the frailties of mankind, he is vainglorious, and his overwillingness to lead may pose a threat to freedom, or at least to existing institutions. There is another distinguished man (Brutus) capable of disinterested public service, but he too is only a man, uncertain about his proper role and already slightly tainted by association. Among the forces either opposing or supporting Caesar will appear the specters of vanity and self-interest.

I, iii

Amidst thunder and lightning Casca tells Cicero of the dreadful portents which have filled the night with horror. He meets Cassius, who recklessly welcomes the omens of crisis. Caesar is to be offered a crown by the Senate on the morrow, and Cassius will die before yielding to subjection. When Casca endorses the sentiment, he is invited to join a band of noble Romans who are meeting this night in a plot against Caesar. Cinna comes with a message that the conspirators are waiting at Pompey's Theatre. When he voices the devout wish that Brutus would join them, Cassius gives him additional inflammatory writings to place in Brutus's way. Before the night is over, an attempt will be made to enlist him in the cause.

1 s.d. The thunder and lightning are stage sounds and pyrotechnics, such as were available for natural storms and might here be pressed into service for this unnatural one. On this same night Brutus will see both stars and 'exhalations, whizzing in the air' (a storm of meteors). For the rest, the eerie effect is produced by the descriptive verse. **1-164** The scene has several curious features, one of them typical of Shakespeare's art, the other less so. There is something we may call 'blurred time.' Cicero's question, *Brought you Caesar home?* (1), conveys the impression that this is the night of the day of the Lupercal games, for the simple reason that we are conscious of no other occasion when Caesar has been *away* from home. Our impression is reinforced by the fact that the position of Casca and Brutus in relation to Cassius's schemes is identical now with what it was then. But gradually we are appraised of the fact that this is the eve of the ides of March, so that a month of calendar time has elapsed. Artistically it is a matter of indifference whether the Feast of the Lupercal is a month or a day before the ides of March. In the next scene (this same night) Brutus will prove to have been reading messages dropped in his way for some time, with the Feast conveniently moved back to its proper place. The dramatic advantage of this blurring of time is that it permits Brutus (with Casca) to be won over to the cause at the last possible moment—thus concentrating into one prodigious night and day momentous decisions and momentous events. The other curious feature is too conspicuous to be equally justifiable. There is in Casca not a trace of that *blunt fellow* who described Caesar's rejection of the crown in such strikingly sardonic prose. Here he is the normal, even naïve man, suitably appalled by the prodigies. His present personality is useful, to be sure; he supplies a norm, since he responds as we would respond to the fearful sights and sounds, in contrast with the responses of others. Cicero is determinedly the judicious stoic (33-35); Cassius is the reckless freethinker (45-52) interpreting everything in terms of his own obsession as Cicero has said men do; Brutus, as we shall see, is impervious. The prodigies themselves, picked up at random from Plutarch, are strangely assorted but have one feature in common, their monstrosity or abortiveness: the rain of fire rather than water, the commonplace slave transformed to a fire-brand, the day-haunting owl, the Capitol-haunting lion (which neglects to prey), the quaking earth, the walking dead. All are given a chilling reality by the tone of the speaker and their reported effect upon a huddle of *ghastly women* suddenly conjured into existence (22-24). Note the concluding emphasis, provided by three different speakers, on Brutus's prestige, nobility, and *worth*.

II, i

Brutus in his garden debates with himself the ethics of assassination. Caesar is a potential tyrant, and if he must die, it is for that reason rather than for any present shortcomings. The page Lucius, who has obeyed an order to light a candle in the study, brings yet another missive of instigation against Caesar. He consults the calendar as directed, and reports that this is pre-dawn on the ides of March. Cassius comes with his fellow-conspirators, Casca, Decius, Cinna, Metellus, and Trebonius, whom Brutus welcomes although he is repelled by their furtive air. He consents to join them, but rejects their proposals to swear an oath of resolution, to enlist Cicero, and to slay Antony as well as Caesar, overriding the misgivings of Cassius on the latter point. The assassination will take place at the

Capitol where Caesar expects the Senate to offer him a crown. Decius will play upon his weakness for flattery to make sure that he appears, and all will attend him on his way. Caius Ligarius, who has a grievance against Caesar, will be added to their number. When the delegation leaves, Brutus refrains from disturbing the sleep of his page. Portia joins him and makes an eloquent plea for her right as a woman of honor and faithful wife to share the thoughts that have been troubling him. Moved by her anxiety and worth, Brutus consents to enlighten her. Caius Ligarius comes to see Brutus as directed, in spite of his ill health, and is told that he might join in a great exploit if his health were better. He is ready to ignore his malady in order to join any action led by Brutus, and the two depart to attend upon the death-marked Caesar on this morning of the ides of March.

1-69   Brutus's reference to the stars, and direction to Lucius to light a candle in the study, serve to fix the place (the grounds outside the house) and the time (past midnight). Lucius's various errands provide stage movement, as well as opportunities for Brutus to soliloquize, to receive and read the missive, to learn that this is the ides of March (ominously mentioned in I, ii), and to indulge in his painful reflections just before and during the arrival of the conspirators. Thus, skillful construction serves multiple ends; our eyes have been occupied as we learn of the place, time, and date; and Brutus's frame of mind at the moment of decision has been conveyed to us in artfully partitioned discourse. His soliloquy (10-34) has been criticized for its disregard of political realities, the chaotic state of Roman affairs and Caesar's qualifications as 'man of the hour.' But such criticism is irrelevant, since we are not reading a history of Rome but a work of art levying upon it. The play creates its own frame of reference, and we have not been told that the social situation is hopeless or that Caesar should be regarded as a symbol of order. The only political issue raised is whether a society which has formerly suffered under the rule of kings should again submit itself to kingly rule. Brutus thinks not, because power corrupts, and he abides by this principle with full recognition of the merits of the present candidate for a crown. In short, he is an idealist and not an opportunist. However, the murderous action known as assassination is a form of opportunism, an ill means whatever the end, and the play by disregarding the peculiarities of the Roman situation at the time, raises the universal question of whether ideal ends can be served by opportunistic means. It is the question that has been tearing at Brutus's soul, although he never states it flatly. He *feels* that they cannot, as we see from a host of signs, but he *acts* as if they can. Why does he act so? Because of intellectual confusion? Because of family pride and the flattering regard of fellow patricians pressing upon him through the machinations of Cassius? Or because he heroically sacrifices personal scruples when he finds them in irreconcilable conflict with the public interest, choosing what he honestly believes is the lesser evil although the more repugnant to himself? Observe how the playwright holds the problem in suspension in the early part of the play by processes of cross-cancelation, as he does later in 'motivating' the actions of Hamlet and Macbeth. Brutus says *Since Cassius first did whet me against Caesar* (61), but we witnessed that occasion, and observed that Brutus was ripe for the 'whetting.' And his *It must be by his death* (10) is the first actual mention of assassination in the play. Human beings are complex, and Shakespeare declines to oversimplify, discouraging us from supplying pat answers to the question of motive, or any answer at all until all the evidence is in. Observe that in Brutus's reflective presence the disturbances of the night persist only in muted form. (Lucius notices none.) Brutus is a rational man and indifferent to omens; in fact he reads by them! (45) His devotion to reason bars him from the passionate utterance which commands sympathy, and he may often seem cold; however the words wrung from him after the knocking at the gate (61-69) reach home to us. The central image of the inner insurrection, the occurrence of such words as *dreadful, phantasma, hideous,* and the 'm' and 'n' sounds which predominate suggest murmurings from tortured depths. **70-228** This is a fascinating meeting, as Brutus touches pitch and struggles to remain undefiled. The sight of conspiracy disgusts him (77-85), and he tries to ennoble the proceedings by condemning the proposed oath, with its suggestion of superstition and fears, and by invoking in its place the binding force of high moral and political aims (114-40). (Brutus employs emotional oratory on the one occasion when its practical value is dubious.) He verbalizes the assassination into a *sacrifice* and intervenes for Antony, whom he wishfully transforms into an inconsiderable trifler. As the council progresses, he begins to assume the proportions of a dictator himself, on the moral plane, and, amazingly, we catch a faint scent of that sycophancy which tainted the air about Caesar. The conspirators begin to reverse themselves like yes-men, as when Casca says, *Let us not leave him* (Cicero) *out* (143), and then *Indeed he is not fit* (153) when Brutus dismisses Cicero with a flick of the wrist. Cassius completely loses the initiative, and gains somewhat in our estimation by refusing to wrangle in spite of his misgivings. Brutus entered this council with a shudder of revulsion at the need of conspiracy to hide its hideousness in *smiles and affability* (82) but ends it with politic injunctions to the conspirators to *look fresh and merrily* (224). How sadly ironical this is, in its recognition of the vulnerability of the armor of human virtue! **229-334** For Brutus is *truly* a virtuous man. He is consistently kind to his boy, an exception to the rule that no man is a hero to his valet. He is a solicitous husband (234-36), with his own nobility reflected in the nobility of his wife. The long interview with her could only have been designed to authenticate, by opening a curtain on his domestic life, the reputation for virtue won by his public behavior. Whatever its limitations, the quality of Brutus is a fine and powerful thing. It seems to work like a miracle upon Caius Ligarius, whose display of absolute trust is both comic and touching. (Observe that, in the interest of economy, we are expected to take the word for the deed, so far as Brutus's confiding his secret to Portia is concerned. She later proves to know it although he is given no chance to tell it.)

II, ii

Caesar rises after the night of ill omen and demands a report from his augurs. Calphurnia, who has dreamed of his bleeding statue, asks him not to go to the Capitol, but he boasts of his courage and indifference to death, as he resists her pleas, and refuses to accept as sinister the report that the entrails of the sacrificial offering lacked a heart. He then consents to remain at home to humor her, but reverses the decision when Decius appears, puts a favorable construction on Calphurnia's dream, and works upon his vanity and ambition for a crown. Brutus and the other conspirators (except Cassius) arrive to accompany him, as do Antony and the senator Publius. Caesar greets them all as friends, and proposes to drink with them before setting forth. Brutus speaks a regretful aside about Caesar's confidence in their friendship.

1-129 In successive speeches Caesar appears at his great-hearted best (32-37) and at his vainglorious worst (41-48). His physical infirmities, his eclectic credulity, his susceptibility to flattery, and, above all, his vanity and arrogance have been unsparingly stressed. (He even vacillates arrogantly.) Yet the portrait never becomes a travesty. The playwright could have observed all of the traits here portrayed in the one ruler he knew (Elizabeth Tudor), yet realized that she was great in spite of them. Caesar is afflicted by the malady of inordinate pride, his wisdom *consumed in confidence* (49), but there is no suggestion that he is a mere braggart, with nothing to be proud about. It is not a malicious or 'debunking' portrait, but a dramatically useful one, since Caesar epitomizes the pride that goes before a fall. His defects serve to make him more credible as a human being, at the same time that they remind us of the extent to which he has lost his sense of proportion. We are in the strategic position of being much better aware of his mere human status than he is.

II, iii

Artemidorus reads his letter of warning against the conspirators, whose names he lists; then he finds a stand where he can deliver it to Caesar as he passes by.

1-16 We are told neither who Artemidorus is, nor how he came by his information. Such facts are superfluous, in view of the 'ad hoc' function of the scene. It introduces an element of suspense, demonstrating that the success of the conspiracy hangs upon a thread.

II, iv

Tormented by anxiety for her husband's well-being, Portia wishes to send Lucius to the Capitol as an observer, but dares not tell him why lest she reveal the secret of the conspiracy. The Soothsayer appears, to repeat his warning to Caesar, and leaves to find a sheltered stand after Portia probes him to see if he knows of any specific danger. She invents a vague reason for sending Lucius and having him return with a report.

1-46 This scene, too, is designed to build suspense—not through the possibility that Portia will give away the secret, but through the infectiousness of her anxiety.

III, i

As he approaches the Capitol with his escort of patricians, Caesar greets the Soothsayer ironically and again disregards his warning. He refuses to read the letter pressed upon him by Artemidorus when told it concerns him personally, giving precedence to a petition resourcefully produced by Decius. As the company arrives at the Capitol, one Popilius surprises Cassius by wishing his enterprise may 'thrive,' then proceeds to converse with Caesar. Cassius fears that the conspiracy is being exposed and is prepared to destroy himself, but he is steadied by Brutus who points out that Popilius is smiling and Caesar showing no alarm. Each of the conspirators now makes his allotted moves. Trebonius draws off Antony, and Metellus kneels before Caesar with a plea for repeal of his brother's banishment. Caesar proclaims his uniqueness as a man of unswerving constancy, and rejects the plea. The others have crowded about him in pretended support of Metellus, and now thrust their blades into him, Casca striking first and Brutus last. Caesar dies reproaching only Brutus. In the subsequent confusion Brutus assumes command, assuring Publius and the other witnesses that no harm is intended them, and bidding his fellows to bathe their arms in Caesar's blood as a token to the people that freedom is now assured. A Servant comes with a message from Antony, protesting his mutual regard for Caesar and Brutus, and offering his support if instructed why the assassination was necessary. Brutus sends a reassuring reply, and Antony comes to confer. By the exercise of great diplomatic skill he simultaneously expresses loyal sorrow for the death of Caesar and wins the confidence of Brutus. Despite the misgivings of Cassius, Brutus gives Antony permission to deliver Caesar's funeral oration, providing only that it follow his own address to the people. When alone, Antony asks forgiveness of the dead Caesar for appearing to temporize with his butchers, then vows to unleash the dogs of war. He warns the servants of Octavius Caesar that their master had better wait outside Rome for the turn of events, then helps bear the body of Caesar to the public market.

1-77 In this scene one part of the stage represents the approach to the Capitol, another part the Capitol itself, perhaps symbolized by a dais with consul's seat and emblems. The tension is skillfully built up as three separate hazards appear (as represented by the Soothsayer, Artemidorus, and Popilius) and pass (1-19); as Cassius falters but Brutus rises to the occasion (20-24); and as the moves in the assassination are precisely charted, with each conspirator playing his prearranged part. Although this is a scene of full and fascinating action, the characters of the persons involved are never forgotten but are illuminated by the events. Caesar's famous last six words (77) poignantly contradict his last long speech (58-73) asserting his high detachment from ordinary human feelings. In his earlier speeches in this death scene, there have been, in spite of the continuing boastfulness, intimations of his genuine judicial probity.   **78-121** Brutus's actions, including the blood-washing, are in line with his expressed conception (II, i) of the assassination as a sacrifice in the cause of freedom. Observe how the play capitalizes upon its own existence in the theatrical image which advertises the importance of the subject matter (111-16); it is a daring device, but so persuasive that fact and fiction seem to coalesce, and we feel as if we are witnessing the event itself rather than its representation. The dazed conduct of Popilius is important to the stage image even though he is given no words to speak. Brutus's words of reassurance are no more than we should expect from him; however, who but Shakespeare would have thought of putting words of charitable concern in the mouth of tough Cassius! (92-93)   **122-297** Antony has been briefly mentioned by a number of different characters and always as a gay pleasure-lover—with one exception, when Cassius called him a *shrewd contriver* with an *ingrafted love* for Caesar (II, i, 158, 184). His emergence as a power and intelligence of the first order is one of the wonders of the play. In a sense he remains the pleasure-lover —his motives personal gratification. He is capable of intense love and loyalty on the personal level, and his grief for Caesar is real and moving, but he seems socially indifferent or irresponsible. The act against Caesar was an act against something he personally valued, and it is his will, his pleasure, to exact revenge regardless of consequences. He acts with an efficiency derived from untapped reserves of ability and complete absence of scruples. There is no hesitation in him; he automatically regards his past bond with Julius Caesar as a present bond with Octavius Caesar.

III, ii

The Plebeians cry for an explanation. Some follow Cassius, who will address them in a neighboring street, and some cluster about Brutus, who has mounted the public rostrum. Brutus dispassionately explains that he held Caesar in high personal regard, but took action as an honorable man because Caesar was ambitious; hence no one should be offended. The crowd approves, and shows a disposition to let Brutus assume power over them in place of Caesar. He persuades them to remain and listen to the funeral oration of Antony, who has entered with Caesar's body. They do so with mutterings that Caesar was a tyrant and Antony had best not speak ill of Brutus. Antony begins in conciliatory fashion, then works upon the emotions of his listeners, gradually altering the emphasis of the repeated words 'honorable' and 'ambitious,' until the people are in tears for the pitiful fate of Caesar and enraged at Brutus. Finally he reads Caesar's will, with its provisions on their behalf, and they rush out to take vengeance upon the conspirators. Antony remains to rejoice over the mischief he has wrought. He welcomes a message that Octavius has entered Rome.

1-271 The merits of this scene scarcely require comment. It is theatrically famous as the one in which the actor playing Antony always 'steals' the play from the actor playing Brutus, and we should scarcely expect a Roman mob to prove less susceptible than Shakespearean audiences. Brutus blunders, but his is the noble blunder of overestimating his audience. Antony does not make this blunder; he understands the audience, in part because he shares its passionate willfulness and its indifference to abstract ideas. Also, he both feels and knows the power of pity. Brutus's rational appeal (of course in prose), which we must confess is almost self-parody in its excessively logical patterning, has no chance against Antony's emotional appeal (of course in verse), with its supplementing properties —the dead body, and the will, of Caesar. And Brutus's sense of fair play has no chance against Antony's unscrupulousness. The content of Brutus's speech is essentially honest, his use of the word *slaves* (23) the one possible deviation and this we are inclined to excuse as hyperbole. The content of Antony's speech is essentially dishonest. The emphasis he gives the word *honorable* in its application to Brutus is, in its sarcasm, an instance of 'suggestio falsi' and, of course, Caesar could be and was *ambitious* (a bad word in the Renaissance) in spite of the services he performed. He instances Caesar's rejection of the crown without mentioning his politic reasons. Still, it is hard to withhold admiration from the underdog who wins, even though he does so by reaching for the throat. As interesting as either of these principals is the third character—the mob. Its weakness is in the brain and not the heart, and it succumbs to moral and not immoral persuasions—admiration, gratitude, pity. It misses Brutus's point entirely, that one must strike against an aspirant to kingship even if he is a good man. It recognizes Brutus as a good man and hence worthy of kingship—*Let him be Caesar* (50). Antony's 'non sequiturs' it accepts—*Therefore 'tis certain he was not ambitious* (113). But observe that it is ready to avenge Caesar for pity alone; Antony is more mercenary than those he addresses, playing what he supposes his trump card, the will, after the game is already won.

III, iii

On his way to Caesar's funeral, Cinna the poet is stopped by rioting Plebeians. He gives a disarming account of himself, and explains that he is not Cinna the conspirator. They 'tear him' anyway; and rush out to lay fire-brands to the houses of Brutus, Cassius, and the rest.

1-38 *Mischief, thou art afoot,* Antony has said a moment ago— and here it is. The force he has unleashed has now neither head nor heart, but only the atavistic impulse to *tear,* to lynch the innocent if the guilty is unavailable. Observe the influence upon the artist of traditional associations: brainlessness suggests clownishness which suggests humor. Grim humor, but it is here.

IV, i

Antony, Octavius, and Lepidus list those who must die by proscription. Lepidus consents to the death of his own brother, and Antony to that of Publius his own nephew. He is light-hearted about this, and casually prepares to increase the yield of Caesar's will to the right parties. He sends Lepidus to fetch it, and when Octavius mildly challenges his contemptuous appraisal of the third member of their 'triumvirate,' he dismisses Lepidus as a mere tool. The two of them prepare to consolidate their position and levy forces against those of Brutus and Cassius.

1-51 This side is hampered with the presence of no idealist. All are eminently practical. Antony now sees different uses for Caesar's will, and views Lepidus himself as a *property* (40). Note that Octavius tosses in none of his own relatives at the bargaining board. He appears to be a cool and efficient youth—frugal even of disdain.

IV, ii (+ iii)

After liaison is effected by Lucilius and Pindarus, the armies of Brutus and Cassius meet at Sardis. The two leaders repair to Brutus's tent in order to canvass in private the breach which has developed between them. When Cassius complains that one Lucius Pellas has been disciplined for petty venality, Brutus rebukes him for having interceded in such a base cause, and suggests that Cassius himself has been guilty of having an itching palm. Cassius is enraged, but Brutus meets his outbursts with flinty disdain, reminding him of Caesar's death and the loftiness of their original aims. Now Cassius even withholds money needed for the support of Brutus's troops. Cassius is reduced to tears by the contemptuous tone of his revered associate, whereupon Brutus grows mild and tells of his private afflictions. Portia has died. The two are now reconciled, and Cassius extends his sympathies. After an intruding Poet is dismissed from the tent, Titinius and Messala enter, the latter with news from Rome. Although Brutus has already told Cassius of Portia's death, he now extracts an account of it from Messala and expresses stoic fortitude. Tactics are discussed, and, overriding the objections of Cassius, Brutus decides that they will march against the enemy at Phillipi. The conference over, Brutus retires after calling Varro and Claudius to sleep in his tent in readiness to serve as messengers. He asks his page Lucius to give him music, but refrains from disturbing the boy when he falls asleep over his instrument. The taper burns low, and the Ghost of Caesar appears. Brutus responds staunchly to the warning that he will see the Ghost again at Phillipi, then arouses the others to ask them if they have cried out. They reply that they have not. He sends Varro and Claudius with orders to Cassius to begin the march to Phillipi.

1-308 The 'armies' appearing in this scene and the next could have been represented by a few symbol-bearers, a sort of color-guard, with the troops extending hypothetically off-stage. The tent could be a canopy set up during the early action. This scene is one of the most striking in the play, and the richest in 'human interest.'

It has been criticized as disproportionately long, but it does more than exploit a quarrel: it reveals the fundamental differences between two men linked as coadjutors by historical accident, and it suggests the tragic erosion of ideals as a 'cause' meets the practical problem of survival. Our sympathy goes out to Cassius, faulty though he is, as he is humiliated by the impregnably virtuous man whose love and approval he craves. He did actually say that he was the *older* soldier, whose seniority should be respected (31), not the *better* soldier, as the effronted Brutus charges (51). He is required to supply funds to this man who is too fastidious to raise them himself (69-75). And his humorous tolerance of the intruding rimester is far more appealing than Brutus's starchiness. The austerity of Brutus would repel if it were not for our awareness that he is a tortured man, bearing up under the collapse of his hopes for Rome and the loss of those who were dear to him. From one fault he should be exonerated. What appears to be a piece of stoic play-acting, when he denies knowledge of Portia's death (181-94), is probably an accidental redundancy in the text, owing to a printer's error in retaining a passage marked for omission in the manuscript. We do not know which of the passages pertaining to Portia the playwright wished to retain, but we hope it was the first, inserted marginally because he was dissatisfied with the one which appears second in our text. (There are a number of instances in the plays where canceled passages have been mistakenly retained.) As if to restore a balance after displaying his public acerbity, the playwright, at the end of the scene, shows Brutus at his kindest and bravest best. He is thoughtful of the comfort of his sentinels, and tender to the sleepy boy. He is a lover of music, always regarded by Shakespeare as a prepossessing trait. The cessation of the music, the reference to the dimming tapers, and Lucius's drowsy cry, *The strings, my lord, are false* (291), are atmospheric touches accompanying the visitation of the Ghost. Like others in Shakespeare this Ghost is ambiguous. It would be represented visually and made to speak even if intended only as a projection of Brutus's subconscious qualms; he feels personal guilt about the death of Caesar, and he senses the approach of his own (see *If I do live*, 265). Such doubts on our part about the reality of a 'character' who has actually made an appearance in the play would be unjustified were it not for Brutus's remarks. The vision fades as his courage rises, and he thinks the voice may have come from one of the sleepers in the tent. We must share his indecision about what he has actually seen.

V, i

Octavius and Antony, at the head of their army, express elation that the enemy is descending from the heights of Sardis to engage them on the plains of Philippi. With imperturbable firmness Octavius reverses Antony's proposal that he lead the left wing; he thus gains precedence. Brutus and Cassius appear with their forces and engage in a parley. This consists of an exchange of invective, with Brutus and Cassius vilified as treacherous assassins, and Octavius and Antony ridiculed as 'schoolboy' and 'reveller.' As their enemies withdraw to take up battle-positions, Brutus speaks privately to Lucilius; and Cassius, whose birthday this is, voices his misgivings to Messala. He has not been in favor of the decision to stake everything upon this battle, and he is disturbed by the evil omens which have appeared, in spite of his skepticism in such matters. He asks Brutus what he will do if the battle is lost, and Brutus replies that, although he opposes suicide in principle, he will not let himself be led captive to Rome. On the chance that they may never meet again, they bid each other farewell.

1-125 The rivalry of Cassius and Antony is forecast (19-20) because the conception of character is three-dimensional, not because it has bearing on the present situation. Octavius is alert and unbending in matters concerning his prerogative even at this moment of crisis, and Antony, who is as generous to those he accepts as he is ruthless to those he does not, yields the point with little protest. The hurling of defiances before battle meets a conventional obligation, but we may wish that the remarks were more in key with the imposing occasion; Brutus barely retains his dignity as a participant in this kind of wrangling. The issues seem to be reduced to matters of personal pique. There have been earlier indications that Cassius and Brutus adhere to different philosophies, and the fact here emerges explicitly. Cassius speaks as an Epicurean, skeptical and fatalistic; suicide, as we have observed, has always been prominent in his thoughts as a resource in case of failure. Brutus speaks as a Stoic, one whose religious and ethical positions is much nearer to that of the Renaissance Christian, but like other characters in Shakespeare in similar circumstances, his instinctive allegiance is to personal honor; he will compromise his principles rather than sacrifice his human dignity. The parting of the partners in this alliance, which has been uneasy since the beginning, is not warmly affectionate, but it is manly and free from bitterness.

V, ii

The alarm for battle is sounded, and Brutus gives Messala orders for an attack on the wing commanded by Octavius, which appears to him to be lacking in morale.

1-6 See under V, iii.

V, iii

Cassius has been trying to stem the retreat of his men, and now hears that Antony's wing has moved in victoriously during Brutus's premature attack upon Octavius. He sends Titinius to bring a report, and orders Pindarus to watch his progress. Pindarus, observing from a vantage point, describes Titinius as surrounded and captured. In despair, Cassius reminds Pindarus of his oath of obedience as bondsman, and appoints him his executioner. He dies from the thrust of the sword which he had used against Caesar, and Pindarus sadly retires from the scene. The report of defeat was mistaken. Titinius was not captured by foes but greeted by friends. He returns with Messala, and when he finds Cassius dead, crowns him with a wreath sent by Brutus, and follows him in death. Messala, who has left to seek Brutus, now returns with him and Young Cato, Strato, Volumnius, and Lucilius. Brutus reflects that Caesar is mighty yet, turning their own swords against them. He pays tribute to Cassius, and rallies the others for a second engagement with the enemy.

1-110 The battle of Philippi is represented with a minimum of on-stage conflict and danger of awkwardness. We hear its sounds as we get fragmentary reports of episodes, so that the fighting may be as vast and complex as we choose to imagine. Cassius dies as he has lived, a victim of his own limited range of vision, but he dies without sordidness. He is himself in error this time, but as the facts are represented to him, Brutus has made a tactical blunder. He utters no recriminations. It is with another, however, his *best friend* Titinius (35) that he is linked in death. Brutus also refrains from uttering recriminations.

V, iv

Brutus appears with Messala and Flavius in a renewal of the conflict. Young Cato and Lucilius divert the attack of the enemy to themselves, the former declaring his identity and dying a heroic death, the latter posing as Brutus. Lucilius is captured and presented to Antony as Brutus, but he is identified at once. Antony orders that he be honorably treated as a soldier of worth. A report of the fate of the true Brutus is to be brought to Octavius's tent.

1-32 The heroism and unswerving loyalty of his followers, whom he has kindled to nobility, go at least part-distance in converting Brutus's defeat into moral victory.

V, v

Brutus calmly accepts defeat, and sounds out the remnant of his officers to find one who will help him die. He speaks of another visitation of the Ghost of Caesar, and says that the death thus presaged is welcome. Clitus, Dardanius, and Volumnius each decline to hold the fatal sword. Brutus expresses gratitude for the fact that he has never experienced betrayal, and pretends to heed the warnings to take flight. He persuades his man Strato to hold the sword, and takes his own life with better will than he had taken Caesar's. As trumpets sound the end of battle, Antony and Octavius appear, with Messala and Lucilius captive. The latter rejoice to see that Brutus has died well, and commend Strato for his service. Antony proclaims Brutus the greatest Roman of them all, and Octavius orders his honorable funeral rites.

1-81 Brutus mourns Caesar's death to the end and views his own as expiation, yet never wavers in his belief in the rightness of his decision to act (36-38). Thus he remains true so far as he can to both of two conflicting codes of morality, personal and political, impaled on their irreconcilability. He has made errors at every turn, but has never sought the easy way, and has consistently tried to shun the major evil, including passivity and abdication of responsibility. He is judged at last by his intention, and the pride in him which Messala and Lucilius express (58-59, 64) is truly moving. It is customary for Shakespeare's victors to speak well of a fallen enemy, but the requirement in this case might have been met by the perfunctory remarks of Octavius, who as ranking leader of the winning side is given the last speech. Antony's speech, expressing quite naturally his generous side, is in a class by itself. It picks up the phrase *general good* which we first heard on Brutus's own lips at his first appearance. It is one of the noblest tributes in literature, and in the last analysis deserved. Although the road to hell may be paved with good intentions, there would be no roads anywhere without them, and Brutus has at least bequeathed the 'memory of an ideal.' The play is censorious of no one, its creator having looked at its people clear-eyed but with charity. The merits of the piece can scarcely be over-estimated. To view it as an elementary sort of play ('beginner's Shakespeare') is to be wide of the mark. One of its remarkable features is its factual density—the wealth of detailed action shown and implied with a masterful economy. Its language is spare and explicit, superbly functional rather than rich. Its beauty, appropriately, is of the classical order.

6

Measure for Measure

:

I, i

DUKE VINCENTIO commends Escalus for his knowledge of statecraft and appoints him second in authority in Vienna. He will serve under Lord Angelo, who will supply the Duke's own place during the latter's absence. Angelo is summoned and told he must substitute the active for the retired life, since virtue is truly virtue only when put to use. The Duke overrules his objections that his worth is untested, and gives him power of life and death in Vienna, with the right to enforce or qualify its laws. The Duke insists upon a private departure from the city, leaving Angelo and Escalus to confer about their new duties.

1-24   Both Escalus and the Duke are introduced with good credentials. The Duke compliments and commands with equal assurance, and demonstrates his sagacity by refusing to parade it. He uses the first person singular by choice, but shifts to the royal plural (9-14, 16-21) when speaking explicitly in his capacity as ruler. He wears with accustomed ease the robes of power, and gives Escalus status by his trust. Angelo is introduced as a more doubtful quantity. The first thing we hear after mention of his name is, *What figure of us think you he will bear?* (16), even before we learn that he is to be regent, and the speech ends with another question, *What think you of it?* (20) The very name *Angelo* is so excessively auspicious as to provoke doubts, and the Duke's *Look where he comes* (24) operates like a third question.   **25-83**   Escalus has given Angelo unstinted praise, but the Duke does not. Indeed his address may be construed as a rebuke. Its first lines (26-29) are ambiguous, since they may mean either that Angelo bears the mark of virtue or the mark of the cloister. What follows is a rejection of 'cloistered virtue' invoking both Christian (*Heaven*) and pagan (*goddess . . . Nature*) sanctions in praise of the life of service. The heart of the speech (32-40) is beyond praise for its dignity and its tonal and connotative richness (see above, p. 22). The remaining speeches of the Duke define the situation: he is delegating power for a limited term while absent on an unspecified mission; what happens in his absence is of vital concern to him although Angelo's power will be absolute. His one generalization, that he loves the people but not popularity (67-72), fortifies our good impression of his judgment. Angelo speaks briefly four times in the presence of the Duke, each time with courtliness and diffidence. His one speech to Escalus is formal and unrevealing. Nothing he says or does provides a glimpse behind a correct social exterior. Escalus is less reserved. The Duke's term *old* seems apt, for reasons hard to define, unless it be a turn of phrase (77-80) slightly reminiscent of York in *Richard II*. He accepts his position as secondary without demur, promptly giving Angelo precedence and a new title of dignity, your honor (83).

I, ii

Lucio engages with several other Viennese gentlemen in an exchange of wit about war, religious grace, and physical health. At the appearance of Mistress Overdone, a bawd, they charge each other with having contracted diseases under her auspices. She laments that Signior Claudio, who is better than any of them, has been arrested for getting Juliet with child, and is to be executed in three days. They turn serious at this news, which tallies with a recent civic speech and proclamation, and go off to seek Claudio. Mistress Overdone is joined by her tapster Pompey, and the two speak of Claudio's offense and of how all the Viennese bawdy-houses are to be pulled down. The bawd is woebegone over the threat to her means of livelihood, but her pander assures her that their trade will continue although their address may change. Lucio and his companions return, accompanying Claudio and Juliet, who are being publicly displayed by the Provost on their way to prison. Claudio speaks penitently, but claims that he and Juliet are man and wife in all but form; they have postponed a public declaration in the hope of winning relatives to approve a marriage settlement. He is the victim of Angelo's revival of a long-dormant law, and he cannot reach the absent Duke with a plea. He asks Lucio to convey a message to his sister Isabella, who is this day entering a cloister, and whose youthful appeal and discursive skill may move Angelo to mercy. Lucio consents to seek her out at once.

1-41 Our first impression of the moral tone of Vienna is obtained from the small talk of three gay worldlings, all cynical, and one, Lucio, satirically aggressive. Mention of a league of Italian city states against Hungary leads to a wish for 'peace at our price' which is given ironical status as a prayer by the word *Amen* (6). This leads to jesting about the way heavenly commandments conflict with earthly business. (See Falstaff's joke in *1 Henry IV*, above p. 199.) The mention of *thanksgiving before meat,* along with the general drift of the talk, brings into play the word *grace* in its central Christian significance as God's mercy and man's state of readiness to accept God's mercy. Lucio's *Grace is grace, despite of all controversy* (24) is a fine utterance—immediately perverted by controversial charges. (In *1 Henry IV* it is Falstaff who brings charges of lack of grace.) The mutual accusations of lack of grace provoke allusions to sexual laxity as evidenced by venereal disease. (Casual as this conversation seems, its chain of ideas proves thematically relevant in a play dealing with sexual laxity vis-à-vis religious austerity, and with ideas of venality and grace, justice and mercy.) **42-77** The joking about venereal disease receives impetus from the appearance of the bawd, whom Lucio greets with something of Mercutio's exuberance in greeting the Nurse. (See *Romeo and Juliet,* above, p. 151.) Note the association of ideas in his speech (52-54): *Sound-hollowness-disease-sin,* with the concatenation suggesting hypocrisy. We first hear of Claudio's and Juliet's plight from the mouth of a bawd. Although their situation proves to be exceptional (Juliet is no prostitute, and Claudio not necessarily a libertine although Lucio's friend), they are initially blighted by atmosphere, that is by the kind of conversation we have been hearing, and by the approval of the bawd. The distinction between their offense, and the grosser vices of the city is thus blurred before it is made. (We must adjust ourselves to the postulates of the play, and not bring 'anti-Victorian' attitudes to bear on it. A sharp distinction is made between sanctioned and unsanctioned sexual relations; the latter are continuously associated with ideas of religious sin and ill social consequences, bastardy and disease.) Our impression of Lucio as an irresponsible man-about-town may be modified by his exertions on behalf of a friend, if they prove disinterested. The nature of the *speech* and *proclamation* affecting Claudio and Juliet is revealed in stages, so as not to jar us into incredulity. **78-111** We have heard the voices of a sampling of the gentry. We now hear those of the non-gentry—represented by a pander and a bawd. The low moral tone persists, with grossness succeeding elegant cynicism. Mistress Overdone deplores war, sickness, teeming gallows, and poverty, not as evils in themselves, but as hazards to her business, which she views as indistinguishable from any other business. Pompey is a cockney sophisticate, certain that vice will survive vice-raids because of administrative corruption; only the bawdy-houses in the poor sections (*suburbs*) will go, not those in the city bringing profits to some pillar of society (*wise burgher*). But Pompey has his virtues; he is cheery and resilient. (Confusions in this scene and elsewhere suggest incomplete revision or imperfect copy. Mistress Overdone addresses *Pompey* as *Thomas Tapster*, and receives as news information about Claudio which she herself has just conveyed to Lucio. Minor factual discrepancies may usually be dismissed as conventional sacrifices to artistic convenience, but these are so conspicuous that they may result from an accident like the one suggested in *Julius Caesar:* see above, p. 263.) **112-88** This is no mere walk to prison but a punitive exposure to public view (112-13), such as was usually reserved for professional and low-class sexual offenders. Thus Angelo's rigor is visually demonstrated while it is being discussed. The Provost (warden), himself low enough in social station to be addressed as *Fellow* (112), might well consider this treatment of aristocracy improper even if he were less humane than he proves to be. (So far as the death penalty for fornication is concerned, it is a donné of the plot, like Shylock's presumed right to claim a pound of flesh in forfeit. This law is an invention, but Shakespeare was not its inventor.) Observe that Juliet neither speaks nor is spoken to, standing pathetically mute, and that Claudio displays no solicitude for her apart from solicitude for himself, referring on one occasion to *me* (166). Typically Shakespearean is the way a critical issue is suspended. Angelo, in spite of his rigor, does not emerge as a persecutor. Claudio uses the term *demigod Authority* (116), and is inclined to think Angelo is merely trying to make a name for himself (166), but he concedes the possibility that the deputy may be obliged by his place to act as he is acting (158). Nor does Claudio, in spite of his situation and suffering emerge as martyr. He is at once indignant and ashamed, self-excusing and self-accusing. His claim that he and Juliet are, in effect, man and wife (140-48) is not valid because, as the Elizabethan spectators would know, there could be no *true contract* without *outward order*. A betrothal was binding, but a betrothal could not be secret. Their offense lies not in having anticipated their marriage ceremony but in having anticipated their betrothal. True they *intended* to become betrothed, and so Claudio's mixed feelings of guilt and innocence are appropriate to his anomalous situation. The seriousness and intensity of his feelings call naturally for blank verse, but the verse is constantly interrupted by Claudio's earthy sallies in prose, with their deflating effect. (As earlier in the scene, characters speak verse or prose according to their mood and nature rather than their social station.) Although the playwright is refraining from letting Claudio benefit fully from the cleansing power of poetry, his imagination is engaged on his behalf: Claudio's words are consistently vital, and, at intervals, they glow, as in the passages following *Our natures* (124-26) and *for in her youth* (177-79).

I, iii

The Duke tells Friar Thomas that he has always cherished seclusion, and has delegated his authority on the pretext of a journey to Poland. During his supposed absence, Angelo, a man of ascetic habit, will have a chance to reform Vienna. The Duke himself cannot do this with good grace since his own laxity in enforcing the law has encouraged vice to flourish. He will now don the garb of a friar and observe Angelo's actions, to determine whether they are consistent with the principles he professes.

1-6 The Duke's opening remark shows that Friar Thomas has assumed that he is seeking *secret harbor* in order to carry on a love affair. The association of friars with clandestine or romantic love was a common motif (see Friar Lawrence in *Romeo and Juliet*). In the Duke's vigorous denial, the playwright, elsewhere so well-disposed toward romantic love, is invoking the conventional moral attitude that it is a folly of *burning youth,* and is thus further establishing this character's rational worthiness. He is governed by 'right reason.'   **7-10** The Duke here testifies to his own love of the cloistered life, against which he had warned Angelo. Are the vices of Vienna attributable to the Duke's own failure to actively employ his virtue?   **11-43** As the facts are here presented the answer must be 'yes,' and the Friar's words (31-32) express our own sense of a weakness in the Duke's position. But it is doubtful if the playwright wishes to attach much, if any, odium to this character. Although he uses a past *fault* (35) to excuse a present evasion (42-43), the irony is not pointed up and may be inadvertent. The primary impression made by the Duke's speeches is that he is distressed by vice in Vienna and is using politic means of combating it. He says that the period of lax law-enforcement has extended for *fourteen years* whereas Claudio has said *nineteen* (I, i, 163), but, although we tend to err in the direction of our desires when we use figures, the discrepancy here is probably accidental. **44-54** This establishes a traditional Haroun-al-Rashid situation (in which a solicitous ruler goes in disguise among his subjects for benevolent purposes), and the concluding lines had best be taken as explanatory of the over-all theme rather than of the speaker's character and motives. If taken in the latter way, they place the Duke in a position which is morally ambiguous indeed; he distrusts asceticism, suspects Angelo of being one of the *seemers* (hypocrites), and is satisfying his curiosity by giving him a chance to betray himself rather than using him as an instrument of reform. If at this point we view the Duke as a symbol of Providence, we would have to suspect religious satire: he has admitted evil into his universe by oversight, and he is leading man into temptation under false pretenses. Observe the use of 'double time.' In the preceding scene Angelo has been in office long enough to put the dormant law into effect, but here the Duke has evidently just left the court on his pretended journey. The logical place for this scene would be just after the first. But this wresting of the time sequence is a familiar convention, and the true question is not why the present scene comes so late but why it comes so early, since a few explanatory lines would account for the Duke's delay in reaching the monastery. The Duke does not actively intervene until later, and the fact of his presence might have been longer withheld. The explanation is that the playwright is giving his audience, if not his characters, all the necessary information for seeing the events in perspective, using the technique of suspense rather than surprise. Since he is writing a play which is to have a happy ending, the comforting presence of the Duke is established just before Isabella, the heroine, is involved in the ugly situation. This mitigating fact is revealed at the last possible moment, *after* Claudio has appeared in apparently mortal danger. Claudio is not the hero, and presumably would not strike us favorably enough for his danger to arouse uncomfortable anxiety.

I, iv

As a novice of the order, Isabella receives instructions from a sister of Saint Clare and welcomes the strictness of the rule. Lucio knocks at the cloister gate, and curbing somewhat his libertine wit out of respect for her vocation, tells Isabella of her brother's arrest. She exclaims that he must wed Juliet at once, but Lucio convinces her that nothing can save him from death except a plea to Angelo for mercy. Hesitantly, she consents to make the plea.

1-15 Isabella's situation is carefully defined. The sisters of Saint Clare comprise one of the strictest of the recluse orders, and she welcomes the austerity of the rule. Since no other reason is given for her retreat from the world, the implied motive is religious ardor. Presumably she already wears the garb of a novice, and is emotionally reluctant to be seen by or to speak to men. But she is still free to go among them since she has taken no final vows.   **16-44** Her youth has been mentioned by Claudio, and her beauty is reflected in Lucio's tone as well as his words *cheek-roses* (16) and *Gentle and fair* (24). The *Hail virgin* suggests 'Hail Mary'; but note that the expression is coupled with the speculative *if you be,* typical of Lucio's mode of thinking. Lucio approves of getting *friend with child* (29) in or out of wedlock, and links the process jovially with good husbandry and the fine fecundity of nature (40-44) whereas Claudio himself had linked it with ratsbane and death (I, ii, 121-26). Lucio proclaims his respect for Isabella in such excessive terms, *enskied and sainted . . . immortal spirit . . . saint,* that she suspects raillery. Her words are perhaps too strong, but it is within Lucio's capacity to *blaspheme the good* (38). **45-49** The use and immediate definition of the word *cousin* indicates that the marriage of Claudio would be feasible socially, and within canon law. Isabella's remedy for the situation is marriage (49)—and this must be remembered in her favor when she connives at another marriage later; she, like the play as a whole, distinguishes sharply between sanctioned and unsanctioned sexual relations.   **50-71** This is a skillfully compact recapitulation, summing up and reinforcing what we have learned about Angelo's disposition, the shift from one extreme to the other in law-enforcement, and Claudio's situation. There is even mention of a distinction between the Duke's published and his *true-meant design* (55) a convenient rumor being created to order so that the summary may be complete.   **72-90** Isabella's words sound apathetic, even banal: *I'll see what I can do* (84), *I will about it straight* (85). There are several explanations for this; the playwright cannot let her enter into this business with alacrity; and, further, he must hold her emotional displays in reserve. (Possibly her expressions were not then the clichés they have since become; observe the oddity noted in the style of III, ii, below, p. 288.)

II, i

Escalus asks Angelo to spare Claudio, arguing that Angelo himself might have erred at some time in his life if temptation and opportunity had coincided. Angelo replies that there is a distinction between being tempted and yielding to temptation, and explains that the law must continue to operate against the detected even though the undetected escape. He orders the Provost to carry out the execution the next morning at nine. Constable Elbow enters with Pompey and a young gentleman named Froth, whom he has arrested on suspicion that Mistress Elbow has been assaulted by Froth in the house where Pompey is employed. Elbow proves a master of malapropism and Pompey of irrelevance as the inquiry proceeds, until Angelo departs in a dudgeon, hoping Escalus will find cause to punish them all. Escalus patiently proceeds. When he learns that Elbow lacks evidence and that Mistress Elbow is herself not above suspicion, he dismisses Pompey and Froth with a warning, and takes measures to replace Elbow with a more competent officer. He invites a fellow magistrate home for dinner, and departs sighing over the fate of Claudio, although conceding that easy pardon nullifies law.

1-31 This is the first of a number of fascinating passages of ethical debate. Angelo's position is theoretically invulnerable. What he says about disregarded laws (1-4) is precisely what the Duke has said (I, iii, 19-31), and what others have conceded (see Lucio, I, iv, 63-64) and will concede again (see Escalus himself, below, 266-68). Escalus properly pleads moderation, but couples this with a plea for special privilege (Claudio is of noble blood) and with ad-hominem allusions to universal human weakness. Angelo returns, with a memorable use of concrete metaphor (17-26), the logical reply—that the law deals with acts, not impulses, and that it cannot adbicate its role simply because its operation is imperfect. If he means what he says in his last lines, about his willingness to be judged as he judges, he will stand above reproach. If he changes his mind, the lines will assume an ironical cast and return to haunt

him.   **32-40**   Angelo's orders are hard and unfeeling. Since we
are appraised of the imminence and certainty of Claudio's execution, Isabella's mission is seen as crucial. Escalus's lament (37-40)
dignifies his merciful impulse and introduces a motif that will recur;
in a world where all men are sinners it is difficult to determine
who should and who should not be whipped.   **41-270**   The remainder of the scene has three functions; it reinforces our impression of a corrupt Vienna, it provides a comic respite, and it makes
a distinction between Angelo and Escalus as judges to the former's
disadvantage. For the first time in the play, an actual rather than a
hypothetical defect in Angelo is revealed. He is irascible and hu-
morless, unlike Escalus, who takes a tolerant pleasure in Elbow's
malapropisms. (Here Angelo plays Brutus to Escalus's Cassius, see
above, p. 263, as a man of principle too preoccupied to unbend.)
More important, he seems more intent on punishment than reform,
hoping that there will be cause to *whip them all* (130). Compare
this with Escalus's patient hearing of the case to its end, his sifting
such evidence as there is, his correct legal judgment, and, particularly, his attempt to restrain the parties from committing further
offenses. He even tries to improve the Viennese constabulary
(253-57), obviously taking his cue from conditions in Shakespeare's
London. This gesture by Escalus comes as near as anything in the
play to suggesting what might properly be done to combat vice in
the city. The scene performs its comic function with imperfect
success, in spite of the presence of comic types which Shakespeare
in other plays has manipulated to perfection—the impudent scamp
Pompey, the dim-witted and word-mangling constable Elbow (see
Dogberry in *Much Ado about Nothing*), and the vapid young heir
Froth (see Slender in *Merry Wives of Windsor*). The trouble lies
in the intractable subject matter; the odor of the brothel stales the
air. Pompey's paradoxes are clever but unpalatable, and the ideas
of adultery, pregnancy, and even assault associated with Elbow's
wife are dampening. The defect is owing less to our disapproval of
the material than to the playwright's failure, possibly because of
his own disapproval, to transmute it—as he had transmuted similar,
but not identical, material in *1 & 2 Henry IV*. Here he tends to
underline his jokes, such as Elbow's malapropisms, with a conse-

quent sense of strain. The funniest part of the dialogue is Pompey's detailed testimony on anything that is beside the point—the way he tries to evaporate the proceedings with, *I hope here be truths* (85-126).

II, ii

Angelo bruskly rejects the Provost's intercession for Claudio, telling him to obey the order of execution or resign his office. Juliet, whose labor pains are beginning, is to be given adequate but not lavish facilities. Isabella is introduced; and she makes her plea with Lucio spurring her on and the Provost fervently wishing her success. She admits her feelings of loathing for sexual license, but suggests that one may condemn sin, yet spare the sinner. Angelo replies that his function is not to condemn sin, which stands pre-condemned, but to enforce the law. She seems ready to accept this judgment, but when Lucio reproves her, she persists, and makes mercy the basis of her appeal. Angelo replies that he shows mercy to men in general by exercising impartial justice. As the imminence of her brother's death is born in upon her, she warms to her cause and eloquently condemns the abuse of power, the immunities of the powerful, and the assumption of righteousness on the part of Angelo himself. Unguardedly she has repeated Escalus's argument that Angelo himself might be capable of sexual misconduct, and she asserts that Claudio should not die for a sin that many have committed. Angelo, who has met her arguments at each point, finds to his consternation that he is aroused by her physical appeal. He promises to consider the case, and tells her to return the next morning. Hopefully, she departs, with Lucio and the Provost, leaving Angelo to commune with himself. He is appalled to discover that Isabella's very purity has provoked him to lust, and that he is capable of committing Claudio's sin.

1-25 The mastery of the blank verse medium is complete. Although the speeches of the Provost and Angelo are written under metrical restrictions, there is no trace of artificiality; and although the metrical restrictions are uniform, the alternate speeches are diametrically opposite in tone. The Provost *sounds* tender-hearted and conciliatory, while Angelo *sounds* harsh and peremptory, his questions and commands all equally curt and monosyllabic. At this point the implication remains that he is moved by a firm sense of duty. Note that he does provide for Juliet's needs (24), sparingly though it may be.   **26-47**   The dramaturgic convenience of his unexplained order to the Provost *Stay a little while* (26) becomes clear later on. No pleader could begin more ineffectually than Isabella, with her expression of repugnance for the offense and her readiness to accept defeat. As in I, iv, it is made clear that the cause is one into which she finds it hard to put her heart, and for the moment the Provost (36) and Lucio (43-47) sound more concerned about her brother than she does. It must be recognized, however, that Angelo's position is finely stated and hard to assail. **48-55**   Urged on to her task, Isabella seems to grope for a basis for a plea, asking what at first seems a pointless question and then prodding to determine the extent of Angelo's discretionary powers. The skirmish over *can* and *will* is interesting. Angelo's reply that he cannot act at his own discretion because he has no wish to do so is really a quibble because Isabella's question referred to his official powers, not to his personal inclinations.   **56-82**   His *too late* (56) is clearly an evasion, and is recognized by Isabella as such. She is now able to sue for mercy, citing sanctions both human (59-63) and divine (72-79). Her allusion to the atonement of Christ is beautifully and movingly expressed, but she has been guilty of a tactical error in assuming, much less guardedly than Escalus had done (II, i, 9-16), that Angel himself might have *slipped* (65) if tempted. His immediate *Pray you, be gone* (66) suggests that he is at this point first physically stirred by her presence. We must feel sympathy for both at this juncture. Constrained by her relationship to the accused, and by the urgings of those who have failed to accomplish what they expect her to accomplish, she cannot choose all her words with care, or refrain from palliating in some measure the offense by arguing its high incidence. She is in a cruelly false position. And for Angelo it must be said, that his defenses of virtue are being undermined by these repeated references to their vulnerability.   **83-102**   The word *Tomorrow* brings home to Isabella the nearness of her brother's death, and she speaks with increasing vehemence, as indicated by the exclamatory and disjointed style and by Lucio's approval. Again she incautiously instances the widespread nature of sexual laxity—a point which Lucio too eagerly endorses (87-89). Angelo wins in this phase of the debate. He makes a telling case for the good achieved by exemplary justice; and his defense of himself as its minister, *For then I pity those I do not know* (101), might well be carved on every judge's bench—providing, of course, that every judge remembered that a man is more than an 'example' and that the immediate culprit is as deserving of pity as members of the unseen throng. There is always the danger that we will be better disposed toward man in the abstract than toward individual men. The oddity of this debate is that both speakers are right and both are wrong. We cannot determine the relative value of mercy and justice, and any debate on the matter resolves itself into a collision of absolutes. We can only discuss the two things meaningfully in connection with the individual case. Isabella should be in a stronger position than Angelo because an individual case is at hand, but, like him, she tends to generalize and to pit one absolute good against another.   **103-44**   Angelo's last point, that execution benefits the sinner by preventing him from committing further sins is beneath the level of anything he has said in the play thus far, a piece of casuistical cant. Isabella is now fully engaged, her language passionate, indeed enraged. One of her speeches (110-23) is the most famous in the play, unforgettable in its intensity, and its close-knit and multiply-suggestive imagery (see above, p. 30); this has both size and scope, ranging from *Jove* to the *angry ape* and linking heaven and earth by a thunderbolt. Such language has authenticating power, and we must accept Isabella's as the voice of wrath and righteousness. But the wrath has its defects: it is hard to detect the relevance of her charges of special privilege, and there is point in Angelo's protest, *Why do you put these sayings upon me?* (133) And for the third time she refers to Angelo's own capacity for lust (137-39). It is at this point, as if her words had activated it, that Angelo's lust is admitted to himself. His first impulse is to get out of her presence (142). His invitation to her to return the next day acts as an automatic stay of execution, since the Provost is present to hear it. We can understand now the earlier command that he stay (26): it was a structural convenience, representing Shakespeare's prescience, not Angelo's.   **145-54** In these few lines the playwright effortlessly affords us glimpses into three minds. To Isabella the word *bribe* (145) means the offer of prayers. To Angelo it means the offer of her body, as indicated by his startled response, the thought being already in his mind. To Lucio it means the offer of money, and we must note that this irresponsible 'fantastic' (whimsical eccentric) recognizes that Angelo is above ordinary bribery. Lucio appears at his best in this scene because of his ardent espousal of his friend's cause, but we must note that his partisanship differs from that of Escalus and the Provost; theirs derives purely from their humanity, his in part from his vested interest in lechery.   **155-87** The most striking feature of Angelo's speech of amazement and self-revulsion is its honesty. He rejects at once the idea that Isabella is at fault as *tempter,* and puts the onus on the *cunning enemy* (Satan) and his own corruptibility. Under the warmth of the same sun, the violet blooms and emits fragrance, while the carrion rots and emits stench. This striking metaphor (166-68) carries his admission that, were it not for his fallen nature, Isabella's virtue would have stirred a virtuous response. That a man of Angelo's experience would be excited to desire more readily by an Isabella than by a *strumpet* (183-87) is entirely credible, and he cannot be dismissed as an habitual hypocrite, or as a symbol of the contemporary 'Puritan.' (The playwright is dealing with something more universal than the presumed traits of members of particular sects.) Angelo is learning about himself for the first time, and may respond in either of two ways—by becoming more tolerant of the weakness of others, or more indulgent of his own.

II, iii

The Duke in his friar's disguise tells the Provost that he has come to minister to the prisoners. He questions Juliet, and finds her truly penitent as well as overwhelmed with grief at the fate of her beloved Claudio.

1-42 The Duke again appears in a scene which is dispensable so far as the actual plot is concerned. True this one draws him into the orbit of the action, but the information it conveys could have been reserved until he begins to shape that action. Its real function, like its predecessor's, is to intimate the conclusion and to mitigate anxiety. Coming as it does just before Isabella is required to make a hard ethical decision, it confers upon her certain fictitious immunities. She is, or should be, given the right in our imaginations to abide purely by the dictates of her conscience, since in this play, as distinct from the actual world, there will be no cruel consequences. Since the play is partly concerned with codes of sexual conduct, the playwright takes this occasion to provide a moral apologue. The Duke prods Juliet to the very limit of our tolerance, but the process is to her advantage in more ways than one. We are less impressed by the fact that hers is a true, not an enforced, penitence than by the assurance that she has truly loved Claudio and is more grieved by his fate than her own. Will we ever get similar assurances about Claudio? The Duke may seem to be endorsing a double standard of morality, but he is not. His statement that Juliet's sin was of *heavier kind* (28) does not absolve Claudio of sin. It may imply many things—that a woman is more capable of restraint, that she has more to lose, and that her capacity for restraint is a husband's only guarantee of the legitimacy of his children. We must keep in mind the visual symbol. Juliet is pregnant —the consequence of her *offenseful act* (26) written large upon her.

II, iv

After vain prayers for strength, Angelo confesses to himself that he would now trade his talents as a statesman for success as a lover. He feels an onslaught of passion as Isabella is announced, and he gives an ambiguous answer to her query about her brother's fate. She is ready to concede defeat, but he prolongs the interview with hints that she might save her brother by sacrificing her own chastity. When she fails to understand him and speaks at cross-purposes about sin and charity, he charges her with insincerity and makes his meaning more clear. He asks what she would do to save her brother, and when she replies that she would do anything except sin away her soul, he accuses her of being as merciless as the law. He reminds her, to her distress, of her having palliated Claudio's offense, and of her own condition as a woman and hence excusably frail. She asks for plain speech, and he proposes that she yield her body to him in payment for a pardon for Claudio. She wrathfully threatens him with exposure, but he convinces her that no one would believe her story. Either she return her consent the next day, or Claudio will be tortured as well as beheaded. When alone, she recognizes her helplessness, but resolves to preserve her chastity. She will tell Claudio to prepare for death, certain of his approval of her decision.

1-17 Although its function is choral (explanatory of the character), the soliloquy is not psychologically incredible in its objective self-appraisal. Angelo might recognize these truths about himself, however unlikely it is that he would express them. His struggle with temptation is lost, yet he wishes to retain prestige. This means that his 'virtue' will henceforth be a façade, and his bitter apostrophe is upon façades in general. The words *Good angel* and *false seeming* are verbal links with the intimations of the theme provided by his name, and by the Duke's remarks on *seemers* early in the play (I, iii).   **18-30** The extended simile illustrating the rush of blood to the heart reminds us of the Duke's aversion to crowds expressed in the first scene; evidently the idea was active in the poet's mind, possibly because the new King at the time (James I) was known to have such an aversion.   **31-33** His salutation to Isabella is jaunty! (30) In his present susceptible state, her word *pleasure* is sexually suggestive to him, and his words *know it* play upon the suggestion.   **34-41** Isabella's resignation to Claudio's death is unalienating, because it is expressed in association with concern for his soul. As a religious, she is more intent upon saving souls than lives.   **42-50** The excessiveness of Angelo's expression of disgust with fornication, linking it with murder, has its intended effect, and Isabella is trapped into repeating her former 'defense' of the act.   **51-81** This is subtly revealing. As they speak at cross-purposes, Isabella is unable to understand the drift of Angelo's remarks, and he is unable to believe that she is as innocent as she seems. His own mind sullied, he assumes that hers must be too, and he brings veiled charges of hypocrisy. Still, to some degree, his mind continues working in its former ethical channels, and, almost inadvertently, he concedes that he is on thin ice when he excludes consideration of the *soul* while speaking of the *body* and *compelled sins* (59-60)—a delicate touch of characterization.　　**82-116**　In speaking *more gross,* Angelo remains indirect and puts a hypothetical case. Isabella is at her best in countering it. Her affirmation that she would rather die than prostitute herself is put in such imaginatively vivid terms that it enforces belief (99-104). Her position is that she will not pay with the death of her soul for the life of her own or her brother's body, and she properly counters Angelo's ingenious casuistry (109-10) that her refusal would be as cruel as his own refusal of pardon. The two things are *nothing kin* (113) because Angelo ignores the factor of motive.　　**117-20**　Her tone softens appealingly as she admits that she has compromised herself in certain of the arguments she has used.　　**121-38**　Note the opposite response of the two to the idea of universal human frailty. To Isabella it suggests that Claudio may appropriately be shown mercy. To Angelo it suggests that others, especially women, may appropriately yield to temptation.　　**139-70**　The debate is swiftly and excitingly concluded. Thwarted in his attempt to rationalize his proposal, Angelo is forced to put it in crude quid-pro-quo terms, and Isabella's response is a stirring denunciation. It should be noted to her credit that, in the midst of her anger, she thinks she has been given a means of saving her brother (152), and we would be straining indeed if we maintained that this exposes her own capacity for blackmail. As Angelo disabuses her mind, and meets threat with hideous threat, his ruthlessness is convincing; he moves with the rush of one who has cast off habitual restraints.　　**171-87**　This speech sums up the situation and carries the interest forward; Isabella's very certainty that Claudio will approve her action creates a doubt in our minds and an eagerness to witness their interview. (It would be unfortunate if we should let this superbly written scene reduce itself in our minds to the terms of the unhappily mechanical couplet

(184-85) which filters out all its ethical and emotional nuances. Much has been written on whether Isabella makes the right or the wrong choice, with attendant attacks upon and defenses of her character. The discussion is irrelevant except in the context of the play. If the play treats the consequences of her choice as fortunate, it is ipso facto the right one. If we extract the alternative offered her and view it theoretically, we recognize that there is no room for a right choice. We cannot countenance coercion, and non-resistance to evil, no matter what act Angelo requires Isabella to perform. That it is of a sexual nature is beside the point; we must accept its gravity from her point of view. However, we cannot countenance either her assumption that her act, any act, performed to save another means the death of her soul, since the assumption predicates a merciless God. Shakespeare has tilted the debate in her favor, denying Angelo some good arguments. All we can say of a dilemma where a good choice is denied one is that one should choose, according to his lights, the lesser evil. This Isabella does. The treatment of the situation is so stimulating that it sends our thoughts exploring, but the over-all intention is clear. In some respects Angelo and Isabella are in the same situation; both discover that it is easier to remain unsullied in the cloister than in the world, but the similarity ends there: Angelo fails the test as Isabella does not. In reward she is rescued from the consequences of her choice. A third alternative is found for her, a means of saving her brother without danger of losing her soul. In Walter Scott's *Heart of Midlothian* Jeanie Deans is similarly rewarded after she has refused to save the life of her sister by committing, not an act of prostitution, but of simple perjury. To couple acts of ideal morality with joyful consequences is a resource available to fictionists. We may justly say that the kind of dilemma here involved is more proper to tragedy than comedy, if the elimination of fortuitous escapes will make for a more satisfying moral conclusion. It is instructive to speculate on the direction a tragic version might take. Classical literature suggests themes. Isabella might sacrifice her chastity, then take her own life; or she might let Claudio die, then take her own life in remorse. In either case, Angelo will be executed by the Duke, who will survive to ponder the consequences of his own initial evasion of responsibility. But those Christian scruples, which give moral dimension to the dilemma in the first place, militate against suicide with its positive proof of the heroine's sincerity; hence the way seems blocked to a tragic treatment of the fable. It is difficult to decide what one might have advised the playwright to do.)

III, i

The Duke prepares Claudio's mind for death by delivering a sermon on the ills of life. When Isabella arrives, he eavesdrops on her interview with her brother. This takes an unexpected turn. After Claudio hears that his life can be saved only by shameful means, he eagerly asks what they are. When she tells of Angelo's proposal, he agrees that she should not comply, but he speaks without conviction and presently begins to waver. To her horror, he begins to minimize the proposed offense, speaks of the terrors of death, and finally asks her to make the sacrifice. In outrage she ignores his pleas to be heard further, and is denouncing him as a dishonorable coward when the Duke intervenes. The Duke tells the contrite Claudio that Angelo was only testing Isabella's virtue, and he must prepare to die. After arranging with the Provost for a private conference with Isabella, he proposes to her a way to save her brother without loss of honor. One Mariana, to whom Angelo is bound by troth-plight, is still in love with him although he has jilted her after the loss of her dowry. If Isabella will pretend to yield to Angelo, Mariana can take her place in the secret assignation, thus consummating a marriage and making it binding. Angelo will pardon Claudio while still under the illusion that he has lain with the object of his present lust. Isabella willingly consents to this plan, and agrees to meet the Duke at the moated grange, where Mariana dwells, after she has made the necessary appointment with Angelo.

1-151 In bidding Claudio *Be absolute for death* (5) the Friar-Duke is not closing the possibility of a pardon, but saying that Claudio will be the better for coming to terms with death whether he lives or dies. The sermon (5-41) is one of the best of its kind in the Mediaeval and Renaissance 'contemptus mundi' tradition, designed to woo men from preoccupation with this corrupt and frustrating world to thoughts of a better world to come. The style is consciously clerical, with the parallel series of negations modulating the rhythm almost in the fashion of a chant, and with its allusions to *death's fool,* the devouring *worm, dust,* the equal miseries of rich and poor, of young and *palsied eld* all properly traditional. True to its kind, this speech denigrates life, but it contains much bitter truth. However, it must be recognized that an ironical element attends its presence in this scene, where it functions in conjunction with Claudio's horrified cry against death (118-32). Like the sermon, this has its distinctive tone, seeming to issue from a throat tight with fright and despair, as the speaker's mind is seared by hideous visions. The two speeches are sufficiently separated from each other for their affiliation to escape suspicion of clever patness, but their complementary nature is indisputable—the gloomy comfort in the words rejecting life, the answering agony in the words rejecting death. The interview of sister and brother is as painful, one is tempted to say as cruel, as anything in Shakespeare. Isabella feels the turn of the screw as she gets the reverse of the reassurance she craves, and there is psychological truth in her almost hysterical outburst of rage. She deserves our sympathy, not our condemnation. But Claudio deserves sympathy, too, as he is subjected to the ultimate in humiliation, passing in a moment through extremes of uncertainty, terror, and self-loathing. The dialogue is managed with matchless skill as it reveals Claudio grasping at straws, expressing his half-hearted approval of his sister's virtue and weak gratitude for her counsel, his faltering rationalizations (in which he instances Angelo's character as a guide to permissible conduct!), his inability to withhold his ignoble plea, then his final sense of abasement—*O hear me, Isabella!* (151); and as it reveals Isabella's initial confidence, her first uneasiness, her horror as she finds herself unable to deflect the course of her brother's thoughts, then her own final loss of control—*'Tis best that thou diest quickly* (151). The impact is tremendous.   **152-261**   What follows is less in need of explication than apology. This play, from II, ii, 1 to III, i, 151, the point we have just reached, contains dramatic poetry as intense, imaginative, and passionately ratiocinative as any to be found in

Shakespeare outside his major tragedies. What preceded II, ii, 1 was adequate as preparation for this central section of the play. But what follows III, i, 151, although there are occasional fine passages, and much interesting subject matter and plotting, gives a general sense of let-down. Why should this be? Perhaps we should first answer a related question. Why should this scene, written thus far in the most vital of blank verse, be concluded in stuffy prose? The Duke's speeches are wordily grandiloquent, and Isabella's sound as if they had been copied from an Elizabethan manual of genteel conversation (157-59, 202-03, 207-08, etc.). One can only hazard a guess. When the Duke steps in to take an active part, the resolution of the dilemma begins and we are on our way to the happy ending. The playwright is forced to recall that he is writing a drama of intrigue, not high tragedy, and he suddenly reigns in Pegasus. He tries to write this portion of the scene, with its plotty developments, in a transitional style—with dignity but without poetry or passion. The result is what we see. (Of course there is a chance that some accident has intervened. The conclusion of the play may represent the hasty salvaging of work left incomplete, or the beginning of the play may represent an interrupted revision. It seems to be Shakespeare's own writing throughout.) Whatever its reason, the result of the shift in tone and technique is that all the major characters suffer in our estimation. The Duke begins to appear as a mere master of intrigue, needlessly devious, telling lies with abandon, and subjecting good and bad alike to groundless apprehension. Angelo, who previously has at least possessed dignity, is diminished in retrospect to a jilt, who has balked at marriage not because of asceticism but because of cash considerations. Isabella falls in with the Duke's scheme almost apathetically, certainly without an ethical qualm. There is nothing wrong with the 'bed trick' as such, granting the propensity of the times to view the propriety of sexual relations in terms of their legality. The trouble is that the playwright does not prepare us emotionally for the consummation. Angelo is disqualified as a husband for Mariana not so much by his villainy as by his indifference to her. Mariana's love, and Isabella's sympathy with it, are insufficiently dwelled upon. We expect the same kind of emotional justification for actions as we have been getting, but the justification is not forthcoming. Even Lucio, amusing though the process is, descends to the level of mere coxcomb. The over-elaborate nature of the action, as compared with what has gone before, will speak for itself.

III, ii

Pompey, who is again in Elbow's charge for pandering, defends his occupation against the Duke's strictures. The Duke approves the arrest, but privately deplores the character of the man who will judge the culprit. Pompey appeals to Lucio for bail, but is greeted by heartless witticisms and led off to prison. Lucio now engages in a long conversation with the Duke, disparaging Angelo's campaign against lechery, and contrasting his frigidity with the alleged lustfulness of the disguised listener. The Duke hears himself traduced as a squire of dames, whom Lucio knows intimately, and a very superficial fellow despite his supposed wisdom. Lucio refuses to withdraw these slanders, and brazenly supplies his name when threatened with reprisals upon the Duke's return. The latter is left musing upon the ubiquity of calumny, when Escalus and the Provost appear with Mistress Overdone under arrest. She accuses Lucio of having informed against her, in spite of her having cared for his illegitimate child by Kate Keepdown, whom he has betrayed with promises of marriage. She, too, is led off to prison. Escalus remains with the Duke, who voices priestly laments over the abuses of the times. He hears a better account of himself from Escalus than he has heard from Lucio, and he receives thanks for his ministrations to poor Claudio. When alone, he soliloquizes upon Angelo's iniquity, and upon the need for pitting cleverness against viciousness.

1-265 In this scene, which is continuous with the preceding, the style of the prose becomes acceptable again—largely because it is again appropriate to the subject matter. The scene provides a pause in the action such as is not uncommon in the plays after a succession of highly-charged dramatic episodes. The term 'comic relief' is less inappropriate here than is frequently the case. The humor is supplied by moral paradoxes, and the quaint humors of Elbow, Pompey, Mistress Overdone, and Lucio. As is usual with the humor in this play, it is overcast by its thematic relevance; the trophies of a vice-raid do not lend themselves to joyousness. Lucio moves into greater prominence as an entertaining 'fantastic,' resembling the 'Vice' character in moralities. The idea that eavesdroppers 'hear no good of themselves' is comically exploited, at some cost to the Duke's dignity as deus ex machina, but, of course, to the advantage of amusing complication. As part of the review of the present situation and preparation for the denouement, Escalus reappears as 'good judge' in apposition to Angelo as 'bad judge,' and his truth-speaking is counterpoised with Lucio's scandal-mongering. The Duke's final jogging couplets strike us almost as a request by the playwright to accept the schematization to come, and not to look for poetic profundity.

IV, i

Mariana is listening to a plaintive song, when she is visited by the Duke, who in his role as friar has been serving as her spiritual advisor. Isabella joins them, and after Mariana withdraws for a moment at the Duke's request, reports that she has arranged with Angelo for a brief midnight assignation in the darkness of his garden. The Duke then summons Mariana and bids her confer in private with Isabella. While they are absent, he muses upon the misconceptions which fasten upon the actions of the great. Isabella returns with Mariana, who has agreed to the substitution if her religious counselor approves. The Duke assures her that it will be no sin since Angelo is her contracted husband.

1-75 The song is lovely, and the blank verse is fine however low-pitched. Considerable care is taken to distinguish between the ethics of Mariana's going to Angelo's bed and Isabella's doing so. Mariana is Angelo's legally betrothed, and the Duke in his priestly role sanctions the act. We must remember, too, the visual symbols: Mariana is not wearing the garb of a votarist. Although the situation is irremediably awkward, no playwright could have handled it more delicately than this one.

IV, ii

The Provost appoints Pompey assistant to Abhorson the executioner, and the two debate the merits of their trades. Claudio is told to prepare for his death in the morning. His fellow prisoner, Barnardine the murderer, refuses to be roused for instructions. The Duke brings the Provost the good news that Claudio may be reprieved, but when Angelo's messenger comes, he brings orders that Claudio be executed as scheduled and his head remitted as evidence. Casting about for a means of meeting this crisis, the Duke inquires about Barnardine and is told that he richly deserves execution but has thus far evaded it by his obduracy in resisting spiritual preparation. The Duke persuades the Provost to postpone Claudio's execution. Angelo can be deceived by the dispatch of Barnardine's head in place of his. The Provost is shown the hand and seal of the Duke, who, he is told, is about to return to Vienna and will certainly approve the ruse.

1-201 See under IV, iii.

IV, iii

Pompey inventories the former customers of Mistress Overdone now languishing in prison. He arouses Barnardine as Abhorson directs, but the felon is obviously in an unregenerate state. When he rejects spiritual admonition, the Duke is unwilling that he be sent to death unprepared. The Provost suggests that they use the head of the pirate Ragozine, who has just died in prison and whose resemblence to Claudio will insure the deception of Angelo. The Duke gladly accepts this proposal, and makes certain that the secret of Claudio's survival will be kept until he himself is ready to discard his disguise. When the Provost has departed with the head of Ragozine, Isabella comes to the prison in expectation of her brother's reprieve. The Duke tells her that Angelo's treachery has circumvented them, and that Claudio is dead. Their only course now is to expose the perfidy of the deputy. The true Duke is returning, and has instructed Angelo and Escalus to meet him at the city gates. Isabella is to carry a message to Friar Peter, who will aid her and Mariana to have their case against Angelo heard. Lucio now visits the prison, and condoles with Isabella over the fate of Claudio, but he proves no more respectful than before in his allusions to the Duke. The latter is unable to shake off his unsavory company, but takes note of his boastful admission of having gotten a woman with child.

1-174　This scene and the preceding function as a unit. The sociocomic matter and the serious intrigue are now permitted to alternate intimately and even to intermingle. Pompey continues to entertain with inverted moralizing as he views life in Vienna from the vantage point of the gutter; the macabre species of humor formerly associated with executioners is levied upon. Observe how the emotional responses of the characters are now reined in by the playwright so as not to impede the plot. Claudio receives final notice of his death without a quaver, indeed with small talk about a fellow prisoner (ii, 61-63). The Duke takes the news of Angelo's treachery in his stride; he gives no answer to the Provost's *What say you to this, sir?* (123) but gets on at once with his plotting. Isabella receives the unexpected news of Angelo's treachery with a single line of empty threat (iii, 117), and the cruelly false news of her brother's death with a few conventional exclamations (iii, 119-20), reminding us of those in the false-death scene in *Romeo and Juliet* (see above, p. 159). It is not unusual for the emotional response of characters to be made proportionate to the facts as known to the audience rather than as known to themselves—psychological plausibility is properly sacrificed to total artistic effect—but, as previously noted, the difficulty in this case is that we remember so well the capacity for emotional response of these particular characters. What the playwright has done earlier is at war with what he is doing now. The sardonic humor involving the unregenerate Barnardine, with the grotesque business of the substituted head, is less gratuitous than it might seem. At least we can guess how the playwright came to include it. If a felon can save his life by the simple expedient of refusing to express the penitence before execution required by custom, we have another illustration of the paradoxes of man-administered justice. Punishment and immunity from punishment go partly by accident.

IV, iv

Angelo and Escalus prepare for the Duke's return. His letters have been contradictory, but it is certain that he wishes them to deliver up their authority at the city gates, having proclaimed beforehand that anyone with a grievance will be heard at once. Escalus leaves to issue the proclamation, and Angelo remains to consult with his conscience. He believes that Isabella's shame will prevent her from exposing him, and that his secret is safe; nevertheless, he realizes the enormity of his offenses and wishes that Claudio, whom he betrayed in order to forestall vengeance, had been allowed to live.

1-32   The situation is, in some measure, rationalized—by conjectural excuses for the Duke's strange proceedings, and by an explanation of Angelo's treachery. It is not unusual for an action to precede the indication of its motive. The token-expression of compunction by Angelo is to prepare us for his penitence and pardon.

IV, v

The Duke in his proper person prepares for his reappearance in Vienna. He coaches Friar Peter in the part he is to play, tells him that the Provost is now aware of the true situation, and sends him with letters to various friends who are to meet him at his lodgings outside the city to form a cortege for him as he approaches the gates. He is joined by one Varrius, who has been aiding him in his preparations.

1-13   Observe the suspense-building, and the creation of illusion. The busy arrangements and the naming of specific places and persons lend an air of plausibility.

IV, vi

Isabella and Mariana on their way to the gates discuss the instructions they have received. Isabella is not to be surprised if the Duke at first responds hostilely to her charges against Angelo. Friar Peter comes to conduct them to a good stand near the gates, through which the leading citizens of Vienna have already passed in advance of the returning Duke.

1-15 This, like the preceding brief scenes, straightens out plotlines as it shows the major characters converging on what is at once a locale and a climax. The function of these scenes may be compared with that of the similar series preceding the assassination scene in *Julius Caesar*.

V, i

As the Duke is commending Angelo and Escalus for their good service, Isabella kneels before him and cries out for justice, then enumerates the crimes committed by his deputy. When Angelo describes her as mad, the Duke agrees that she must be so, but remarks upon her rational manner of speaking and lets her continue her story. She does so, interrupted by Lucio, whose quips continue in spite of the Duke's rebukes. At the conclusion of her accusations, the Duke professes disbelief and orders her to prison for conspiracy to commit slander. Her presumed accomplice is one 'Friar Lodowick' whom Lucio describes as a scurvy fellow whom he has encountered at the prison making slanderous remarks about the Duke himself. Friar Peter steps forward to defend this 'Lodowick,' who, he explains, is too ill to appear in person, and offers to produce a witness who will aver the falsity of Isabella's charges. As Isabella is led off, Mariana enters veiled. She describes herself as neither maid, wife, nor widow, and makes other statements which mystify the company and provoke Lucio to further efforts of wit. Angelo orders her to unveil. She reveals her identity and her role in his supposed assignation with Isabella. When she and Angelo give conflicting accounts of their broken troth-plight, the Duke pretends that he believes that she, too, is guilty of slander, and orders the Provost to produce the mysterious 'Friar Lodowick.' Angelo and Escalus are to conduct the inquiry while he himself retires. He resumes his disguise off-stage while Escalus is questioning Lucio, then returns in the company of the Provost and Isabella, who has been summoned back to the scene. As 'Friar Lodowick' he replies to the questions of Escalus by saying he has nothing to fear and by inveighing against the corruption of Vienna. Escalus accuses him of inciting the women to slander, and orders him and them to prison, whereupon Lucio grows abusive and tears off his friar's-cowl. As the Duke stands revealed, Lucio tries to slink off, and Angelo confesses his crimes. The latter is ordered to marry Mariana at once; and, while the ceremony is taking place, the Duke begs Isabella's pardon for failing to save her brother. He condemns Angelo to die, as 'measure for measure' since he has procured the death of Claudio. Mariana pleads for the life of her new husband, and in charity Isabella joins in the plea. The Duke finds a pretext for sending for Barnardine, and the Provost produces both him and a second prisoner whom he has reprieved. When this proves to be Claudio, Angelo, who has penitently asked for death, is pardoned along with Barnardine. For his calumnies against the Duke, Lucio is ordered to marry his whore, a fate which he considers worse than the whipping and hanging that have been threatened. In conclusion the Duke declares his intention to sue for the hand of Isabella.

1-534   There can be no denying the success of this conclusion as a theatrical tour de force. Its effectiveness goes far to justifying the Duke's devious methods of keeping all the cards in his own hands; he has, comedy-wise, subjected characters to temporary pain before giving them joyous relief. Its splendidly written blank verse is sufficient to obliterate the rough structural joints as the characters shuttle in and out on arbitrary and quickly-performed errands. The succession of delayed revelations and gratifying exposures is calculated to provide maximum delight. But we cannot deny either, that the excess of contrivance prevents us from taking this conclusion very seriously. It lacks the moral impact and inevitability that the theme of the play would seem to demand. The various marriages with which it is capped (as a proper comedy) are all sullied, and entered into under constraint. Probably Isabella and the Duke would leave the stage hand in hand, thus signifying without need for an embarrassing declaration on her part that she is destined to become a duchess instead of a sister of Saint Clare. Such things are permissible in a comedy of intrigue, but not in a Christian allegory such as this is often taken to be. True, religious notes are struck to the end, but we cannot, in honesty, accept the Duke as a symbol of Providence, or defer to him as a great spiritual force, in view of the ambiguity of his own actions and the way he has shrunk in stature through his involvement in petty intrigue and his collision with a petty person like Lucio. A jester may gambol about a king but not about a Christ-symbol. Only in one detail can the Duke's sleight-of-hand be defended as anything more than good entertainment—it does give Isabella a chance, while still believing she is wronged, to plead for her oppressor Angelo, thus returning good for evil and validating by her acts her own earlier words in praise of mercy. Again Isabella passes a test. *Measure for Measure,* then, is a problem play in more ways than one. It is so, in the usual sense, because it makes us constantly debate in our minds the ethical issues it treats. It is so in another sense, because it presents us with an artistic problem. Although indubitably a success as one kind of play, it defeats our hopes of a success of a higher kind. Although created with great skill, it fails to crystallize into inevitable form like Shakespeare's other masterpieces. It lacks homogeneity, and promises more than it performs. Oddly enough, our final impression is that parts of it are too good for the *kind* of play it is.

IV

Death and Poetry

1

Aspects of Good and Evil

:

Hamlet, Othello, Macbeth and *King Lear* are bright particular stars in the poetic firmament. They have shown uncanny vitality in the theatre, with productions abundant even in periods when whole clusters of Shakespeare's comedies and histories were dropped from the repertory. Although *King Lear* was acceptable only in adapted form for a century and a half after 1680, at least its semblance was constantly staged; and its fellow masterpieces have been the least affected of all Renaissance literature by 'changing climates of sensibility.' These are the plays which first carried Shakespeare's fame abroad. The wine of his humor and fantasy does not always travel, and the conspicuously 'native' orientation of his histories has proved a limiting factor, but the tragedies, especially these four, have been adopted as their own by most national and ethnic groups. They are now performed in scores of languages all over the world, from outposts in Arctic Siberia to kraals in southernmost Africa.

Gabriel Harvey, a pundit of Shakespeare's own times, remarked that *Hamlet* has something in it 'to please the wiser sort.' The wiser sort have been occupied with it ever since. It was *Hamlet* which first induced Coleridge to exercise his 'turn for philosophical criticism,' and it was this play along with *Othello, Macbeth,* and *King Lear* which provided the substance of Bradley's famous lectures on Shakespeare early in the present century. These four plays account for more than half of the vast body of Shakespearean criticism in existence. The flow of commentary has by no means abated; indeed now more than ever before 'definition' of Shakespearean tragedy is the literary critic's bow of Achilles. Whether great tragedy (or great art in general) is susceptible to definition is a moot point, but the attempts have often been illuminating as well as valiant. They will not be rivaled here; however a brief note on Elizabethan conceptions of tragedy may be helpful to the reader.

Most discussions begin or end with quotations from Aristotle's *Poetics,* but the Aristotelian definition of tragedy had little currency in Elizabethan England, and no influence whatever upon the popular playwrights. Aristotle had analyzed Greek tragedy with the acumen of an intellectual genius, and although he did not succeed in defining it, he perhaps came as close as a logician could. Since Shakespearean and Greek tragedy have some (although by no means all) features in common, some of Aristotle's comments apply, coincidentally, to the plays we are considering, but they are a poor point of departure for arriving at a basic conception of them. Of necessity, his remarks apply even less perfectly to *Hamlet* or *King Lear* than to *Oedipus* or the *Oresteia.*

When Shakespeare's King Richard invites his faithful remnant to sit upon the ground and 'tell sad stories of the death of kings,' he is invoking the concept of tragedy inherited by the Renaissance from the Middle Ages. A tragedy was the sad story of the death of a king or someone comparably eminent. Death was the nexus—as it was not in Greek tragedy. The first adjustment the modern reader must make in achieving rapport with our older literature is to accept death as a fitting subject for contemplation. We tend to think of death as something in rather poor taste, its traces to be genteelly disguised and its inevitability to be put out of the mind. The idea that the death of the protagonist must be shown, illogically, as *deserved* was not originally part of the concept of tragedy. Most of the victims in the 'tragedies' narrated by Chaucer's Monk were as virtuous as they were eminent. Tragedy dealt with eminent men and 'unnatural' death because the stories were available and imposing. There is no essential difference between reversal from great affluence and power and reversal from hale middle age. If even kings must suffer and die, all men must suffer and die. Tragedy was designed to make men come to terms with this great reality.

During the late Middle Ages and early Renaissance, 'tragedy'— first in narrative poetry and then in drama—tended to become morally and politically utilitarian. The more acceptable tragic stories were those which displayed suffering and death as the wages of sin or abuse of power. In Sidney's definition, 'high and mighty tragedy' castigated vice by showing its consequences to the vicious, and taught kings 'not to be tyrants.' If a playwright in Shakespeare's time treated a story of crime and punishment in high places, interspersing his treatment with lofty moral sentiments, he was meeting all the presumed obligations of the tragic poet. Ben Jonson followed this prescription as did most other playwrights; a few were daring enough to make sin even in middle-class homes the subject of their dramatic homilies.

However, the basic conception of tragedy was never wholly lost to view, and the virtuous might die in tragedy without bewildering audiences or evoking cries for 'poetic justice.' A second, somewhat later and less common, modification of the basic concept actually made moral capital of virtue rather than vice. We might call this 'inspirational' tragedy. A woman who died in defense of her honor, or a man who died in defense of his country, might appear as a theme of praise and object lesson in the way to win lasting fame. The ethical and patriotic bias of this species of Elizabethan tragedy distinguishes it from the hagiologic drama of the Middle Ages, but the vast contemporary literature of religious martyrdom, Protestant and Catholic, provided a propitious climate. The dramatic treatment of English history encouraged the portrayal of self-sacrificing national heroes, like Shakespeare's Lord Talbot in *1 Henry VI,* and the currency of classical literature encouraged the portrayal of secular heroines such as Lucrece and Virginia or their more modern counterparts. This inspirational tragedy, with its emotional commitment to ideas of martyrdom and sacrifice, was apt to be written by playwrights of the humbler sort, and much of it has perished.

The range of tragedy was great in this permissive age, and we are apt to encounter anything from occasional religious allegories, like Marlowe's *Doctor Faustus* to theatrical 'dreadfuls' like the same author's *Jew of Malta*. A tragedy might encorporate many things: it might be a thrilling spectacle of bloody criminality, 'gladiatorial' in appeal, and yet show its mediaeval heritage by seriously contemplating death. It might represent the suffering of some of its characters as just retribution for evil actions, and the suffering of others as sacrificial atonement. It might defer to both 'Stoic' and 'Christian' moral sentiments, not always easily distinguishable. It might resemble on the one hand a Senecan revenge play, and on the other a mediaeval morality. It might be, and often was, a curious conglomerate of villainous intrigue and moral philosophy.

Shakespeare was the one, and almost the only one, who fully succeeded in synthesizing the disparate elements of 'Elizabethan tragedy.' With him, especially in the four major examples, tragedy became the vehicle of expression for most of what men have felt and thought about the human predicament. Death is the central mystery. Of all earth's creatures man is the only one aware of inevitable death and curious about the value of life. From awareness of mortality comes the conception of immortality; and from the life-death antinomy come ultimately all religious and moral codes, including Shakespeare's eclectic code of affirmation. What is on the side of life is good. What is on the side of death is evil. Good men believe in life after death—if not life for themselves, at least life for others. Evil men believe that the universe ends when they end. To create is good, to destroy is evil. Kindness is good, cruelty evil. To take but never give, to use but never nurture, to hate but never love—these things are evil. To contain animal appetite within the bounds of reason, to cherish the welfare of others, to meet the obligations of membership in the human community by cultivating the generous impulses of fidelity, gratitude, mercy—these things are good. The tragedy of life is the persistence of death and evil. The consolation is that good survives, and life goes on.

Shakespeare's tragedies are filled with tremendous conviction.

The good is so manifestly preferable that the power of evil, like the power of death, is viewed as a dreadful mystery. It remains the same mystery in all four plays, but it changes its aspect from one to another. *Hamlet* progresses in the shadow of past transgressions; evil is a haunting memory, and good an aspiration. In *Othello* evil is personified in one diabolical character who has not, and has never had, any good in him. In *Macbeth* it is a growth from within, rotting tissue which once was good. In *Lear* it is a combination of these things with others, its dimensions truly terrifying. But as the power of evil grows, so also does the power of good, which also appears in many guises. As these plays take hold of us, we feel a strengthening of our spiritual sinews. And yet they are never mere allegories of warfare between abstractions. They are enthralling stories acted out, filled with human interest in the most familiar sense of the term. They are also filled with poetry. Rather they *are* poetry, which can only be defined by itself.

2

Hamlet

:

I, i

IN A midnight changing of the guard, Francisco is relieved by Bernardo and Marcellus, the latter accompanied by Horatio, who has come to share their vigil. He cannot believe their story that for the past two nights, at the stroke of one, a spirit has appeared in the likeness of the late King Hamlet. As Bernardo is rehearsing the circumstances, the Ghost again appears, but silently stalks off as Horatio charges it to speak. They wonder what this visitation augurs for the troubled times. Denmark is arming against young Fortinbras of Norway, who has raised forces for a lawless bid to retrieve the territories forfeited by his father, conquered and slain when he dared to challenge King Hamlet to combat. The Ghost again appears. Horatio adjures it to reveal its wishes, but it guiltily retreats as the cock crows, defeating their attempt to intercept it. They speak of the power of the herald of the morn to banish ghosts to their confine, and of the legendary banishment of evil spirits the whole night long on the anniversary of Christ's nativity. They feel sure that the Ghost would speak to the young Prince Hamlet, and they resolve to tell him of it.

1-20 To Bernardo's *Who's there?* Francisco's *Nay, answer me,* with the stress falling on *me,* is the right soldierly response. His challenges and the replies (2-3, 14-15), varied though they are, have the ring of military ritual and suggest the faithfully guarded citadel. This, with the comradely regard shown by these dutiful men for each other, produces a 'comfortable' effect—of human solidarity and intimacy, fortified by Horatio's humorous nayword *A piece of him.* But the 'comfortable' is immersed in the 'uncomfortable.' Vigilance spells danger, and it is midnight, cold, and dark (they can scarcely discern each other). Francisco's *'Tis bitter cold, And I am sick at heart* comes naturally enough from the lips of a sentinel after a lonely watch, but it also, like a note struck on a tuning-fork, supplies the tragic pitch. Soon Hamlet, indeed Denmark itself, will appear *sick at heart.*   **21-51** Horatio's *What, has this thing appeared again tonight?* induces the 'shivery' feeling noted by Coleridge because *this thing,* like the later uses of *it,* locates the apparition in the non-human realm of the cold and the dark, where this cluster of warm and well-disposed men stands as a small beach-head. Horatio's skepticism objectifies our own, and delegates it; we are ready to be convinced when he is convinced and, like him, to be harrowed with *fear and wonder* when the Ghost appears. The others wish Horatio to speak to it because he is a *scholar* (42)—that is, proficient in Latin, the language used in exorcising evil spirits. Evil is thus immediately associated with this spirit, but there is countering suggestion: it wears the *fair and warlike form* of Denmark's late King, and when Horatio addresses it as no subject should dare to address a king, it is *offended,* but unaggressively *stalks away* (50).   **52-125**   The opening moments, rich in atmosphere, and daring to a degree in immediately creating a tension difficult to sustain, are followed by a brief expository respite. Our attention is held by the vividly pictorial language describing the nation urgently arming (71-79), and by the suggestion of an ominous connection between the past events being narrated and the ghastly visitant just seen. Note the compact recapitulation (113-20) of the portents which had appeared in *Julius Caesar,* still fresh in the poet's mind, and the way Horatio's terms create a sense of general unease: *some strange eruption to our state* (69), *this posthaste and romage in the land* (107), *A mote it is to trouble the mind's eye* (112). Physical affliction is being levied upon in the imagery, and the word *sick* (120) is repeated.   **126-57**   There has been no hint that the Ghost would return, and this second appearance is more startling than the first because our skeptical defenses have been breached. The wordplay of Horatio's *I'll cross it* (i.e. 'oppose it' and 'confront it with the sign of the cross') is visually paralleled: the unusual stage direction *He spreads his arms* indicates that Horatio puts himself in the posture of opposition, and also that his body assumes the form of a cross. Although not an exorcism, his speech has ritualistic features, with its three *If* clauses punctuated by short lines: *Speak to me . . . Speak to me . . . O speak* (129-35). It admits the possibility that the Ghost is not evil: three motives commonly associated with haunting spirits are mentioned, and one of these is that the dead may return because of earthly business left incomplete—some *good thing to be done* (130). The attack with partisans both demonstrates the Ghost's immateriality and provides occasion for a bit of stage deception: as the eyes of the audience followed one running figure crying *'Tis here,* then another crying *'Tis here,* the Ghost *faded* (157). The question of whether it is evil remains in suspension. Marcellus thinks they may have done it wrong, being *majestical* (143), and yet it started at the cock-crow *like a guilty thing* (148) since it belongs to the unwholesome night.   **158-75**   The tone of the speakers alters as fears recede with the cleansing approach of dawn. Their recent experience with life after death lends appropriateness to the allusion to Christ, and we get the lovely lines on Nativity night, *So hallowed and so gracious is that time* (158-64). As a rational man, Horatio believes in miracles only with reservations—*in part* (165)—just as he believed in ghosts, but two of his lines evoke in our minds the recurrent miracle of the dawn (166-67). This great opening scene of this great play poses the first of the cumulative questions posed by the work as a whole: Is this Ghost good or evil, and what does its visit portend? The scene ends with the first mention of the titular character, in terms which set him apart from ordinary men: this spirit *dumb* to others will surely speak to *young Hamlet*.

I, ii

King Claudius reminds his court of how his grief for his brother's death has been discreetly tempered: with the consent of his councilors he has taken his sister-in-law to wife. He then disposes of various items of state business, sending Cornelius and Voltemand on a mission to the bedridden King of Norway, who is scarcely aware of the warlike intentions of his nephew Fortinbras; giving Laertes, son of his trusted minister Polonius, permission to return to France; and finally addressing words of advice to his stepson Hamlet. Both he and Queen Gertrude remonstrate with the young Prince for his excessive mourning. Hamlet responds ironically to Claudius's display of regard, and to his mother's question about his inconsolable grief over the loss of his father; but he consents to remain at court instead of returning to the University at Wittenberg. In elation Claudius dedicates the remainder of the day to carousing, and Hamlet is left communing bitterly with himself. Disgust with life makes him wish that suicide were no sin; within two months his admirable father has been succeeded on the throne by this detestable uncle, and his own mother has forgotten King Hamlet's love and hurried into an incestuous marriage. The Prince is joined by Marcellus and Bernardo, whom he greets courteously, and by his dear friend from Wittenberg, Horatio, whom he welcomes to Elsinore. He alludes satirically, then sadly, to the almost simultaneous death of his father and remarriage of his mother, and grows instantly intent when told of the apparition. When assured by his probings that it indeed wore his father's form, he agrees to watch with them this night and question it if it reappears. He urges secrecy, and, when they have left, voices his suspicions that the visitation means that there has been foul play.

1-41 The cunning rhetoric of Claudius sugar-coats the pill, so that his marriage to Gertrude (incestuous in canon law, as well as precipitous) is made to seem an act of virtue—a means of properly moderating two passions, grief and joy. The balancing off of the two in pat figurative phrases (10-13) terminated by the bluntly literal *Taken to wife* (14) is special pleading verging upon travesty. There is no sign that the pill proves hard for this court to swallow; the *sometime sister, now our queen* (8) is nearly brazen, and the fact is made clear that the court has *freely gone . . . along* (15-16). There is, perhaps, suspicious over-protestation in the repeated *dear brother's death* (1, 19), but Claudius's dispatch of state business is efficient and reasonably terse.   **42-63** The address to his envoys, *good Cornelius . . .* (34), *We doubt it nothing. Heartily farewell* (41) may not have exceeded normal royal courtesy, but the voice now becomes conspicuously ingratiating. Claudius has the politician's awareness of men's love of the sound of their own names, and his repetition of *Laertes* five times in twelve excessively polite lines (42-49, 57, 62-63) sounds almost obsequious.   **64-128** Hamlet's first speech in the play is a single line inserted as an aside between Claudius's unctuous salutation and his question. It punningly denies any similarity in nature between himself and Claudius or feeling of good will (*less than kind*) in spite of the double relationship the other has stressed (*more than kin*). His second speech, also a single line, punningly expresses a distaste for being addressed as Claudius's son and for being exposed to the sunshine of his royal favor (*too much in the sun*). The effect of these quick shots at Claudius's words on the wing is to establish at once the fact of Hamlet's mental agility and aversion for his uncle-stepfather. Gertrude's address sounds sincere (68-73), but as Hamlet picks up her word *common* (72, 74), we feel that he is using it in a sense different from hers because he has already made two slurring puns. There can be no doubt about his intent with the next word he picks up, *seems* (75, 76), which he immediately wrests into its pejorative sense of 'falsely appears,' so that in defending the sincerity of his own display of grief (76-86) he implies that that of certain others (unspecified) is hypocritical. Like his opening speech, Claudius's lengthy injunction (87-117) hovers just this side of travesty. Its patterned sententiousness stamps it as a public address, uttered for effect rather than for the immediate comfort of Hamlet, but the terms of endearment threaded through it are obviously intended to conciliate. Hamlet, whose tone changes with each speech, yields to their persuasions in a single lackluster line; and Claudius's effusive response, with his plans for a carouse and artillery salutes, seems absurdly incongruous; Hamlet's consent may have been *fair, gentle, unforced,* but it was certainly not *loving.* (The initial impression made by Gertrude is not unfavorable—she has at no point over-protested, and her words have sounded natural as well as solicitous. The initial impression made by Claudius is less unfavorable than might be—he has appeared eloquent and intelligent, capable of making wise observations, and the notes of insincerity in his remarks, with his over-desire to please, might well be excused if he proved, in the upshot, merely a diplomatist coping with a delicate official and domestic situation. At this point the one irrefragable fact counting against this pair is their precipitous marriage in the teeth of canon law and their presumed grief as loving wife and loving brother of the recently deceased.)   **129-59** Hamlet's accent is so individual that it brings his living presence before us. His words pour from him in surges of emotion, the frustrated longing for death (129-32), the disgust that seems to reach out and infect his world (133-37), the love tremulously expressed for his father and for the way his father had cherished his mother (138-42), the amazed disillusionment with his mother (143-55) evoking mental images shifting from classic dignity (*Niobe, all tears*) to lampoonlike indignity (*post With such dexterity to incestuous sheets!*). The magic of this language, so far as it can be analyzed, lies in the way thought combines with passion, concrete illustration with abstract interjection, broken utterance with continuous harmony—these are sobs to music. Psychologically, there is nothing puzzling about the emotions so far as their kind, as distinct from their strength is concerned; they are such as any sensitive young man would feel in similar circumstances. Hamlet's use of *Hercules* as illustration of his own opposite (153) is suggestive: Hercules was a doer, performing with dispatch the labors laid upon him. **160-83** Observe how Hamlet shifts almost instantaneously from tortured spirit to social adept, observing the amenities with equable grace. Are these shifts in mood indicative of instability, or heroic efforts of self-control? In either case they make unparalled demands upon an actor. In two lines (180-81) he makes a high-spirited ironic jest, and in the next two (182-83) the sob is back in his voice, all irony gone. **184-258** (We will have accepted in our stride the improbability that Horatio has been at Elsinore unseen by Hamlet until now.) As the message is conveyed, we get at the outset one of the glimpses into a mind by means of which the playwright produces his three-dimensional effects: Hamlet's figurative mention of seeing his father (184) provokes Horatio's startled *Where, my lord?* (185) because his experience of the previous night makes the words seem to him more than a figure of speech. Hamlet's rapid-fire questions, at one point resembling a cross-examination (228-30), have double value—they signal his anxious concern, and they dissipate in our own minds any lingering doubts about the reality of the Ghost. Also contributing to the air of plausibility is the slight disagreement among the witnesses (237-39). Hamlet's *Foul deeds will rise* (257), through proverbial association, suggest that murder has been committed. We may take this either as choral foreshadowing or as evidence of the speaker's already-aroused suspicions, but his insistence upon secrecy suggests the latter. (This scene has, of course, aroused our curiosity about the relations of Claudius and Gertrude, but the chief question it poses is on the nature of Hamlet. His melancholy, since it has already led him to thoughts of suicide, may strike us as abnormal. His grief is natural, as is his feeling of repugnance about the remarriage of his mother. It is only the strength of his emotions which suggest morbidity. But those in the scene who have insisted that his feelings of grief are too strong are the very ones whose own feelings of grief appear to have been somewhat weak, so that their opinion is cross-canceled. Again a question is left in suspension.)

I, iii

As he is about to embark for France, Laertes warns his sister Ophelia that she should view Hamlet's advances with caution. As a member of the royal family, he is beyond her reach, and however innocent his present intentions, she lies in danger of seduction. She promises to heed the warning, and bids Laertes to be as mindful of his own virtue as he is of hers. Polonius comes to speed him aboard, but delays him long enough to deliver a speech of good counsel. When left alone with his daughter, he repeats Laertes's warning in more arbitrary terms, and orders Ophelia to avoid Hamlet's society. She promises to obey.

1-54 This dialogue between brother and sister is not without charm. Laertes is fair to Hamlet as he explains the social obstacles to an honorable love-affair between him and Ophelia, and the didacticism of his words is relieved by fresh and poetic expressions (7-9, 36-37, 39-40), as is that of her counter-warning to him against the *primrose path of dalliance* (50). Laertes has the gentlemanly gift of speech, and may, so far as we can at present see, prove a force for good in the story; he is evidently a loyal brother and son, even accepting *as* a blessing a second blessing from his father.   **55-86** There was no sign of folly in Polonius in the last scene, nor is there immediately in this one. His advice is good advice, admirably expressed, and to view it as platitudinous is to be wise after the fact; to be sure the counsels are of ancient vintage, as good counsels are apt to be, but if the expression sounds stale, it is because it has since been staled by quotation. If there is an element of mockery here, it lies in the fact that Polonius speaks at such time-consuming length after warning Laertes to hurry.   **87-135** Unless we count his share in the venality of a court acquiescent to a shady royal marriage, Polonius's defects begin to obtrude only at this point. In contrast with the moderation and reasonableness of Laertes' warning, his sounds petulant, nagging, suspicious. In place of the gracious metaphors of youth, we hear the labored conceits of age. Observe the speaker's smug satisfaction in his play on the word *tender* (105-09). Has Polonius reached the age when one fortifies himself with conceit and assertiveness against the recognition that one's faculties are in decline? Ophelia has much less to say than either of these others although the attention is focused on her. What she says is consistently mild in purport and gentle in expression; indeed her docility is almost disturbing.

I, iv

Hamlet keeps midnight watch with Horatio and Marcellus, as trumpet-flourishes and cannon-salutes sound the wassail kept by Claudius. The Prince deplores this drunken custom, and speaks of how a whole body can corrupt from a single defect. The Ghost reappears. Hamlet calls for heavenly protection, but in defiance of his fears he addresses the Ghost as father and begs it to reveal its purpose. When it silently beckons him to follow, he rejects the warning of Horatio that it may madden him and tempt him to death. Throwing off the restraining hands of his comrades, he follows the Ghost, leaving them to trail anxiously behind.

1-38 The atmosphere of the first scene is swiftly recreated, with the off-stage sounds reminding us of the court subsequently glimpsed—a court where recent death can be followed by *swaggering* revels. Horatio appears to be a detached cosmopolite, a traveling humanist to whom Danish customs must be explained. Hamlet, too, seems in a measure detached, a thoughtful spectator of a society he is in but not morally of. His speech is of the 'philosophical' generalizing kind, proceeding, with parenthetical addenda resembling footnotes (24-26, 31), from a particular Danish drinking bout, to Danish drunkenness, to blighted Danish honor, to the blighting of honor generally by single defects generally. There is such stress upon the insidious operation of *the stamp of one defect* (31), *the vicious mole of nature* (24), *the o'ergrowth of some complexion* (27) in undermining men otherwise *pure as grace* that we are bound to wonder if the words can be thematic, and apply in some fashion to the speaker himself.   **39-57** The cry to interceding heavenly agents for protection is in harmony with the mediaeval setting of the legend, Roman Catholicism serving as the official faith of the play. The ambiguity of the Ghost, its undetermined status as good or evil, is explicitly recognized in a series of alternatives (40-42), and Hamlet seems aware of fearful risks in addressing it. His words have immense incantory power, with their images of the tomb, of the armored corpse revisiting the *glimpses of the moon* (magical phrase), and of the mortals quaking with fear. The last questions (57) come out spasmodically, like gasps.

58-91 At the moment there is small suggestion that the Ghost can be anything but evil and dangerous. Horatio's warning relates it to dreadful things—madness, suicide, dizzy heights, roaring seas— and Hamlet's bristling threats (84-86) and physical struggle with friends concerned only with his good make his act in following it seem one of desperate frenzy.

I, v

Alone with Hamlet, the Ghost solemnly reveals itself to be the spirit of his father, condemned for a term to expiate sins committed in life by burning in purgatorial fires by day and wandering the earth by night. Hamlet's cry of sympathy is cut off by an injunction to exact revenge. Although it has been given out that King Hamlet died of a serpent-bite, he was murdered by his brother Claudius. This is as young Hamlet suspected, and he cries out his intention to speed to his revenge. The Ghost continues with an account of the hideous crime. Claudius, having won Gertrude to his lust, poured poison into the ear of her sleeping husband, sending him unshriven to a lazarlike death. Denmark's throne must no longer be possessed by this incestuous, murderous villain; Gertrude, however, must remain unharmed, her punishment left to her conscience and to heaven. As the Ghost departs, Hamlet swears to wipe all things from his memory but his father's command and his uncle's guilt. When Marcellus and Horatio appear, he greets them with hysterical gaiety, returns evasive answers to their questions, and asks them to swear secrecy. With the Ghost echoing his words from below, he demands that they swear upon his sword, moving wildly about and shouting jaunty responses to the supernatural voice. They are to preserve absolute silence, and if he chooses hereafter to pretend to be deranged, they are never to hint that they know the cause. When they have obeyed his and the Ghost's commands to swear upon the sword, Prince Hamlet's passions suddenly subside, and his final words are subdued, plaintive, tender.

1 s.d.   The stage is vacant only for a moment before this re-entry; use of the convention of 'double time' permits this pair to reach a removed location considerably in advance of Horatio and Marcellus.   **1-23**   The Ghost's concession to Hamlet's fears, the very fact that it begins to explain itself, serves, along with the listener's ready pity (4), to reduce the sense of danger; but the supernatural atmosphere is sustained by the quality of the language. This has enormous force, and indeed a sepulchral sound. The Ghost's first words, *Mark me* (2) and first full lines (2-4) are rich in 'm's' and 'n's' as well as long vowels, lending themselves to a hollowly reverberant delivery, slow-paced and sonorous. This tonal quality persists in the longer speech, and, linked with the images of suffering and violent fear, produce a unique effect: we hear the voice of anguish, fierce resentment, and purgatorial suffering. The scent of brimstone is in the air.   **24-41**   Hamlet's ejaculation, punctuating the initial charge against Claudius, remind us of his prior suspicion of foul play (I, ii, 256). Observe, in adjacent speeches, Hamlet's image of revengeful action *swift As meditation* (29) and the inciting spirit's highly-wrought image of extreme lethargy and tardiness (32-33)—a suggestive juxtaposition.   **42-91**   This speech alone could account for a considerable amount of erratic behavior on the part of any hearer personally involved and emotionally responsive. It is a strange and wonderful thing, combining elements individually impressive but mutually incompatible. This spirit seems both Christian and pagan, devoted to the sacraments but subject to the dictation of the cock-crow and rising sun. It expresses fierce hatred of one of the partners in crime but lingering tenderness for the other, and demands action in one quarter, inaction in the other. It is highly moral, even citing past marital fidelity (47-50), and fervidly religious, mentioning with horror the denial at death of the last rites of the church (76-80), and yet it is immorally and irreligiously demanding vengeance, thus compounding the sins for which it is at present suffering in purgatory. But having conceded these effronts to our reason, we must observe that there is no effront to our emotions. The detailed description of the awful effects of the *juice of cursèd hebona,* the *leperous distilment* (61-73), and the speaker's tone—like a sustained cry of pain—wins our sympathy and enforces a conviction that a terrible wrong has been done which should recoil upon the doers. Passion and poetry, at least for the moment, rationalize the irrational.   **92-112** Something similar may be said about Hamlet's speech in reaction. His groping for realms to swear by (92-93), his repetitious resolves to remember (95-104), and his practical precautions lest he forget the unforgettable (107-110) verge upon the ridiculous, especially since his extravagant words are obviously accompanied by extravagant actions—his grasping of his head as he speaks of *this distracted globe* (97) and his ostentatious scribbling in his notebook. But the shock he has just received, tantamount to the destruction of his past and his future, cancels any chance to respond with propriety; his display of almost childish bluster has its own kind of decorum. **113-40** If we have ever witnessed the symptoms of near-hysteria in certain high-strung persons reacting to sudden grief, terror, or disaster, we will not be puzzled by these lines. The shrill clowning (116), the wanton rudeness (119-31), the apologies which are more than half mockery (134-40)—indeed all these *wild and whirling words* are far from 'unnatural.'   **140-81** But to effect a liaison between this quite credible mood and the very agency which has induced it, to let Hamlet continue his clowning with comic sallies evoked by the receding voice of the Ghost itself— *truepenny . . . this fellow in the cellarage . . . old mole* (149-51, 156-57, 162-63)—and at the same time to pursue the practical end, with the Ghost's cooperation, of obtaining an oath upon the sword, is an act of creative imagination which defies critical analysis and can be justified only by its success. All we can say is that momentarily we are drawn wholly within that phantasmagoria where Hamlet himself momentarily resides, and that we emerge with him all amazement spent.   **182-90** His sudden gentleness, *Rest, rest, perturbèd spirit* (181) is singularly affecting, as it contrasts with his cavalier treatment of the Ghost just before. This characteristically swift change in mood makes us see Hamlet, as we may not have done before, as a youth terribly victimized. An immense load has been laid upon him, and our sympathies go out to him as he expresses his yearning for human companionship: *Let us go in together* (186) . . . *Nay, come, let's go together* (190). (Apart from the dubiety attaching to this inconsistent Ghost, two questions arise at this point: Why is Hamlet insistent upon secrecy? Why is he planning to *put an antic disposition on* (172), that is, presumably, to simulate madness? The play has provided no answers, and the commentator has no right to do so. He may, however, without presuming to speak for playwright or play, indicate the nature of his own speculations. Perhaps secrecy is necessary if one is to be successful in a course of action against a king who controls legal procedures. We have learned that Hamlet already suspected Claudius—*O my prophetic soul!* (40)—and are reminded that he enjoined secrecy (I, ii, 246-50) when he first mentioned *foul play*. His present insistence upon it is endorsed by the Ghost. There is the further consideration that Gertrude is not to be exposed. So far as simulated madness is concerned, we may guess that it will confer immunity and make for more freedom of action. Without trying to rationalize everything in the work of art, we should recognize that speculation and suspended judgment are more fruitful to appreciation than blunt conclusions—such as that the playwright is merely duplicating source material, or that Hamlet is simply crazy, or the play itself simply a crazy-quilt. It is proper to refer to the questions raised because the question-raising itself is, in this play, integral to its nature as a work of art, but we should try not to view the work as a puzzle to be solved. If no precise answers are provided for the questions, we should assume that this is part of the artistic design. Meantime we must recognize the intrinsic merit of each part of the play, the sustained fascination, the 'variety' which Dr. Johnson noted. Each scene caps its predecessor, and apart from the wonder of the language, each is full of action—both in the sense of striking developments and of interesting movement upon the stage.)

II, i

Polonius commissions his servant Reynaldo to deliver money and messages to Laertes in Paris. He gives Reynaldo superfluously minute instructions on how to gather gossip among the resident Danes about Laertes's moral conduct. Ophelia comes to her father in fright, and describes the strange appearance and conduct of Hamlet. He has visited her in a state of pitiful disorder, and gazed at her long and silently. Polonius is certain that Hamlet is mad with love, his condition brought on by Ophelia's refusal to receive his addresses. Polonius now believes that his strictness with Ophelia was ill-advised, and prepares to tell Claudius of the situation.

1-74 After the tension of the preceding scenes, this relaxing interlude is welcome. The humor is neither boisterous nor cruel as this oldster, teetering on the edge of senility but still mentally animated, takes childish delight in his guile. Never has anyone been so amusingly tedious. Mere prolixity would be boring, but that of Polonius is, if such a thing be possible, a concentrate of prolixity, symbolizing its counterpart in actual life. Such details as the midpoint derailment of his train of thought—*What was I about to say?* (50)—bring us the joy of recognition. Incidentally, the defect of Polonius appears to be vanity and waning intellect rather than ill will. He is not so completely divested of dignity as he might have been, since Reynaldo remains consistently respectful.   **75-120** Ophelia's description gives Hamlet all the attributes of the love-sick swain as conventionalized in Elizabethan literature, but one of her phrases, *As if he had been loosèd out of hell* (83) associates disturbingly with our memory of his visitor from purgatory. This, together with the compelling account of his long scrutiny of her face, prevents us from viewing his conduct as a mere *antic* pose. Neither can we view it as a symptom of frustrated love—for the simple reason that foolish Polonius does.

II, ii

Claudius and Gertrude welcome to the court two former comrades of the Prince, Rosencrantz and Guildenstern, who have been sent for in the hope that they may divert him in his melancholy and perhaps learn its cause. Polonius announces the return of the ambassadors to Norway, and promises that he will later explain fully the cause of Hamlet's condition. Claudius is anxious to hear, but Gertrude doubts if there is any cause but the obvious one, his father's death and their own 'o'erhasty marriage.' The ambassador Voltemand reports that the King of Norway has curbed his nephew, young Fortinbras. The latter will lead an expedition against the Poles instead of the Danes, and Claudius takes under advisement a request that he be granted right of passage through Danish territory. Polonius now, in his most circumlocutionary style, declares that Hamlet is infatuated with Ophelia, and reads a love-letter sent her containing a mixture of florid prose and bad verse. Polonius is willing to stake his reputation for acumen upon the soundness of his diagnosis: the Prince, denied access to Ophelia because of Polonius's fatherly prudence, has declined into madness. The truth of his theory may be tested by letting Ophelia meet with him while Claudius and Polonius observe their encounter from concealment. As Hamlet enters reading a book, the others withdraw, leaving Polonius to engage him in talk. Hamlet's remarks are such that they may be regarded as symptomatic of love-madness by Polonius, but actually they ridicule the old man, suggest the vulnerability of his daughter's virtue, and express the speaker's own longing for death. Polonius is succeeded by Rosencrantz and Guildenstern, whom Hamlet greets cordially, and with whom he converses rationally although in sardonic vein. He wrests from them the admission that they have been sent for to observe him, and he tells them what they may report; he has lost his mirth, and the wondrous universe now appears to him foul, while neither man, the lord of creation, nor woman either is able to please him. Rosencrantz remarks that, in his present mood, the troupe of players about to visit the court will have small chance of pleasing. Hamlet is curious about why they are traveling, and is told that a company of child actors in the city have launched a satirical attack upon 'common players,' with the result that theatrical activity there is disrupted. Hamlet deplores the episode as indicative of the specious appeal of novelty, tells Rosencrantz and Guildenstern that they are as welcome as the actors, and comments cryptically on the degree of his 'madness.' As Polonius returns, to announce the arrival of the actors, Hamlet resumes his ostensibly mad vein of persiflage, but he greets the actors themselves soberly and shows an informed interest in the drama. The leading Player delivers at his request a passionate speech on the slaying of King Priam from a play which missed popular success. After bidding Polonius to see the company comfortably lodged, Hamlet speaks privately to their leader. Next day they will perform the play called 'The Murder of Gonzago' and include in it a brief speech written by Hamlet himself. As all are leaving, he warns the members of the company not to mock at old Polonius. Alone, he marvels at the facility of the Player in showing deep emotions of grief over a purely fictitious death, while he, with every motive for passion, remains idle and lethargic, open to charges of villainy and cowardice. He cries invectives against the murderous uncle against whom he has failed to take vengeance, then rails at himself for merely blustering. He will have the players perform something like his father's murder, and will observe Claudius's response. The Ghost may have been a devil, lying to entrap his soul. If the play traps Claudius into exposing his guilt, Hamlet will know what course to follow.

1-39 Claudius's courtesy is not excessive, and no air of furtiveness marks his arrangement with this pair. Although he expresses a wish to know the cause of Hamlet's madness, as Gertrude does not, the attitude of both may be taken as purely solicitous. **40-85** If we take Claudius's impulse to probe as a sign of guilt, we must take Gertrude's freedom from the impulse as a sign of innocence, and yet the Ghost has accused both. The news from Norway is introduced for its future utility and has little present interest; hence it is slipped into an interval in Polonius's report, which does have present interest. **86-158** Here Polonius achieves full stature as ass-absolute, his frivolous pomposity a wonderful comic conception. The wordplay to which he is addicted is a caricature of Shakespeare's own, distinguished from it by utter inanity. The verbal juggling, as in *day, night,* and *time* (88-89), and in *pity* and *true* (97-100), exploits no variations in meaning, and places words in no novel perspectives, but proves on analysis to be exercise in pure redundancy. The cream of the jest is Polonius's own relish, his conviction that he is being clever as well as wise; in the context of his speeches such phrases as *brevity is the soul of wit* (90) and *a foolish phrase* (98) are explosively relevant. Yet these *are* his phrases, arguing the survival in his addled head of a residue of true wit and perceptiveness. Note that he sets up here—*'beautified' is a vile phrase* (111)—and later, when the Player recites, as quite a critic of language. Has the folly of Polonius any function other than that of providing incidental entertainment? We may say that whatever theory he holds about Hamlet will be ipso facto wrong, or that Claudio's wiliness is illustrated by his selection of so easily hoodwinked a counselor, but we have little confidence in these answers. The humor is present for its own sake, but it is not intrusive because it derives from a trait in the character (officious obtuseness) which does indeed have an organic function in the play. Hamlet's letter, with its lamentable verse so different from anything we would expect of him, must be viewed with caution as a clue to his character and mental state. Is its style, and very existence, part of his *antic* pose? Or is it conventionally ill-written because, like Orlando, he is an amateur love-poet? Or is it simply attracted into a semi-comic vein because it has fallen into the hands of a comic character?   **159-67** The primary purpose of these lines is to engage our interest in a promised piece of stage action; however we may feel that Claudius's readiness to spy is suggestive of his guilt. **168-217** Since this is Hamlet's first appearance since his encounter with the Ghost, we are bound to view him with great curiosity. In the preceding scene it was intimated, and in the present one confirmed, that considerable time has elapsed since he declared his readiness to *sweep* to his revenge (I, v, 31). Why has he not done so? The bafflement of Polonius, Ophelia, Claudius, and Gertrude, even though they are less well-informed about him than we, communicates itself to us. We have heard of his intention *to put an antic disposition on,* but have had no reason to expect that it would involve Ophelia; hence we are not certain that his reported 'madness' is play-acting or that it is related to his delay in taking action. In the present exchange with Polonius we are quickly satisfied on one point; his overt irrationality is play-acting, since under its cover he is gibing at the old man. But we are not enlightened about its purpose, and through his pose we detect a genuine harshness, and a genuine obsession with Ophelia (181-85) as well as with death (205, 214-15). **218-309** The shift from *These tedious old fools!* (217) to *My excellent good friends!* (222) marks one of his characteristically quick shifts in mood. He drops the *antic* role as he greets this pair, and meets his social obligations with an exchange of levity. But here too we detect an underlying consistency of tone —the melancholy is real. The complexity of his nature becomes increasingly evident: suspecting that he is under surveillance by Claudius, he prods ruthlessly and successfully to get the truth from his visitors, but in the midst of the process comes one of his heartfelt expressions of craving for sincerity and comradeship (280-85). Since they need something they may report, he ironically fubs them off with the obvious—that he is in heavy spirits—but in doing so gives classic expression to a noble view of the universe and mankind, together with a poignant demonstration that philosophy is futile as a comfort to the soul in distress. Linked with this famous 'apostrophe to man' (itself introduced as a pretext) is a mechanical comment designed to introduce the subject of visiting actors—the playwright seems not to have realized that he had just written a passage of deathless prose. **310-531** This episode is intrinsically entertaining, as well as highly suggestive of the playwright's attitude toward his profession and toward the actual theatrical situation in 1599-1601 when there was a war of satire among the theatres. In a measure Shakespeare has made Hamlet his own spokesman in deprecating the slurs cast upon the *common players* (338-44) such as himself. Polonius continues to exhibit his folly and Hamlet his intellectual agility and human many-sidedness. Observe his kindness to the players, his sudden reference to universal sinfulness (515-17), and his concern lest others follow his example in mocking Polonius (529). At one point the vogue of the child actors is unexpectedly equated by Hamlet with the popularity of the new King Claudius (355-59) whose *picture in little* commands such high prices. (It is not irrelevant to point out here that the theatres of the actors 'in little' charged high admission rates, and that Shakespeare would naturally have viewed his own kind of company as of pre-Claudian meritoriousness.) Hamlet's allusion to Polonius as *Jephtha* (393-408) is significant, in view of the fact that Jephtha sacrificed a beloved daughter and that Ophelia is, however unwittingly, sacrificed by her father. The Player's speech provides occasion for a display of histrionic passion which Hamlet will later remark upon, but its length is much greater than this simple function necessitates and one suspects the presence of an element of parody in the stiff rhetoric and bombastic metaphor. (It was the repertory of the child actors which normally contained plays designed to please *not the million*.) However distended in treatment, this episode with the players serves the useful purpose of showing the inception of Hamlet's device in trapping his uncle with the play-within-the-play.   **532-91**   As Hamlet refers to the Player's 'passion' as a reproof of his own lethargy, he is given lines infinitely more 'passionate' than the Player's. Observe the artistic cunning in the juxtaposition of the two long dramatic speeches by the two different speakers. The Player was merely an actor, his passion simulated, whereas Hamlet (although also an actor—some other member of Shakespeare's company) is presumably real—and his passion is made to sound real indeed. The illusion is created by the language. Although the same metrical form is used in the Player's speech and Hamlet's soliloquy, in the latter the verbal artifices are concealed instead of paraded, and the rhetoric becomes dramatic poetry and living speech. To what extent does the soliloquy answer the questions that have been raised in our minds? We get mutually incompatible answers: the first, that Hamlet is *dull and muddy-mettled* (552), perhaps even *pigeon-livered* (562); the second, that he is not certain that Claudius is guilty since the Ghost may have been an agent of damnation. We are hesitant about accepting the first because it is so intemperately expressed and the language is the reverse of *dull* and *muddy,* and we are hesitant about accepting the second because it comes as such a surprise. True, a great suspicion of evil was originally associated with the Ghost, and the memory of this may have reasserted itself since we have had as yet no confirmation of its charges, and since the atmosphere at court in these recent scenes has not seemed conspicuously corrupt. The authenticity, or at least the reliability, of the Ghost may be recessive in our minds as it appears to be in Hamlet's. But observe that there has been no mention at all of the practical difficulties involved in taking revenge on Claudius (but not Gertrude), and that Hamlet does not explain why he has been pretending to be unbalanced—if it is truly pretense. Thus we have no definitive answers at all, but only issues held in suspension, so that we must remain observant—and spellbound.

III, i

Rosencrantz and Guildenstern report that Hamlet has told them of his melancholy but not its cause. They tell of his pleasure at the coming of the Players, and Claudius agrees to attend the performance planned for the present evening. As he and Polonius prepare to carry out their plan of espial, Gertrude speaks kindly to Ophelia as if she might welcome her as a daughter-in-law. Polonius instructs Ophelia to make her solitude seem plausible by reading a book of devotion. He adds a moral reflection about false displays of piety which draws an aside from Claudius—to the effect that his conscience is troubled by his 'deed' and his consequent hypocrisy. Hamlet enters and at first fails to see Ophelia, the only character now remaining in view. He deliberates upon suicide, enumerating the ills of life and concluding that men bear them only because of fears of the life to come; conscience deflects them from suicide and from other momentous actions. Upon seeing Ophelia, he asks to be remembered in her prayers, then suddenly becomes distant and finally hostile. When she offers to return his tokens, he denies having given her any, speaks ambiguously of her beauty and virtue, bids her go to a nunnery, and, with increasing vehemence, blackens his own character, ridicules her father, and wildly attacks calumny, women's coquettishness, and marriage. He concludes with a veiled allusion to one married man who must die, and with the repeated command that she enter a nunnery. Ophelia is left alone bewailing the decay of his noble mind when Claudius and Polonius emerge from their hiding place. To Claudius Hamlet has appeared to be neither in love nor truly mad, but in a mood that threatens danger. Polonius agrees with the proposal that he be sent to England until his condition mends, but suggests that he first be questioned by his mother. Again Polonius will act as eavesdropper.

1-49   While the act of spying is never an agreeable one, it cannot be deemed villainous if the motive is truly what it here purports to be. Polonius's conviction that love is the cause of Hamlet's malady seems to rule out his knowledge of any other possible cause, while Gertrude's remarks (10, 14-15, 37-42) show an interest only in a cure.   **49-55**   For the first time in the play we get confirmation of anterior wrong-doing, and it applies only to Claudius: he is guilty of something, but we are not told of what, or of the extent of Gertrude's complicity.   **56-89**   Hamlet's famous *To be or not to be* soliloquy shows him musing not upon revenge but upon suicide—to exist or not to exist. The self-contained nature of this speech, its meditative tone, and its inventory of human ills in general rather than the speaker's in particular—indeed those very features which, in combination with the beauty of the language, have made it a favorite 'memory piece'—may seem to make it somewhat extraneous, and it has been described as a detached 'lyric.' We must remember, however, that it was part of the play before it became a 'quotation' and that it is therefore presumably functional. It does two things: it enlarges the speaker, as does his 'apostrophe to man' (II, ii, 292-305), to the stature of a Humanity Figure, with whom we can identify; and it prevents us from accepting as conclusive his explanation in the preceding scene that he has failed to take vengeance upon Claudius because of doubts about his guilt. The *conscience* which inhibits him from taking his own life may be inhibiting him from taking Claudius's. However obliquely expressed, this idea is obtruded upon us (83-88). At some point in the course of Hamlet's procrastination, we were bound to ask if a man of his sensibility would not recoil at the idea of answering evil with evil. That the issue would have occurred to the playwright and his audience goes without saying; and the fact that Hamlet never explicitly condemns vengeance upon ethical grounds must be weighed with the fact that there is much else in the play which is only tentatively expressed. **90-149** Hamlet's tirade against Ophelia has been attributed to his catching sight of Claudius and Polonius in hiding, but there is nothing in the text to indicate that this is so, and the arbitrary assumption flattens out his character. We have noticed that sudden fluctuations of feeling are characteristic of him, and the present episode, left just as it appears to be, is quite in line with the artistic strategy of the play—the strategy of multiple suggestion. An unknown has been introduced, in the matter of Hamlet's mental state. Since he was already highly disturbed (and contemplating suicide) before he spoke of adopting an *antic* pose, and what appears to be the pose resembles his original state exaggerated, we cannot always distinguish between pretense and non-pretense. His antics with Polonius are surely pretense, and his self-recriminations just as surely are not, but there is an indeterminate zone, as in his present treatment of Ophelia, where we cannot be quite sure; it is possible that he is both highly-overwrought and 'acting' so. How he truly feels about Ophelia is another of the questions which the play poses but fails to answer; and again the commentator can only describe his own reflections. Perhaps the disillusion, suspicion, and disgust engendered in him by the conduct of his mother has rubbed off on all women (143-47) including Ophelia, so that she both attracts and repels him; or perhaps he wishes to divorce her for her own sake from his own cursed life (121-30) and the infectious world. His injunction to her to get *to a nunnery* (121) is repeated five times. The word 'nunnery' was sometimes used as slang for 'house of prostitution,' but as here first introduced into the dialogue, it seems to mean 'nunnery' and no more—*Why shouldst thou be a breeder of sinners?* (121). **150-88** Ophelia's speech affords a glimpse of the pre-tragic Hamlet, before he had been afflicted by the *cursèd spite* of coping with something rotten in the state of Denmark. There is an inconsistency in her lament, in that it includes no allusion to the fact that it has been not Hamlet but herself, in docile obedience to her father, who has initiated the break between them. It would be hard to better Claudius's shrewd diagnosis of Hamlet's 'madness' (163-65). Polonius continues to impress us as being free from guilty knowledge; indeed he seems innocent of everything except being a vain busybody.

III, ii

Hamlet instructs the Players in the proper delivery of the speech he has written and in the art of acting generally. As members of the court gather to hear the play, he compliments Horatio on his stoic equability, and asks him to observe Claudius closely for signs of guilt such as may confirm the Ghost's accusations. He declines to sit by his mother, but reclines with his head in Ophelia's lap. Resuming his 'antic' pose, he addresses satirical remarks to Claudius and Polonius and bawdy ones to Ophelia, who turns them aside with gentle propriety. The play is performed with interjected sallies by Hamlet: first, a dumbshow, showing a King and Queen in loving relationship, the King left alone to sleep, a Murderer poisoning him through the ear, and then the Murderer wooing and winning the Queen; second, the early part of this action duplicated in rimed dialogue up until the point where the murderer (now named Lucianus) pours the poison in the sleeper's ear. In the dialogue the stress has been upon the player Queen's insistence that she would never marry again if widowed; and, in reply to a question by Hamlet, Gertrude has commented that 'The lady doth protest too much.' Claudius has asked, just before the poisoning episode in the spoken portion of the performance, if there is any offensiveness in the plot, and Hamlet has replied that there is none for innocent persons like themselves. As the act of poisoning occurs, Claudius rises, crying for lights and rushing out, with all but Hamlet and Horatio following. Hamlet speaks in high glee of his success in play-making and in detection, then calls for music. Rosencrantz and Guildenstern report that Claudius is highly disturbed and Gertrude wishes to speak with Hamlet in her chamber. When they again try to discover the cause of Hamlet's mental state, he asks Guildenstern to play upon a recorder, and when this agent of Claudius proves unable to do so he mockingly demands if he himself is thought of as more easily played upon than a pipe. Polonius comes to summon the Prince to his mother's chamber and, as usual, is subjected to 'antic' ridicule. Alone, Hamlet proclaims his bloodthirsty mood, but resolves to upbraid his mother without doing her physical harm.

1-42 As in his previous interview with the players, Hamlet shows a greater interest in the drama than this particular dramatic occasion requires, and we may legitimately object that the author is interloping; however, unlikely though it may be that Hamlet would demonstrate the fact at this crisis in his affairs, he proves a fine connoisseur of acting. **43-86** He has evidently confided in Horatio, whom he admires for the qualities which he himself lacks. **87-129** His *I must be idle* (87) is a clearer signal than we usually get that he is about to resume his mad pose; as usual, he employs the pose less as a means of furthering his designs, or safeguarding himself, than as cover for licensed jesting, for shooting his barbs of satirical innuendo. **130-260** We need not be disturbed by such inconsequential details as the fact that the *King* of the play-within-the-play is referred to by Hamlet as a *Duke* (231), that the preceding dumbshow is untypically complete, or that Hamlet's purposes are served by more than an inserted (unidentifiable) 'speech.' We need not be disturbed either about Claudius's failure to expose himself during the dumbshow. We may, if we wish, assume that he is inattentive, or exercising great self-control, but the point is immaterial. Even during the spoken playlet, he exposes himself not when he naturally would, but when it is dramatically convenient; and such delayed responses are a common enough convention. More significant is the fact that neither dumbshow nor dialogue suggests that Gertrude was party to the murder or involved in adultery with the murderer. This disparity with the account of the crime given by the Ghost (I, v, 42-57) injects a new element of uncertainty into the situation, since we do not know whether she is guilty, and being protected from exposure; or whether she is innocent, and the earlier version of the crime unreliable. The whole device of the play-within-the-play, the watchful impressario, the detected criminal leaping to his feet and crying *Give me some light* (259) is a grand coup de théâtre.   **261-84** Anticlimax is avoided as our interest focuses upon the one who has sprung the trap. He runs the whole emotional gamut once more, from hysterical gaiety, through aloof contemptuousness, to over-demonstrative bloodthirstiness.

III, iii

Claudius directs Rosencrantz and Guildenstern to convey Hamlet to England at once since his madness is dangerous, and they deferentially consent. Polonius announces that he is on his way to conceal himself behind the arras in Gertrude's chamber, since her maternal partiality may prevent her from reporting accurately on her interview with Hamlet. Alone, Claudius speaks of his rank offense in murdering his brother. He craves forgiveness but knows of no way to pray for it so long as he retains the fruits of his crime—Gertrude and the crown. Torn between his impulse to remain in criminal possession of his winnings and the impulse to repent, he kneels in an attempt to pray. Hamlet enters with sword bared, but forgoes the opportunity to slay Claudius. His father was slain with his sins upon his head, and this murderer must be slain while sinning so that he will die body and soul. He goes to his mother. Claudius rises, unable to direct his thoughts to heaven.

1-98 We learn from his own lips that Claudius is guilty of fratricide (36-38) but not whether Gertrude was party to, or aware of, the crime. Observe that Claudius is conscience-racked, and hence a villain of a different stripe from an Edmund (*King Lear*) or a Iago (*Othello*). This capacity for redemption in him is calculated to make us none too eager for his extermination, and hence tolerant of Hamlet's delay whatever Hamlet's reasons. The reasons he gives for failing to take advantage of the present opportunity are logical, horribly logical. It seems gratuitous to doubt them, and yet we are bound to do so—in view of the evidence of more mysterious reasons for failure to act coming both before and immediately after. It is foolish to say that he refrains from slaying Claudius here because the act would end the play. The playwright could have omitted this episode entirely, or, if he had wished to stress the difficulty of getting 'at' Claudius in general, could have given prominence to the guard of *swissers*. Unquestionably Hamlet's procrastination is integral to the whole dramatic design.

III, iv

Polonius tells Gertrude to deal sternly with her son, then conceals himself as Hamlet enters. Gertrude is so frightened by his initial threats that she cries for help. When Polonius takes up the cry, Hamlet mistakes him for Claudius, and runs his sword through the arras and slays him, pretending that he thinks he is slaying a rat. He castigates Gertrude, showing her pictures of his father and his uncle as he praises one and execrates the other. He charges her with perverse lasciviousness as she cries for merciful silence. The Ghost returns and reminds him of his 'almost blunted purpose'—presumably in reference to his failure to take vengeance on Claudius, since it continues to show its former solicitude for Gertrude. Since she is unable to see or hear it, she supposes that Hamlet's addresses to it are madness, but he warns her not to take comfort in such a belief. He pleads with her to abstain from further intercourse with Claudius, harping upon the subject with terrible vividness. He repents the slaying of Polonius, viewing the act as heaven's punishment of him as heaven's own scourge. He tells his mother he is being cruel to her only to save her, and warns her not to be seduced by Claudius into revealing the secret that his madness is only pretended. After she has promised to keep his secret, he tells her that he is to be sent to England accompanied by his two false friends, whose craft will be undermined by his own. He makes ironical comments upon the unaccustomed silence of Polonius as he drags away his body.

1-218 Since the slaying here is not premeditated, but seems no more than an impulsive reflex action, it does not eliminate the possibility that Hamlet is a reluctant killer. In fact this scene contains another of his obliquely expressed concessions that vengeance is sinful (173-76): heaven scourges its own scourger. The modern critical stress upon the 'Oedipus complex' as explanatory of Hamlet's psychology leans heavily upon this scene, in which he does indeed display an excessive concern with his mother's sexual life. The analysts suggest that his passion is interpretable as jealousy provoked by his own unconscious incestuous drives, and that Claudius has been Hamlet's own surrogate in slaying the father and possessing the mother; hence his attitude toward this figure exhibits a powerful and yet inhibited sense of outrage. The suggestion should not be discounted entirely, but we should try to retain our sense of critical proportion. Whatever the basic scientific reason, sons in general tend to view sensuality in mothers as repugnant; and Hamlet's responses are excessive in other areas as well as this one: he is 'abnormally' responsive to, and articulate about, phenomena as varied as Polonius's folly and the Player's acting. There is danger that an anachronistic interpretation will be given his abhorrence of the idea of sexual laxity in his mother; in former times the idea was more closely linked than now with ideas of family honor, and men were more active and vocal than seems to us decent in their guardianship of the chastity of mothers, wives, sisters, daughters. Observe the concern of Polonius and Laertes (surely not unconsciously incestuous) about the chastity of Ophelia. More interesting actually, because more certainly a part of the conscious artistic design, is the ambiguous role of Gertrude. She is as great a mystery as Hamlet. To precisely what degree of guilt is she admitting? (89-92, 95-97) Just what has she done—other than promptly wedding the inferior brother after enjoying the love of the superior one? Hamlet's charge of murder is against Claudius, not her; and everything she says and does in the play is reconcilable with a genuine love of her son and concern for his welfare. Since the Ghost has previously revealed itself to others as well as Hamlet, we cannot conclude that it is a figment of Hamlet's imagination merely because Gertrude cannot see it; however, whether or not it be regarded as such a figment on the present occasion, its reference to Hamlet's *almost blunted purpose* (112) casts doubt on Hamlet's explanation of why he refrained from slaying Claudius in the scene immediately preceding.

IV, i

Gertrude, having asked Rosencrantz and Guildenstern to withdraw, answers the questions of her husband about Hamlet's whereabouts and her own perturbation. Her son, she says, is surely mad. When she describes the stabbing of Polonius, Claudius says that they will be held accountable since they have let Hamlet go at large. She describes his grief after his act of violence as evidence of his underlying purity. Claudius tells her that they will send him away and cover up for him as best they can, then calls Rosencrantz and Guildenstern to bid them fetch the body of Polonius into the chapel. A council of friends will be called to assist in averting a scandal.

1-45 We have here another of the many choices of interpretation offered by the play. Is Gertrude keeping Hamlet's secret (recently entrusted to her) that he is only pretending to be mad? Or, as seems more likely, does she believe that he is mad indeed? If the latter is the case, does it argue her relative innocence, since she truly views his accusations as mere raving? Or is she, in his terms (III, iv, 146) using a wishful belief in his madness as *unction* to her soul?

IV, ii

Hamlet refuses to tell Rosencrantz and Guildenstern what he has done with the body, and gibes at them in barely intelligible terms. He demands to be taken to Claudius.

1-30 No explanation whatever is provided for the action of Hamlet in concealing the body of Polonius, and it is hard to regard the action as either a precaution against detection or a new way of pretending to be mad. Is this no more than a gruesome demonstration of his emotional affinity with death?

IV, iii

Claudius informs a group of courtiers that Hamlet is too dangerous to remain at large, and yet is so loved by the populace that the law cannot be invoked against him. The sending of him away must appear judicious policy. Rosencrantz and Guildenstern report that he refuses to disclose the whereabouts of the body. He is brought in, and is questioned by Claudius, to whom he replies in the same erratic fashion as he has done to the others; however, he lets it be known where the body may be found. He continues to utter insinuating nonsense as Claudius tells him he is to be conveyed to England for his own good. After he has left, closely guarded by those who are to see him off, Claudius says in soliloquy that the English, who are subject to the Danes, will receive orders to end his life.

1-67 Hamlet's preoccupation with death and its leveling power (16-36) is in the same vein while he plays the *antic* with Claudius (if that is what he is doing) as while he later talks rationally with Horatio at Ophelia's grave (V, i). Observe the sudden collapse of his resistance to revealing the whereabouts of the body (36)—like the equally sudden collapse of his resistance to remaining at court (I, ii, 120). The coldly ruthless plan of Claudius for disposing of Hamlet is one in which he has no accomplices; the reason he gives for the journey to England are such as might be endorsed by Gertrude, or any others well-disposed toward the Prince. The question arises of why Rosencrantz and Guildenstern seem more and more sinister as the action unfolds, when nothing they ever do or say is actually villainous. One answer is that we distrust them because Hamlet does, but it is not the full answer. They exude a kind of evil, the evil of negativeness, because they constantly reappear as a pair (like a brace of hunting dogs) and never display any will or initiative of their own. They are completely subservient to the will of the greatest temporal power in their vicinity. Since they are nothing in themselves, they begin to appear as elongations of Claudius, his tentacles so to speak.

IV, iv

Fortinbras passes with his army, leaving a Captain to greet the Danish king and to arrange for the promised free march through his territory. This Captain is accosted by Hamlet, who is being escorted by Rosencrantz and Guildenstern to his ship. When Hamlet learns that the Poles and the Norwegian forces of Fortinbras are about to engage in a death struggle for a small piece of worthless land, he sends his escort ahead and reflects upon the example. It is another reproach to him and a spur to his revenge. Man's power of reasoning is useless unless applied in the world of action. Whether through lethargy or over-scrupulousness, he himself has failed to act, whereas this army led by a cultivated Prince is prepared to sacrifice lives and treasure purely for fame. To fight for trifling causes when honor is at stake is to be truly great; yet he, with a father killed and a mother stained, does nothing about it. Henceforth his thoughts must be bloody or admittedly worthless.

1-66 Although not canceled out, our own explanations of Hamlet's inaction are periodically thwarted by his own utterances, which attribute it simply to his personal inadequacy. In this remarkable soliloquy there is one elliptical passage (52-56) which makes sense only if we recognize that the *not* (54) is doing double duty and must be read '*not* not.' But, so read, it commits Hamlet to a somewhat superficial conception of *honor*—as something best demonstrated by deeds performed in trivial causes. However, perhaps we should cooperatively fill out the thought and deduce that he believes true greatness to consist of acting for the preservation of honor whether the cause be great or trivial. At least we can understand the admiration, even envy, of this man tortured by doubts for a serene extrovert like Fortinbras.

IV, v

A Gentleman describes Ophelia as distracted by grief over the death of her father. Gertrude is reluctant to see her, but when Horatio points out that her ravings may spread suspicion, Ophelia is admitted. Gertrude remarks in an aside that every trifle now seems ominous to her sin-infected soul. Ophelia's disjointed words bear out the report that she has been deranged by the death of Polonius; but some of the snatches of ballads she sings have a ribald cast, suggesting that her frustrated love for Hamlet may be a contributory cause. Claudius has joined them, and after Ophelia has left with Horatio attending her, he reviews the ill state of their affairs. The secret burial of Polonius was a blunder; the people are racked with suspicion, and Laertes, who has secretly returned from France, is being incited by the current rumors. At this point Laertes breaks in upon them supported by a rabble hailing him as king. Gertrude restrains the angry youth while Claudius, invoking the sanctity of his royal office, coolly reasons with him. Ophelia returns, and Laertes is heart-broken as she repeats her mad performance, distributing flowers among them and singing a mournful song. Claudius declares to Laertes that he will satisfy him and his friends about the circumstances of Polonius's death. Although Laertes speaks bitterly of the obscure funeral and the omission of public tributes, he consents to hear what Claudius will have to say about fixing responsibility and punishing guilt.

1-217 Gertrude's reference to her *sick soul,* to *sin,* to *guilt* (16-20) seems to argue for a transgression greater than a mere 'o'erhasty marriage,' but again she is not explicit. She is more self-assertive in this scene than elsewhere, except perhaps when she insists upon drinking to Hamlet in the final moments of the play. Claudius's words indicate that she grasps hold of Laertes, and her *you false Danish dogs!* (110) sounds venomous. But note the bearing of the speech: these dogs are on a *false trail* (109) because they should be giving their voice to young Hamlet rather than Laertes as Denmark's rightful king. Ironically, it is Claudius who remarks upon Ophelia's madness as an illustration of the repercussive effects of evil-doing (78). The display of madness, so rich in dramatic poetry and pathos, suggests authentic aberration in a way which Hamlet's never quite does, although it too is marked by meaningful recurrence of allusion. It is the madness of the bereaved, but also of the lovelorn, and some of the songs (47-66) throw a startling but not incredible light upon the nature of her past yearnings. If we ask whether Polonius was worth her grief, or worth Laertes's vengeful resentment, we can only answer that he must have been. It is a critical custom to heap invectives upon erring dramatic characters, but as we reflect upon the matter, we must recognize that Polonius has never been portrayed as a man who could not command affection.

IV, vi

Horatio is visited by sailors, who bear a letter from Hamlet instructing him to procure them access to Claudius. Presumably they are pirates armed with Hamlet's testimony that they deserve reward. During a piratical attack upon his vessel at sea, he boarded the attacking vessel and was captured, but he has been honorably treated and returned to Denmark. Horatio is to come to him and hear strange tidings about Rosencrantz and Guildenstern, who remain on the ship bound for England.

1-32 With the return of Hamlet to Denmark, the play is set upon its last swift tack. This scene, coming as it does between rather than before those in which Claudius manipulates Laertes, makes the murderous plot against Hamlet seem a piece of opportunism, a clever improvisation.

IV, vii

Claudius has told Laertes that Hamlet killed Polonius and wished also to kill Claudius himself. When Laertes asks why there has been no punishment, Claudius explains that he has had to be circumspect because of the love of Gertrude for her son and the love of the people for their Prince; however, he has never intended to let Hamlet off. At this point a letter is delivered announcing the latter's return, and Claudius proceeds to enlist Laertes in a plot. He tells of how a visiting Norman expert in horsemanship has praised Laertes's skill in fencing in such terms as to arouse Hamlet's spirit of rivalry. If Laertes has truly loved his father and is willing to act against Hamlet, he can use this circumstance as a means of obtaining safe and secret revenge. When Laertes declares himself ready to stop at nothing, Claudius proposes that a fencing match he arranged, in which Laertes will use a foil with the protective button removed.

Laertes not only agrees, but resolves to dip the point in a deadly poison. Claudius adds one more refinement: a cup of poisoned wine will be provided for Hamlet to drink in case he is not pierced by the point. A sound of lamentation is heard, and Gertrude enters with the news that Ophelia is drowned. She was weaving fantastic garlands and hanging them in a willow tree, when a limb broke and let her fall into the stream below. She floated for a time on the water, still singing her plaintive songs, then sank into the deep. Laertes tries to restrain his tears but cannot. When he is gone, Claudius tells Gertrude that now he must begin all over again to pacify him.

1-193 All these preliminaries about the Norman expert (suggestively named *Lamord*), and Laertes's skill in fencing, may seem supererogatory, since, logically, it is Hamlet rather than Laertes who would need to be persuaded into engaging in this match. But Claudius's circumstantial approach to his proposal makes the match itself seem plausible, and we are lulled into taking Hamlet's consent for granted. Laertes's alacrity in falling in with the plot, and improving upon it with the use of poison—as heinous as cutting Hamlet's *throat i' th' church* (125)—place him clearly enough in the category of 'men of action,' and we are invited to consider whether we really prefer the type. Still, Laertes is not debased to the rank of utter villain. At the news of Ophelia's death, so poignantly described by Gertrude, he is so strongly affected that he engages our sympathy, and we are reminded of the strength of his provocation. In his last lines (191-93), designed to hoodwink Gertrude, Claudius becomes the complete Machiavellian, subtle and supple: he has been using strange means indeed with Laertes to *calm his rage* (191).

V, i

Two Gravediggers gossip about the inquest upon Ophelia. Since she is to have Christian burial although suspected of suicide, they feel that the gentry enjoy special privileges in this matter of self-destruction. They speak of their own kinship with Adam the delver, and of the gallows and the grave as the most durable works of man. One goes to fetch drink, and as Hamlet and Horatio enter and find the other singing at his work, they are struck by his ease in the company of death. As skulls are tossed up and pounded with the spade, Hamlet muses upon the common lot of politician, courtier, lawyer, whose heads these may once have been. The Gravedigger proves a master of chop-logic as Hamlet questions him, but he condescends to identify one of the skulls as that of Yorick the court jester, dead these twenty-three years. Hamlet descants upon the present state of this bright spirit, who was a joy of his childhood. To this state everyone must come; the loam of Alexander may stop a bunghole, that of Caesar a chink in a wall. He and Horatio step back as familiar figures approach in a funeral procession. Laertes is complaining of the scanty rites, and angrily rebukes a priest who says that even these are a special concession in view of the doubtful circumstances of Ophelia's death. When her body is lowered into the grave, Gertrude strews it with flowers and speaks of her past hopes that Ophelia and Hamlet would wed. Laertes leaps into the grave for a farewell embrace, and demands in a frenzy of grief that he be buried too. At this, Hamlet steps forward, leaps in beside him, and matches his protestations of grief. Laertes seizes him by the throat, and they grapple until separated by attendants and drawn from the grave. Horatio and the rest try to calm Hamlet, who talks wildly of his love of Ophelia, mocks at Laertes's 'rant,' and then protests that he has always loved him. Claudius and Gertrude assure Laertes that Hamlet is mad, and Gertrude tries to excuse him. When the others have preceded them out of the churchyard, Claudius reminds Laertes that vengeance is close at hand.

1-204 We may say that the passing of Polonius has left a vacancy, and that new characters are introduced to take over the function of providing intervals of relieving laughter—the Gravediggers in this scene and Osric in the next. Although valid so far as it goes, this critical observation does scant justice to the artistry of the play. The humor is never purely gratuitous. Observe that Polonius, the First Gravedigger, and Osric all serve as foils to Hamlet, who is the 'humorist' in chief. The present episode is a visual and verbal 'memento mori' and appropriate in a play whose protagonist is so consistently preoccupied with death that he is often emblemized as a black-clad figure with skull in hand. The skull is that of Yorick— a 'character' we remember although created in a few brief lines of reminiscence. Yorick, the First Gravedigger, and Hamlet—jesters all three—are a troupe who appear to be performing in a shadowy verge shared by the living and the dead. Observe that the minds of the Gravedigger and Hamlet are not unlike in their workings. The delver and the prince, each in his own idiom, is a dealer in paradox, and the riddle of the first (38-39) is generically akin to the half-formulated riddle of the second (106-09). This Gravedigger is one of the playwright's most memorable clowns, thumpingly clever, unawed by the living or dead, patronizingly knowledgeable in speaking of his own craft, and durable as the tanner's skin (154-57). Owing to his sturdy imperviousness to death, and Hamlet's intellectual vigor in expatiating upon it, the present episode, however macabre, does not strike us as morbid; in fact it has a curious vitality, like the mediaeval representations of the 'dance of death.' **205-85** Hamlet's concluding generalizations in rime effect a transition from the prose of the grave-making episode to the blank verse of its fantastic sequel. There can be little doubt that this outburst of Hamlet, who will admit no rivals in his all-compassing grief (241-44), is an authentic lapse in rationality, as Horatio himself seems to believe (252). He and Laertes have had no prior encounter in the play; and it was fitting that they have at least one before their fatal match. It was fitting too, if we were to remain fully aware of Hamlet's inner turbulence, that the encounter should have this nightmarish quality. Observe that Hamlet is the offender in all ways but one; it is Laertes and not he who reaches for the throat.

V, ii

Hamlet tells Horatio that, before the attack by the pirates, he had secretly opened the commission of Claudius borne by Rosencrantz and Guildenstern and had found that it contained orders to the English that he be beheaded, whereupon he turned the tables by replacing it with a forged substitute ordering the death of the bearers. Horatio exclaims at the perfidy of Claudius, and Hamlet reviews his crimes. News of the death of Rosencrantz and Guildenstern will soon reach Claudius from England, but the interim belongs to Hamlet. Osric, a fop of the court, comes with the proposal of the fencing match. Claudius is ready to wager six barbary horses against the six rapiers with accoutrements waged by Laertes that Hamlet will not be bettered by more than three hits in twelve passes. With mockery of Osric's precious manners and parody of his affected diction, Hamlet consents to engage. A Gentleman comes with a message from Gertrude, urging Hamlet to treat Laertes courteously before the match, a request he is more than willing to grant. He is confident of his ability to win at the odds, and yet he feels presentiments of disaster; however he is ready to trust to Providence and accept whatever befalls. The court gathers, a table with wine cups is set out, and the spectators ceremoniously take seats. Hamlet offers Laertes apologies for his conduct at Ophelia's grave, attributing it to his madness, and Laertes professes his willingness to accept the apologies if assured by the best judges that his honor will not be compromised. They select foils, and Claudius orders that healths be drunk to the tune of drum-beats, trumpet-calls, and cannon-salutes if Hamlet wins in the early passes. Hamlet claims the first hit, Osric confirms the claim, and the ordained signals sound. Claudius offers his stepson a cup of wine with the gift of a precious pearl, but Hamlet wishes to proceed at once to another bout. He gets also the second hit, and Gertrude, who has been eager for his success, offers to wipe his brows. She then drinks his health, choosing, to the consternation of Claudius, the cup containing the poison. Laertes, although he expresses compunction in an aside, is now ready to exercise his full skill and wound Hamlet with his poisoned point. He does so, but in an ensuing scuffle, the foils are exchanged and he also receives a poisoned wound. At this moment Gertrude cries out that she is poisoned, and then collapses in death. Laertes admits his own treachery and implicates Claudius. Defying the cries of treason among the courtiers, Hamlet pierces Claudius with his foil and forces him to drink from the poisoned cup. As Claudius dies, Laertes begs Hamlet's forgiveness, and then follows his accomplice in death. Horatio, knowing that

Hamlet is doomed, tries to drink the dregs of the poisoned cup, but Hamlet wrests it from him, beseeching him to live and report aright the story. A march is heard from afar, and when Hamlet learns that it is Fortinbras returning in victory from Poland, he gives this Prince his vote as successor to the Danish throne. Hamlet dies, with Horatio bidding him good night and wishing him heavenly rest. Fortinbras enters with his officers, his arrival coinciding with that of English ambassadors who have come to report that the sentence of death against Rosencrantz and Guildenstern has been carried out. Horatio asks that the bodies of the dead be placed high on a stage, so that he may publicly recount the circumstances at this moment of general excitement. Fortinbras, who soberly anticipates his election to the throne, gives orders that the body of Hamlet be borne to the stage by four captains; then speaks his epitaph and bids the soldiers fire a salute.

1-80 The playwright gives small moral emphasis to the fact that Hamlet sends Rosencrantz and Guildenstern to their deaths, *Not shriving time allowe*d (47). Horatio merely asks how the commission was sealed, and our attention is focused on the luck and ingenuity of Hamlet as a counter-intriguer. The death of the pair is treated, on the whole, as a rather neat arrangement. The treatment illustrates quite clearly the distinction which must be made between the significance of acts in real life and those same acts in works of art. In real life Hamlet's casual dismissal of this pair to hell would eliminate him from our serious consideration as a moral symbol. In the work of art it does not, because the artist does not intend it to do so. Rosencrantz and Guildenstern have been presented less as human beings (with souls to be lost or saved) than as shadows of King Claudius. Their elimination is incidental; and when Hamlet professes that they are not on his *conscience* (58), we are required to agree that they need not be. The morally significant act remains to be done—the premeditated slaying of Claudius, and although Hamlet seems prepared to perform it, he is still asking a question, *is't not perfect conscience . . . ?* (67). Observe that Horatio does not answer this question.   **81-185** Who could have predicted that the grand finale would be preceded by this comic interlude, exploiting a stock theme of Elizabethan social satire? And yet it belongs. Osric is a 'front.' He is the false emissary of a false master, who is mustering the court to witness a false match (which Osric will referee). Behind the confrontation of a Hamlet and an Osric stands a tradition of allegorical drama: Master True confronts Master False.   **186-213** In speaking of his impulse to open the commission, Hamlet has mentioned *the divinity which shapes our ends* (10), and now, in speaking of his premonitions, he mentions the *special providence in the fall of a sparrow* (209). In both instances the reference is to his own fate, not Claudius's. He never renounces his professed intention to take vengeance, but he has never convinced us that he will carry out this intention; and his *The readiness is all* (211) is so broad in its implications that we feel that he may be reconciled to a passive role. What follows is not willed by him, but by the Providence he has twice invoked.   **214-392** The spectacularity of the conclusion —the crowded stage, the elaborate sound effects, the sword-play, the multiple deaths, the pageantry—fulfills a promise, meets a theatrical obligation. Like an orchestral crescendo, the ending grandly caps the work. But as the violent action subsides and the echoes die away, quiet words return to haunt us: Hamlet's own, *the rest is silence* (347), Horatio's, *Now cracks a noble heart. Good night, sweet prince* . . . (348), and Fortinbras', *For he was likely, had he been put on, To have proved most royal* . . . (386-87). The final judgments of the most reliable witnesses, Horatio, pattern of the reasonable and well-disposed man, and Fortinbras, symbol of a preservative normality, tally with our own impressions. There have been, throughout the play, intimations of the kind of man Prince Hamlet basically is—gentle, just, noble—and his evident defects of character, his evident futility in action, have been no more than symptoms of his pain. He is the scapegoat, the human sacrifice. Had he not lived, and cared, and suffered, the whole of Denmark must needs have sickened to its death. Evil, as concretized in fratricide, conjugal betrayal, and usurpation would have been vindicated by success. The implication is that such cannot happen so long as a Hamlet exists, regardless of the form his protest takes. By his death something of value has been lost and something of value has been gained. The play will leave other readers with other thoughts, and these will have their own validity. If in *Julius Caesar*, the method was 'classical,' in *Hamlet* it is 'romantic' to a degree—suggestive, expansive, strange. The play has been interpreted for centuries, and will be interpreted for centuries to come. It invites us to collaborate with its author in 'forging the conscience' of mankind. Whatever we think of its message, we must surely agree about its distinction as a work of art. At every moment of its creation, its creator was fully engaged; throughout its great and turbulent length, there is not a shoddy line.

3

Othello

:

I, i

I A G O assures the whining Roderigo that he has not betrayed him, and that he has equally good reasons for hating Othello. He has been fubbed off with the rank of ensign while Michael Cassio, a mere tyro, has been appointed the Moor's lieutenant. Whatever service Iago renders will be in his own interests. Roderigo's grievance is of a different kind. Its nature becomes apparent as he follows Iago's lead and joins in a boisterous outcry to rouse the sleeping household of Brabantio. The Venetian senator appears at a window and angrily bids Roderigo be gone, reminding him that he has been rejected as a suitor to Desdemona. Iago returns ribald shouts that Desdemona is at this very moment clasped in the arms of a black-amoor, then leaves Roderigo to explain. Having searched his house and found his daughter gone, Brabantio joins Roderigo in the street and learns to his horror that she has eloped with Othello. He thinks she must have been seduced with love potions, and prepares to muster his kindred to help him bring the Moor to justice. Roderigo is prepared to lead the way to the inn of the newly-married pair.

1 s.d. Neither the opening stage directions nor the opening lines (1-66) indicate where and when this dialogue occurs. Unless there was a Prologue, one of the speakers must have carried a torch; they are isolated by darkness and self-preoccupation, the strained vehemence of the voices imparted by the need to keep them hushed in spite of urgency and vexation. **1-34** We cut into the conversation further along in its course than usual, a characteristic of a number of the scene-openings in this play, in harmony with the forward rush of its events. Beneath the prevailing tone of moral indignation, we detect the paltriness of the speakers: Roderigo is the sponged-upon, complaining to the sponger; Iago's mode of asseveration, *Abhor me* (6), *Despise me* (8), suggests the game he habitually plays, in which his counters are 'Love me,' 'Admire me.' Observe the contradiction in his account of the appointment of officers: he made his bid for the lieutenancy through influence—*Three great ones of the city* (8)—yet missed it through base favoritism. His complaint is the traditional one of the unpromoted: 'practical' men are passed over to the advantage of mere 'theorists.' Both speakers are losers expressing envious contempt of winners. **35-65** In a moralistic vein Iago perverts morality, and reverses familiar Elizabethan tenets—that men should serve for love and duty regardless of reward, and that men should be what they seem. His praise of self-interest and hypocrisy is a Machiavellian manifesto. **66-67** We have become conscious of someone who can appoint officers in Venice at his own discretion, and who has defeated the hopes of Roderigo as well as Iago. This man is here alluded to as a lucky *thick-lips* (66), the first of a number of unmistakable indications that the Moor's physical characteristics are negroid. We must reckon at once with the fact that he is racially alien, valued and yet socially stigmatized. **68-81** There is no practical need for this clamor. Iago moves into action with almost orgiastic excitement, relishing disorder for its own sake, loving the mischief of the moment. **82-143** Something of the atmosphere of a licentious charivari attends this episode. An elderly dignitary is aroused from his slumber and pelted with obscenities about his daughter. The animated destructiveness of the action has an insidious appeal, but to the extent that we find it comic and enjoyable we are involved as accomplices, touched by Iago's corruptiveness. Note the workings of his imagination as he pictures the sexual union of the white Venetian and the black Moor *Even now, now, very now* (88), in images prevailingly bestial (88-89, 91, 110-13, 116). Amidst this sadistic aggression, which he so obviously enjoys, comes one of his habitual moral generalizations (108-09). (Never have famous lovers in literature been first obtruded upon our attention in circumstances of such indignity. The ultimate impression made upon us by the love of Othello and Desdemona stems in a measure from the initial impression it has canceled.)   **143-58**   Here Iago sets the pattern of his later behavior, darting away from the turbulence he creates.   **159-82** Brabantio's words are calculated neither to attract nor repel. The broken and exclamatory style of his speech, in which concern for his daughter is intermingled with concern for himself (159-66), is uningratiating but not unnatural; the idea that Othello has used love-potions occurs to him as a buffer to his pain. His sudden regard for the formerly despised Roderigo (174, 182), now that another has taken her, is a very human touch. We must note that in Venetian social as opposed to military circles even a Roderigo is preferable to an Othello.

I, ii

Iago tells Othello that, were it not for his moral scruples, he would have run Brabantio through for speaking so insultingly. He is powerful in Venice, beloved of the Duke, and will do his best to retrieve his daughter and exact revenge. Othello replies that he himself has served the Venetians well and is a man of royal lineage; his claim to Desdemona rests upon his merits and upon his great love for her —he has not lightly relinquished his cherished single state. Cassio and other officers arrive with a summons from the Duke. Urgent messages from Cyprus have forced an emergency session of the senate. As Othello steps inside to take his leave, Iago begins to give

Cassio a facetious account of the marriage, but he is interrupted by
the return of Othello and the arrival of Brabantio's party. Swords
are drawn on both sides, but Othello calmly bids all to keep the
peace. Brabantio charges him with prevailing upon Desdemona
with magic charms since no one of his frightening visage could
otherwise have won a maiden so fastidious and shy. He demands
that Othello submit to arrest, but when told that this would contravene the Duke's summons, he decides to attend the session of the
senate and make his accusations there.

1-17 Iago advertises his moral rectitude with glancing allusions to
his *conscience* (2), his lack of *iniquity* (3), his *godliness* (9), mod-
estly described as *little,* but his visions of 'yerking' someone (anyone) *under the ribs* are remarkably concrete. He affects the brusk
tone of the manly soldier as he plays sycophant to the one he has
already betrayed; evidently he has called Othello from the inn
where his marriage with Desdemona is to be consummated to
'warn' him of Brabantio's threats.   **17-33**   Othello's opening
lines are not wholly free of agitation, but his voice is serene as compared with those we have heard thus far. He will be massive and
finely attired but indubitably black; his physical characteristics, like
those of Shakespeare's other Moors (Aaron in *Titus Andronicus,*
Morocco in *Merchant of Venice*) will suggest fierce pride and reckless bravery rather than bondage or jungle savagery, but they cannot be ignored. As the playwright was well aware, ideas of mis-
cegenation, of exotic sexual attraction, are bound to attend the
contemplation of his winning a Venetian maiden for his bride.
Othello is as conscious as Morocco (see above, p. 180) that his race
prejudices his eligibility although he refrains from mentioning it as
he speaks of his services, his royal lineage, and the disinterestedness
of his love (24-28). Observe that he finds it necessary to repeat
that he is a man of parts, legally wedded to the fair aristocrat, and
easy in his conscience (31). But his refusal to evade a meeting with
Brabantio—*Not I; I must be found* (30)—while consistent with
his apparent character, as intimated by his composure and spacious
mode of utterance, is scarcely consistent with his situation. Has not
his marriage been clandestine? The character of Iago as Machiavel-

lian hypocrite is drummed in upon us relentlessly: he even swears by the (two-faced) *Janus* (33); of course the oath may be given an impersonal application, since the fact he is commenting upon wears a different face from what he had at first supposed. **34-54** The Moor's prestige is enhanced by this summons; we get a sense of crisis and of his being the man of the hour. A mercenary taint attends his marriage, at least in the minds of Roderigo (I, i, 66) and of Iago, who likens it to an act of piracy (51); if he can hold his prize, *he's made forever*. We incline to doubt that his motives were truly predatory, but the ambiguities are multiplying. **55-99** The drawing of swords seems to release Othello's latent powers: he is at ease in his métier, and his *Keep up your bright swords* . . . (see above, p. 34) requires nothing in the way of threatening gesture to be instantaneously effective. Observe that Iago is alert to all opportunities, and, in a single breath, both clears himself of complicity with Roderigo the informer and chooses a safe opponent in the possible fray (58). Brabantio's suspicion that Othello has used charms and drugs to weaken the will of Desdemona has hardened into a certainty. His indictment, while it fails to induce belief, nevertheless whets our curiosity by its characterization of Desdemona. Why *has* she shunned the *curlèd darlings* of her nation to run to the *sooty bosom* of the Moor? Othello's unruffled response, his courteous handling of his accuser, his readiness to answer for his actions, do more than anything he has directly affirmed in predisposing us to believe in his *perfect soul* (clear conscience). We already sense the fact that he is cut from no petty mold.

I, iii

The Duke of Venice is discussing with the Senators the contradictory dispatches on the strength and movement of the Turkish fleet when a final messenger informs them that it has made rendezvous at Rhodes and is now bearing down on Cyprus. Othello must be sent to take over the command of the defenders from the trusty but less-experienced Montano. When Othello and Brabantio arrive with their several parties, state business pauses until the dispute between them is heard. To Brabantio's charge that he must have used foul means to win Desdemona, Othello replies that he will fully describe his courtship. As a welcome visitor to Brabantio's house, he was asked to tell the story of his life, and Desdemona, having heard it only in parts, one day asked him to repeat it to her. She fell in love with him because of the hardships he had endured, and he with her because of her tenderness. To the Duke this explanation seems plausible, but Brabantio refuses to accept it. When Desdemona, whom Iago has been dispatched to fetch hither, confirms the story and professes her deep love of the Moor, her father denounces her bitterly and rejects the Duke's proffers of comfort. Othello is commissioned to proceed at once to Cyprus, with Desdemona following in another ship under the escort of Iago. Brabantio's parting words are a warning that she may deceive her husband as she has her father, but Othello is ready to stake his life upon her faith. When all the others have departed and Roderigo declares that he will drown himself for grief, Iago ridicules the idea since Desdemona will surely soon tire of the Moor and seek another lover. Roderigo need only follow to Cyprus disguised and richly supplied with money. Alone, Iago speaks of this dupe from whom he extracts money, then of Othello whom he craves to destroy. Rumor has it that the Moor has been familiar with Iago's wife, and he will act on the assumption that it is true. Since he covets Cassio's place, he will weave his designs to entrap them both. Cassio is handsome, and perhaps Othello can be persuaded that Desdemona finds him desirable. Since the Moor is innocent and unsuspecting, he will prove defenseless against devilish schemes.

1 s.d. These early scenes are so articulated that the action seems continuous: at the end of the first the characters set out for Othello's inn, and at the beginning of the second we were at that inn awaiting their arrival; at the end of the second they set out for the senate chamber, and we are now in that chamber ready to observe their arrival. **1-46** The prolonged and circumstantial treatment of the Turkish threat to Cyprus contributes to the prevailingly realistic atmosphere. The mysteriousness of Othello, Desdemona, and Iago is accentuated by the hard and sharply outlined background.

47-75 All eyes focus on Othello, twice addressed as *valiant* by these statesmen who stand in present need of his valor. The Duke covers with an apology—*I did not see you* (49)—his slip in failing to give Brabantio precedence in his greeting. This is an unpropitious moment for bringing charges against a valued commander. When Othello is named the miscreant, just after the Duke has declared that the *bloody book of law* will be invoked, the senatorial response is almost comically tepid—*We are very sorry for't* (73).   **76-127** Othello's style is as limpid and spacious as the skies over the desert wilderness where he has passed so many of his days. Were we to concentrate upon content alone as he opens his defense, we might judge him to be wily (because of his deferential address to *potent, grave, reverend, noble,* and *approved good* judges, his eloquent claim that he lacks eloquence, his timely allusion to his warlike experience), but it is the music of the words that really speaks to us. Their formality bordering upon the quaint, their stately pace, their utter clarity, their harmony of sound convey an impression of complete candor; surely anyone who speaks so purely must himself be pure. But if Othello is guileless, his creator is not, and we have here a prime instance of artistic 'misdirection' of attention. Had Brabantio accused Othello of violating the laws of hospitality by stealing a marriage with the daughter of the house, denying the father the chance to use even his powers of dissuasion, it is hard to see what Othello's defense could have been. Instead of being forced to defend what really needs defense, he is permitted to dismiss the subject with a few easy words of admission, *That I have ta'en away this old man's daughter, It is most true* (78-79). Brabantio's original frantic notion that the Moor has used magic charms has so grown upon him that he brings an unfounded charge. Othello can honestly plead his innocence, Desdemona can be summoned to verify his testimony, and the Duke can gently rebuke Brabantio (105-09) who has been jockeyed (by the playwright) out of his position as injured party into that of false accuser. Still these are defensible tactics. The purpose of the episode is not to provide a judicial consideration of the rights and wrongs of the elopement as it affects Brabantio, but to convince us of the innocence of the love of Othello and Desdemona and to rebuke the suspicions whispering in our minds. The most operative part of Brabantio's indictment is his characterization of his shy and modest daughter— *A maiden never bold . . .* (94-106). Conveyed though they were by suspect witnesses, impressions of sexual perversity in the bride and mercenary predation in the groom attached themselves to this marriage as it was originally presented to us, and we were bound to wonder why a lovely Venetian aristocrat should elope with a middle-aged Moor.   **128-71** Othello's great speech provides the only conceivable answer that would induce belief. As he provides this magical panorama of his past, he becomes a creature of wonder by association with things of wonder, trailing clouds of glory from his *hairbreadth scapes* and his sojourns midst *anters vast and deserts idle.* Dreams of travel and adventure are associated in our minds with the health and innocence of youth, and the original fabric of Desdemona's love could have been woven of no more disarming stuff; we have been charmed as she has been charmed. Add to this the faint note of pathos sounding through the speech. From childhood Othello has been homeless and exposed, so that, despite his strength, he bears scars of deprivation appealing to the maternal instinct. All is summed up in the lines, *She loved me . . .* (167-68) so perfectly expressing so perfectly credible a phenomenon that our cynicism cannot survive, and our response concurs with the Duke's *I think this tale would win my daughter too* (171).   **172-89** Brabantio is again used by the playwright as an implement in his design to remove suspicions of baseness in this marriage; here he is made to ask the wrong question instead of bring the wrong charge. Had he asked his child why she had failed to trust him with the truth of her love, her position would have been awkward. Instead he asks her to whom she owes obedience. The question is in the present tense, and Desdemona, whose marriage is a fait accompli, can answer with perfect truth and propriety (180-88), indeed in the very terms in which Cordelia will later answer a similar question. The effect is to place her solidly in the right, Brabantio in the wrong; she has invoked the ethical code actually incorporated in the marriage vow.   **189-220** The feelings of fathers are expendable in circumstances such as these, but the playwright is aware, as we all are, that Brabantio has been ill-used. Here he is given his innings. He at least is not made to accept passively the Duke's consolations; these are lent an air of patness by the use of rime (202-09), and Brabantio's bitter and apt rejoinder (210-20) is given, by its continuation of the rime-scheme, the effect of parody. **221-300** The transition to the subject of practical arrangements is appropriately effected by the Duke's speech in prose. The desire of Othello and Desdemona to remain together is expressed in adjacent speeches of equal length (248-59, 260-74) which function almost as affidavits of belief in their mutual love, compatibility, and integrity. As Iago is entrusted with the custody of Desdemona, he is described as a man of *honesty and trust* (284) and soon thereafter addressed in the fashion that proves recurrent, *Honest Iago* (294). This is ominous enough, but a richly suggestive cluster of speeches as the company disperses (290-94) is even more indicative of the direction the tragedy will take. Why is Brabantio permitted his *Look to her, Moor . . .* speech (292-93) in parting? Partly, of course, to evoke Othello's *My life upon her faith!* with its ironic implications. But further than that it serves as a reminder that this marriage, virtuous though it is in essential respects, stands slightly blemished at its inception. Brabantio's mistaken objections have more than once adumbrated valid ones. Although the playwright has been at pains to combat initial impressions made by the mixed character and surreptitiousness of the marriage, he has refrained from sponging the slate completely clean. Because this marriage is idealistic and 'innocent,' it does not follow that it is in all respects a good one. This untainted pair have not willfully intended to hurt Brabantio, but in respect to him, and perhaps to other things as well, they have acted with a certain obliviousness. **301-98** We deceive ourselves if we deny the presence in Iago of qualities that amuse and attract. He is sprightly, energetic, intellectually vital; and we feel small concern for his present victim. Roderigo will deserve what he gets, and Iago's present role is that of the comic confidence-man who entertains rather than disgusts; the very frankness of his deviltry is engaging. However, the groundwork is being laid for impressions of a quite different kind. Although uniformly villainous, Iago does not evoke a uniform emotional response, and one of the striking features of the play is the manner in which our sense of attraction modulates into a sense of revulsion. (Observe how his entertaining antics thin out as his victims begin to suffer.) That he is only twenty-eight (311-12) does not mean that he is young; by Renaissance standards he is middle-aged and is here implying as much. He continues to identify love and animality, with his reference to Desdemona as *guinea hen,* so that the distinction he claims between his *humanity* and the *baboon* is unconsciously myopic (315-16). His essay on reason and the passions (319-31) is orthodox moral philosophy, but we need not dismiss it as 'insincere.' Iago has no present need for insincerity, and might express such views when alone. as, in fact, the Machiavellian Edmund does in *King Lear* (I, ii, 115-24). The value of such views varies with the nature of the speaker; on the lips of good men they indicate virtuous self-responsibility; on the lips of evil ones, vicious self-sufficiency. The beginning and end of the speech provide sufficient clues: *Virtue? a fig!* denies the existence of the transcendental values which make the distinction between love and lust (330-31). The repeated *Put money in thy purse* during the long injunction to Roderigo (333-67) is a telling theatrical trick, but a more significant kind of reiteration appears in these speeches—in the allusions to corruptibility. Iago is the epitome of the Evil-thinker. This fact, already intimated, is established explicitly after Roderigo leaves. Merely to call Iago 'cynical,' or to discuss his suspicion that Othello has seduced his wife as 'motivation' is to do scant justice to the symbolic significance of his mode of thinking. Obviously he believes, and enjoys believing, that everyone is seduced or seducible. Anyone of *a free and open nature* (393) like Othello, that is anyone not an Evil-thinker, is his natural opposite and natural prey. That evil-thinking creates evil, or rather that evil-thinking *is* evil, and need only be communicated in order to multiply evil, will presumably be the theme of the play. We have already been introduced to human symbols of vulnerable innocence (Othello and Desdemona) and of insinuating evil (Iago). If we seek a mythic point of reference, Adam and Eve and the Serpent will do as well as any. The final 'choral' couplet (see above, p. 82) identifies Iago as an emissary from Hell. Although in the guise of an Italian ensign, his qualities are reptilian: he is bright, resilient, swift, covert, as he hisses his lies and darts his poison into bodies and souls, striking from ambush to kill. (Observe that he later prevents Othello from using literal *poison*. *Poison* must remain a metaphor, and exclusively his own.)

II, i

Montano speaks with several Cyprian Gentlemen about the fearful storm raging offshore, perhaps playing havoc with the Turkish fleet. A third Gentleman brings news that the enemy is indeed in distress, and that a ship has arrived bearing Cassio, the lieutenant of Othello. Cassio himself joins them, and all express hope for the safety of the valiant Moor. Shouts and a cannon-salute signal the arrival of another ship, and as Cassio is telling of the marriage of Othello to the lovely Desdemona, she is escorted in by Iago, his wife Emilia, the disguised Roderigo, and others who have just debarked. As greetings are exchanged, more shots and another cannon-salute signal the arrival of a third ship, which perhaps bears Othello. The interim of waiting is filled with social pleasantries. Cassio gives Emilia a kiss of greeting, and Iago discourses satirically upon her qualities and those of women in general. At Desdemona's request, he improvises rimes on various types of women, including the type completely innocuous and hence vapid. As Cassio acts the gallant with Desdemona, Iago muses to himself that such civilities may help hoist him out of his lieutenancy. Othello now enters, safe, with his attendants. He announces the end of the Turkish threat to Cyprus and exchanges loving greetings with Desdemona. All prepare to celebrate joyously the peace and this happy reunion. Iago lingers behind with Roderigo to set a plot in train. He convinces his gull that Desdemona is ready to transfer her passion to Cassio. Roderigo must aid him in disgracing the latter and removing him from the running. He can do this by provoking the hot-tempered lieutenant to a quarrel as soon as Iago creates an occasion. Alone, Iago reviews his suspicions and tentative plans. He chooses to assume that his wife Emilia has been the object of Cassio's lust as well as Othello's, and that Desdemona is the present object of Cassio's as well as his own. His jealousy prompts him to use jealousy as the means of ruining both the Moor and his lieutenant, letting the plot take shape as it proceeds.

1 s.d. The only major time-and-space gap is closed by the same device noted earlier as contributing to our sense of the forward rush of the action. Again a preceding scene ended with an exodus to a stated destination, and again the succeeding one places us at that destination awaiting imminent arrivals. We shall see that in a sense Venice has moved to Cyprus, or rather that the two have coalesced, since no new major characters are recruited from the Cyprians. What later may seem a confusion of time in the action is the result of the sea-voyage's being treated sometimes as a time-vacuum, sometimes as a ripening period, with references to the actions of the characters reaching back into a very elastic past. We need not be disturbed by the problem of whether Roderigo has had *time* to spend his money, Cassio to conduct his liaison with Bianca, Iago to nag Emilia to steal the handkerchief, and the like. Similarly irrelevant is whether Desdemona should be exonerated by Othello simply on the grounds of her bridal virginity and subsequent lack of opportunity.   **1-82** The noise and bustle of the offshore storm, with the cries of sail-sighting, the cannon-salutes, and the successive arrivals of groups of characters are fine and exhilarating stage business. We can scarcely add this to those Shakespearean stories symbolizing parallel upheavals in the macrocosm and souls of men since it is really a very cheery business: it has *banged the Turks* (21) but spared the Venetians, and it emphasizes the joys of reunion. The dialogue is studded with enhancing allusions to the *brave Othello;* and Cassio's speech on his marriage to the *divine Desdemona* (67-82) is a virtual epithalamion.   **83-175** Cassio's *Hail to thee, lady!* and subsequent lines suggest a prayer to the Virgin as all kneel. Note that her first words are of Othello. Like other gracious ladies in Shakespeare, she is willing to supply a jester his leads, as she and Iago improve the social occasion. Iago, in his stock animadversions upon his wife and all womankind, and in his improvised rimes, is playing the part of a very mild cynic indeed —a most innocuous *slanderer* (113). This is incidental entertainment, but it throws light on Iago's reputation for *honesty.* Publicly he is *profane* and *liberal* (licentious) within limits which inspire confidence. A man's man this! (162-65). But as he watches the courtesies paid to Desdemona by Cassio (166-76) his gaiety drains away, and his words (obviously timed to accompany their pantomime) are muttered with a vindictive leer. Note that he fastens upon each physical contact with an almost obscene absorption, like a peeping-tom.   **176-96** Presumably Othello will be given an entrance as imposing as Desdemona's so far as gestures of homage are concerned, but after Cassio's *Lo, where he comes,* all are silent as he and Desdemona meet. This is their moment of greatest felicity. As they speak of the perfection of their union, in terms both heroical and devout, we are invited to look upon something which is about to be assailed; the tableau stands in contrast with that of the fatal conclusion when the kiss of love becomes the kiss of death. (No interim kissing is indicated in the text, and producers should take note.)   **197-279** Othello's words have been filled with foreshadowing suggestion; the image of the kiss as discord is picked up by Iago who will make it truly so. Even Roderigo is convinced of Desdemona's purity, and Iago waxes evangelical in his effort to convert him to a different way of thinking. He is resourcefully plausible in his systematic disparagement, and his concluding soliloquy again reveals his belief or craving for belief in the evil he propounds. The reference to his jealousy as a *poisonous mineral* gnawing his *inwards* (291) may seem to contradict Coleridge's dictum that his is the 'motive-hunting of a motiveless malignity,' but if there is anything misleading in this famous phrase, it is the 'motive-hunting' rather than the 'motiveless.' We are never convinced that he seeks self-justification, his early allusions to his 'motives' serving only to parry for a time our growing awareness that he has none and needs none. He has assumed human ways of speaking and acting along with his human form, the vengeful and hypocritical ways of the conventional villain, and they provide a façade as deceptive as the façade of honesty and kindliness. At the core is mysterious evil, a wanton cruelty and destructiveness ultimately directed against those (such as Desdemona) from whom he never even claims to have received injury.

II, ii

Othello's herald proclaims that the hours from five to eleven will be devoted to feasting and revelry, in celebration of the destruction of the Turkish fleet and the nuptials of the new commander.

1-11 The next scene (9-10, 15-17) places this announced period as occurring on the day of arrival. The *nuptial* (7) is the consummation of the marriage.

II, iii

About to retire with Desdemona, Othello bids Cassio supervise the setting of the guard. It still lacks an hour to curfew, and although he has a bad head for drinking, Cassio is persuaded by Iago to take a cup of wine with some gentlemen of Cyprus. As he steps out to greet Montano and several others, Iago gloats at the prospect of making him drunk and quarrelsome. The wine is passed about, and Iago leads the company in drinking-songs while Cassio becomes increasingly surly and thick of speech. When he withdraws, protesting his sobriety, Iago tells Montano that drunkenness is his nightly habit. Roderigo appears and is instructed by Iago in an aside to follow Cassio and provoke a quarrel. He comes racing back with the enraged lieutenant at his heels. When Montano tries to intercept this pursuit, Cassio turns violently on the peacemaker and wounds him. The alarm bells sounds and draws Othello and attendants to the fray. He angrily demands to know its cause, and Iago, who has followed Roderigo and returned, states the facts with a great show of reluctance. Othello strips Cassio of his rank, orders Montano cared for, and comforts Desdemona, who has been aroused by the alarm. Cassio remains with Iago and speaks from the depths of his humiliation, inveighing against wine and bewailing the loss of his reputation. Iago makes light of the loss, assuring him that he need only enlist the aid of Desdemona in order to be restored to his office. As Cassio goes off comforted, Iago soliloquizes upon the 'honesty' of his advice since Desdemona is sure to make an ardent intercessor. But he will see to it that the intercession arouses Othello's suspicions. Roderigo returns complaining of the beating he has taken and the money he has lost, but Iago cheers him with the fact of Cassio's disgrace—Roderigo need only be patient. Alone again, Iago resolves to enlist the aid of his wife Emilia in drawing Desdemona on. He will bring Othello to where he can watch Cassio solicit her assistance.

1-11 This glimpse of Othello and Desdemona on their bridal night is appropriately fleeting and devoid of intimacy. We need put no sinister construction upon the mercantile image (9-10) of the consummation. (A similar one occurs in *Romeo and Juliet,* III, ii, 26-28.) The general tactic of the playwright is to play down the physical aspects of this marriage except as they incite the imagination of Iago, and we should not let this suggest 'inhibitions' on the part of Othello; it is in the nature of the artistic design that this match be treated as both ardent and 'chaste.'   **12-25** Observe the decency of Cassio, his refusal to be drawn into any lickerish conversation about it.   **26-318** In this first successful ruse of Iago, he employs mainly practical manipulation of persons, so that the stage is filled with fascinating action. Everyone behaves according to character and with great naturalness. Since we are aware of Iago's designs at every point (are, so to speak, viewing the events from back-stage), we may get the impression that the ruse is transparent and the victims easily fooled. However, if we watch and listen to Iago from their point of view, we observe that he offers no loophole for suspicion. He makes no move that seems otherwise than correct, tells no lie that can be detected. For instance, on the pretext of following Roderigo, he relieves himself of the later necessity of explaining why he failed to come to Montano's assistance, and at the same time insures that the alarm bell will be rung. Thus he both creates occasions and improves upon accidents. His virtuosity as intriguer gives the play a spectacular interest which may or may not serve its ultimate tragic ends. The advice Iago gives is sensible advice, and the truth he tells with such a masterly show of reluctance is the strict truth as the others are in a position to see it.

This is the *honest* Iago. This is also the *kind* Iago. We can under-stand why the quality of good-will is attributed to him in his circle almost as habitually as the quality of honesty. Observe how club-bable he is with his jests and his drinking-songs, how tolerant when Cassio grows truculent (100, 104), how generous in praise of a comrade in arms *fit to stand by Caesar* (116) (were he not, alas, an habitual drunkard), how sound his moral comment (295-96), how out-giving he is with comfort and advice (299-310). And the advice would be excellent were it given with good intent. In his soliloquy, he gleefully calls attention to the innocent exterior he has so successfully maintained: *And what's he then that says I play the villain* (319). Just as he has spoken repeatedly of using Othello's virtue of trustfulness in order to destroy him, so he now speaks of using Desdemona's virtue of kindness: he will make the net *out of her own goodness* (344). It has actually been Cassio's goodness that has just served his purpose—not proneness to drink, which Cassio fears and abhors, but desire to be courteous to the gentlemen of Cyprus. Only with Roderigo does Iago count upon stupidity, and we are reading awry if we speak of the 'stupidity' of Othello, Desdemona, and Cassio. Iago's constant explanations *to us* of his machinations, going considerably beyond the need of the occasion and the playwright's usual methods, may result in our con-sidering his victims obtuse, but they have a different artistic end; it is disturbing to be taken so completely into the destroyer's con-fidence as if we were trusted accomplices.

III, i

At Cassio's direction, musicians play an aubade before the cham-ber of Othello and Desdemona, until a clownish servant puts an end to the performance with witticisms and a gift of money. Cassio bribes the Clown to procure him an interview with Emilia, but Iago appears and offers to send her while he himself draws off Othello. As Cassio is speaking in praise of this kind and honest Florentine, Emilia comes to him, expresses her sympathy, and seems to offer assurance that his suit will succeed. Othello has had to take stern action because of the high regard in which Montano is held in Cyprus. She will conduct Cassio to where he can present his suit to Desdemona.

1-55 It is appropriate for Othello and Desdemona to receive an aubade on this particular morning, but Cassio's motives as sponsor are so open to question that the device is indubitably awkward, especially since the recipients are so unresponsive. The episode seems to have been introduced simply to let the audience listen to music for a restful interval. The jokes of the servant, whom the playwright fails to name except with the generic tag 'Clown,' serve a similar purpose and are similarly awkward from a functional point of view; certainly this is the most intrusive of Shakespeare's clowns. The present scene and the next are utilitarian and makeshift, serving merely as lead-in to the great crucial scene of the play.

III, ii

Othello bids Iago to dispatch certain letters to Venice and then rejoin him; he is about to accompany several gentlemen in an inspection of the Cyprian fortifications (1-6).

III, iii

While Desdemona is assuring Cassio that she will do her best to persuade Othello to restore him to favor, Emilia remarks upon the Moor's approach with Iago, whereupon Cassio retreats in embarrassment. Iago insinuates that there is something suspicious about this, and as Desdemona pleads the case of the discharged lieutenant, her husband seems preoccupied. However, he yields to her importunities to consider the matter soon, and after she and Emilia have left, he fervidly declares the strength of his attachment to her. Iago proceeds to make leading remarks about the relations of Desdemona and Cassio until Othello is impelled to demand his meaning. He protests his unwillingness to speak, moralizing upon the vileness of suspicion, slander, and jealousy until Othello is thoroughly aroused. As if under duress, Iago then cautions him to be mindful of Desdemona's honor, instancing her perversity in her choice of a racial alien as husband, the sensuality of the Venetians, and the like. Under his skillful manipulation, Othello is more moved than he cares to admit, and when Iago has left, he remarks upon the prevalence and horror of cuckoldry. When Desdemona and Emilia return, he greets his wife ambiguously and complains of a pain in his forehead. She offers him her handkerchief to bind his brows, but he puts it aside so that it falls to the floor. When they have left, Emilia takes up the handkerchief with the remark that her husband has been nagging her to procure for him this first love-token given by Othello to Desdemona. Iago returns and receives it from her, refusing to tell why he wants it; but after she has left, he remarks that he intends to plant it in Cassio's lodgings. Othello now returns, and Iago notes with a fearful relish that the throes of jealousy are upon him. A violent interview ensues. Othello expresses his present agony, turns savagely upon the informer, and demands proof of Desdemona's guilt. In defending his role as well-meaning friend, Iago manages to fan Othello's passion with a succession of skillful lies; he tells of Cassio's erotic dreams of Desdemona and of the handkerchief she has given him. Othello is thoroughly possessed, and kneels to vow vengeance upon the lecherous pair, with Iago kneeling beside him. He commissions Iago to murder Cassio within three days, addressing him as his lieutenant. He himself will give swift death to the fair devil Desdemona.

1-92   Desdemona undertakes Cassio's cause with the naïve alacrity of the young bride, welcoming a chance to prove her power and, at the same time, to do her husband and another good. The poignance of the situation derives from her generous optimism and sense of security in Othello's love; she is quite without armor. Her importunate methods should not offend us; they are of a 'wifely' kind. Iago's opening gambit, *Ha! I like not that* (35), is startlingly recognizable. He invents none of his tactics. All are as universally current as slander itself, *tricks of custom* in Othello's phrase (122), the more frightening for so being as Iago musters them with the deadly precision of a master strategist. In the betrayal of Cassio (II, iii) he used practical demonstration; here he uses psychological suggestion, and the significant action of the scene occurs in Othello's mind. His asking Desdemona to leave him (85) indicates that he is already affected, without quite knowing how or why. His over-emphatic protestation of faith after she leaves contains the unconsciously prophetic oaths, *Perdition catch my soul* (90), *Chaos is come again* (92).   **93-129** Iago dangles familiar bait— 'unguarded' questions, 'evasive' responses, 'absent-minded' repetitions. We can picture his excessive blankness of expression when challenged. Othello's angry challenge confirms our impression that Iago's first shaft struck home (109). Why, we may ask, has Iago been able to *fright* him (120) so quickly if he is not prone to jealousy? There is a curious paradox here. Jealousy is compounded of possessiveness and suspiciousness. Othello is, of course, possessive, and no one, including Desdemona, would consider the trait a fault. But if he were suspicious, he would surely suspect Iago. The instrumentality which creates his jealousy exonerates him of the charge of being jealous by nature. What we mean when we say that he is not naturally jealous is that he is not, like Leontes in *The Winter's Tale,* the kind of man in whom the malady would generate from within. So far as the speed with which Iago succeeds is concerned, we must reckon with the synoptic nature of dramatic art; this single session must symbolize a process which in 'real life' would consume weeks or months.   **130-92** In giving his testimony on Cassio's brawling, Iago maneuvered himself into the position of having to have the truth dragged out of him; here he repeats the device and since, in the case of Cassio, his testimony proved strictly in accord with the demonstrable facts, he is in a most strategic position—again the reluctant *honest* witness. He fortifies his position with a display of moral fervor, actually preaching to Othello; and observe that his homilies on the rights of mental privacy (133-41), decent reticence (145-51), stolen reputations (155-61), and the horrors of jealousy *the green-eyed monster* (165-70) are all eloquent and true!   **193-289** The commitment he extracts from Othello, *To be once in doubt Is once to be resolved* (179-80) is, by a familiar shyster's trick, wrested into an invitation to speak with *franker spirit* (193-95) and to plant, not resolve, a doubt. He capitalizes upon all the possible uncertainties of a man in Othello's position—the Moor past his youth who has won the love of a beautiful young woman reared in a supersubtle milieu quite alien to his own. Iago expresses the thoughts that he would have were he in Othello's place, engrafting his own imagination upon the other's imagination, entering in a very real sense into his victim's mind and making the pure impure. To argue Othello's predilection to jealousy (which, at the very most, is no greater than that of the average man) is to reduce the impact of the scene. This is a 'temptation' scene with 'innocence' lost through partaking of the fruit of the tree of a certain kind of 'knowledge.' We witness the appalling process until Othello becomes, like Iago, the Evil-thinker. Swift though the process is as measured by literal time, an amazing verisimilitude is achieved. Othello is infected by stages, with Iago hovering like a diabolic physician alert to arrest any symptom of recovery; the weak affirmation *I do not think but Desdemona's honest* (225) is quickly countered with *Long live she so! and long live you to think so!* with its insidious *think*. The slightest opening, *And yet, how nature erring from itself*—(227) invites the darting lunge, *Ay, there's the point!*, with new jets of poison pouring in—*Foh! . . . a will most rank, Foul disproportion, thoughts unnatural.* The comicality is gone. The vision is stark and merciless.   **290-329**   The intrigue involved in the use of the handkerchief as 'material evidence' adds to the story-interest of the play, but we shall see that it does so at a certain cost.   **330-32**   There is a truly Satanic sublimity about these lines of Iago; never has such pure delight in pure cruelty been so beautifully expressed. The sounds of the words tell us of that *sweet* and healing *sleep* which the sense of the words tell us Othello will never know again.   **333-73**   We may respond in many ways to Othello's violent eruption of rage. We may scold him for his egotism, his apparent concern only with his peace of mind and the blow to his pride. There is a wonderful elegy to a lost love (348-57)—not Desdemona, but *glorious war* with glorious Othello in its midst. But this is a little like scolding a man in his death throes, and although Othello is here shown feeling in a certain way, we cannot conclude that it is the only way in which he feels. Besides, there is a stranger side to this episode. We have been led to think of Othello as the untamed, the natural man. At this moment when he acts most untamedly, most naturally, he presses nearest to the truth. Instinctively he lashes out against his new 'knowledge.' If he had *nothing known* (335-47) he would indeed be *happy,* since there is actually nothing to know. Were the *If* omitted from one of his speeches (368-73), it would be a perfect summary of the situation, and were he to follow through with his impulse to choke Iago, who seems truly terrified (373-75), justice would be served.   **374-90** He is charmed back into submission with the talismanic word *honest.*   **391-479** The scene rises to its climax as Iago fills Othello's mind with gross images and maddens him with ever-bolder lies. The ruthless daring of the conclusion, with the two kneeling in devotion, suggests a witches' sabbath, with the convert hideously devout, the evangelist hideously elated. The perversion is underscored by Othello's reference here, and frequently hereafter, to Desdemona as a *devil.*

III, iv

Desdemona sends the clownish servant to bid Cassio come to hear of the progress of his suit. She remarks to Emilia that she is distressed at the loss of the handkerchief given her by Othello; fortunately he is free from jealousy and will not view its absence with distrust. But as Othello enters, his manner belies her confidence. When she begins to petition him on behalf of Cassio, he interrupts with complaints of a cold and a request for her handkerchief. He refuses the one she is carrying and demands the other, which he describes as a magical heirloom with the property of insuring the mutual fidelity of receiver and giver. Frightened, she tries to conceal its loss, using the worst possible means of distracting his attention, by persistently referring to Cassio. He grows harsher and harsher in his demands, and finally leaves in a rage. Bewildered, she wishes she had never seen the handkerchief, and Emilia remarks ironically upon her husband's alleged freedom from jealousy. When Cassio arrives in the company of Iago and speaks of his hopes, Desdemona dolefully explains that her efforts have been thwarted by Othello's angry mood. Iago expresses surprise that he could ever be angry, and leaves to seek him out. Desdemona comforts herself with the thought that her husband may have received vexatious official news; he cannot possibly be jealous because she has given him no cause. She tells Cassio to wait while she goes to renew his suit. Cassio is accosted by Bianca, who has come to reproach him for neglecting her. He explains that he has been low in spirits, but will renew his attentions soon. Meanwhile she may do him the favor of copying out the designs on a handkerchief he has found in his lodgings. Anxious not to be seen in this courtesan's company, he conducts her on the first stage of her departure, giving her placating assurances that she still possesses his love.

1-201   The play might conceivably have proceeded, with little intervening action, from III, iii, where Iago succeeds in converting Othello to IV, iii, where the consequences of his success begin to take active shape. Scenes III, iv, IV, i, and IV, ii constitute a distension or prolongation of the situation which may be compared with that occurring in *Hamlet*. In both plays the distension results from the ostensible need to verify guilt. In *Hamlet* the incidental sense of 'delay' contributes materially to our conception of the protagonist's nature. But the Moor of Venice is not, like the Prince of Denmark, given to thinking 'too precisely on the event'; in fact he has proclaimed the opposite—'To be once in doubt Is once to be resolved.' His *My mind misgives* (89) represents an illogical return to mere suspicion after the certainty he has expressed at the end of the preceding scene, and we may legitimately ask why, since he is a man of action and apparently 'resolved,' does he now appear 'in doubt.' Obviously the playwright wishes to provide us with opportunity to observe Othello in his fallen state and to contemplate its horrors before we witness the fatal denouement. The plot development, involving the handkerchief and Cassio's liaison with Bianca, gives rise to some brilliant theatrical episodes starring Iago as intriguer, but its thematic relevance is dubious. The three scenes in question have both dramatic virtues (as they reveal Othello's state) and theatrical virtues (as they reveal Iago's skill), but these virtues are uneasily combined. Again the jokes of the Clown are shrewdly placed (1-20) immediately following a scene exhaustingly tense, but again they are singularly unamusing. Emilia's bare-faced lie about the disposition of the handkerchief—*I know not madam* (24)—and, even more, her persistence in standing silent while Desdemona suffers cruelly during Othello's demands for it (75-98) may suggest for the moment that she is a fit mate for Iago. We have been given no chance to form conclusions about her character and hence are not nonplussed by her conduct; later, when she emerges as heroically loyal, we have happily lost sight of the present episode, or are inclined to believe that she is insensitive to anything but the most jolting moral stimulus. It is well to ignore the inconsistencies and to submit to the over-all impression, which is, in fact, highly poetic and dramatic: Othello himself is now Evil-thinker, victimizing the innocent. Observe how Iago-like he has become, given to sexual innuendo (39-44) and deviousness of action (51-97). His strength has degenerated into rude burliness.

IV, i

Pretending to offer comfort, Iago tortures Othello with images of adultery. When he insinuates that Cassio has boasted of his conquest of Desdemona, Othello grows incoherently passionate and falls in a swoon. Cassio enters as Iago is exulting over his stricken form, and is told to return when this fit of 'epilepsy' has passed. Iago returns to the attack as soon as Othello recovers. He arranges for him to observe from concealment Cassio's demeanor as he talks of Desdemona. Actually Iago induces Cassio to talk of Bianca, and Othello mutters imprecations as he watches what is obviously an account of a successful amour. Bianca returns, having had second thoughts about copying out the design, and angrily returns the handkerchief to Cassio with the charge that he must have received it from a new mistress. When the two have departed, Iago tells Othello that he must accept the testimony of his own eyes: Cassio jests publicly about Desdemona and has given her love-token to his whore. A lingering tenderness for the woman he has loved contends with Othello's lust for revenge, and it is Iago who maps out the course of action—he will dispose of Cassio, and Othello will strangle Desdemona in her bed. A trumpet sounds, announcing the

entrance of Lodovico, who is accompanied by Desdemona and attendants. He is Desdemona's kinsman, bringing a letter from
Venice; Othello is to return, leaving Cassio in command at Cyprus.
As Othello reads, he hears Desdemona speaking to Lodovico about
Cassio's merits. He ironically choruses her remarks, then strikes
her in a fit of rage. Bewildered and crushed, she turns to leave the
company. In amazement, Lodovico exclaims that this would not be
believed in Venice, and urges Othello to recall and comfort her.
Othello calls, but only to make her act of obedience occasion for
further insult, then rudely orders her to be gone. He speaks civilly
to Lodovico, accepting the mandate he brings, but departs uttering
cryptic oaths. Lodovico asks Iago whether this amazing conduct is
madness or a mere fit of ill-temper provoked by the message, and
Iago replies that Othello is no longer the man he was.

1-275 Othello appears in this scene at his most base. It is well
to resist pat identifications of mythic symbolism, but it is hard to
resist the idea that his *swoon* is calculated to suggest to us the 'fall
of man.' Since his agony is so authentic, and in one marvelous exchange is, almost inadvertently, expressed in terms of his past love
and idealism—*O Iago, the pity of it, Iago* (175-92)—our sympathies are not wholly alienated, but no other tragic protagonist in
Shakespeare comes so near to overstepping the limits of our tolerance and arousing disgust. He is now completely malleable in Iago's
hands, open to every evil suggestion (1-43); his speech is violent,
incoherent, coarse; he is placed in the ignominious posture of eavesdropping, with eyes (109-67) and with ears (218-27); his actions
are both brutal, as when he strikes Desdemona, and mean, as when
he bullies her with his order and his foul innuendo. Some of his
very expressions are Iago's—*Goats and monkeys!* (256; see III,
iii, 403). To attempt to establish a psychological consistency by
tracing the traits of the present Othello to those of the past Othello
is critically supererogatory. That he possessed his present potential
is, of course, true but this would be equally true of any other man.
The artistic intention seems obviously to be that this is *not* the
past Othello—the open, the magnanimous, the generous Othello.
In Iago's superbly ironic understatement, *He is much changed*

(261). One of the remarkable qualities of the scene is its preservation of Desdemona's feminine appeal, despite the inciting effect of her unconscious tactlessness, and the preservation of her dignity, despite the contemptuous usage to which she is subjected. Observe how the human lineaments of Iago are becoming progressively blurred; less and less he seems the gay artist in deviltry, more and more the mere factotum. At one point (45-47) he is amusingly used by the lesson-teaching playwright as ventriloquist's dummy, when he remarks upon the effect of slander upon *worthy, chaste,* and *guiltless* dames (in whose existence he cannot believe).

IV, ii

Othello interrogates Emilia, who protests that he lacks the slightest occasion for jealousy. He sends her to fetch her mistress, then bids her watch at the door as if she were bawd in a brothel. Othello subjects Desdemona to an inquisition, and although he weeps and gives passionate expression to the strength of his love, he proves wholly impervious to her pleas of innocence, and concludes the interview with further cruel allusions to her as inmate of a brothel. Desdemona is stunned into near-apathy. She asks Emilia to lay her bed with her wedding sheets, and to call Iago hither. She pleads with him for reassurance, and Emilia tells him of Othello's charges, inveighing as she does so against the slanderous rogue who must have poisoned his mind. Iago curtly shuts up Emilia, but pretends to sympathize with Desdemona, telling her that her husband's distemper has been caused by the vexations of office. A trumpet signals the hour of supper, and Iago counsels them to go in and preserve appearances before the messengers from Venice. He is joined by Roderigo, who is in a state of petulant rebellion: Iago has defrauded him of his money and jewels on the pretense of corrupting Desdemona with gifts, but he is as far from enjoying her favors as ever. Iago counters with assurances that success is within reach. However, Roderigo must cooperate in removing the last obstacle. Since Othello has been replaced by Cassio in the command at Cyprus, he is planning to take Desdemona to Mauretania. He can be prevented from doing so only by making the change of command impossible. Cassio is supping this night with a courtesan, and may be waylaid between twelve and one; Roderigo must join with Iago in putting him out of the way.

1-241 In his prying questions, and in the ugly charade into which he forces Emilia and Desdemona, Othello remains the repugnant figure into which he has been transformed; however, there is here a beginning of the necessary restoration of tragic stature. In a series of magnificently imaginative speeches (48-81) our ears catch again the large accent with which we were first impressed. The note of egotism remains, and the morbid suggestibility, as when he plays on the word *committed* (70-80), but there are lines so overpoweringly indicative of the value he has placed on Desdemona (57-60) that they alone seem to answer her question, *Am I the motive of these tears . . . ?* (43) The lines *O thou weed, Who art so lovely fair . . .* (67-69) so combine the thoughts of love and loss, and sound so beautiful and heart-broken that our defenses against the speaker crumble. Emilia here establishes herself as on the side of right, but it is a curiosity of the play that her tirade against *some eternal villain* (130-48) is intended to amuse because it is unwittingly directed to that very villain. Here, as occasionally elsewhere, a standard theatrical 'effect' is introduced in a situation of such gravity as to render it somewhat grotesque; we do not care whether or not Iago is subjected to momentary discomfort, nor do we believe that he is capable of moral discomfiture. At no other point in the play does Iago seem more remote from the human community as when Desdemona turns to him for sympathy—*O good Iago* (148-68)—and he continues busily plotting her destruction. Iago is alone among Shakespeare's villains in never experiencing a single qualm.

IV, iii

The company in the chambers of Othello is dispersing. He accompanies Lodovico on his way, after bidding Desdemona to retire and dismiss her attendant. As Emilia helps to prepare her mistress for bed, they speak hopefully of Othello's calmer deportment.

Desdemona's love for him is undiminished, and she expresses the wish that, if she dies early, her wedding sheets will be her shroud. Her mind is haunted by memories of her mother's maid Barbary, who was forsaken in love and died singing the song of 'Willow.' Desdemona herself begins singing verses of the plaintive song as she engages Emilia in desultory conversation. She asks if there are really women who play false with their husbands, and Emilia makes humorously worldly replies. Desdemona cannot conceive of such conduct, even if the price were the whole world. Emilia argues that such a price might be sufficient, and places the blame for the infidelity of wives upon the wayward conduct of husbands. Desdemona rejects this view in a brief concluding prayer.

1-104 From the opening commonplaces of farewell—including Othello's *'twill do me good to walk* (2)—to Emilia's gossipy homily on the rights of woman (83-102), there is a low-pitched and homespun quality in this scene, rendering all the more chilling the ominous notes—*Hark! who is't that knocks? . . . It is the wind* (51-52). The song of the 'Willow' contributes both to the atmosphere of hearthside intimacy and of foreboding. We customarily speak of the 'pathos' of Desdemona's singing, but we should observe her own awareness of the whimsicality of what she is doing, her curiosity about its compulsive nature. There is nothing cloyingly sweet about her lines or actions; indeed, melancholy though she feels, she is dauntless in defense of her love and her ideals. She is the pure to whom all things are pure. Emilia's humorous common sense and moral temporizing are pleasing, but the palm goes to the young girl (and she here seems young indeed) who knows no compromise. Her last lines, rebuking worldly wisdom, are very moving—one of the best examples of the playwright's 'capping couplets.'

V, i

Iago stations Roderigo where he can thrust his rapier through Cassio; then steps aside, remarking to himself that it will be to his advantage whether either or both are slain. Cassio's coat is proof against Roderigo's thrust. He wounds his assailant, but is cut in the leg by Iago, who darts out from hiding and then flees. The two wounded men call for help. Othello appears on the scene just long enough to verify the fact that Iago has played his part against Cassio; it is now his turn to follow suit against Desdemona. Lodovico and Gratiano, a fellow-messenger from Venice and kinsman of Brabantio, are drawn hither by the cries of pain, but fear to enter what may prove a trap. As they stand by, Iago approaches with a lantern, pretends to discover the victims for the first time, and grasps the opportunity to finish off Roderigo. He then joins Lodovico and Gratiano in examining Cassio's wound. Bianca enters and, when she bewails the misfortune of her paramour, is accused by Iago of being party to it. Cassio is borne off in a chair. Emilia enters, hears Iago's version of the crime, and joins him in vilifying Bianca. Iago sends her to notify Othello and Desdemona of the attack, then follows with Bianca in custody. He remarks in an aside that this night's work will make him or break him.

1-129 As in *Hamlet* and other tragedies, there is here, after a preceding pause, an acceleration of physical action just before the end. Again Iago both plans and resourcefully improvises, but this time with incomplete success. Cassio's undercoat of mail, like Emilia's later intransigence, is a factor he has not reckoned with. If we seek Iago's 'motives' in his words, his glancing comment on Cassio, *He hath a daily beauty in his life That makes me ugly* (19-20), comes closest to satisfying us; we can understand the need to obliterate distinctions, to create a community of evil where the evil one may feel at home. The 'daily beauty' in Cassio's life must be taken largely on trust. He has shown only negative virtues, doing nothing and saying nothing to impugn his standing as an honorable and right-thinking soldier, but his status as petitioner and his necessarily furtive relations with Bianca have prevented him from playing a very imposing role; we must rely on the esteem in which he seems generally held. Observe that Roderigo, whose mental and moral feebleness have been consistently portrayed, is permitted a word of compunction (8-10), semi-comic like himself, before his predestined end. Othello adds a new word to his habitual characterization of Iago—*and just* (31)—intimating the spirit in which he thinks he himself is about to act.

V, ii

Othello bears a light to the bedside of Desdemona and speaks of the irrevocable nature of what he is about to do. Still loving this woman he must kill, he pauses for a farewell kiss. As he repeats the kiss, she awakens, and he bids her say her last prayers. She realizes that he intends to murder her, and she desperately pleads her innocence. He cites the evidence of the handkerchief, rebukes her for her denials, and tells her of Cassio's death. Her horror at the tidings seems to him only additional evidence of guilt, and, ignoring her pleas for the mercy of a little delay, he proceeds to smother her. As Emilia calls for admission, he stands in indecision before closing the bed-curtains and bidding her enter. Emilia tells of the attack, unconsciously tormenting Othello with the news that Cassio has survived. A murmur from the bed draws her to her mistress's side. Desdemona uses this moment of revival only to commend herself to her kind husband and exonerate him of her death. For a moment Othello seems willing to profit by this loving lie, then brands the speaker a liar destined to burn in hell, and declares that he has killed her. Emilia heaps execrations upon him, and when he cites Iago as his informant, she curses her husband and raises the cry of murder. Iago enters with Montano, Gratiano, and others, and is greeted by Emilia's charge. Othello throws himself on Desdemona's bed and tries desperately to disbelieve what he is hearing, as Emilia defies Iago's attempts to silence her and exposes his ruse with the handkerchief. There follows a moment of violent action. Othello is disarmed by Montano as he lunges at Iago; the latter stabs Emilia and flees. Montano leads the pursuit, leaving Gratiano to guard the door. Emilia dies upon the bed of her mistress, after repeating a few words of the 'Willow' song and reproaching Othello once more. He secures another sword and commands Gratiano to enter, but instead of using the weapon against him, stands speaking in abject shame and remorse. Montano returns with Iago prisoner, accompanied by Lodovico and by Cassio borne in a chair. Othello wounds

Iago with the sword, but is again disarmed. As the evidence of the calumny is reviewed, he asks that Iago be made to reveal why he has ensnared him body and soul, but the destroyer retreats into morose and savage silence. Letters found on the person of Roderigo have exposed the details of the plot and further exonerated Cassio. Lodovico decrees that Iago will be tortured to death, Cassio left in command in Cyprus, and Othello conducted to Venice for trial. Othello calls for a pause, speaks of his service to the state, and asks that the story be told, without extenuation or malice, of one who loved not wisely but too well and threw a pearl away dearer than all his tribe. He then stabs himself and kisses Desdemona as he dies. Lodovico speaks the concluding words: he bids Iago look upon his victims before the bed-curtains are drawn; he designates Gratiano as the Moor's heir, Brabantio having died of grief; he appoints Montano as Iago's judge; he himself will bear the heavy tidings to Venice.

1-372 Othello's reiterated word *cause* (1-3) admits of more than one interpretation, but the least debatable sense in which he is using it is 'grounds of action'—that is, adultery, the naming of which would offend the *chaste stars*. He is persuaded that he is performing an act of justice, serving as judge and executioner, not as vengeful murderer. He is meting out heavenly as well as earthly justice; his tears are such as God might shed in paying the wages of death to a sinner (21). The monstrosity of this delusion is matched by his conviction that he is being merciful, sparing the beauty of her body (3-5) and the redeemability of her soul (31-32). At the same time that he assumes these postures, he is enraged by the pleas of the defendant—his eyes *roll* (38) and he gnaws his *nether lip* (43)— so that we have the same visible travesty of righteousness as when he kneeled in wrath and made his *sacred* vow (III, iii, 460). The irony in this play has sometimes seemed too abundant and facile, but not so in the present case. Partly this is owing to the power of the language. Partly it is owing to the fact that Othello's passionate craving to think of himself as just contributes to our sense of his agony when he learns what he has really been. Also prefiguring the intensity of this agony is his awareness, beautifully expressed

(7-15), of the finality of his action and the persistence of his love. The 'lift' of the scene is effected by the indestructible goodness of Desdemona (125-27), the heroic loyalty of Emilia, and, deny this who will, the final deportment of Othello himself. It seems pretty certain that his creator considered his account fully squared when he gazed in horror at the truth, and felt no inclination to add a few figures to the debit column. We may feel that we could teach Othello better ways to die and to speak before dying, but his farewell speech was not set down *in malice*. He tries to pick up the shreds of his human dignity, as do other of Shakespeare's offenders, but this is not the last thing that he does. A stage direction is implied in the last lines; he takes himself by the throat as he took the malignant infidel—the *dog* whom he smote *thus*. His last thoughts (359-60) are not of himself but of Desdemona. If there is a defect in this play, it lies not in the stature of the tragic hero. There is not the same thorough integration of theatrical fiction and dramatic vision, of action and idea, that there is in the other great tragedies. Although the proven effectiveness of the play on the stage renders somewhat irrelevant both attacks and defenses of its plot, the concession must be made that it is more 'plotty' than need be in respect to its great theme. The machinations of Iago, fascinating though they are to watch, give us too much of a good thing, with the excess at the expense of a better thing. There lacks a perfect balance of emphasis upon what Iago does and what he is; his mystery is submerged in the intrigue. Perhaps this was inevitable since Iago is, after all, nothing. His answering snarl *What you know, you know* (304) to Othello's incredulous *Why* is all we can ever expect to get when we ask Evil to explain itself.

4

Macbeth

:

I, i

IN FOUL weather, on a barren heath, three witches plan to return and meet Macbeth when a battle now raging is over.

1 s.d.   Stage thunder and lightning signal the opening of the play;
black clouds, erupting into periodic violence, seem banked over
Scotland throughout its course.   **1-11**   The *or* (2) is equivalent to 'and'; it is raining now and will be raining still at the meeting with Macbeth—auspicious weather from the Witches' point of
view. The rime words *again-rain* (1-2) lend themselves to intoning,
in a manner suggestive of the whining of the wind, the cadence of a
chant. The lines are short, and the pattern of stress reverses the
normal iambic order. Everything about the Witches, for whom *fair
is foul, and foul is fair* (10), reverses the normal. The cat, the toad,
and the unnamed creature associated with the third Witch are
'familiars' (lodging places for their devil 'contacts') but, in a sense,
also pets; instead of calling their pets, their pets call them. The
battle, slightingly termed a *hurlyburly* (3) will be *lost* (by one
side) *and won* (by the other), as all battles are; the Witches view
the outcome with inhuman detachment. They leave to *hover* in the
air, vulture-like, ready to descend upon the one who carries the
scent of spiritual death. This is *Macbeth* (8). Banquo they do not
mention.

I, ii

A wounded Officer, who has saved Prince Malcolm from capture, describes the progress of the battle to King Duncan. The valiant Macbeth has hacked his way to Macdonwald and carved him up, thus turning the tide against the rebel and his island mercenaries; but King Sweno of Norway has seized upon this opportunity to lead an assault upon the Scots. Macbeth and Banquo have turned furiously upon the new foe. Faint with his wounds, the speaker is led off to the surgeons. The Thanes of Ross and Angus enter, and Ross describes the final outcome. Although close to victory, and joined by the treacherous Thane of Cawdor, Sweno has been subdued by Macbeth and held for ransom. Duncan pronounces sentence of death upon Cawdor, and decrees that his title be conferred on Macbeth.

1-67 The opening words *What bloody man is that?* (1) are hard and naked. As this bloody man paints his bloody picture, we see no bright armor, curveting steeds, or fine pageantry, but only ferocious forms contorted in struggle, their steel smoking with *execution* (18). The battle is brutal, its hero's acts all acts of butchery: he rips *from the nave to th' chops* (22); his very name is made to rime with *death* (64-65). But he is unmistakably hero—*valor's minion* (19), *Bellona's bridegroom* (54), *noble Macbeth* (67). It is he, not his royal master, who has saved the realm, with Banquo as his mere assistant. The savagery of the battle suggests a primitive era in a harsh and craggy land, where violence is lethal and treachery black, but where virtue also may assume epic dimensions. What we have learned of Macbeth is that he is evidently loyal and indubitably formidable. We may wonder if the title stripped from a traitor, *Thane of Cawdor,* is the most fitting reward that the grateful Duncan could bestow.

I, iii

The Witches reappear, one of them cackling over her design to act
as succuba to a sailorman as she delays his voyage home. At the
sound of an approaching drum, they whirl in a ritualistic dance.
When Macbeth enters with Banquo, they hail him as Thane of
Glamis, Thane of Cawdor, and future King of Scotland. Banquo
demands that they prophesy also for him, and they hail him as father of future kings. Macbeth is eager to know more, but the
Witches vanish, leaving the pair to wonder. Macbeth knows that he
has become Thane of Glamis upon the death of his father, but he
believes that Cawdor still lives in good repute. At this juncture
Ross and Angus bring the greetings of King Duncan, and the news
that Cawdor is impeached and Macbeth invested with his title.
Macbeth is enraptured at the thought that the third title named by
the Witches may also become his, and, as Banquo warns him against
the blandishments of the instruments of darkness, his imagination
shapes frightening visions of securing the crown by assassination.
He suggests to Banquo that they speak of these matters hereafter,
as they go off to join the King.

1-88 The Witches are finely conceived. A grotesque combination
of the repellent and the ridiculous, they startle and fascinate but
fail to awe. Their malice is infinite but it is pettily manifested: they
afflict cattle (2), stir up ineffectual tempests (24-25), and en-
viously commit acts of sexual predation (4-5, 18). As epitomes of
the perverse, they sail in the least seaworthy of vessels, the sieve
(8)—just as they traditionally fly on the most earth-bound of im-
plements, the broom. Although aged, they dance vivaciously; although women, they are bearded. Withered, skinny-lipped, chapped,
bedraggled (40-47), these are the musty crones of popular superstition, not ministers of fate. Nevertheless they are redolently evil,
hell's converts, zealous in the cause of infiltration. When Banquo
accosts them, the fingers on lips is a visual sign that their business
is not with him. When Macbeth accosts them, they shrill out their
All hails (48-50) on cue. Here and in their supplementary proph-

ecy (62-69), their lines are formalized and chanted in rotation like a ritual. It is apparent why they have singled out Macbeth; he is ripe for *soliciting* (130). When addressed as *King hereafter,* he starts and *seems to fear* (50-51) like one whose secret thoughts have been surprised. He stands *rapt withal* (57), and then becomes morbidly intent: *tell me more* (70) . . . *Speak, I charge you* (78) . . . *Would they had stayed* (82) . . . *Went it not so?* (87). Each of these utterances is strongly stressed on the first syllable, as if blurted out in eagerness. Banquo, in contrast, sounds curious but unperturbed, half amused, even patronizing. There is a largeness about his manner which should attach by rights to the greater chieftain.   **89-116** We have anticipated the moment when Macbeth would hear that he is truly *Thane of Cawdor.* The slow approach to this moment in the formal speeches of Angus and Ross increases its dramatic impact, as does Macbeth's astonished doubt. Observe the mystery attaching to this unseen Cawdor—a *prosperous gentleman* (73) and trusted minister of the King (I, ii, 64) who *labored his country's wrack* (110-16) from motives never revealed.   **117-56** As Macbeth moves in and out of his trance-like absorption, the lines are filled with suggestion. At his first appearance in the scene, he spoke of the day as *foul and fair* (38), and, although his thoughts were evidently of the military success achieved in stormy weather, the words sounded an echo to the *foul is fair* of the Witches in their profession of perverse faith (I, i, 10). Now, in thinking of their promise of kingship (which Banquo has just warned him to distrust), he juggles the words *ill* and *good* (131) in a manner suggestive of his precarious spiritual state. Apparently the Witches' prediction has not newly created an impulse to murder Duncan (139) but has reactivated an old one; he excuses his preoccupation by describing his brain as wrought *With things forgotten* (150). The thought of murder is horrible (138), and presumably he has been formerly restrained by the horror. He would prefer to obtain Duncan's title blamelessly, as he has obtained Cawdor's, but he mentions the chance of doing so only as a possibility (143-44). We can imagine the workings of his mind, the form of its confusion or dislocation. One sense of the word *good* (desirable) is invading another sense of the word *good* (ethical).

His becoming Cawdor was *good*—desirable and ethical—and his becoming King will be *good*—whether ethical or not. Of course he knows that this is not so, but he is losing his grip on this knowledge. Perhaps the most remarkable feature of this episode is the simultaneous evidence that he is struggling with his conscience and that the struggle is already lost. He seems aware that he must form a party, must court friends and enlist adherents. Observe his overtures to Banquo (153-55), and, even more revealing, his repeated thanks to Ross and Angus, interpolated in the very midst of his musings: *Thanks for your pains* (117), *I thank you, gentlemen* (129), *Kind gentlemen . . .* (150-52), *Come, friends* (156).

I, iv

When Malcolm reports that Cawdor has gone to his death nobly and penitently, King Duncan remarks that he had trusted this thane utterly. He is reflecting that there is no way to read a man's character in his face as Macbeth enters with Banquo and Angus. Although both the victorious generals receive high praise and promise of reward, it is Macbeth who is singled out as special object of the King's loving trust and who replies with the greatest ardor. But as Duncan names his son Malcolm as heir apparent to the throne, Macbeth broods to himself that another bar has been placed between him and the prize he desires. The King proposes to tax his hospitality at Inverness, and Macbeth rides ahead to make preparations.

1-14 The comment upon the past Thane of Cawdor applies also to the present Thane of Cawdor, as signaled by Macbeth's timely entrance (see above, p. 89). The irony of Duncan's second bestowal of misplaced trust would be lost upon us if the playwright had not sufficiently intimated *the mind's construction* in Macbeth. Evidently he assumed that he had done so, not reckoning with the possibility that the visitation of the Witches would be viewed as cause rather than symptom of Macbeth's decay.   **15-58** The corruption of the second Cawdor is as mysterious as that of the first. The image of planting, growth, and harvest (29-33) is one of a number of fertility and infertility images that recur through the play. Macbeth's potential for good is, or has been, real; he is not the born destroyer like Iago, but the born creator who destroys. Duncan's naming of Malcolm as Prince of Cumberland (and hence heir to the throne) acts as a spur to Macbeth's *black and deep desires* (51) by lessening the possibility that chance will make him King (I, iii, 143). We would not suppose at this moment that he will need instigation from his wife.

I, v

Lady Macbeth reads a letter from her lord, describing his meeting with the Witches. She exults at the prophecy of kingship, but knows that her husband has qualms about using bloody means. When a Messenger brings word that Duncan will lodge this night at Inverness, she prays for the murderous ruthlessness that will let her incite her husband to seize the opportunity. When Macbeth himself arrives, she hails him by his titles, present and to come, and begins combating at once his reluctance to murder. The King coming hence must never go hither; the planning may be left to her.

1-12   If we insist upon asking when this letter was written, which mentions the meeting with the Witches but not the visit of Duncan, we must answer that it was during a pause in the ride from the blasted heath to the King's headquarters at Forres. (But the question is actually as immaterial as that concerning Brutus's opportunity to inform Portia of the conspiracy. See above, p. 255). We have witnessed the fact that Macbeth, as he here writes, *burned in desire* (3) to question the Witches further. That he expects to wear the crown is manifest from his elated address to his *dearest partner in greatness* (9), but there is no inkling in the letter of how he expects to get it.   **13-51**   Lady Macbeth's opening speech indicates that the idea of her husband as king is not a new one, and that his scruples have been a subject of previous debate. Her own apparent lack of scruples do not necessarily prove that she has been from the first the one who lusts after power and hopes to obtain it through her husband. The situation admits of a different interpretation—that she knows her husband wants the crown, and, as a thorough-going pragmatist, thinks he should put his mind at rest by taking it. Our stage tradition tends to overstate her initial ferocity. Her *Thou'rt mad to say it!* (29) suggests that, much as she has preferred action to dreaming, this suddent chance to act comes to her as a shock. Like her husband, she 'starts and seems to fear' (I, iii, 51). The speech invoking the murderous spirit of hell (36-52) is descriptive less of what she is than of the monster she wishes, for the occasion, to be, and its extravagant dreadfulness is in a measure atmospheric. She could scarcely pray for release from womanliness and capacity for pity unless she supposed that she possessed these traits.   **52-71** As the two face each other and refer obliquely to what is in their minds, we seem to be witnessing something like the embarrassment of a nuptial. As she greets him in the way that must gratify him most (53-54), and he her as his *dearest love* (56), there is no doubt in our minds about their mutual attachment; this is a loving couple, with what that should imply. They never mention by name the 'act' which will destroy life rather than create it. Her word is that Duncan must be *provided for* (65). His weak demurrer, that Duncan goes tomorrow *as he purposes* (58), is weakened further by his *We will speak further* (69). He seems less reluctant than shy.

I, vi

King Duncan and Banquo commend the delicate air of Inverness as the royal entourage arrives. Lady Macbeth greets her guest with protestations of devotion, before conducting him in to the host whom he admires and loves.

1-31 The *pleasant* site, the *delicate* air, the *temple-haunting* swallows of Macbeth's castle are as deceptive as the external appearance of its occupants. The beautifully expressed procreation image (4-8) functions as an ironic commentary upon the entering Lady Macbeth, who breeds not life but death. (See the fertility image earlier associated with her husband, I, iv, 28-29.) In the exchange of civilities Duncan repeatedly speaks of his and his host's *love* (11, 12, 23, 29)—a word which Lady Macbeth refrains from using, although her protestations of gratitude and anxiety to rended *serv-ice* are perfervid enough.

I, vii

Supper is being served within, and Macbeth, who has left the table, soliloquizes upon the heinousness of the projected murder. His Lady joins him and cautions him to return. When he speaks of the honors he has lately received and of other considerations which deter him, she accuses him of unmanly weakness. He was willing enough to broach the subject of killing Duncan before the opportunity arose; had she sworn as he then swore, she would more willingly dash out the brains of her own infant than forgo this chance to win the coveted crown. They need only make Duncan's chamberlains drunk, kill him in his sleep, and blame the deed upon them. Praising her for her fierce resolution, Macbeth consents to carry out the plan; and they return to their guest with false smiles of affability.

1-28 Lady Macbeth in her soliloquy (I, v, 36-52) aligned herself with the *ministers* of hell. Macbeth is correspondingly unevasive. The thoughts, the images, the very sounds of this magnificently-wrought avowal all speak of *deep damnation* (20)—and of sure retribution in this life, regardless of the life to come. He inventories the virtues of the victim and the obligations of himself, as subject, kinsman, and host, so that the mere riskiness of the deed seems nothing as compared with its intrinsic monstrousness; the universal horror and grief which must follow are describable only in apocalyptic terms. What can be said on the other side? Only that he wants the crown. All this follows upon the reflection that the deed had best be done quickly—as if doing it will relieve him from the horrible thought of doing it. That there is a fundamental irrationality about the situation—that no two people so aware of the hideousness of what they are doing, and so possessed of traits suggesting opposite inclinations and capabilities, should proceed with the plan —goes without saying. But the enormous impact of this play derives from this very irrationality. This is not murder committed in revenge, sudden rage, or rash desire, but slowly, deliberately, with eyes wide open. This is murder-pure. It is no part of the design to make it seem rational. **29-82** But it is part of the design to make it seem real. The play deals with an absolute, but not with an abstraction. Pure evil is concretized and domesticated. In expressing his reluctance now, Macbeth mentions none of the mighty considerations which occupied him a moment ago, but only that he is already doing rather well and would like to remain popular. And Lady Macbeth launches her passionate argument not against moral scruples but only against unmanly shilly-shallying. It is as if a husband were being shamed into making good his boast that he dared ask his employer for an increase in salary. And the plan is ultimately embraced on the basis of its mere practicality! This shift in focus is veiled by the continuing impressiveness of the language, the tropes remaining as somber and grand in the treatment of petty particulars as in the treatment of great universals. If we have read the earlier scenes attentively, we are not surprised to learn that the murder of Duncan had been contemplated some time prior to Macbeth's meeting with the Witches (51-54). This does not reduce the mystery of his infection but rather increases it, giving greater size to the idea of evil by rendering it invisible; the Witches are not the thing itself. Lady Macbeth's assertion about dashing out the brains of her smiling babe (54-58) and Macbeth's *Bring forth men-children only* (72), like Macduff's later *He has no children* (IV, iii, 216) which may or may not apply to Macbeth, have led to much speculation about whether or not the couple are childless, and, if so, why Macbeth resents the thought of the crown passing to Banquo's line. Whatever conclusions are reached about the literal state of affairs, the significant point is that they are never associated with children as are the other ranking characters, Duncan, Banquo, and Macduff. Poetically at least, they are childless. Lady Macbeth's vow is so particularized and vivid that, so far as our emotions are concerned, the babe she says she would slay she has already slain. And Macbeth kills the children of Macduff, tries to kill the child of Banquo, and fervently wishes he could kill the children of Duncan. They are killers of posterity. Their love should make their union fruitful; but destroyers cannot be creators.

II, i

It is past midnight as Banquo bids his son Fleance goodnight, and speaks of his fear of evil dreams. Startled by someone's entrance, he reaches for his sword, then relaxes as he recognizes Macbeth. They speak of Duncan's largess, then of their meeting with the Witches and of the way that part of the prophecy has been fulfilled. Macbeth proposes that they find leisure to confer together, and Banquo consents to discuss anything that will not smirch his honor. Macbeth bids Banquo and Fleance goodnight, and orders a servant to ring the bell when his drink is ready. Alone, he gazes at an imaginary dagger which marshals him the way he must go. His mind fills with visions fitting this evil time of night and the awful task before him. The bell rings, and he goes in to send Duncan to his death.

1 s.d. Banquo and Fleance are being lighted to their chamber across the courtyard, off which open both the gate to the castle and the entrances to its various living and sleeping quarters; thus they can look up and allude to the moonless and starless sky. (This interior courtyard is the place of action of the whole of the present and the two ensuing 'scenes,' which are continuous and form a single dramatic unit although divided in most texts. It is the most harrowing 'murder scene' in drama although we see no murder committed. We are forced to dwell with the *idea* of the act before, during, and after it occurs, there being no single decisive physical action to trigger the dissipation of attention.)   **1-30**   The opening lines set the time (the witching hour), place, and mood; bad dreams (6-9) belong to this particular night, but Banquo's have their special shape (20). There are inklings that he has escaped evil infection at the cost of some exertion of will-power. Macbeth's words (22-24) again reveal an impulse to draw him in and make common cause, and Banquo's (26-29) again reveal that the attempt would be vain. Another calculated entrance for Macbeth, and fine bit of stage business, occur here. Fleance is helping his father remove sword and belt before retiring. As Macbeth's form appears,

Banquo scents danger and reaches for his sword, then relaxes when he recognizes his host; he was, of course, right in his first instinctive fear. **31-64** As Macbeth sees the dagger, tries to grasp it, then sees it still ahead of him so that he must step forward to reach it, he is like a somnambulist being literally *marshalled* toward Duncan's chamber. As he draws his actual dagger, he sees the other covered with *gouts of blood* (46) as his own is soon to be. This double vision is characteristic of Macbeth, and makes the choral type of soliloquy especially appropriate on his lips; he both is, and sees, Macbeth. In the remainder of the present episode he seems actually disembodied, a spirit watching its own body—a cadaver, *withered murder* (52), moving upon its prey *like a ghost* (56). It moves *thus,* with *stealthy pace* (54) but, contradictorily, with *Tarquin's ravishing strides* (55), the restraint of movement contrasting with the violence of purpose. The uncanniness of the effect is indescribable. Sounds and silences heighten the terror of these scenes—those evoked verbally, such as the howl of the wolf, and the muffled footsteps (57), and those supplied theatrically, such as the ringing of the chamber-bell (32, 61 s.d.) and, later, the knocking at the gate, the clang of the alarm.

II, ii

Lady Macbeth enters and hears her husband cry out as he returns from the chamber of Duncan. She has drugged the chamberlains' possets and would have thrust in the dagger herself had not the old King resembled her father as he slept. Macbeth enters with bloody hands. He has heard some sleeper cry out for God's blessing and, although himself much in need of blessing, has been unable to say 'Amen.' And he has imagined he heard a voice proclaiming that he who has murdered the sleeping Duncan has also murdered sleep; Macbeth will sleep no more. His Lady tries to restore his courage, and reproves him for bringing away the incriminating daggers. Since he is unable to look again at his victim, she goes to return them and to smear the chamberlains with blood. A knocking on the gate startles Macbeth as he stands alone gazing at his eternally bloodstained hands. Lady Macbeth returns with her hands likewise stained. As the knocking on the gate is repeated, she draws off her husband so that they may cleanse themselves and present an appearance of innocence. Macbeth follows her in, devoutly expressing the wish that the clamor at the gate could awaken Duncan.

1-18 It is the Lady who has resorted to physical stimulants; she has been consistently presented as the practical one, flesh to Macbeth's spirit. But now, unexpectedly, in the midst of her references to 'arrangements,' comes a sign that she, too, has imagination and conscience (12-13). Her words have the additional value of summoning up the image of the sleeping victim as a helpless, benign, and patriarchal figure. Verbal sound-effects persist—the *shriek* and *scream* of the owl, the *cry* of the crickets (3-15)—with the sound-words suggesting pain. There have been voices within, real and imaginary, but now we hear heavy-laden silence as the pair strain their ears between breathless monosyllables: *Did you not speak? . . . When? . . . Now. . . . As I descended? . . . Ay. . . . Hark!* (16-17).   **19-42** Tension has been released by no sight of violence, but we confront the physical fact of murder as the blood drips from Macbeth's hand. This is the most terrible moment of all as we watch him awakening from nightmare and learning that it was real. His bewildered repetition that he could not say *Amen* when a sleeper *cried God bless us* is pathetic and naïve, his *But wherefore . . . ?* the quintessence of irony. The stunned repetition continues as he bids farewell to sweet and healing sleep: *Macbeth does murder sleep* (38), *Glamis hath murdered sleep* (41). The words sound like a tolling bell: *Sleep no more. . . . Sleep no more. . . . Sleep no more. . . . sleep no more* (40-42). **43-73** The Lady's practical mind can conceive only of actual voices—*Who was it . . . ?* (43)—and she is querulously intent, like any housewife, upon completing the task and tidying up. Her *gild-guilt* pun (55-56), like Desdemona's 'whore-abhor' pun (*Othello,* IV, ii, 161-62) in a context equally grave, will seem intrusive to modern ears, but such puns must be accepted as a rhetorical device employed for emphasis, intrinsically no more frivolous than rime or alliteration. Macbeth is alone when the knock sounds at the gate. As he starts, we start too. It is one of the mysteries of our response to dramatic art that we can identify emotionally with one whom we rationally abhor: at this moment we *fear* that he will be detected. The knocking at the gate recurs three times after Lady Macbeth's return, bringing threat of imminent discovery and giving her mingled directions and admonitions an aspect of fearful urgency. Her reference to *a little water* (66) which will obliterate the evidence and make all things *easy,* stands in apposition to Macbeth's *multitudinous seas* (61) which will fail to obliterate their guilt, her obtuseness throwing his awareness into relief. Like Faustus he repents before, while, and after he signs away his soul, and his *Wake Duncan with thy knocking! I would thou couldst* (73) seems to come from the depths of his heart. It is doubtful if anywhere else in literature is represented an action at once so imposing and so unglamorous, so awe-inspiring and sordid, as this furtive, messy, and irreparable deed. This, says the poet, is *Murder.*

II, iii

As he prepares to open the gate, the Porter pretends that the knocking is by newcomers to hell, and he characterizes the hoarding farmer, the treasonous equivocator, the cheating tailor. He jokes about the drinking at last night's feast as he admits Lennox and Macduff, who have come to keep an early appointment with the King. Macbeth enters to greet them, and, as Macduff goes to Duncan's chamber, he stands listening to Lennox's account of the strange portents of the night. Macduff returns crying out with horror. Macbeth and Lennox rush off to verify his report that the King is murdered; the alarm bell sounds, and Lady Macbeth and Banquo enter and receive the fearful tidings from Macduff. As Macbeth returns with Lennox and Ross, he voices extravagant lamentations and tells Malcolm and Donalbain, who have joined the others, that they have the death of a father to mourn. Lennox describes the evidence that points to the guilt of the chamberlains, and Macbeth admits to the rash action of slaying them out of hand, his passions having overcome his reason. In pretense or in reality, Lady Macbeth swoons and is borne off-stage. In asides to each other, Malcolm and Donalbain communicate their sense of imminent personal danger. After Banquo calls for all to dress to attend an inquiry, Macbeth appoints the great hall as their meeting place, and all but Malcolm and Donalbain withdraw. These speak of the ease with which grief may be simulated, and agree that they should flee without ceremony, Malcolm seeking refuge in England, Donalbain in Ireland.

1 s.d.   The knocking at the gate links this 'scene' temporally with the preceding, the stage standing vacant only for a moment between the exit of the Macbeths and the entrance of the Porter.   **1-38** The Porter's comic routine, quite apart from the appositeness of the *hell gate* conceit, is not gratuitous. The glum jocularities, the cadging for a tip, the subsequent ribaldries, draw a boundary between night and day, between hell and earth, isolating the Macbeths in their monstrous universe and returning us to a seamy but sane normality. He opens the gate not into but out of inferno, and we are able to breathe again. It is fitting that Macduff should make his first appearance at this juncture. More than any other single character, he symbolizes the human norm—the tissue which will close over the Macbeth lesion.   **39-142**   The swift succession of entrances and exits, the cries of horror, the clanging of the alarm, the fainting and carrying out of Lady Macbeth, create a stir proper to the occasion, and forestall anticlimax. This is the releasing display of physical action hitherto withheld, but the words spoken are in character. Macbeth emerges as the inexpert politic dissembler, and Macduff as his single questioner: *Wherefore did you so?* (103). Oddly, the most restrained speakers are Malcolm and Donalbain, drawing together in chilled apprehension. The device is immensely effective; this place is too dangerous to allow them the leisure to mourn.

II, iv

An Old Man speaks to Ross of the dreadfulness of the murder, and of the prodigies in nature attending it. They are joined by Macduff, who reports the findings of the inquiry. The murder was committed by the chamberlains, who may have been suborned by Malcolm and Donalbain since their flight seems a suspicious circumstance. Duncan is to be buried at Colmekill, and Macbeth is to be crowned king at Scone. Macduff, who is not attending the coronation, guardedly expresses his hopes that it will not prove inauspicious.

1-41 The dialogue between the Old Man and Ross, like a speech by Lennox in the preceding scene (50-57) underscores the direness of the event by mention of ominous perversions in nature. These choral speeches belong to the poem, and, with their strange images and sonorously violent diction, are stylistically alike regardless of speaker. But observe the distinctive accent of Macduff. Terse, literal, flat, his statements self-style themselves as the 'official' version of the crime, in which he may or may not believe. His failure to attend the coronation is an inkling of the recalcitrance which will later disturb Macbeth.

III, i

Banquo suspects that Macbeth has played foul for the crown; yet the prediction of the Witches has been fulfilled, and he wonders if they spoke true when they said that he himself would become father of kings. Macbeth and his Lady enter as King and Queen, with Ross, Lennox, and others in attendance. Banquo is to be their honored guest at this evening's feast, and Macbeth questions him closely about the hour of his return from a day of riding. When the court empties, Macbeth sends a servant to summon in two men who are awaiting his pleasure. He reveals in a soliloquy that he feels insecure in his throne so long as the astute and valorous Banquo lives; moreover this throne for which he has sold his soul means little if, as the Witches predicted, it is the issue of Banquo who will succeed. When the two men enter, Macbeth reminds them of a previous interview in which he has told them that Banquo is responsible for all their misfortunes. If they are men of mettle, they should welcome revenge. It will be to his advantage as well as theirs if they put Banquo out of the way. They agree to undertake the murder, and he instructs them to waylay both Banquo and Fleance as they approach the castle this evening after their day of riding. They are to stand by and await further instructions.

1-142 Sufficient time has elapsed for the coronation to lie in the past; henceforth Macbeth appears as King. We rarely think of him as such, less because he is a usurper than because the playwright has scanted him royal title and ceremonials. Banquo's soliloquy (1-10) is ambiguous. We are permitted to infer that, although he suspects Macbeth, he is content to play a passive role in the hope that the remaining prediction of the Witches will prove true and the crown will revert to his house. If such is the case, Macbeth's fears are groundless and his second murder wanton. We can understand the dramatic usefulness of this, but the device is so damaging to Banquo's character and so contrary to our prior impressions of him that we are left in a state of uncertainty. As Macbeth addresses him, the questions insinuated at intervals, *Ride you this afternoon?* (18), *Is't far you ride?* (23), *Goes Fleance with you?* (35), are sinister in effect—again we catch the scent of murder. Macbeth's soliloquy (48-72) provides a chart of things to come. While Banquo lives, Macbeth can say *There is none but he Whose being I do fear* (54-55), but the very prolixity of his reasoning renders it suspect. His fears and his victims will multiply since he is reaching for the unreachable—the sense that his royal robes are rightfully his: *To be thus is nothing, but to be safely thus . . .* (48). Elsewhere in Shakespeare hireling assassins are sent to their tasks with a word, and we may wonder why here they are treated to such lengthy persuasions (73-142). Clearly the episode is not offered as entertainment through display of villainous technique, as are some of those in *Othello*. The purpose seems to be that, as in the murder of Duncan, all air of casualness must be avoided; again the act is fully premeditated, the fruit of both emotion and deliberation. It is characteristic of this moralistic murderer that he should use the kind of arguments he does.

III, ii

Disturbed by the brooding of her husband, Lady Macbeth seeks him out and advises him to cease thinking of what has been done. He replies that they had better be at rest with Duncan than to live in perpetual fear, instancing the danger presented by Banquo and Fleance. She agrees to flatter Banquo at the evening's feast, but hints that there are other ways of dealing with him. Macbeth, without giving her the particulars, boasts that he has in mind a deed of dreadful note. He invokes the approach of black and lethal night.

1-56 A wonderful variety of impressions is conveyed by the somber poetry of this scene. Retribution has come to the offenders even though there has been, thus far, no hint of practical opposition to them; they take no pleasure in their royal status, and each in turn expresses envy of the dead (6-7, 19-26), Macbeth in elegiac lines of singular beauty. And yet despite the penitential undertone, their major concern seems not their sin but their fancied insecurity. The concluding lines (38-56) express the same fierce ruthlessness as those preceding the murder of Duncan; the speakers are obviously set upon curing themselves by succumbing further to their disease. The speeches are full of expressions of mutual tenderness as if the crime had drawn the speakers closer together; yet Lady Macbeth asks *Why do you keep alone . . . ?* (8) and we sense the loneliness of both, their alienation from the rest of mankind and their impending alienation from each other. Finally, we observe that the initiative is passing from the Lady to Macbeth, as he promises his *dearest chuck* a deed she will *applaud*. At this point alone does his voice rise in elation. Many contrarieties are packed into the half-hundred lines exchanged here between these maimed mortals; tenderness-brutality, insight-stupidity, repining-tenaciousness. The writing is beautiful—and grim.

III, iii

The two Murderers, joined by a third, lurk outside the castle grounds and hear the approach of Banquo and Fleance. The travelers dismount and approach on foot, lighting their way with a torch. The Murderers overcome Banquo, but as the torch is knocked down, Fleance escapes in the darkness, spurred on by his dying father. The Murderers go to report their partial success.

1-22 We need not be disturbed by the fact that there are three Murderers instead of two; Macbeth's *perfect spy o' th' time* (III, i, 130) may be taken to mean that his agent would be present to direct them. The deputized killings, here and in IV, ii, are frighteningly swift and brutal. In both instances the animal ferocity stands in contrast with a token of human love and solidarity; the dying victims are mindful of the safety of others: *Banquo. O, treachery! Fly, good Fleance, fly* (17); *Son. He has killed me, mother. Run away, I pray you!* (IV, ii, 84)

III, iv

Macbeth prepares to mingle with his guests at table while his Lady sits in state. One of the Murderers comes to the door and tells him of the death of Banquo and escape of Fleance. He draws what comfort he can from the removal of the more dangerous of the two, and, at his wife's bidding, resumes the role of gracious host. But the Ghost of Banquo, whose absence he is pretending to deplore, has entered and occupied the one vacant place at table, invisible to all but Macbeth. When he recoils and addresses it in terror, Lady Macbeth excuses his conduct to the guests as a customary seizure and goes to him with pleas that he control himself. As she does so, the Ghost vacates the stool and Macbeth recovers his courage. But as he proposes a toast to Banquo and again tries to take his place at table, he sees that the Ghost has returned. It removes itself again as he hurls defiances at it, but his ravings have so disturbed the assembly that Lady Macbeth ceases pleading with him and bids the guests disperse. He now complains that Macduff has refused to attend his feast; he knows of his disaffection because he keeps spies in the houses of all his thanes. Tomorrow he will go to the Witches to learn what the future holds. Already deep in blood, he is ready to wade still deeper. He will cease to be haunted by fantasies as he becomes more hardened in crime.

1-144 The double role of Macbeth as bloody actor and appalled observer of his acts is epitomized in his sardonic praise of his agent, *Thou art the best o' th' cut-throats* (17). This self-awareness exists side by side with impregnable self-delusion; again he expresses the conviction that the life of a single man is all that stands between himself and heart's-ease; perfect felicity lies only one murder away (21-23). Retributory suffering (anticipating practical reverses) is most spectacularly displayed in this haunting scene. There is still no evidence of any party forming against the usurpers, but they sleep-walk on the edge of a knife. The Ghost of Banquo, seen only by Macbeth, may, like the bloody dagger, be taken as a projection of his imagination. Aware of the edict that *blood will have blood* (122), Macbeth experiences overwhelming fear—fear in the abstract. His immediate response is to objectify and limit this fear: his mind fastens upon Macduff. A great wonder of this play is the way its hell-bound protagonists never relinquish their sway over our sympathetic imaginations. They struggle and suffer, and their language retains as points of reference the hopes, fears, and moral and religious perceptions of common humanity. The supernatural trappings, the fantastic and superficially contradictory details, cannot obscure the basic logic of the working out of the situation. Were there no moral law, Macbeth would feel no guilt, and if he felt no guilt, Macbeth would be safe. He is driven by guilt to further guilt, to ultimate destruction. We approve the trap, yet pity the wretch who is caught in it.

III, v

Hecate chides the three Witches for trafficking with the thankless Macbeth without her guidance. Tomorrow morning they are to prepare their magic gear; and when Macbeth comes to consult them, he will be enticed to his ruin by artificial demons distilled by Hecate from drops of the moon. The scene ends with music and a Witches' song.

1-37   A reader should have no trouble in detecting this as a non-Shakespearean interpolation. Not only is the verse scheme different from that of the earlier Witch-scenes (substituting iambic meter and a longer line), but the very texture of the language is sleazy in comparison. We need not inquire into who wrote these tame verses; anyone could have written them.

III, vi

Lennox speaks ironically of Macbeth's grief over the death of Duncan and Banquo, and accusations against their heirs; he is thankful that the latter have escaped the tyrant's power. To his question about Macduff, a Lord replies that he has defied the summons of Macbeth and gone to England to petition the good King Edward to take action in the cause of Malcolm, to whom he has given refuge. The two pray that the English warriors Northumberland and Siward will be commissioned to join Macduff and Malcolm in an expedition against Macbeth.

1-49   For the first time we hear of active opposition, in the fine sarcasms of Lennox's review (1-20), and of gathering forces of resistance; hence the scene represents a turning point in the play, and prepares us for the ambiguous prophecies that Macbeth will get from the Witches. This, rather than the preceding scene, is the proper preparative for the interview.

IV, i

The three Witches drop loathsome ingredients into their boiling cauldron and repeat an incantation. Hecate enters with three more Witches, who join in a dance about the brew and in a song of 'black spirits.' When they have left, Macbeth enters to the original three.

and recklessly demands to know the future. The Witches offer to reveal it through the mouths of their masters; then conjure up an Armed Head, which tells Macbeth to beware of Macduff; a Bloody Child, who tells him he need fear no man born of woman; and a Child Crowned with a tree in his hand, who tells him he will never be vanquished until Birnham Wood comes to Dunsinane. Macbeth is cheered by these prophecies, but demands to know further if Banquo's issue will succeed to the throne. The Witches then torture him with a spectacle of eight kings marshalled in by the bloody Ghost of Banquo—the latter's descendants who are destined to rule in Scotland. The Witches then dance again and vanish, whereupon Macbeth calls in Lennox to ask if he has seen them. Lennox has not, but he tells of couriers who have just arrived with news of Macduff. When Macbeth learns that he has fled to England to enlist forces, he regrets that he has not acted more promptly to destroy him. He will at least seize upon Fife and put Macduff's family to the sword.

1-156 The bizarre spectacularity of this scene is a theatrical treat. The Witches remain semi-comic gargoyles rather than sybils, and the grandeur of Macbeth standing on the lip of inferno is undercut by his displays of petulance and credulity. The objects dropped into the cauldron to the ceremonial chant of *Double, double, toil and trouble* illustrate the inversion motif mentioned earlier in connection with the Witches. This charm-making is parodic cookery: it would be hard to imagine a more resourceful shopping-list of inedible and repulsive ingredients than those which make this gruel *thick and slab . . . firm and good* (32, 38). A perfect opportunity to compare the writing of Shakespeare with that of the interpolator is provided by lines 39-43, 125-32 which were obviously inserted to float added singing and dancing. Insipid prettiness succeeds to inspired ugliness; Shakespeare's *secret, black, and midnight hags* suddenly diminish to *elves and fairies in a ring* (42). Macbeth, now a reckless invoker of chaos, is seen momentarily with Lennox, whom we already know to be disaffected, and then, from this point on, is never seen again with anyone we have previously encountered in the play, not even with Lady Macbeth—until he is slain by

Macduff. No other character in Shakespeare has been subjected to this degree of isolation.

IV, ii

The wife of Macduff complains that her husband has shown small regard for his family in going to England. Her kinsman Ross tries to comfort her, arguing that Macduff's motives are good. He then takes melancholy leave of her and her small son. These two engage in a whimsical conversation about the missing head of the house, the wife pretending to attack him and the child cleverly catching her up. A Messenger enters in breathless fear, and lingers only long enough to warn them that they are in imminent danger. He is followed by Macbeth's assassins. The wife refuses to divulge the whereabouts of Macduff, and the boy bravely defies them. They murder him as he pleads with his mother to flee; then follow her in pursuit.

1-84 With a few deft strokes the playwright reminds us of all the charm and decencies of normal civilized life—and then lets the firmament crack. We have come full cycle. The sign manual of Scotland's savior—*noble Macbeth*—is now this butchered child.

IV, iii

Malcolm tells Macduff that he dare not trust him: his leaving his family in Scotland while undertaking this mission appears suspicious; he may be the agent of Macbeth. When Macduff protests his good faith, Malcolm admits uncertainty and proceeds to blacken his own character, admitting to vices that would make him an even worse ruler than Macbeth. Macduff tries to palliate the seriousness of the confessed defects, but is at length driven to declare that Malcolm is fit neither to rule nor to live. Convinced by this display of moral fervor, Malcolm explains that he has falsely accused himself in order to test Macduff; he is ready to accept him as his ally in an invasion of Scotland, for which ten thousand English levies under old Siward are already prepared. A Doctor makes a momentary appearance, providing Malcolm with an occasion for telling Macduff of the miraculous power to cure sickness possessed by the saintly King Edward. Ross appears with news of the multiplying woes of Scotland, and after much hesitation tells Macduff of the slaying of his wife and children. Macduff receives the blow in silence, but at Malcolm's urging finally gives words to his grief. His loved ones have suffered because of him; he longs for the day when he will meet the tyrant face to face upon a field of battle.

1-240 This long and discursive scene provides a pause in the action. What proceeds and what follows is so packed with energy, and so emotionally taxing, that the respite is necessary. Although the pace slackens, the interest does not flag. Malcolm's 'test' of Macduff, and Macduff's response to the news of the atrocity are more than enough to hold our attention while we are being made aware of the alliance forming among the Scottish noblemen and between them and the good King Edward. The focus of attention is always Macbeth—this is not a 'history' play—but at least some slight stress had to be put upon the formation of the forces destined to crush him. The tenders offered, the mutual suspicions overcome, the deliberative councils held—all these have had to be symbolized in this single scene. (The play is silent upon the issue of Macduff's responsibility for the death of his undefended family. Of course he did not know that they would be killed, but he left them at a risk. Presumably it was a chance he took as a patriot. Although he is not exonerated on these theoretical grounds, his grief and his successful act of vengeance have a vindicating effect. It is characteristic of Shakespeare that he portrays neither Banquo nor Macduff as free from human defect, even though they function in the play as antitheses to Macbeth.)

V, i

A Gentlewoman describes to a Doctor the sleep-walking of her mistress, but she is afraid to repeat the latter's incriminating words. The Doctor is able to see and hear for himself as Lady Macbeth enters carrying a taper which she now keeps always by her bedside.

Her eyes are open but sightless as she tries to wipe imaginary blood from her hand. Her broken words reveal that she is reliving in a dreadful dream the nights when Duncan and Banquo were murdered. The spectators stand pitiful and appalled, the Doctor aware that this patient's illness is not of the body but of the soul.

1-74 The use of prose is appropriate to the realistic, almost clinical, atmosphere. The hush of night is in the scene; and the anxiety of the watchers communicates itself to us. Lady Macbeth's entrance, like a living corpse, and her hand-washing and fragmentary duplication of words spoken in scenes still vivid in our minds, are a perfect means of projecting her inner agony so that the episode is tremendous in effect. Usually it is too strenuously played, with the Lady as aggressive in her collapse as she was in her health. The whole point lies in the contrast—she is now weak, sick, broken. Curiously, although she was still masterful when we last saw her (III, iv), and there has been no intervening mention of a change, we are not surprised by it; we have already surmised that her apparent ferocity was in a measure bravado, was sustained by an effort, that she was not a fiend by birth. Curiously too, we share the sympathy of the watchers for her: *God, God, forgive us all!* (70)

V, ii

Lennox, Angus, and other Scottish lords appear with their forces prepared to join the army from England at Birnham Wood. Macbeth, so savagely defiant that some consider him mad, is entrenched in his stronghold at Dunsinane. His soldiers serve him without love. His days as usurper are numbered.

1-31 We are often given glimpses of the converging forces in scenes preceding a battle, but the present one is far from perfunctory. It projects a picture of the wolfish marauder gone to ground, defiant though doomed, and of the crusading spirit of those hunting him down—including the beardless youths protesting *their first of manhood* (11). The mention of *Birnham Wood* (5) and *Great*

Dunsinane (12) serves as reminder of the seeming promise of immunity given Macbeth by the apparitions, thus sustaining suspense.

V, iii

Macbeth refuses to listen to further reports on the melting away of his forces, and takes comfort in the supernatural assurance that he is invulnerable to any man born of woman. He curses a Servant who comes to him with news of the ten thousand English troops, and calls Seyton to help him on with his armor. His mood is a mixture of despair and defiance as he speaks to Seyton of the invasion and to the court Doctor of his wife's malady. He is as sick in mind as she. He declares that he need not fear death until Birnham Wood comes to Dunsinane, and orders Seyton to follow him with the remainder of the armor. The Doctor wishes himself far away from this ill-starred fortress.

1-61 This is the Macbeth who has just been described by the Scottish lords—madly ignoring the facts and proclaiming his immunity, yet terrorized and snarling in rage. The guarantees of the apparitions are now specifically cited (2, 5). Observe his solitude: although 'King' he has no visible retinue except the anonymous Servant and the colorless Seyton (whose name is suggestive in sound). But this is still also the other Macbeth—imaginative, reflective, even sensitive—fully aware of all the precious human values he has violated. Two of his speeches, *My way of life Is fall'n into the sear, the yellow leaf* (22-28) and *Canst thou not minister to a mind diseased* (40-44) are sad and beautiful; this is truly the poetry of the soul in anguish.

V, iv

Malcolm enters in command of the united forces of English and Scots, with Siward, Siward's young Son, Macduff, Monteith, Caithness, Angus, and others. He orders the soldiers to screen themselves with the boughs of Birnham Wood so as to conceal their numbers as they approach Dunsinane.

1-21   We see now how Birnham Wood will 'march to Dunsinane,' and we can expect to see soon how Macbeth's nemesis will be a man 'not born of woman.' (Often a new sub-plot or tangential action appears late in a Shakespearean play so that interest will be sustained as it progresses toward a forgone conclusion. In the present play nothing of the kind is necessary since the 'riddle-solving' interest suffices.)

V, v

Macbeth orders his soldiers to hang out the banners and prepare to withstand a siege. He hears a cry of women such as once would have made his blood run cold, and sends Seyton to learn its cause. When Seyton returns with word that Lady Macbeth is dead, his only comment is upon the noisy idiocy of life. A terrified Messenger reports that Birnham Wood is moving toward Dunsinane. Macbeth rages first at him, then at the fiends who have given him false assurances. He orders a sortie from the fortress—at least he will die fighting.

1-52   The play continues to rise upon a firm foundation of logic Macbeth has been driven from crime to crime by his craving for an unattainable sense of security. Now he abandons his best chance of real safety (withstanding a siege) when the assurances upon which he has relied prove fictitious. He is consistently the victim of his own desperation, every move he makes increasing the precariousness of his situation. He is like a man struggling violently to mount a slope, and as a result of his efforts slipping ever more swiftly toward the abyss. Thus the play is at once a practical demonstration of cause and effect, and an allegory of the 'pursuit of evil.' The *To-morrow, and to-morrow, and to-morrow* soliloquy (17-28), denying the primary tenant of human faith (that human life has meaning) is an ultimate expression of despair. Macbeth's response to the news of his wife's death, *She should have died hereafter* (17), is one of those strokes of genius which define the Shakespearean imagination. It conveys an impression of absolute desolation and spiritual aridity. She was dead to Macbeth before she died. We have been convinced earlier of the original genuineness of their love; but love is creative and cannot survive in the destructive heart. Macbeth himself is dead before he dies; he knows he has lost everything, and is filled with a vast emptiness.

V, vi

Malcolm orders his army to cast down the boughs and prepare for battle. Siward and his Son will lead the first onslaught, with Macduff and Malcolm himself deploying their forces as planned. Siward bids them a brave farewell, and Macduff orders the trumpets to sound.

1-10 From the first sounding of the *Alarums* (10 s.d.) until the *Retreat and flourish* (V, viii, 34 s.d.) the episodes succeed each other continuously on a stage representing the whole battlefield outside the fortress; thereafter we are within the walls.

V, vii-V, viii, 1-34

Macbeth fights doggedly, repeating to himself the assurance that he can be slain by no man born of woman. The young Son of Siward dares to engage him despite the terror of his name. Macbeth slays him, with the comment that he was born of woman; then goes to seek further foes. Macduff, who has refrained from engaging any lesser man, enters in search of the murderer of his wife and children. A tumult offstage guides him to where he thinks Macbeth may be. Malcolm enters with Siward, and receives the report that the castle is surrendered; many of Macbeth's soldiers have shifted to the side of his enemies. When they have left to enter the castle, Macbeth and Macduff enter and confront each other. Challenged by Macduff, Macbeth shrinks from killing the man he has already so cruelly injured. When attacked, he speaks of the charm which protects his own life from all men born of women. Macduff replies that he was not born as other men, but was taken prematurely from his mother's side. Knowing that the fiends have again played him false, Macbeth feels fear and tries to withdraw from the conflict, but he rallies when

Macduff taunts him. He resumes the fight, and dies by Macduff's sword.

1-29 Macbeth's mood both is and is not suicidal; he seems to know that he is doomed, and yet his vision remains clouded by the diabolic assurances. His lips seem drawn back in the grin of the engrossed gambler as he boasts, slays young Siward, and dryly remarks, *Thou wast born of woman* (11). **V, viii, 1-34** Shreds of the Macbeth that he once was and might still have been cling to him to the end. He can still feel pangs of conscience, *My soul is too much charged With blood of thine already* (5-6); he can still shudder with fear (17-22); and he can still be desperately brave: *Yet will I try the last. . . . Lay on, Macduff* (32-34). The original stage direction, usually modified in modern texts, is curious: *Exeunt fighting. Alarums. Enter fighting, and Macbeth slain* (34 s.d.). Evidently Macbeth was slain in sight of the audience, and it is difficult to see why his death was preceded by an exit and reentrance unless some special effect was intended. Although Shakespeare does not usually feature ignominious deaths, it is possible that Macbeth re-entered flying in terror and was stabbed by Macduff in the back. The only textual suggestion of this possibility, other than the oddity of the stage direction, appears in the next and final scene, when we hear that young Siward, *God's soldier,* had his death-wound *on the front* (47).

V, viii, 35-75

The victors gather to the flourish of trumpets. When Malcolm notices that Macduff and young Siward are missing, Ross reports that the latter has been slain. They offer sympathy to the bereaved father; but he accepts his loss without complaint when he is assured that the youth died facing the enemy. Macduff enters bearing Macbeth's head, and hails Malcolm King of Scotland. The others join in this salutation, and Malcolm makes the concluding speech. He creates his thanes earls, the first in Scotland, and promises to pacify the land. The exiles will be called home, and the agents of the tyrant and his lady, who is rumored to have taken her own life, will be searched out and brought to justice. He gives thanks to all, and invites them to see him crowned at Scone.

35-75 Stripped down to essentials throughout, the play ends with simple dignity. Victories cannot be won without casualties, and the fate of the brave young Siward symbolizes the cost. There is no generalizing about the evils of murder and tyranny—nothing but the display of the *usurper's cursèd head* (55) and a reference to the suicide of his *fiend-like queen* (69). There was no need to point the moral. The flourish of trumpets, the ceremonial *Hail, King of Scotland!* and the valedictory assurance by King Malcolm that *The time is free* (55) provide all that is needed. Thus ends this flawless tragic poem. A great though simple truth has been invested with tragic splendor. We feel that we have been witnesses of the continuing creation of moral law.

5

King Lear

:

I, i

T H E Earl of Gloucester speaks with the Earl of Kent about King Lear's plan to partition Britain, then introduces his son Edmund, jocularly explaining that the youth is a bastard and yet no less beloved than his legitimate elder brother. A sennet sounds, and King Lear enters in state, attended by the Dukes of Cornwall and Albany and by his daughters, Goneril, Regan, and Cordelia. After bidding Gloucester to usher hither the King of France and the Duke of Burgundy, Lear announces that he is retiring from active rule, and is placing one part of his realm under Albany, husband of Goneril, one under Cornwall, husband of Regan, and one under France or

Burgundy, depending upon which of these rival suitors wins the hand of his youngest daughter, Cordelia. First the daughters must declare their filial love so that he may dower the most devoted with the largest share of land. Goneril and Regan make fulsome declarations, but Cordelia refuses to comply. When she persists in declining to advertise her love, Lear falls into a rage and disowns her. Kent protests at this rash injustice, and is summarily banished from the realm. Gloucester conducts France and Burgundy into the presence. Burgundy withdraws his suit when he learns that Cordelia is dowerless, but France wishes to know how she has offended, and she begs that he be told. To France it seems no offense but an added proof of her worth, and he gladly takes her without dowry. As the court withdraws, Cordelia takes leave of her sisters, admonishing them to match their words with deeds and treat their father well. Their response is hostile, and when alone they agree to combine forces in curbing Lear's headstrong will.

1-32   The opening dialogue, in chatty prose, supplies one salient fact about each of the twin protagonists of the play: Lear is about to split his kingdom according to the whim of his affections; Gloucester has a son whose bastardy sits lightly on his conscience. Although so weighty in implication, these facts are mentioned casually: Kent is non-committal about the first, and socially pliant about the second—*I cannot wish the fault undone* . . . (6). The exchange exposes glancingly the fissures in a fracturable world. For the presumed effect of Gloucester's remarks in the presence of Edmund, see above, p. 83, their primary function is to provide expository preparation for the opening of the second scene.   **33-82** This gains by contrast with the low-pitched courtly conversation preceding it. Flourish of trumpet, formal announcement—*The King is coming* (33)—and processional pageantry (31 s.d.) give ceremonial character to Lear's appearance and pronouncement, as does the shift from prose to verse. It is fitting that his first words should be a command (34), good stage strategy that the entrance of France and Burgundy should be postponed. No aged tremor sounds in the voice declaring Lear's *darker purpose* (36-54): the King speaks like a king, with masterful economy and decisiveness. The fine rounded periods in which he makes his bequests (63-68, 79-82) lend him an air of power and grandeur; his size seems to match in spaciousness *all these bounds* he is giving away. The symbolic character of the proceedings is signalled by the schematization, with the speeches occurring in parallel sequences—Lear-Goneril-Cordelia, Lear; Lear-Regan-Cordelia-Lear. The falsity of her sisters would be evident without Cordelia's prompting asides; the protestations of love, while less crass than they might be, are nevertheless excessive and pat. Moreover, they are self-stigmatizing; the non-negotiable is being negotiated, 'love' being bartered for land. **82-119** Lear's own words become truly affectionate only when he turns to Cordelia—*Now, our joy* . . . (82)—and he at first seems dazed by her reproof, the stages in his deflation punctuated by repetition of the harsh word *Nothing* (87-90). It is possible to construe Cordelia's acerbity as a fault—as irritable reaction to the hypocrisy of her sisters, with her father bearing the brunt—and yet Cordelia acts as we ourselves at this moment would have her act. It is the function of the true to speak truth; and it is an absurd refinement of criticism nicely to weigh degrees of responsibility for consequences unforeseen. Observe that Cordelia is not asked to declare her love as love, but as a means of drawing *A third more opulent* than her sisters' (86), and not asked to mend her speech because it hurts her father but lest it may *mar* her *fortunes* (95). She is revolting not against an attempt to breach her natural reticence but against a demand to participate in an auction. Lear's explosion of wrath (108-20) and total rejection of one he has just greeted as his favorite child may be rationalized as evidence of either surprised resentment or of splenetic old age, but we must be cautious in applying 'psychological' theory at this stage of the action. Much of the play (and this scene especially) is highly synoptic in character, representing as 'happening' things which over a number of years 'might have happened'; only by this means could its expansive materials have been compressed into present compass. **120-87** Kent too might better have served Lear's interests by holding his tongue and biding his time, but we never consider this possibility. We are in a poetic world of elemental emotions, not of politic maneuvers, and we see Kent simply as an honest, brave, and loyal man. He is as recklessly strong-willed and passionate as his master, where his sense of right and wrong is concerned, and we can understand the affinity of the two although the one is so right and the other so wrong. What a grand stirring clash this is, as Lear roars like a baited lion and Kent refuses to give an inch—*What wouldst thou do, old man?* (146) In its course, essential information is being obliquely conveyed: Lear, in bestowing Cordelia's share upon her sisters, details the impossible bargain he thinks he is making— surrendering up his power and revenues, yet retaining the *name, and all th' addition* (prerogative) *to a king* (136). He parts a token coronet between Cornwall and Albany, but retains the crown of Britain. We must remember, in assessing Lear's later responses to slights, that he has never ceased to be king. The episode is rounded off by Kent's summarizing couplets (180-87). **188-266** As in an allegory, the characters continue to take stands clearly and swiftly on the side of right or wrong. There is humor in the embarrassed dilemma of *wat'rish Burgundy* (258) when offered a bride without a dowry; a 'spirited' plaintiveness in Cordelia's insistence that the record be set straight; and a fine human quality in the responses of the King of France. Few characters have established themselves in our esteem so instantaneously as this urbane, fair-minded, and generous man, whom we see only this once; his *She is herself a dowry* (241) following his tribute to disinterested love is the perfection of compliments. Observe that, despite Lear's outrageous treatment of Cordelia and Kent, and the folly of his jurisdictional scheme, he never impresses us as naturally cruel or obtuse. He is partially excused in our eyes by the angry unpremeditation of his acts, by his good intentions, and by other more subtle factors; for instance his basic preferences are for the better of the juxtaposed characters, Albany (1-2), Cordelia (82-83), France (208-10), and he has been loved as a father by such a man as Kent. (Later we learn that he is the god-father of Edgar.) We might call this 'innocence by association.' Above all, he is imposing: the grand sweep of his language invests even his petulance with dignity. **267-306** Cordelia is concerned with what will happen to her father rather than with what has happened to herself: Goneril and Regan are concerned with themselves. Observe how this self-interest is expressed in adverse 'moral' judgments patently self-contradictory: Cordelia has *obedience scanted* (278) and Lear has with poor judgment *cast her off* (291). The scene ends as it begins in low-pitched prose, casually exposing cracks in the firmament.

I, ii

Edmund proclaims 'Nature' as his goddess, speaks with cynical relish of his bastardy, and resolves to dupe his brother Edgar out of his inheritance. When Gloucester enters, distraught over Lear's rash actions, Edmund pretends to conceal a letter so that his father will ask to see it. It appears to come from Edgar and to hint that the two brothers might well dispose of their father and split his wealth at once. Gloucester is persuaded by Edmund's ostensibly reluctant words that his elder son is plotting against his life, and he agrees to eavesdrop upon an interview in which Edmund will put the matter to a test. He speaks with horror of the portents in nature which indicate the approach of general moral disruption. When alone, Edmund speaks mockingly of the alleged influence of the stars, and proclaims his own conduct to be self-determined. However, as Edgar enters, he echoes Gloucester's remarks about astrological portents, thus whetting his brother's curiosity. He then informs Edgar that their father is violently incensed against him, so that he had better go armed. If he will repair to Edmund's lodgings, proof will be provided of Gloucester's dangerous mood. Alone, Edmund triumphs over the ease with which he will trick his credulous father and foolishly innocent brother.

1-22 Edmund's soliloquy is an exhilarating composite of wit and wickedness: his defense of bastardy (9-15) is humorously paradoxical, but it is imbedded in a declaration of contempt for moral law. The *Nature* invoked is the goddess of the godless, giver of the law of the jungle. (The word 'nature' and its derivatives will constantly recur, usually in a sense opposite to Edmund's: what is 'natural' is what is 'human' and heaven-ordained.) For the moment, despite his coarse rapaciousness, the speaker's bravado

amuses us.   **23-114** Edmund's hoodwinking of Gloucester
provides a Iago-like display of Machiavellian technique, and the
appeal remains intellectual, at once shocking and comical. We are
not repelled by this ingenious deviltry since little stress is placed
upon Gloucester's suffering. His worried comments on Lear's behavior (23-26) and the dire portents of the time (101-14)—fair
game for Edmund's parody—establish at once his benevolence and
futility. His *O villain, villain!* (74-76) as he takes Edmund's bait
and cries out against Edgar lacks the passionate energy of Lear's
corresponding rejection of Cordelia; he seems gullible, almost ludicrous. Nevertheless his duplication of Lear's error at the very moment he is deploring it gives that error the authority of the commonplace: we seem to be witnessing *the bond cracked* between fathers
and children in general.   **115-33** The fine vigor of this speech,
and its seductive rationality, cap a similar one by Iago (see above,
p. 349); again, to admire the sentiments is to be trapped, although
we must admit delight in that *maidenliest star* that might have
twinkled at Edmund's bastardizing (128). Observe Edmund's conscious showmanship at the entrance of Edgar (129-33)—the virtuoso's smirk at the audience.   **134-77** Although Edgar rises
as readily as his father to Edmund's slanderous bait, the effect is
not the same. This is partly because Edgar remains relatively calm,
partly because he does not inveigh against his father but places the
blame (accurately) elsewhere: *Some villain hath done me wrong*
(159). The distinction is made explicit by the astute Edmund in
his reference to *A credulous father, and a brother noble* (172).
Like Iago, Edmund works upon vulnerable innocence, *foolish honesty* (174), but he is a villain of a different stripe—in some respects
better, in others worse. He is the body, not the soul of evil, the ruthless materialist striving for tangibles: power, possessions, and the
delights of the flesh. Although he will tolerate it in any degree as a
means to his ends, cruelty for its own sake does not interest him.

I, iii

Goneril complains to her steward Oswald of Lear's unruly manners,
and gives instructions that he be slighted. She is resolved to put the

old man in his place, and to write to Regan so that they may present a united front.

1-26 Since the account of Lear's misconduct comes from one whom we have seen in an unfavorable light, we will wish to discount it somewhat; however it receives at least partial confirmation when he appears in person—Lear is no easy house-guest. We are apt at this point to equate him with all the cantankerous oldsters we have known, and to feel sympathy for Goneril's evident wish to preserve order in her household. But there are details which warn us to suspend judgment—the slyness of her methods, the docile readiness of her man, and the rancor of her judgment, *Old fools are babes again* (19).

I, iv

Kent, disguised, hopes he may win a place in Lear's retinue and thus continue to serve. The King enters with his attendants from the hunt, impatiently demands dinner, and asks the stranger his business. Kent's ruggedly direct way of speaking wins approval, and he is promised dinner and possible employment. Lear sends for his Fool, then questions Oswald on the whereabouts of Goneril. The steward ignores the question and fails to obey when a Knight is sent to bid him return. When the Knight refers to the recent decline in deference, Lear admits that he has observed it but has been trying not to notice. He is also unhappily aware that his Fool has been pining since Cordelia's departure for France. He sends again for the Fool, and for his daughter. Oswald re-enters, responds impudently to Lear's questions, and is rewarded with a blow. When he protests, Kent trips him up and hustles him from the chamber. The action wins Lear's thanks and a token of acceptance into service. The Fool now appears, and in a series of bitter jests and cryptic rimes reproves the old King for his folly in dividing his kingdom and submitting himself to the power of his elder daughters. Goneril enters, and complains of the Fool's licensed jesting and of the disorderly conduct of her father's train. Lear's heavy attempt to show ironical incomprehension is met with a direct demand that he reduce his train, and behave like the old man he is. Lear is enraged, and orders his horses saddled so that he may depart. As Albany enters and tries to placate him, he defends the civility of his knights and laments the folly that made him prefer Goneril to Cordelia. In a towering passion, he calls upon Nature to curse this thankless child with sterility, then rushes from the room. He returns almost in tears, crying that Goneril has already dismissed fifty of his followers. He will go to his other daughter, on whose kindness he can rely, and Goneril will learn to repent her conduct. Goneril coolly sends the Fool packing after her father and Kent, then calls for her steward. She directs him to carry a letter to Regan and to supplement it by word of mouth. Condescendingly she dismisses Albany's plea for moderation.

1 s.d. Kent enters upon the stage just vacated by Goneril and Oswald, the sound of hunting-horns as Lear approaches (I, iii, 12; I, iv, 7 s.d.) indicating that the two 'scenes' are continuous in time and place; yet by a convention of compression, the scheme to slight Lear which we have just seen initiated proves to have been operating for some time (55-68).   **1-42**   Lear's wants are simple—food and fun, his dinner and his Fool—but he wants them instantly: *Let me not stay a jot* (8). Goneril has complained that he *still would manage those authorities That he hath given away* (I, iii, 17-18), and in the domestic realm he is peremptory enough: *go, get it ready* (8); *Go you and call my fool hither* (42). We can understand Goneril's point of view. But Lear is still king, with *Authority* in his very countenance (26-29); and the right to command personal service was not among the things he has *given away;* there is no sign that he has violated the actual deed of gift by trying to retain administrative authority or revenues—he is *poor enough* (21). Suavity of manners are not valued in his milieu; he is the rugged leader of primitive times, and Kent offers those things he values: simplicity, honesty, strength, fidelity—and very homespun humor. We need not accept his values as all-sufficient, nor deny that he is a domestic nuisance. His treatment of Cordelia and Kent looms large in the debit column, and we may wish to see him taken down; nevertheless we are required by the playwright to limit our disapproval. Faulty as the old man is, we cannot line up with an Oswald in opposition to a Kent.   **43-89** Lear's rudeness to Oswald—*You, you, sirrah* (43)—and abusive epithets for him— *the fellow, the clotpoll, that mongrel* (45, 48)—are deplorable, and it requires an effort of the imagination for us to see them in their context: a king is being slighted by a groom, and by the type of groom for which this particular king would feel a natural anti- pathy. Oswald is the pliant gentleman-usher, a smooth character smoothly performing his mistress's will; the very correctness of his external demeanor is an offense—he dares to be aloof! But again there is counter-balancing. We cannot admire Lear and Kent as they rough this menial up. Shakespeare, as only Shakespeare would, consciously places the better side in the poorer light. Compare Lear's billingsgate, *you whoreson dog, you slave, you cur!* (77-78) with the Steward's restraint, *I am none of these, my lord* (79); and the dignity of the Steward's *I'll not be strucken, my lord* (81) with Kent's subsequent piece of bullying. Our perceptions must sift this complex data, distinguish between appearances and realities. At the moment Lear and Kent seem merely uncouth; in the upshot we may wish that they had killed the snake, not scotched it. Another current, barely perceptible, is flowing beneath the surface. Burly as his manners may be, Lear is not insensitive. He has *perceived a most faint neglect of late* (65) which he has striven to ignore. He is well enough aware, through fellow-feeling, that his Fool misses Cordelia: *No more of that; I have noted it well* (72).   **90-179** The Fool exercises to the limit his privilege to say what others dare only think. He does all the things expected of his kind—play-acts, sings, asks riddles, and contrives paradoxes and jingles—but his theme remains fixed: Lear's folly in giving himself into the power of Goneril and Regan. The King winces, *A pestilent gall to me* (108), *a bitter fool* (129); and he threatens, *Take heed, sirrah— the whip* (104), but he offers no real resistance as the Fool keeps boring in. He is like one conditioned by long habit, looking for pleasure from one who has given him pleasure in the past, and refusing to recognize what he receives as pain. He is staunch in his affection for this creature, and it is an article of his faith that the tongues of licensed fools should not be bridled: *An you lie, sirrah,* *we'll have you whipped* (172). The Fool himself is a fascinating conception. He has been, and to an extent remains, the professional irresponsible, with quick, clever, perversely irreverent mind, but he has ceased to be typical. He has become an earnest fool, a moral fool, so aware of the disaster overtaking his master that his aberration now resembles monomania. He nags compulsively, as if he might restore Lear to what he was by harping on what he is. This Fool is at once a wag, a fury, and a pitiful defective.   **180-284** Goneril's rebuke is cold and complete, as efficient as a scalpel, mingling veiled threats with a catalogue of her father's social misdemeanors and personal defects. It is wounding beyond expression, especially as addressed to one who thinks of himself as her benefactor and king as well as her father. His attempts to answer with irony (209-26) are lamely ineffectual—in this kind of warfare he is completely outgunned—so that his only resource is rage. The writing is implacable. Much of what Goneril says is true, but it is terrible that she should say it. Lear's wrath is understandable, but it takes a terrible form. His curse of sterility has the frightening beauty of volcanic flame. It is a miracle of the scene that the poetic intensity does not eradicate homely details—'natural touches.' It is when the quality of his retainers is impugned that Lear's anger explodes (241-42). He returns to this subject (253-54) as later he keeps returning to the subject of the mistreatment of his courier (II, iv). Remorseful thoughts of Cordelia again rise briefly to the surface of his mind—*O most small fault . . .* (257-58). His attention is so concentrated upon Goneril that he addresses her confused and temporizing husband in an absent-minded aside—*It may be so, my lord* (265).   **285-339** We must not judge King Lear's servant requirements by our own. The hundred knights he has stipulated in his bargain are the visible sign of his royal dignity, and the dismissal of half of them in the first fortnight of his retirement must be accepted as an outrage. His speech at the discovery summons up his image—stunned, shamed, helpless, with his bursts of anger now a defense against tears. The irony of *Yet have I left a daughter* (245) is repeated, *I have another daughter* (296), and we catch our breath at mention of the *kind and comfortable* Regan. Observe Goneril's icy poise.

I, v

Lear sends Kent on as courier to Regan, then stands in tortured distraction. With one part of his mind he replies to the gibes of his Fool, with another to his own self-reproaches and fears. A Gentleman announces that the horses are ready for the journey.

1-46 The number of Lear's attendants is a kind of hypothesis in the play, a number we merely hear of as diminishing; he is already virtually deserted, followed from this point on only by Kent, the Fool, and a few anonymous 'Gentlemen.' After Kent leaves on his mission, the stage picture is freighted with meaning, as the one who has ruled a nation stands alone except for one improvident 'subject.' The latter recognizes the need to divert him, and jokes with dogged persistence still turning the knife in the wound. And Lear recognizes the need to be diverted: *Ha, ha, ha* (11). His responses are patiently habitual, mechanical and absent-minded, as he stands locked in the grip of regrets and fears. In wonderful fashion, the playwright lets us see inside his mind by means of words which escape his lips with an irrelevant relevance that stuns: *I did her wrong* (21) . . . *So kind a father!* (28) . . . *To take't again perforce* (34) . . . *O, let me not be mad, not mad, sweet heaven!* (40). This 'slight' scene is one of the greatest in dramatic literature.

II, i

Edmund is informed by one Curan of rumors of impending wars between Albany and Cornwall. The latter, accompanied by Regan, is visiting Gloucester this night. Alone, Edmund expresses elation over the timely visit which will abet his plot against Edgar. He calls his brother and warns him to flee at once; his hiding place is known, and the animosity of his father is supplemented by the additional danger of Cornwall's suspicion of treason. First he must draw his sword, since Edmund dare not let him escape without pretense of a fight. Edmund makes a noisy business of this mock combat and, after Edgar has been hustled into flight, wounds himself in the arm.

Thus, when Gloucester enters with Servants, he is able to tell a convincing story about Edgar's murderous ferocity. Gloucester proclaims Edgar a wanted outlaw and, under Edmund's cleverly suggestive guidance, promises that ways will be found to make the bastard son capable of inheriting the estate. Cornwall and Regan arrive and join with Gloucester in condemning Edgar, who will receive condign punishment, and in praising Edmund, who will be taken into the Duke's service as the first of the trusted retainers he now needs. Regan explains their sudden visit as a politic one connected with a matter upon which they need Gloucester's counsel: Lear has quarreled with Goneril, and Regan and Cornwall have thought it best to be away from home when confronted with the old King's complaints.

1-129 Edmund's plot against Edgar has remained conveniently immobile during the considerable lapse of time since its inception, and now levies upon intervening developments. The predictable rift between the rulers of the divided kingdom, Cornwall and Albany, is obtruded upon our attention with strategic casualness (6-13) since it will become important in the plot only after considerable delay. Edmund's methods (like Iago's) shift from psychological to practical manipulation. The playwright never forgets his obligation to provide stage entertainment, and the poetry and passion of the preceding scenes is here followed by a display of intrigue and exciting action. Observe, however, that the appeal is no longer, as in Edmund's initial appearance, in any degree comic. The villain has ceased to indulge in, or invite, chuckles, but confines himself to brazen lies and purposeful acts of aggression. (The medium is now verse instead of prose.) With insidious adroitness he plants a seed in Gloucester's mind with a term of abuse invented by himself, *unpossessing bastard* (67), and the seed promptly sprouts—*I'll work the means To make thee capable,* i.e. of possessing Edgar's birthright (84-85). The ineffable righteousness of Cornwall and Regan is a nice ironic touch: Regan seizes on the chance to link Edgar's perfidy with her father's knights, and Edmund is quick to oblige: *Yes, madam, he was of that consort* (97). Although the characters are princely and the canvas huge, the substance of the play is basically familiar, intimate, domestic—such as greets the common experience of Everyman. The petty meanness of Goneril's methods, in prompting a servant to snub Lear, is matched by those of Regan and Cornwall, in being not at home when he calls.

II, ii

Kent and Oswald arrive at Gloucester's castle at the same time. Enraged at the sight of the time-serving steward, Kent attacks him with words, then blows. Oswald's cries for help draw out the occupants of the castle, Edmund with his sword drawn. Kent is ready to fight this newcomer, but Cornwall commands them to keep the peace. Regan identifies the couriers, and Cornwall demands an explanation. Kent anathematizes Oswald as a servile instrument of corruption, and shows no deference to Cornwall himself, treating with mockery the latter's charge that he is only a posturing ruffian. Cornwall accepts Oswald's version of the quarrel and, with Regan's approval, orders Kent to be bound in the stocks. Since he is a king's messenger, this is lese majesty as both he and the worried Gloucester observe. Nevertheless, the sentence is allowed to stand, and Kent is trussed up in the stocks and abandoned. He accepts the ignominy stoically and, before falling asleep, comforts himself with phrases from a letter by Cordelia, indicating her concern about her father's plight.

1-169 As in his previous appearance, we are apt to misconstrue Oswald. His remarks sound civilized, decent, in comparison with Kent's brutal tirade. But quite apart from the fact that, in the acting, the gentility of Oswald's speech was probably intended to accompany a mincing manner, our favorable impression is here subject to rapid revision. This is one of the instances in which the playwright provides action first, explanation afterward. We understand Kent's rage fully when we learn that Oswald has been the one to prompt Regan and Cornwall to confront the aged King with locked doors after his wearying journey (II, iv, 37-38), but even here his repellent portrait is sufficiently blocked out—his cowardice

(36-39), falsity (57-58), and his effeminacy and supercilious smile (62, 77). The portrait is framed by Kent's masterful diatribe against all panderers to the vices of their masters. (Ultimately we share Kent's detestation: of all of Shakespeare's subsidiary villains, Oswald is the slimiest.) Kent's display of hostility to Cornwall and Regan—*I have seen better faces in my time* (88)—is in some degree anticipatory, although here too he has sufficient reasons. An odd diversion is provided by Cornwall's good, but misapplied, sketch of those who affect honest *bluntness* (90-99), and by Kent's (somewhat forced) parody of courtly speech. The treatment he receives has a significance partially lost upon modern readers, despite his obvious surprise and Gloucester's consternation. It is a barbaric violation of custom: in no civilized nation would a king's courier, friend or enemy, be stocked. From this point on Kent appears to be resigned to the facts. He does no more bristling, but works quietly and tenaciously in his master's cause. (Time is compressed as in *Richard II,* see above, p. 129, with Cordelia preparing to redress wrongs which, logically, she has not had time to hear about.)

II, iii

Edgar appears for a moment, having emerged from a hiding place in a hollow tree. He speaks of his outcast and hunted state, and resolves to evade capture by disguising himself as a mad beggar.

1-21 After Kent falls asleep and before Lear arrives, Edgar makes this momentary appearance, so that the action is continuous and scenes ii, iii, and iv comprise a single structural unit. Edgar's soliloquy is expository and descriptive but not purely utilitarian. The image of Tom o' Bedlam as man *Brought near to beast* (9) is vividly evoked, and in resolving to assume this shape, Edgar reveals his awareness that by a single spin of the wheel he has been brought next to *nothing* (21)—subject, as Lear is about to be, to *The winds and persecution of the sky* (12). Yet he speaks without recrimination or self-pity: *Whiles I may 'scape, I will preserve myself* (5-6). At the end, he tries out the canting whine of the Bedlam beggar—*Poor Turlygod, poor Tom* (20)—but *That's something yet* (21) and better than *nothing*. Edgar opposes himself to despair from the beginning; he is a balancing moral symbol of great importance in the play.

II, iv

Arriving at Gloucester's castle with his Fool and a single Attendant, Lear is shocked to find his courier in the stocks. Kent tells him of how he came there, and how Cornwall and Regan have withdrawn here upon news of his approach. Lear goes to demand an explanation, while the Fool remains with Kent and continues to utter his shrill mockeries. Gloucester returns with Lear, plaintively explaining that Cornwall and Regan say they are too weary and ill to greet him. Lear fluctuates between bewilderment, rage, and desperate attempts to believe in the excuses, but the rage overcomes him as he looks at his courier in the stocks. When he threatens to beat at their door, Gloucester goes to them again and this time succeeds in producing them. Kent is set free, and Lear tries to ignore the affront he has suffered as he turns to Regan for love. To his confusion and grief, she responds coldly and tells him to return to her sister. When he asks if he must kneel to Goneril as petitioner for bed and board, illustrating his words with action, his gesture meets only with contempt. A trumpet sounds and Goneril herself arrives, announced by Oswald. Lear recoils, then stands appalled as the sisters join hands and confront him. As Regan proposes that his train be reduced to twenty-five men, he tries to return to the protection of Goneril. Goneril then declares that he needs no train at all but can be cared for by the servants of the house. In anguish he speaks of the needs which cannot be measured, then reminds them of his generosity, of their kinship, of the bargain they have made, until their stony response brings full awareness of the extent of their rejection and of his helplessness and humiliation. Fighting his tears and his fear of madness, he dashes into the gathering storm, followed by Gloucester, Kent, and his Fool. Goneril and Regan assure each other that they have acted with wisdom and propriety. Gloucester returns to say that the land is barren, and that the old man will find no refuge from the raging elements. Cornwall and the daughters reply that he has brought his troubles upon himself. They go in to shelter themselves from the storm, ordering Gloucester to shut his doors.

1 s.d.   It is the genius of the play that it keeps compelling us to revise our judgments. In this scene the shape of the tragedy alters in our eyes; whereas previously we have been weighing circumstances and viewing Lear's reverses at least partly in terms of his faults, and his children's actions at least partly in terms of their provocation, we now cease to do so. Our emotions instruct us that the disaster is not traceable to measurable faults, or misunderstandings, or unfortunate circumstances, but to immeasurable evil. **1-87**   As Lear discovers Kent in the stocks, the choral jesting of the Fool is animated, almost gleeful—the Fool knew better than his betters. Lear opposes his will to the facts—*No. . . . No, I say. . . . No, no, they would not* (14-26); fights back grief and panic—*Hysterica passio, down . . .* (55); and tries to reassure himself of his power of command—*Follow me not; Stay here* (58-59), *Fetch me a better answer* (87).   **88-121**   Gloucester we can see wringing his hands as he expresses his anxiety in well-meaning commonplaces: *I would have all well betwixt you* (115). Lear's tone keeps shifting abruptly, reflecting his dazed incredulity, his hopes that the situation is explainable, his lapses into rage. Observe how the sporadic outbursts are touched off. When Gloucester suggests that he, the King, must be tactful with the *fiery Duke* who has been duly *informed* of his arrival, he cries *My breath and blood! Fiery? The fiery Duke, tell the hot Duke that—No, but not yet. May be he is not well* (98-100), and then, at the very moment of this effort to control his wrath, his eye falls on Kent in the stocks—*Death on my state! Wherefore Should he sit here?* This is the kind of thing the old critics had in mind when they said that Shakespeare 'gives no imitation of nature, but nature itself.' Although baffled and breaking, Lear is still a king.   **122-77**   But he is also any failing old man, desperately needing aid and affection. After forcing himself to utter conventional greetings and to put the treatment of his courier from his mind—*Some other time for that* (128)—his voice breaks as he reaches out to his daughter—*O Regan!* (132).

It is Goneril who is the unkind one, only Goneril. His ears refuse to take in Regan's initial rebuke—*Say? how is that?* (135)—and he treats her successive rebuffs as if they came from Goneril, channeling his response into curses of her. His awkward essay of irony as he kneels in mock-supplication for *raiment, bed, and food* (147-51) meets the same flinty disdain from Regan as had his similar one from Goneril (I, iv, 209-26). So painful to us is his insistence that Regan's eyes *Do comfort, and not burn* (165-76) that his sudden resurgence of wrath comes as a positive relief: *Who put my man i' th' stocks?* (177). **177-281** Goneril is unaccompanied by Albany, who is being saved by the playwright from contaminating participation in this episode. The brawny Cornwall, whose sensitivity is that of the boar, looks acquiescently on. What we hear now as Lear turns from one to the other is a proud man begging for mercy; what we see is his ultimate humiliation as he is treated like a beggar. As these daughters flog him with their detestable common sense, we feel instinctive revulsion—something deep in our natures cries no. We are ready to join our voices with the simplest of our kind and say, he is old, he is your father, he meant well, he trusted you, he gave you what you have, he is a reverend king; our lips shape reasons, but they do not really count. Our protest is against anyone letting what is happening happen. No man should be tortured like this. Our irrational compassion has something of the quality of religious experience, altering our perspectives. We may consider ourselves lucky to possess *raiment, bed, and food,* and yet recognize as calamity Lear's loss of his ridiculous bevy of knights. We lose ourselves in another's suffering, and see needs in another's terms rather than our own. This man needs what he is used to, needs what he expects—*O reason not the need!* (259) In a larger sense his needs are also ours and everyone's; he needs mercy and love, and these relentless realists, his flesh, his blood, his daughters (216), have no mercy or love in their hearts—there is the ultimate evil. The sound of thunder comes with Lear's collapse into tears—*No, I'll not weep* (278 s.d.)—and wild retreat lest they be seen. His parting cry is to his Fool—familiar, faithful, associated with Cordelia—and his final words express his terror, *I shall go mad!* The moral order, the vault of heaven, and the mind of **Man** are simultaneously cracking.   **282-304**   Cornwall, Regan, and Goneril express their own fear, of getting wet, and express their own regrets, that Lear should be so unreasonable and his retinue so inconvenient. To Gloucester's timid protest—the night is coming, the winds are rising, and for miles about *There's scarce a bush*—each makes the same response: *My lord, entreat him by no means to stay* (294); *Shut up your doors* (299); *Shut up your doors, my lord. . . . My Regan counsels well* (303-04).

III, i

As they meet in the storm, a Gentleman tells Kent that Lear defies the elements as he wanders about with his still-jesting Fool. Recognizing the speaker as a friend, Kent instructs him to go to Dover to establish liaison with Cordelia and her French forces. An invasion is impending because of the treacherous treatment of Lear and the impending dissensions between Cornwall and Albany.

1-55   Lear's exposure on the heath is first vividly described (4-14) before being shown, so that in our final impression it is something both heard about and seen. This method of reinforcement is used elsewhere in the play, as in the description of Cordelia's solicitude for her father (IV, iii) and subsequent portrayal of it (IV, viii). Double impact by parallel plots is effected by the play as a whole.

III, ii

The Fool doggedly jests on as Lear addresses the elements in passionate diatribes against ingratitude and secret corruption. Kent finds him and persuades him to seek shelter against the dreadful wind and rain in a nearby hovel. He will try again to make those in the castle open their doors. Lear grows gentle, and as he consents to do as advised, he alludes to his failing mind and to the sufferings of his Fool. They follow Kent, the Fool only lingering long enough to deliver a paradoxical prophecy.

1-96   Again we are forced to revise our judgments. As Lear appears self-described as *A poor, infirm, weak, and despised old man*

(20), he seems more impressive than ever before. There is something in him uncrushed and uncrushable, and his magnificent addresses to the warring elements, the gods, and the sly sinners of the world lend him the stature of spokesman for erring, suffering, aspiring mankind. His view is extending beyond himself, and his own defects are taken into account even as he proclaims, what is true, that he is *More sinned against than sinning* (59). Strangely, he becomes more real to us upon the purely human plane at the same time that he grows in symbolic size. He is both titan and old man in distress, both grand and pathetic; and his admissions of weakness, *My wits begin to turn,* and unexpected display of tenderness, *How dost, my boy? Art cold?* (67-73) are very moving.

III, iii

Gloucester complains of the cruelty of his guests, and Edmund agrees that they are savage and unnatural. Gloucester reveals the fact that he has received a letter concerning a rift between Cornwall and Albany, and a power on foot to restore Lear. He and Edmund must adhere to the King's side. In spite of the orders he has received, Gloucester intends to steal out and try to relieve the present distress of his old master. Edmund must tell Cornwall that he is ill and has retired. Alone, Edmund resolves to make his fortune by informing Cornwall of the letter and his father's designs.

1-23 Gloucester is very 'ordinary'—with the one virtue which the term implies: he is fundamentally decent. We have been plunged into a world where acts of decency must be furtively performed, where they expose the performer to treachery.

III, iv

As Kent tries to persuade him to enter the hovel, Lear says that his physical sufferings counter-affect his sufferings of mind; he fears that the thought of his unnatural daughters will drive him mad. Speaking with his new gentleness, he bids his Fool go in first; then utters a lament for the unregarded sufferings of the shelterless poor.

The Fool retreats in fear as someone mutters within the hovel. Kent orders the creature to come forth, and Edgar appears disguised as Tom o' Bedlam, near-naked, and raving of sin and devils. Lear's reason shatters, and he insists that this pitiful creature has been betrayed by ungrateful daughters, then equates him with Man in his 'natural' state. Gloucester enters bearing a torch, having prepared a warmed and lighted house in the precincts of his castle where he may shelter Lear. Appalled by the sight of the Bedlamite and the demented king, he says that he, too, is near madness at the thought of the treachery of his beloved son. Lear consents to go to the shelter only if he may take along his wise philosopher, the Tom o' Bedlam.

1-175 There is no sentimental exploitation of Kent's faithful services. His lines are spare. Goodness in action is convincing. Observe the interwoven strands of good and evil in the fabric of the play as a whole; in its most harrowing scenes we witness acts of kindness as well as cruelty. In successive speeches Lear dwells on his own injuries, fears, and resentments (5-52), and then, with his new-born awareness, on the miseries of his Fool and all *Poor naked wretches* (23-36). The latter speech is alone sufficient to cancel any suggestion of 'nihilism' in the tragedy; during the onslaught of viciousness, reserves of virtue are tapped. Lear learns by feeling *what wretches feel* that he has *ta'en too little care,* and that the justice of heaven can only be revealed through the acts of men (35-36). Edgar's imitation of a religiously-crazed Tom o' Bedlam supplies a jumbled heap of images of eerie nature, and of persecution, degradation, moral transgression, and devil-haunted sensations of guilt. With his entrance, and Lear's lapse into madness, which is triggered by it, the scene assumes the character of a grotesque charade. As the heavens rage, and the trio of Fool, mock-Bedlamite, and demented King enter into fantastic intercourse, we stand on the verge of chaos, with allusions to the morality, religion, and philosophy of the world of order tossing about like bits of wreckage. Lear's madness, like all his attributes, is both 'natural' and symbolic. In its latter aspect it often seems prophetic, inspired, a kind of super-sanity yielding searing insights, as in the lines following *Is man no more than this?* (97-102) Gloucester's lament over the consequences of Lear's error is infiltrated with evidence of his own corresponding error, and is multiply ironic since it is unknowingly addressed to Kent, *Poor banished man* (155), and spoken in the presence of the son he himself has banished—*I loved him, friend . . .* (159). Imagine the stage effect of Gloucester's address to Edgar himself: *In fellow, there, into th' hovel; keep thee warm* (165). Later, IV, i, 32-35, we learn that at this moment he was close to recognizing the outcast.

III, v

Having informed against his father, Edmund is endowed by Cornwall with the Gloucester title and estates, and is sent to apprehend the culprit. He hopes to incriminate the old man further by catching him in the act of aiding Lear.

1-24   In the present sequence of scenes we watch the progress of the betrayal of Gloucester in alternation with the results of the betrayal of Lear. The rising and falling actions cross and lend terror to each other.

III, vi

Gloucester conducts Kent and his afflicted charges into the house and then departs. Lear's mania now takes the form of lust for retaliation. He appoints the others judges, and conducts a trial of two joint stools which he addresses as his daughters. The Fool falls naturally into his role, but Edgar is so affected with pity that he can scarcely keep up his pretense. Just as Kent finally succeeds in persuading Lear to lie down and rest, Gloucester re-enters with the warning that his very life is sought. He must be placed on a litter and borne to Dover. After he is carried out, Edgar speaks of his own sufferings as of a lesser order than Lear's.

1-113   The grotesque charade resumes, with the contorted image of justice succeeding those of religion, philosophy, and morality.

This is a species of comedy, gruesome comedy, infernal comedy, during which Lear's madness continues to flash with moments of fierce illumination: *Is there any cause in nature that makes these hard hearts?* (75-76). The fact that Lear is hounded from his refuge and repose by a *plot of death upon him* (87) comes to us as no surprise. Edgar's pedestrian couplets (100-14) resemble an epilogue and perhaps marked an interval in the stage production. (After this point the Fool is seen no more. There is no need to rationalize his disappearance, as is sometimes done in productions, by letting him expire in this scene; as a matter of fact, he shows considerable vitality. Like other sustaining roles in Shakespeare (for instance that of Adam in *As You Like It*) this one is expunged when it has served its purpose. In one of his several aspects, the Fool has served as surrogate for Cordelia, and would only be in the way when Lear comes into her orbit in Dover. It is to Cordelia to whom Lear refers in his own dying speech, *And my poor fool is hanged* (V, iii, 306). Much has been said, and justly, about the artistic functions of Lear's Fool, but we must not forget his function simply as clown of the play. There is no reason to suppose his comic prophecy (III, ii, 81-96) an interpolation, and even in the present scene some of his quips are purely a bid for laughter—*Cry you mercy, I took you for a joint-stool* (51). This is Shakespeare's way, and we need neither deny it nor quarrel with it. From now on in the present play, as in the last scenes of *Macbeth,* he bids no more for laughter.)

III, vii

Cornwall makes Goneril his messenger to her husband Albany. They must unite to resist the invading French. Edmund is told to accompany her since it would be unfitting for him to witness the punishment of his father. Oswald enters with the information that Lear has been conveyed toward Dover, and is ordered to fetch his mistress's horses. After Goneril and Edmund have left, Gloucester is brought in bound in a chair, and is charged with treachery. Regan rails at him and plucks his beard as Cornwall cross-examines him. He ceases to defend himself, and declares that he has sent Lear to

Dover to save him from their cruelty. Cornwall gouges out one of his eyes and stamps upon it, and Regan urges him to gouge out the other. One of Cornwall's servants demands that they cease, and draws his sword to defend Gloucester. He succeeds in wounding Cornwall before Regan stabs him in the back. As Gloucester's second eye is gouged out, he cries for Edmund, and is told by Regan that it is Edmund who has informed upon him. He knows at once that Edgar has been falsely judged, and he asks the gods to forgive him and prosper his true son. Regan orders him pushed out of doors to smell his way to Dover, and Cornwall orders the body of his rebellious servant cast upon the dunghill. After their master has left, leaning upon Regan, the remaining servants speak with horror of what they have seen. They agree to poultice Gloucester's bleeding face and to get Tom o' Bedlam to guide him.

1-107 The repugnance aroused in us by Regan, Goneril, and Cornwall in II, iv, proves to be not in excess of the author's intention; those capable of the kind of cruelty portrayed there are capable of the kind portrayed here. Regan and Cornwall commit the atrocity, Goneril first proposes it—*Pluck out his eyes* (5)— and Edmund, the victim's son, is ultimately responsible. This is the most revolting scene in the whole range of poetic drama, but its artistic rightness cannot be challenged. The scene as it is belongs in the play as it is, projecting unshrinkingly a vision of evil absolute. Where the *flesh and blood is grown so vile That it doth hate what gets it* (III, iv, 135-36) the mutilation of parental flesh is the inevitable symbol. To gloze this action by treating it as a metaphor of Gloucester's passage from moral to physical blindness is to mutilate the play. Gloucester proves a worthy martyr, refusing to cringe—*I must stand the course* (53). He refuses to repudiate his kindness to Lear (56-66), and he accepts at the height of his agony responsibility for injuring Edgar—*Kind gods forgive me that, and prosper him* (92). The Servant—and observe that it is Cornwall's own (73)—has a just claim upon us as the most cherishable of Shakespeare's heroes, defender of our human faith.

IV, i

As Edgar is consoling himself with the thought that fortune has done its worst, he comes upon his blinded father and recognizes his error. Gloucester is being led by an old tenant whom he is trying to persuade to desist lest the act of fidelity be punished. The meeting with Edgar, who has forced himself to resume his mad chatter, suggests a solution. If the peasant will supply clothing to cover this creature's nakedness, Tom o' Bedlam can serve as his guide. He wishes only to be led to the cliffs overhanging the straits of Dover, after which he will need no more aid.

1-79 Gloucester's *As flies to wanton boys are we to th' Gods; They kill us for their sport* (36-37) expresses the despair from which Edgar is ordained to save him, but the wording is so compelling that the sentiment is almost irresistible. Gloucester surrenders, as Lear never does, but he has made a similar discovery. Compare his *Heavens, deal so still!* . . . (66-71) with Lear's *Poor naked wretches* . . . (III, iv, 28-36). The idea is identical but the mood is as different as the characters of the speakers: Lear is still *involved,* whereas Gloucester passively states a conclusion.

IV, ii

At the end of their journey, Goneril and Edmund learn from Oswald that Albany is incensed against her and seems indifferent to the French invasion. Goneril speaks of her husband with contempt, says that she will assume command, and sends Edmund back to Cornwall. She gives him a parting token and kiss in earnest of future favors. When Albany enters and upbraids her for the inhumanity shown her father, she accuses him of softness so insolently that he can scarcely refrain from striking her. A Messenger arrives with the news that Cornwall has died of the wound inflicted by his servant. Albany views the death as an instance of heavenly justice when he learns of the circumstances of Gloucester's blinding. He vows to avenge the atrocity. In an aside Goneril has expressed mixed feelings about the death of Cornwall. She thinks it may clear the way for supreme rule by herself and Edmund, but fears that the widow Regan may become her rival in love.

1-97   With the death of Cornwall, Albany becomes de facto ruler of Britain, obliged to resist the French invasion despite his sympathy with Lear. This curious 'political' situation, with the tentative alliance of Albany, Edmund, Goneril, and Regan, which forms and dissolves simultaneously, is lightly but adequately sketched in. The emergence of Albany as defender of the right has been sufficiently prepared for. It was inevitable that lust should appear in the parade of deadly sins, and that Goneril and Regan should turn upon each other. The circumstances have an ironic logic of their own: Edmund is unique, the only 'soul mate' for each of them.

IV, iii

A Gentleman reports to Kent that the King of France has been forced to return home, and has left his forces under command of a marshal. He describes Cordelia's distress at the account of Lear's treatment by Goneril and Regan. Kent explains that the King is here in Dover, but although fitfully aware of the new turn of events, he is too much ashamed of his past unkindness to Cordelia to meet her face to face. The forces of Albany and Cornwall are afoot, and Kent will in due time make his own identity known. Meanwhile he conducts the Gentleman to where he may join those attending upon Lear.

1-55   This scene was omitted from the folio version of the play, and although no doubt present in Shakespeare's draft, it is in fact dispensable. Cordelia's virtues speak better for themselves in IV, iv and vii than this Gentleman is able to speak for them; indeed we may be a little put off by his ecstatic vein.

IV, iv

Cordelia, who has come upon her father madly decked with weeds, orders her troops to spread out and find him. A Doctor assures her that a cure is possible, and she prays that it may be effected. She is aware that the British forces are approaching but remains serene: France has sent its troops only to aid her in her father's cause.

1-40   No other work of art has surmounted so many built-in obstacles as this one. Cordelia appears in the best of causes under the worst of auspices—at the head of invading Frenchmen. She must proclaim the purity of her motives, and the playwright lets her levy upon the Gospels: *O dear father, It is thy business that I go about* (23-24).

IV, v

Regan and Oswald exchange information on her military preparations and those of Albany and Goneril. The condition of Gloucester is turning hearts against them wherever he appears, and Edmund has gone to end his misery. Regan tries to persuade Oswald to let her see Goneril's letter to Edmund, whom she jealously claims as her own. The interview ends with Oswald eagerly agreeing to kill Gloucester if he comes upon him.

1-40   The rivalry between Goneril and Regan, the plot upon Gloucester's life, the exposure of treachery through evidence provided by Goneril's letter to Edmund, and the preparations for battle —all these complex developments remain subsidiary to the central interest, the reconciliation and death of Lear and Cordelia. The episodes of intrigue are treated with maximum brevity—they simply whirl by—while the episodes of tragic passion are treated at length. The effect is that of a vortex, with the movement swiftest away from the center.

IV, vi

Edgar describes an imaginary abyss at their feet as he persuades Gloucester that they stand on the cliffs of Dover. Gloucester rewards him, prays for forgiveness, and flings himself forward in an attempt to end his life. As he awakens from a swoon, Edgar makes him believe that he lies at the foot of the cliffs miraculously preserved, and that the guide to the scene of his attempt was actually a devil. Gloucester resolves henceforth to bear his affliction patiently. Lear enters and engages in a mad colloquy with his blinded subject, in which he expresses his frenzied disgust with the evils and inequities of human life. He escapes from the searching party sent out by Cordelia; and Edgar and Gloucester learn from the Gentleman who leads it that the battle between French and British is soon to be joined. As Edgar prepares to lead his father to a place of haven, Oswald enters and makes an attempt upon the blind man's life. Assuming the dialect of a stalwart, peasant, Edgar engages the steward and slays him. A letter found on his body contains Goneril's directions to Edmund to win her as his wife by murdering Albany. A drum sounds afar off, and Edgar conceals the letter before leading his father away.

1-281 The ruse employed by Edgar in saving his father from the damnation of suicide and converting him from despair is an interpolated 'wonder' made memorable by superb descriptive writing (11-24, 49-59, 69-72). The playwright seems to be drawing upon endless reserves of the creative imagination. The encounter between the blinded Gloucester and the maddened Lear bring the two central stories together for mutual commentary. The intensity of the writing is equal to the demand of this moment of fusion, and the impact is tremendous. It is here that Lear's 'madness' in its aspect of terrible revelation reaches maximum power. Observe that the medium reflects the dual aspects of the madness: the personal and 'realistic' speeches are mainly in prose (86-104, 133-52), the 'inspired' ones mainly in verse (107-30, 154-84). As Lear appears here, just before his temporary reprieve, he is both credible human being and lacerated scapegoat, *every inch a king* and every inch a spokesman for protesting humanity. Some of his words burn themselves into our memories forever.

IV, vii

Cordelia thanks Kent for his care of her father. He has disclosed his identity to her, but wishes, for the time being, to remain incognito. A Doctor announces that Lear, whom they have recovered and re-robed, has slept long and may now be wakened with healing music. He is borne in on a chair, and as the music plays, Cordelia kisses him and speaks incredulously of the cruelty of her sisters. His first dazed impression when he awakens is that he is a soul in purgatory, and Cordelia an angel in heaven, but recognition gradually comes. She kneels for his benediction. He humbly asks her forgiveness, but she replies that there is nothing to forgive. After Lear has been escorted away, Kent learns from a Gentleman that Edmund is the General of the deceased Cornwall's forces, and that Edgar and himself are presumed to be living in exile. Kent replies that the day's battle will be bloody. Alone, he adds that the success or failure of Lear's cause means the life or death of himself.

1-97 The turning away of Lear by Goneril and Regan was orchestrated by sounds of *deep dread-bolted thunder* (33), his reception into the arms of Cordelia by the strains of *music* (25). The play which contains the cruellest scenes in dramatic literature contains also the most exquisitely tender. Cordelia's eager out-giving is suggested by the simplest of verbal devices: *And so I am! I am!* (70). The words which create the image derive their power from the image created, and her *No cause, no cause* (75) seem the loveliest we have ever heard. It should be noted that if the play were characterized by a narrow didacticism, if its primary object were to show Lear's being 'taught a lesson,' it would have to end here. No human being could value another more than he now values Cordelia, and none could be better schooled in humility: *I am a very foolish fond old man* (60) . . . *Pray you now, forget and forgive. I am old and foolish* (84). What more could one ask?

V, i

Edmund and Regan appear with their army. Edmund sends an Officer to learn the intentions of Albany, who is proving a reluctant ally; then responds to Regan's overtures of love and her jealous questioning by denying that he has enjoyed Goneril's favors. Albany and Goneril appear with their army, and a brief council ensues. Albany indicates that he is present to oppose the French, not the native rising in the cause of Lear. As the stage clears, Regan contrives to keep Goneril in her own company so that she will not be present at the further conference of Edmund and Albany. Before Albany has made his exit, Edgar, still disguised, hands him the letter taken from Oswald and revealing Goneril's murderous proposal to Edmund. Edgar declines to wait until the letter is read, but promises to reappear at the proper moment when summoned by a herald. Edmund returns with a reconnaissance report and tells Albany that the enemy is in view. The scene concludes with a soliloquy by Edmund, in which he reveals his private plans. Whichever of the infatuated sisters he takes (if either), he will see to it that Albany dies after he has served his purpose in helping to repel the French, and that no mercy will be shown to Lear and Cordelia.

1-69 Observe that all the complex business of this scene is transacted in fewer lines than was the preceding simple episode of reconciliation.

V, ii

An alarm sounds, and the French army moves into action, with Lear in the charge of Cordelia. Edgar places Gloucester by the shelter of a tree, and leaves to join the fighting. He returns with news of defeat, and leads his father off, cautioning him not to succumb again to despair.

1-12 The conflict between British and French, with the defeat of the latter, receives only token treatment, with the fate of Lear and Cordelia prefigured by the renewed harassment of Gloucester and Edgar. The action here is continuous with what follows.

V, iii

Edmund enters victorious, with Lear and Cordelia prisoners. Cordelia grieves at her failure to save her father, but he refuses to lament; no misfortune can touch them now that they are reconciled.

When they have been led off to prison, Edmund sends a Captain after them with written instructions, and a promise of reward for ruthlessness. Albany enters with Goneril and Regan, and demands that the prisoners be delivered to him at once. When Edmund demurs, Albany stigmatizes him as a base-born upstart and asserts his own supreme authority. Regan challenges the claim, naming Edmund as Cornwall's successor in command and her own prospective lord and master. As she wrangles with Goneril over possession of Edmund, she begins to sicken of poison secretly administered by her sister. Albany now denounces Edmund as a traitor. He has dismissed Edmund's army and is prepared to engage him in arms unless another champion appears. As Regan is led off, a trumpet sounds and a herald issues a call. Edgar enters armed, and after an exchange of defiances, fights Edmund and mortally wounds him. When Goneril begins to rail, Albany confronts her with the letter instructing Edmund in murder, and she runs out in desperation. Edgar now reveals his identity, tells his brother that he has met with just retribution, and describes how old Gloucester has died joyfully after learning that it was his own rejected son who had been ministering to him. The dying Edmund is moved by the account, and tells his brother to speak on. Edgar then speaks of meeting the heart-broken Kent, who has been secretly serving the King. A Gentleman enters with a bloody knife, and news that Goneril has taken her own life after confessing the poisoning of Regan. Edmund remarks sardonically that he and his rival mistresses will be married in death, as Albany orders the bodies of the sisters brought in. The entrance of Kent to take final leave of his master reminds Albany that he has not received custody of Lear and Cordelia. Edmund now confesses that he and Goneril have ordered that Cordelia be hanged and charged with suicide. Before he is borne out, he gives them his sword to be carried as a token to the Captain that the order is countermanded, and an officer hastens on the mission. Before he can return, Lear enters crying out in anguish and bearing Cordelia in his arms. He knows that she is dead, but he tries to find signs of life. Wildly he accuses the assembly of murder, then speaks of Cordelia's gentleness and of how he has slain the one who hanged her. Dazedly, he tries to respond with courtesy

as the identity of Kent is explained to him. When
enters to report that Edmund is dead, Albany dismiss
as a trifle; then promises that Lear will be restored and
Edgar rewarded. His words fail him as his eye falls upon t
of Lear bending over his daughter. Lear's heart breaks, ⌊ ⌋
dies. Kent says that he will soon follow them, and after a few
words from Edgar, the bodies are borne out in a death-march.

1-327 The magnitude of the ending fits the magnitude of the
whole. In a succession of swift, spectacular, interwoven actions
everything comes to resolution. Gloucester dies in the joy of reconciliation with his son, and Lear appears momentarily as comforter
of his daughter (8-25) firm in his redemption and indifferent to all
things but their love. Goneril and Regan perish as symbols of self-
consuming evil, and the false son Edmund falls, in ceremonial
fashion, at the hands of the true son Edgar. Rule in the land rests
in the hands of the just (Albany) flanked by the faithful and merciful (Edgar and Kent). Viewed in the large, this ending represents
a triumph of right: the threat of chaos recedes, and a future for
mankind in a world of order seems possible. But this ending frames,
in effect enshrines, another ending. It is this other ending which
validates, renders meaningful, the play as a whole. Without it, the
victory of right would seem fortuitous and false, and the emotions
we have felt exorbitant and irrelevant; indeed the work would soon
fade from our minds as a grotesque curiosity. The play ends as it
has to end. We must witness the cost of victory in human sacrifice.
Our eyes must focus on those who have loved and suffered most, on
the good and the worshiper of the good, on the dead Cordelia and
the dying Lear. Each reader must come to terms with this ending
in his own way, and with it he should prefer to be alone.

V

Valediction

1

Works: 1607 to c. 1613

:

I N 1607 Shakespeare was in his forty-third year. There is no evidence that the writing of the great tragedies had left him spiritually spent, just as there is none that they were inspired by personal sorrows. So far as we know he was well, prosperous, and in good repute. Nevertheless he had passed into what was then, if not now, full middle age, and we can assume a diminution of energy. He was increasingly concerned with the stabilization of his position as a man of means in Stratford, and with the obligation to see his daughters suitably married. The elder, Susanna, made an excellent match with Dr. John Hall of Stratford in 1607, but the protracted spinsterhood of the younger, Judith, until the year of the poet's death was probably a cause for concern. He was not spared normal human vicissitudes. His mother died in 1608, having survived his father by seven years. Like most Elizabethans, he was occasionally involved in property suits. There is some indication that the publication of the *Sonnets* in 1609, unauthorized and hence unprefaced, may have been an embarrassment to him; some of the poems recorded a liaison, real or fictitious, with a married woman, and neither Shakespeare nor his age would have viewed with equanimity a public admission of adultery: there was no second edition until some years after his death, the erection of his monument in the church of the Holy Trinity, and the publication of his collected dramatic works. His wife Anna was still living when he died; we know nothing of their rapport or lack of rapport. It is unfortunate that the most widely-known fact about his life—that he left his 'second best' bed to Anna—is also the most wildly misconstrued. This provision in the will was a kindly one, meaning simply that the wife was to have legal possession as well as use of an object she evidently prized.

The face of the theatrical world was changing. With the rising tide of Puritanism, the middle classes were beginning to desert the theatres, and the acting companies to depend more and more upon the patronage of the gentry. By 1608-09 Shakespeare's own company was operating at the Blackfriars 'private' theatre as well as the Globe; and although the Globe was rebuilt when it burned down in 1613, the King's Men were destined to view it before long as their secondary theatre as they shaped their wares to the tastes of an increasingly sophisticated clientele. It is quite possible that by 1613 a formidable sector of the available audience considered Shakespeare a little old-fashioned, and preferred the clever young man, John Fletcher. It must be remembered that by 1607 the King's Men, with twenty-nine of his plays in their possession, were well-equipped to offer 'Shakespeare' whether or not he wrote anything new.

What we see is what we might expect to see, in view of the dramatist's age, his domestic preoccupations, and the theatrical situation. His rate of production declined. In the seven-year period 1607-1613 he brought to completion only five plays wholly his own. He left one play in what appears to be an unfinished state, and he wrote parts of three others. To write in whole or in part nine plays in seven years can scarcely be described as idling, but Shakespeare's pace was slower than it had formerly been, and quite slow when measured by Elizabethan standards. By 1612 he seems to have given up his lodgings in London, having ceased acting considerably earlier; between 1613 and 1616 he was living in full retirement in Stratford.

There was no decline in creative power so far as quality as distinct from quantity is concerned. Among the late plays are some of the best. Shakespeare shows a continuing tendency to strike out in new directions, and to continue in a certain mode, competing with his own achievement, until he had reached a self-determined artistic goal. Such sense of direction, the mark of all true artists, is perceptible throughout his career despite our inability to establish a precise chronology.

The problem of dating the later plays is complicated by the fact that only one of them was published before the folio collection appeared in 1623. *Pericles* was printed in 1609 in a quarto bearing Shakespeare's name on the title page. It was excluded from the folio, but there is no doubt that Shakespeare was the author of its last three acts, the spectacularly superior portion of the play. Also excluded from the folio was *The Two Noble Kinsmen,* first published in a quarto of 1634 as by Shakespeare and Fletcher. It is probable that Shakespeare contributed, about 1613, several scenes to this Fletcherian play, just as Fletcher, about the same time, contributed the prologue and several scenes to Shakespeare's belated history play, *King Henry VIII.* The latter was included in the folio, not inconsistently. It contains no extended sections so conspicuously non-Shakespearean as the opening of *Pericles* or the bulk of *The Two Noble Kinsmen.* The latter is a somewhat dubious item in the Shakespearean canon. It is based on the friendship romance of Palamon and Arcite, as told by the Knight in Chaucer's *Canterbury Tales.* It is a fair specimen of Jacobean tragicomedy, less dramatic than theatrically showy, and marred by patches of Fletcher's refined prurience.

Although *King Henry VIII* is properly viewed as primarily Shakespeare's, it lies off the main line of his artistic development; it bears the mark of an occasional piece, perhaps written for some banner day in the theatre when patriotism and pageantry were in order. It elevates Henry into a champion of justice, and a defender of England against ambitious prelates, unscrupulous politicians, and an arrogant Pope. Cardinal Wolsey falls when Henry finds him out, and Archbishop Cranmer rises when Henry astutely recognizes his worth and supports him against insidious enemies. The King's divorce from Queen Katherine and marriage with Anne Bullen are placed in a favorable light indeed; however it must be said that the play does not traduce Katherine: her predicament as victim of the tender religious conscience of her husband is treated with sympathy, and she as well as Anne is portrayed as a royal worthy. The most memorable character in the play is proud Wolsey, the climactic event the auspicious birth of the Princess Elizabeth Tudor. Although the play is quite stageworthy, and has had a distinguished career in the theatre, it is, it must be confessed, inferior to the earlier histories in dramatic interest, and it makes us uneasy, as they do not, by its air of special pleading.

A tentative chronology has been established for the remaining plays, which divide themselves into two groups. There are the three tragedies or classical histories, deriving mainly from Plutarch, *Timon of Athens, Antony and Cleopatra,* and *Coriolanus,* probably written in that order by 1608, and four dramatic romances, *Pericles, Cymbeline, The Winter's Tale,* and *The Tempest,* probably written in that order between 1608 and 1612.

Timon of Athens, c. 1605-08, is the most puzzling. There is no mention of it before its appearance in the folio in 1623, and it is doubtful if it was ever performed. Its 'dating' is guesswork based upon the style of its best portions, upon the resemblance between Timon's passionate invectives and Lear's, and upon the fact that its story comes from the same general sections of Plutarch as do those of Antony and Coriolanus. The play suffers as a work of art from a hiatus between mood and material. Shakespeare seems to have begun with the assumption that Timon, like Lear or Macbeth, was a legendary figure whose story could be made symbolically meaningful. Unfortunately the private reversals of this hero were as commonplace as they were painful, and hence, in the play, great passion is touched off by petty action: Timon resembles Molière's Alceste behaving like Shakespeare's Lear. He alters from philanthrope to misanthrope (or, as we are more apt to see it, from sentimentalist to cynic) when he falls in debt and is abandoned by those who have enjoyed his largess; and his disillusionment turns to mania when a sudden accession of new riches, after he has become a hermit, induces his fellow Athenians to reopen welcoming arms. He rages with true tragic splendor, but we should prefer more adequate occasions, just as we should prefer a hero whose initial idealism had been expressed in larger ways than in giving lavish parties. His extraverted young friend Alcibiades is also unsatisfactory—a somewhat tarnished champion who brings Athens properly to its knees, but from extremely dubious motives. Timon's faithful servant Flavius is an appealing character, and Apemantus, the cynic-born, is an arrestingly abrasive one, but both fit rather awkwardly into the frame of the fable. One would guess that the dramatist realized that this work was not crystalizing into effective form, and so decided to abandon it. The writing fluctuates unpredictably between prose and verse, both very uneven in quality, as if large parts of the play remained in 'roughed out' form.

It is conceivable that the material of *Antony and Cleopatra,* 1606-07, might have led the author into another impasse. One part of the story appears, theoretically, too big for the other part. It treats of a struggle for power with the whole Roman Empire at stake, at the same time that it treats of the final infatuation of an aging libertine. Councils of state alternate with the stratagems of a tenacious coquette, and mighty battles with boudoir wrangles. Antony is at once a great world figure and an amorous fool, Cleopatra an irresistible enchantress and a strident scold. The combination should not work, but miraculously it does—and without recourse to sentimental fictions. There is no glorifying of 'private' codes of morality, no prostitute with 'heart of gold,' no pseudo-heroic preachment on the text of 'all for love and the world well lost.' By some alchemy of its own the play succeeds in being both glamorous and astringent. The vast canvas and majestic rhetoric, which might have reduced to absurdity the tawdry love affair, actually give it size; and we are left at last with a sense not of its folly but of its power. The coldly politic Octavius Caesar is winner on the world stage, as he deserves to be, but Antony is not his foil. We forget his fatal imprudence, the decay of his strength, and the messiness of his suicide, and remember his warmth, magnanimity, and capacity for human attachments. He is loyal to what he values, and, muddled and misdirected though it is, his loyalty creates loyalty. We can understand why Enobarbus, the comrade who deserts him, dies of a broken heart, and why Cleopatra fills out her robes of majesty only at the moment when she resolves to join him in death.

Antony and Cleopatra is not a tragedy of the same order as *Hamlet, Othello, Macbeth,* and *King Lear.* Good and evil do not appear in it as polarized essences. It is secular and documentary, rather than religious and allegorical. The spirit of its creator is calm, contemplative, relatively detached. This is even more true of *Coriolanus,* 1607-08, another play in which a struggle for power goes against a naturally superior man because of his failure to accommodate himself to reality. Coriolanus pits himself against the Roman populace and its tribunes, insisting upon his right to rule as a patrician and military hero regardless of their suffrage. When he is expelled and makes league with Aufidius, general of the Volscians whom he has formerly defeated, Rome finds itself at his mercy. He is dissuaded from vengeful destruction only by the pleas of his mother Volumnia, and is himself destroyed by Aufidius and his resentful new allies. The treatment of cause and effect is logical, and the questions raised still relevant—on the proper qualifications of leaders, and on the vulnerability of both popular and dictatorial forms of government. It has more intellectual, less emotional, appeal than the other Roman plays, primarily because of the character of its protagonist. Although Coriolanus is in some ways admirable, he is difficult to admire; he has every right to be proud, but he exercises this right to the point of absurdity, finally ignoring both his own and the public good. He says too much too often, until his pride bores as well as repels. Actually we are able to attach our sympathies to none of the characters in the play—not the populace, the tribunes, the Volscian General, or Coriolanus's aristocratic family and friends. The people of Rome are foolish and fickle, their tribunes theoretically right but practically wrong, and always devious or untimely in their policy. Volumnia is too much her son's mother to command our affection, and his wife Valeria is too supine. His humorous friend Menenius first appears as an amusing character, but turns plaintive as the play proceeds. This absence of human attractiveness in the characters, and the unrelieved somberness of tone have prevented the play from being a favorite with readers and playgoers despite its vital theme and its stylistic excellence.

The sense of creative poise conveyed by *Antony and Cleopatra* and *Coriolanus* is conveyed also by the dramatic romances, but with this interesting distinction, that it seems to emanate increasingly from the very heart of the works. Shakespeare himself is *in* them, as he was *in* the great tragedies, but his mood is not the same; whether or not the man has found peace of mind, the artist chooses to contemplate those aspects of existence which contribute to peace of mind—the general phenomena of creation and growth, rebirth and renewal, and particular instances of restoration, redemption, fulfillment, providential intervention, realized hopes, and sheer good luck. Characters are reconciled to their lives and each other in a way which reconciles us to life. The material is identical with the material of the tragedies—the deadly sins are on the prowl— and we feel, as in the tragedies, that the human condition is being allegorized, but the allegory invites a new interpretation. In the tragedies, good resists evil, whose ministers are finally expunged, but at the cost of dreadful suffering and waste. In the romances the resistance is more passive, yet less costly, and good succeeds evil instead of merely surviving it. These are plays of the second chance.

Pericles, 1608-09, is par excellence a tale of prolonged ill-fortune finally turning to good. Old Gower, contemporary and rival of Chaucer serves as Chorus as the story unfolds. Its completely blameless hero, Pericles Prince of Tyre, is hounded from land to land in consequence of guessing the guilty secret of the incestuous King of Antioch. After enduring a series of catastrophes, including the apparent death of his wife Thaisa in childbirth, and the loss of his infant daughter (named Marina because born at sea), Pericles is finally blessed. His daughter, who has grown into a lovely and gifted maiden, has preserved herself from contamination after falling into the hands of a Myteline brothel-keeper; and his wife, who has been revived by the skillful physician Cerimon after being buried at sea and washed ashore, has become a priestess of Diana at Ephesus. The three are reunited, the parents provided with a throne and the daughter with a presumably eligible husband. Much of the latter part of the play is concerned with Marina. In the brothel, which is portrayed with a realism both horrifying and comical, she redeems sinners by her very presence, and when she is found by her wretched father, her nature acts upon him as a cure. She is at once a charming young girl and a symbol of cleansing forces. Father, mother, and daughter in this 'strange and worthy' history are all afflicted because of their virtues, then rescued from affliction because of these same virtues and the solicitude of the gods. *Pericles* is a peripatetic piece with a number of quaint features, but it contains entrancing parts. It introduces most of the themes developed in its superior successors.

Cymbeline, 1609-10, like *King Lear,* deals with turmoil in a royal family of ancient Britain and contains an arresting number of story elements in common with that famous tragedy—including the alienation of erring father and superbly virtuous daughter, the persecution by ambitious and lustful villains, the temporarily successful ruse of a Machiavellian slanderer, the exposure of the virtuous to the hardships of life in the wilderness, even a sketchy foreign invasion although by Romans rather than French. It is as if the former play had been fragmented and put together in a new way, with supplementary parts supplied by romantic and realistic fiction. An important distinction from the basic situation in *King Lear* is that the good and evil members of the family are not of the same blood. Although the royal house is split down the middle as before, Cymbeline's vicious Queen is his second wife, and hence her vicious son Cloten is only Imogen's nominal brother; her true brothers, Guiderius and Arviragus, lost in childhood and here restored, prove as virtuous as herself. The evil characters, Cloten and the Queen, perish; the erring ones, Cymbeline and Imogen's husband Posthumous are redeemed; and the good ones triumphantly vindicated. Imogen is chief of the latter: tender and charming, yet hardy and brave, her invincible honesty baffles the predatory schemes of the Queen and Cloten, who come between her and her father, and the cruel slanders of the Italian villain Iachimo, who comes between her and her husband. Her purity, like Marina's, purifies.

Cymbeline is a better play than *Pericles,* and would be valuable, if for no other reason, because of the characterization of Imogen, and the lovely dirge 'Fear no more the heat of the sun'; nevertheless it is not entirely successful. It is overloaded with imperfectly integrated action so that it lacks a clear-cut 'story line.' Shakespeare brought to perfection the dramatic romance, not in this play, but in *The Winter's Tale,* 1610-11, and *The Tempest,* 1611-12, treated at length in the following pages. Perdita in the first and Miranda in the second are the successors and equivalents of Marina and Imogen. The commanding presence of the vernal maiden in each of the four plays is only one of their features in common. All treat of a father-daughter bond, and conclude with the reunion of the separated or estranged. All stress transgression, expiation, redemption. All contain an element of the supernatural. All contain 'resurrections'—instances of the supposedly dead returning to life, often in mystical or religious circumstances. It is hard to evade the conclusion that Shakespeare, in his own oblique and unaggressive way, was communicating a faith. He was at least leaving his London audience with something beautiful to remember him by, and we may trust that it was inclined to grant the plea concluding his farewell play (see below, p. 481).

In the last of his three years of retirement in Stratford, he made a will, providing justly for all members of his family but entailing the principal of his estate upon his eldest daughter and a putative male line. At the time, his single grandchild was Elizabeth, born to Susanna and John Hall in 1608. It is pleasant to think of this infant girl as belonging in Shakespeare's imagination to the line of Miranda, but no doubt he wished it were a boy. The safest biographical conjecture about the poet is that the greatest tragedy in his life was the death of his only son Hamnet at the age of eleven in 1596. On April 23, 1616, William Shakespeare died.

2

The Winter's Tale

:

I, i

D URING an exchange of civilities between Camillo and Archi-
damus, we learn that the King of Sicilia is being visited by his boyhood companion the King of Bohemia, and that nothing could
sever the bond between these royal friends. When the Bohemian
courtier congratulates Camillo upon the great promise of his master's little son, Camillo replies that Prince Mamillius is the joy of all
Sicilia.

1-43 This is casually suggestive exposition, not unlike the opening
of *King Lear*. There may be a hint of parody of the courtly style in
this prose (8-15); its rhetorical sheen prevents us from assuming
that all things are precisely as they are said to be. Nevertheless, one
note is struck (42-43) which proves recurrent in the play: the hope
of one generation in the next. The idea is obtruded, however
whimsically, of old life abiding until new life is insured.

I, ii

King Leontes invites King Polixenes to extend his visit, and asks
his wife Hermione to add her persuasions. When she succeeds
where he has failed, Leontes shows that he has fallen prey to
jealousy. As Polixenes and Hermione converse apart, he voices his
gross suspicions that they have made him a cuckold. His child
Mamillius to whom he addresses his bitter insinuations only dimly
apprehends what he is saying. When the others have gone, Leontes

summons his counselor Camillo and upbraids him for failing to take cognizance of what has been going on. Camillo earnestly defends the honor of Hermione but is unable to alter his master's deadly rancor. He finally accepts the commission to poison the drink of Polixenes. However, when the latter returns, puzzled by the sullen silence with which Leontes has just passed him, Camillo tells of the plot, and the two agree to issue secret orders to the Bohemian ships so that they may flee Sicilia in the night.

1-59 Although the jealousy of Leontes is 'unmotivated' (as it must be, in view of its function in the play as symbol of mysterious evil), it does not follow that the onslaught is so sudden that we witness its very inception here. Leontes at his entrance was probably intended by the playwright to appear preoccupied, even sullen. We are apt to be misled by the contrast between our own standards of good manners and those of the Renaissance, and to mistake Leontes' brevity for sincerity. Polixenes in his expression of gratitude truly extends himself; he is ingenious and elaborate, thus making social intercourse amusing and intellectually stimulating as a gentleman was expected to do. In contrast, Leontes, who is obliged of course to protest against a guest's departure, does so in a style so laconic as to seem half-hearted. We must accept as literally true Hermione's words of rebuke, *You, sir, Charge him too coldly* (29-30). Compare how she, like Polixenes, truly extends herself, and is just as ingenious and elaborate in her insistence that he stay as he in his insistence that he must go. Yet, interestingly, it is Hermione who in passing provides him with the best excuse for going at once —to see the child he has left at home (34-37).   **60-119** This is one of the most fascinating examples in Shakespeare of poetic dialogue proceeding upon a surface, and a countering sub-surface level. It is ostensibly an exchange of banter, in which a charming and witty woman displays her interest in her husband's boyhood and her joy in her marriage to him. But it is also, through imagery and allusion, an allegory of the fall of Man, a commentary upon *Genesis,* 3:1-5. We first hear of a State of Innocence, before the fruit of the tree of knowledge of good and evil had been tasted: *we knew not The doctrine of ill-doing, nor dreamed That any did*

(69-71). Had that state endured, *we should have answered Heaven boldly 'Not guilty,' the imposition cleared Hereditary ours* (73-75). This is an explicit allusion to Original Sin, incurred when Man fell. Hermione's word is the humorously delicate *tripped* (76). The idea that the Fall consisted of yielding to the sexual *temptations* (77) of an Eve (as figured forth by the wives of Leontes and Polixenes) is suggested and withdrawn. Hermione will answer for it that wives are not *devils* (82) if husbands have *sinned* (84) first and only with them. Indeed marriage, which distinguishes man from beast, is a means of salvation: *'Tis Grace indeed* (105). (This acceptance of sexual union as pure when properly sanctioned is Miltonic as well as Shakespearean.) Of what then does evil consist? What was the Fall? What is meant by the deadly fruit of the tree of knowledge? The mind of the playwright has often occupied itself with these questions, and he has sometimes suggested the same answer —that with the knowledge of good and evil comes the possibility of confusing them, and *evil* may be *evil*-thinking. Eve is the temptress in being the unwitting occasion for evil-thinking, with the latter epitomized in a husband's unfounded suspicion of adultery. It is no coincidence that immediately following Hermione's gracious words comes Leontes' *Too hot, too hot!* (108). Here is fallen man—his good 'knowledge' corroded by evil 'knowledge.' Its dreadful consequences, upon the most familiar plane of universal experience, is driven home to us in the last words of Leontes' first 'jealous' speech as he turns suddenly on his child: *Mamillius, Art thou my boy?* (119) **120-46** The gruffly affectionate terms, revealing this father's great fondness for this child, are invaded and distorted by the vile thoughts assailing his mind, as if a clear fountain were growing roiled. The brooding language is abstract, but the images subtending it are terribly concrete; his *Affection, thy intention stabs the center* (138) is both a generalization about the pervasiveness of the sexual impulse and an image of the sexual act; even the erotic dream (139-43) is taken as evidence of irresistible sensuality. **147-84** The family as symbol of creative good is a central point of reference in the play, and Polixenes' charming lines on the joys of fatherhood (164-69) provide an ironic comment upon the situation of Leontes, who is in no position to agree, as he does, that the *childness* of his son cures *Thoughts that would thick my blood* (169-70). The account of the Fall in *Genesis* again informs the imagery when Hermione says of herself and Polixenes *We are yours i' th' garden,* and Leontes insinuatingly replies, *You'll be found, Be you beneath the sky* (178-79).   **185-210** The grossness of Leontes' language is doubly exacerbating because he is addressing himself to a child: *Go play, boy, play. Thy mother plays* . . . (186). The subtlety of Shakespeare's creative imagination is evidenced in touches which could have appeared in the writing of no one else—for instance, the boy's pathetic half-comprehension of what is happening, *I am like you, they say* (207), and the father's affectionate return to an honest use of the word 'play,' *Go, play, Mamillius. Thou'rt an honest man* (210).   **211-348** Something beyond the presentation of Leontes' plot to murder Polixenes is accomplished in this interview. The possibility is removed that there can be any rational basis for Leontes' suspicions: Camillo, like every one else in the play with the single exception of Leontes, considers her guilt 'unthinkable.' The mental state of Leontes is adroitly revealed by the style. Compare his language with Camillo's, which is consistently straightforward and lucid. Not only is Leontes morbidly suggestible—*Didst perceive it? [Aside] They're with me already, whispering* . . . (215-16); *Satisfy the entreaties of your mistress? Satisfy* . . . (232-33)—but his words issue spasmodically, in short thrusting phrases, harsh images jostling each other as his mind boils and bubbles. He is able to express, or half express, a multitude of aspects of his fixed idea in brief compass, and the style, although here put to a very special use, comes nearer, in its suppleness and condensation, than that of Camillo in being the style of the play as a whole.   **349-62** Since Camillo is about to disobey a royal master, and transfer his services to another, every justifying sanction must be explicitly invoked.   **363-463** The style of Camillo's language is no longer being used for purposes of contrast, and both he and Polixenes speak the 'normal' language of the play. It is wonderfully quick, compact, expressive—with the rhythms so keyed to the relevant emotions that we are scarcely aware that we are reading 'iambic pentameters.' The lines flow into each other and are filled with internal stops. Measured stress and significant stress (see above, p. 62) neither jog placidly together nor keep separate pace but stretch each other as a racing team. Observe that Polixenes' estimate of Hermione is identical with Camillo's, and that although the official religion of the play is pagan, a Christian metaphor comes naturally to his lips at the thought of betrayal: had he seduced Hermione he would wish his name *Yoked with his that did betray the Best* (417).

II, i

Hermione and her ladies in waiting talk playfully with Mamillius, who is told that he will soon have a rival for their attention. Leontes breaks angrily into their midst and takes Mamillius from the side of Hermione. He charges her with adultery, and declares that the child in her womb is the bastard of Polixenes. Hermione replies with dignity when she recovers from her bewilderment, but she is sent unceremoniously to prison. The Lord Antigonus earnestly joins with another Lord in protesting against this indignity, but Leontes cannot be moved; the flight of Polixenes and Camillo have convinced him that there has been a conspiracy against his honor and even against his life. To remove all doubts he will send Dion and Cleomenes to consult the Delphic oracle.

1-32 Mamillius (like the son of Macduff and cute children in drama generally) seems knowing beyond his years, but he is also appealingly childlike. Summoned up is an image of happy domesticity, soon to be brutally shattered. Included in the image is the frank rejoicing in Hermione's pregnancy—*She is spread of late Into a goodly bulk* (19-20). Mamillius's 'winter tale' is of *sprites and goblins* (25-26)—a ghost story, which he begins to tell in a frightening whisper (30) like children in all times and places. It is a different kind of 'winter's tale' that Shakespeare himself is telling, generically allied through its source with popular offspring of Greek peripatetic romances of persecution, adventure, and recovery of the lost.   **33-125** Leontes is afflicted by what in Greek tragedy would be called 'hubris.' He is utterly certain of himself, construing even the things which he himself has brought about (such as Camillo's flight with Polixenes) as confirmation of his *just censure,* his *true opinion* (37). In his rank imagination a new suspicion (of an attempt on his life) buds on the first without so much as a hint of reason. We must imagine the implied stage action, as he strides amongst the women and snatches away the child: *Give me the boy* (56). The playwright is always at his best when portraying a true woman falsely accused. Hermione's speeches increase in length and deepen in emotional tone as realization of her situation is gradually borne in upon her. At first she sounds only startled and vexed, *What is this? sport?* (58), then only indignant, as she might be at some minor slur (62-64), then truly angry and shocked (78-81, 95-100), and, finally, hurt to the heart (105-24). Her dignity grows with her sense of pain, and her parting words are both moving—*Adieu, my lord, I never wished to see you sorry . . .* (122-23)—and majestic—*My women, come; you have leave* (124). **126-200** This admirable 'Lord' speaks—*Beseech your highness, call the queen again* (126)—as Lodovico spoke when Othello dismissed Desdemona with similar cruelty under similar circumstances—*I do beseech your lordship call her back* (IV, i, 242). This Lord and Antigonus are sensible, just, and courageous in their opposition to Leontes; like Camillo and Polixenes earlier, they establish the 'right-thinking' norm from which Leontes deviates in his evil obsession. Antigonus is characterized as the 'humorous man' by his salty home-spun diction, but the quaintness is laid lightly on—he has a sharp and forceful mind. Leontes continues to speak in the clipped, violent phrases of compulsive, reckless unreason. He is not by nature and habit tyrannical; were he so, he would feel no obligation to state his present absolutist doctrine (161-70). He must consult the oracle of Delphi—this is a donné of the story—but the playwright achieves consistency by giving him precisely the right reasons: although a forgone conclusion, the answer from Delphi will *Give rest to th' minds of others,* abate *ignorant credulity* (191-92). As for himself, he is *satisfied*—he knows what he knows (189-90).

II, ii

The Lady Paulina visits Hermione's prison and sends in a Gentleman to summon the Gaoler. When she is denied admission, she asks to see Hermione's attendant Emilia. Emilia brings news that her mistress has just been prematurely delivered of a baby girl. Paulina persuades the Gaoler to let her take the infant to Leontes; perhaps the sight of its innocence will bring him to his senses.

1-66 Why must a Gentleman be sent to fetch the Gaoler, the Gaoler Emilia, and Emilia the babe, and why must the Gaoler be present at the conference and the Gentleman dismissed? This handling of the episode provides stage bustle, and creates the proper atmosphere by hedging Paulina's visit with restrictions: when the babe emerges, it seems actually to come from a prison. Paulina's character as the managing sharp-tongued matron, totally secure in her sense of respectability, is deftly created in a few lines of dialogue. She is a fit wife for Antigonus, her surface eccentricities overlaying, like his, a mine of human goodness. The stress on familial attachment and joyous fecundity persists, in the assumption by Paulina, Emilia, and even Hermione and the Gaoler, that the sight of *a goodly babe, Lusty and like to live* (26-27) should restore anyone to his right mind.

II, iii

Leontes reflects savagely that he will be able to take vengeance upon Hermione even though Polixenes and Camillo are beyond his reach. When a Servant brings word that Mamillius has spent a restful night, he speaks of how his child has sickened in consequence of his mother's disgrace. Paulina enters with the babe, defying attempts to exclude her made by her husband Antigonus, his fellow lords, and Leontes himself. She stoutly defends Hermione, and lays the child at the King's feet in spite of his invectives at her and at the husband who cannot control her. When she is finally ousted from the room, Leontes orders Antigonus to take out the child and burn it. All protest, and he alters the sentence to exposure in some wild spot outside his domains. As Antigonus departs sorrowfully with the child, a Servant enters to announce the approach of Dion and Cleomenes from their mission to the Delphic oracle. Leontes rejoices at their speedy return, and announces that their report will be heard during a public trial of Hermione.

1-25 Leontes has something in common with other of Shakespeare's obsessed characters: like Macbeth he craves *rest* (8) and thinks he may find it by perpetrating an atrocity; like Lear he has futile yearnings, obliquely expressed, to wreck military vengeance on his enemies (18-22). But Leontes' obsession has its own kind of consistency; no other character in the plays is so prone to wrest everything into line with his own distorted vision; he cannot conceive of Mamillius as sickening because of the way he himself has treated Hermione, and confidently assumes that it is because of the way Hermione has treated him. This is the arrogance of total self-righteousness, more frightening in a Leontes than in, for instance, a Coriolanus, because rooted in total error. **26-129** Paulina's 'great scene' provides a unique combination of the heroic and the ridiculous. In some respects it resembles any noisy household wrangle, with the violent shoving about, with Leontes' shouts of billingsgate, and with Paulina's familiar termagant threat, *Let him that makes but trifles of his eyes First hand me* (62-63). In its midst comes a joke on the prevalence of hen-pecked husbands (109-11). Nevertheless Paulina cuts an imposing figure, as the grandest scold in drama. **130-92** By an economical stroke the playwright makes the intrusion of Antigonus's wife (together with a commutation of sentence from burning to exposure, and the convenient oath by Antigonus which follows) the means by which a good character may be conscripted to carry out evil orders. Observe that Leontes is consistently shown to be recoverable. His answer to Paulina's near-charge of tyranny is valid, *She durst not call me so If she did know me one* (122-23); and his yielding to the entreaties of his lords in the matter of the disposal of the babe is, though a small favor, treated as a concession, *I am a feather for each wind that blows* (153). **192-206** The irony of the situation is epitomized in the words of Leontes when the return of the messengers to Delphi is announced: he will hold a *just and open trial* (204)—to find Hermione guilty.

III, i

Cleomenes and Dion speak with reverence and wonder of the ceremonies they have witnesses at Delphi. They hope that the words of the oracle, which have been given them in a scroll sealed by a priest, will clear Hermione, whom they are sure has been falsely accused.

1-22 The position of this brief scene, just before the trial of Hermione, represents the same kind of structural tactics as the position of the scene showing the Duke to be present in Vienna (*Measure for Measure,* I, iii), just before Isabella is put to her test. It signals a fortunate outcome regardless of immediate adversity, and mitigates the painfulness of witnessing cruel proceedings. We receive reassurance less from the certainty that the oracle will pronounce in Hermione's favor than from the postulated existence of the 'pagan' equivalent of divine Providence. Were the play to end tragically, it would make a mockery of the ecstatic description of Delphi, where *The climate's delicate, the air most sweet* (1). Like all the rest of the Sicilians except Leontes, the messengers are convinced of Hermione's innocence. No other play of Shakespeare has a larger proportion of well-disposed characters, and this gives to the malady of Leontes an interesting definition. Evil is treated as an inner growth, as in the case of Macbeth, and formidable enough, but it is restricted to a single character, and restricted even in him, so that the over-all impression is of the health of human tissue.

III, ii

Leontes opens the trial, and the indictment is read—that Hermione has committed adultery with Polixenes, plotted with Camillo against her husband's life, and connived in the escape of her fellow conspirators. She enters and defends herself movingly, but Leontes is obdurate and threatens her with death. She replies that death has no terrors for her, now that she has been disgraced by the one she loves, separated from her son, and deprived of her new-born daughter who has been sent away to perish. Only her good name is of consequence to her now, and she calls for the revelation of the oracle. An Officer takes the oath of Dion and Cleomenes that they have received the oracle from the priest at Delphi and have not broken the seal. When it is read, it declares Hermione, Polixenes, and Camillo innocent, and Leontes a jealous tyrant, who will die without issue unless the lost be found. He cries out against the truth of the oracle, whereupon a Servant enters and announces that Mamillius has died. Hermione swoons and is borne out by Paulina and others. Leontes prays to Apollo for forgiveness of his profanation. He confesses the error of his suspicions, and the fact that he had commanded Camillo to poison Polixenes. He will try to make reparation. At this point Paulina re-enters and announces that Hermione has died. She heaps execrations upon the King, then softens as he stands crushed by guilt and sorrow. He says that he has deserved her condemnation more than her pity, and vows to spend the rest of his life in penitence.

1-129 When guilt or innocence is to be determined by a document containing supernatural testimony, there can be no 'trial' in any meaningful sense of the word, and we may feel that the trappings of legal procedure give this scene a borrowed impressiveness. There can be no doubt that theatrical capital is being made of ceremonial —the opening of sessions, the call for silence in the court, the reading of the indictment, the swearing in of 'witnesses'—but the hollowness of these forms is not, after all, inappropriate. The trial would be a mockery, indeed more of a mockery, even if no oracle were available. One can scarcely maintain that this is a calculated effect—the forms are valued for their own sake—but the scene would not have been permitted to stand as it is unless its details, even though by accident, served the over-all intention. (See the remarks on 'serendipity' above, p. 85.) No one knows better than Hermione what the declaration of the oracle must be—*if powers divine Behold our human actions, as they do* (27-28)—and her fine speeches are essentially no plea of innocence but a public statement of her wrongs. She is not trying to avert penalties, but is protesting against the penalties already unjustly inflicted. As usual, the playwright has been able to enter imaginatively into his character and express emotion such as would be felt: written large in Hermione's words is her sense of offended dignity, and we accept without social perturbation the idea that her degradation, like that of another of Shakespeare's royal sufferers, would be 'most pitiful in the meanest wretch, Past speaking of in a' *Queen*. Her self-defense functions in the play not as an answer to the false indictment against her, but as a true indictment against Leontes. Observe that he is immediately afterwards 'found guilty.'   **131-241** The swift-moving succession of events, with the moment of joy when the oracle is read followed by a double catastrophe, is powerful in dramatic impact. The word of his son's death comes pat upon Leontes' blasphemy, yet this seems no theatrical trick; it is thus that the gods should throw their thunder-bolts. At the same time it makes psychologically plausible Leontes' complete recantation. Were the play to end with his *Prithee, bring me To the dead bodies of my queen and son. . . . Come, and lead me Unto these sorrows* (232-41), it would, in its length, in the straight-forward simplicity of its movement, and in its subject-matter, resemble Greek tragedy. We are reminded of Oedipus as he confidently searches out a criminal, and finds that criminal to be himself. But the resemblance to Greek tragedy (even if III, i, were omitted) would be only superficial, because of the absence of retrospective and fatalistic commentary. Nowhere is there suggestion that the disasters are foreordained, or are what man must be schooled to expect. We may extend this observation and say that the setting of the tragic events is non-tragic, that they are so presented as to demand a happy denouement. The play does not split in the middle, but is actually quite unified. Recognition of its unity depends upon sensitivity to its under-theme. As previously noted, it is full of religious suggestion, and, as we might expect in view of the time and place of its creation, the frame of reference is Christian, despite the machinery of the Delphic oracle and the imagery drawn from pagan fertility myths. For instance, Leontes, although he addresses

Apollo (151-70) meets the full obligation of the Christian penitent as formulated in church doctrine: he openly confesses, he repents, he amends his life. When news of the second disaster comes, followed by the reproaches of Paulina (173-212), he meets the test of his return to grace by responding with neither bitterness nor despair but with deeper contrition. An affecting human touch is provided by Paulina's sudden softening (219-30) when she looks at his bowed figure.

III, iii

A Mariner warns Antigonus that he must hasten because the skies threaten a storm, then leaves to stand by in his ship, glad to be done with his part in this business of exposing a babe. Antigonus speaks in soliloquy of a dream in which the weeping Hermione has instructed him to name the child Perdita and leave it in a remote part of Bohemia. Before vanishing with anguished moans, the visionary figure cried that he would never see his wife Paulina again. Antigonus believes that Hermione must be dead, and that the child he has brought to Bohemia may, after all, have been sired by Polixenes. He places it tenderly on the ground, with writings and a store of treasure. A savage roar frightens him, and he runs off pursued by a bear. An old Shepherd enters looking for lambs scared from the flock by the hunt. He finds the babe and takes it up, as his clownish Son enters with great tidings. Antigonus has been slain by the bear, and the ship offshore has sunk in the storm. They discover the treasure left with Perdita, and rejoice in their own good fortune. They will bury the remains of Antigonus, and take the child home to rear.

1-57 The vision of Antigonus (14-45) makes the bringing of Perdita to Bohemia seem not purely fortuitous but directed by divine will. The *Exit, pursued by a bear* (57 s.d.) is Shakespeare's most notorious stage direction, but its abruptness does not argue an abruptly created bear. It has been prepared for by the Mariner's warning that the place is famous for beasts of prey (11-12); and its sudden appearance and ferocity are later rationalized by allusions to the hunt which have harassed it and driven it to the shore. But why a bear at all—when Antigonus could have been disposed of with the others in the wrecked ship? Possibly the playwright refrained from deleting it because of nostalgic fondness for the dragons which infested the drama of his boyhood, but it can be justified on more material grounds. Its presence demonstrates, emphatically, the dangers to which the babe is being subjected; and its discrimination, in going for exposer rather than exposed, demonstrates the partisanship of the gods. Finally, and this is the essential justification, it brings living and dying into sharp juxtaposition, so that the Shepherd may say, *Now bless thyself! thou mettest with things dying, I with things new-born.* (106-07). **58-128** Humor, of course, enters with Shepherd and Son. We are ready for it after the somberness of the preceding scenes, but the actors who perform the play should match the restraint of the author. The humor is not slapstick, and if the old man and the youth are quaint, they are also natural and good—although not oppressively good. Perdita could have fallen into worse hands.

IV, i

Time enters as Chorus, and tells us that sixteen years have elapsed, and we are now in Bohemia where Perdita has grown in grace as a shepherd's daughter and where King Polixenes has a son Florizel.

1-32 Someone, probably Shakespeare, believed that this choral speech was necessary to get us over the sixteen-year interval while Perdita is growing up. It is appropriate that the speech should be in couplets, since they are exceptional and it is extraneous; and it has been maintained that it is also appropriate that they should be halting, since they are spoken by aged and halting Time. Halting they surely are.

IV, ii

Polixenes urges Camillo to remain with him in Bohemia as his indispensable counselor, and not, as he yearns to do, return home to

Sicilia at the plea of his penitent master Leontes. He speaks then of his son Florizel, who has been spending much time at the cottage of a humble shepherd. This shepherd has grown unaccountably prosperous, and has a daughter of rare note. Camillo agrees to join Polixenes in donning disguise and visiting the shepherd's cottage to discover what is going on.

1-51 Camillo's desire to return to Sicilia prepares us for his later readiness to cooperate with the eloping Florizel and Perdita. The utilitarian review and exposition in this scene is written in utilitarian prose.

IV, iii

The rogue Autolycus, cast-off servant of Prince Florizel now reduced to rags, sings merrily as he keeps an eye out for linen to steal and simpletons to cheat. He spies the Shepherd's Son on his way to buy sweets and spices for the sheep-shearing feast which is to be presided over by his sister Perdita. Autolycus lies on the ground pretending to have been beaten and robbed by a foot-pad. He steals the purse of the guileless youth who helps him to his feet, and, in describing his imaginary assailant, gives his own name and autobiography. Alone again, he resolves to attend the feast and gather further spoils, then goes off singing another song.

1-121 The events of sixteen years ago ended with funerals, a court in mourning, and skies blackened by a death-dealing storm. Now the morning sun, which bleaches the white sheets on the hedge, arches the sky with a rainbow. The time of year actually is autumn, but it is right that the song should be a song of spring and that Autolycus should be the one to sing it. Harvest time, teeming time, is the season of saturnalia, and at least one irresponsible bounds-breaking figure must mingle among the morally exemplary shepherds and shepherdesses. This effervescent rogue, with his songs, his tricks, and, later, his peddler's pack of knick-knacks and ballads, is one of Shakespeare's most engaging symbols of the festive spirit. He is provided, incidentally, with a life history of his own, with work to do in the plot, and with some of Shakespeare's most delightfully inconsequential lyrics.

IV, iv

Florizel in the attire of a country swain and Perdita in her finery as queen of the shearing-feast exchange their vows of love, despite the shepherd-maid's misgivings about accepting the courtship of a prince. The old Shepherd enters with his Son and the latter's rival loves, Mopsa and Dorcas. Admonishing Perdita to do her part as hostess bravely, he introduces the strangers who have come to grace their feast (Polixenes and Camillo in disguise), and Perdita distributes flowers to them and to the rest of the company. She and Polixenes engage in a debate, in which she condemns hybrid gillyvors as artificial products of man's art, and he defends them as improvements of nature made by natural means. In so doing he justifies the union of baser and nobler stock, but Perdita refuses to compromise. As she gives Florizel flowers, they move out of hearing of the others, and express the ardor and purity of their love. Polixenes and Camillo find the charm and beauty of Perdita most fetching, and as the music plays and the shepherds and shepherdesses dance, Polixenes questions the old man about her suitor 'Doricles.' A Servant enters describing the arrival of a peddler with a rich supply of trinkets and ballads. The Shepherd's Son gives permission for him to be admitted, and Autolycus enters singing his wares. He synopsizes some of the mint-new ballads in his stock, and joins with Mopsa and Dorcas in singing a sample, then follows them and their rustic escort, again crying his wares and prepared to mulct all comers. The company is now entertained by a dance of twelve herdsmen costumed as satyrs, after which Polixenes decides to bring things to a head. He asks his son why he gives Perdita no trinket, and Florizel replies that she is above such trifles. Moved by the excitement of the feast, he and Perdita openly avow their love; and Polixenes and Camillo are asked to serve as witnesses to a formal betrothal. As the old Shepherd is presiding over this ceremony, Polixenes remonstrates with Florizel for not inviting his father to participate, and when Florizel lightly dismisses the suggestion as impractical, he angrily reveals his identity. He orders his son back to court, and threatens Perdita and her foster-family with dire punishment for so inveigling a Prince. Camillo remains behind, and when he learns that Florizel is determined to elope with Perdita by sea, he persuades them to sail to Sicilia and promises them his assistance. To escape arrest Florizel exchanges clothes with Autolycus, and the latter whimsically decides to do his former master a service. He uses his new clothes to sustain him in a new role as man of influence, and stops the old Shepherd and his Son from following Polixenes to court and revealing the fact that Perdita is a foundling. After frightening them badly, he promises to act as intercessor and uses this ruse to lure them aboard Florizel's ship.

1-824 This is one of the longest scenes in Shakespeare and one of the most delightful. Again we have spring in autumn, with Perdita cast as Flora, *Peering in April's front* (3). She is exquisite—dainty as the flowers in her lines, which are the perfection of poetry; staunchly adverse to impurity, even if she is unreasonable in defining it; and, for all her daintiness and purity, warmly eager for the consummation of her love. No doubt remains about the nature of the thoughts which bring blushes to her cheeks: Florizel strewn with flowers, she says, will be not like a *corse* but *like a bank for love to lie and play on,* and not *buried,* except *quick and in mine arms* (130-32). She is both·delicate princess and sturdy shepherd-girl, a *queen of curds and cream* (161) such as might have issued from Polixenes' hypothesized marriage of *gentler scion to the wildest stock* (3). Florizel is her male counterpart, the two together emblemizing all that is most gracious and promising in youth. A remarkable feature of the image is the way it contains ideas of fecundity and husbandry, concupiscence and moral propriety. As the creation of life is guaranteed by the sparkle in their eyes, so its proper nurture is guaranteed by the firmness of their lips—their intentions are *most* honorable. The allusion to the myth of Persephone (116-18) whose annual return from Hades brings springtime and renewal of life, is in harmony with the context, but we would be fully aware without it that Perdita is a renewal figure. She will not remain *lost* but will be restored to wintry Leontes as balm and salvation according to the terms of the oracle. Sin and death will be redeemed by virtue and life. Yet the allegory is never intrusive. These are real people at a real party. The scene has wonderful variety and vitality—with the dancing of the shepherds and shepherdesses, the singing by Autolycus and hawking of ballads, and the *homely foolery* of the herdsmen-satyrs, one of whom can jump *twelve foot and a half by th' quire* (332). And the story-interest never lags. We can imagine the consternation of Polixenes when he finds himself serving as witness to an actual betrothal ceremony (such as would be legally binding in Shakespeare's England) between his royal heir and a shepherd-girl. The episode has an interesting feature typical of the author's universalizing touch: although Polixenes in his rage lashes out at the lowliness of Perdita and her family—at misalliance, such as he himself has unwittingly justified in his defense of gillyvors—it is actually Florizel's cool dismissal of himself that has gotten under his skin. He is not *bedrid,* he is not *childish* (394-95), and a father, *whose joy is nothing else But fair posterity should hold some counsel in such a business* (401-03). The discovery—*Mark your divorce, young sir* (410)—is a fine coup de théâtre; and Perdita's plaintive bravery (434-43) is amusing as well as touching. The conclusion of the play is shaped by some ready plotting, on a serious level by Camillo and a comic one by Autolycus. One of the precious bits of drollery is the innocent question of the old Shepherd's frightened Son after Autolycus dwells on the horrendous fate awaiting a certain old man: *Has the old man e'er a son, sir, do you hear, an't like you, sir?* (769-70). The scene has everything—poetry, philosophy-in-suspension, human interest, song, dance, drama, and fun. This is as it should be, since it stands in the play for the return from death to life.

V, i

In Sicilia Leontes is told by Dion and Cleomenes that his long penitence has won the forgiveness of heaven, and therefore he should forgive himself. They wish him to re-marry and provide the kingdom with an heir, but Paulina reminds them that, according to the oracle, there can be no heir unless the lost be found. Leontes accepts her rebukes as she praises the virtues of Hermione, and he promises never to marry unless she provides him a wife of equal worth. A Servant enters with amazing news: Prince Florizel has come to visit Sicilia accompanied by a maiden of matchless beauty. Cleomenes is sent to escort the visitors in, and as the youthful pair stand before him, Leontes is saddened by the thought that he might have had a son and daughter of just their age and excellence. Florizel fabricates a tale that Perdita is a Princess of Libya, and that he has stopped to pay his father's respects before taking her home to become his bride. But at this point a Lord enters and announces that Polixenes himself has debarked with Camillo, having followed hither his son and a shepherd-girl with whom he has fled. He is even now sternly questioning the girl's father and brother who have accompanied the runaways. Florizel and Perdita stand crestfallen, but Leontes sees in the lowly shepherdess something that reminds him of his beloved Hermione; and he promises to intercede for them.

1-232 The complaint that, in redemptive comedy, Shakespeare's transgressors (such as Angelo) are too readily redeemed and forgiven cannot be made in the case of Leontes. After sixteen years he is still grieving—and listening patiently to lectures by Paulina. In this scene we receive our first hint that perhaps his career as a married man is not quite closed (75-81). The mournful tone of the proceedings, just before Florizel and Perdita appear, lends a relish to subsequent joys. Leontes could not win our good will better than by his reply when Paulina scolds him for casting admiring looks at Perdita when he should be thinking of Hermione: *I thought of her Even in these looks I made* (226-27).

V, ii

Autolycus learns from a Gentleman that a strange tale has been told by the old Shepherd to Polixenes and Camillo. A second, then a third Gentleman enters to amplify the report. The identity of Perdita has been revealed by tokens and letters found with her, and Leontes is overjoyed. Although Paulina is grieved by the account of Antigonus's death, and Perdita by the fate of her mother, all rejoice over the fulfillment of the oracle, the reunion of the royal friends, and the impending marriage of the Prince and Princess. They are about to repair to see a statue of Hermione which has been many years in the making, in a certain removed dwelling never visited by anyone but Paulina. The old Shepherd and his Son enter in fine attire, elated over the sudden accession to favor and their re-birth into the gentry. They promise to put in a good word for Autolycus with their royal relatives, then invite him to join them in watching the unveiling of Hermione's statue.

1-165 We are told of the recognition and restoration of Perdita instead of being shown because the playwright is practicing conservation. We are to be eye-witnesses of another recognition and restoration. The prose, like some of Shakespeare's ecstatic prose elsewhere, is overwrought (41-87). He was a poet and dramatist; and, as noted before, much better at representing emotion in action than in describing it. Some words of apology, as if he were a little embarrassed by his material, appear here: *This news which is called true is so like an old tale that the verity of it is in strong suspicion* (27-29). This would suggest that his title, *The Winter's Tale,* is deprecatory, somewhat on the order of 'the old wive's tale,' but we cannot be sure on this point: like the myth of Persephone, this tale of winter is also a tale of spring.

V, iii

Having shown them the art works of the house, Paulina leads her royal company to the statue of Hermione. Perdita kneels before the image, and Leontes stands in a rapture of remembered love. It is so life-like that he wishes to embrace it, but Paulina warns that its colors are not yet dried. Finally, however, she tells them that the statue is able to move; and, as music plays, the living Hermione descends from the pedestal and embraces her husband and child. She has remained alive in Paulina's care, in the hope that the oracle had implied that Perdita would be restored to her. Leontes bestows upon Paulina Camillo as a new husband, as she has bestowed upon him Hermione as a new wife. He bids Hermione to greet Polixenes, asking pardon for his old suspicions, and presents to her Florizel as her new son.

1-155 Critical discussion of the 'statue scene' in which Hermione proves to be alive is often marked by uneasiness; and the scene is sometimes excused because it 'goes' so well in the theatre. It was, of course, intended for the theatre, and to treat its success in the theatre as 'excuse' is somewhat curious. On no basis, the play being the kind it is, does the scene need apology. It is true that we have, in a sense, been tricked—that we were given no hint at the time it was reported (III, ii, 170-241) that Hermione's death was anything but real. Paulina's words were, *I say she's dead; I'll swear't. If word nor oath Prevail not, go and see* (201-02), and her laments, unlike laments in other plays for those only supposedly dead, had in them the ring of truth. We may say that the playwright has been dishonest, or at least has used the dubious tactic of substituting surprise for suspense. But against this judgment stands the fact that the play has been progressing on several levels, one of them allegorical. We have been getting with the story, by what might be called subliminal means, in imagery and allusion, an encompassing story which is essentially religious. The playwright might have wished to introduce an actual miracle, an actual resurrection, but he was denied this resource by his secular medium and auspices. What he has done has been to create the atmosphere of a miracle, the atmosphere of a resurrection, and this would have been impossible had he employed his usual method of withholding no facts from the audience. When the royal company moves from the *gallery* (10) into the *chapel* (86), Perdita kneels: *And do not say 'tis superstition, that I kneel and then implore her blessing. Lady, Dear queen* . . . (43-44). This is unmistakably a sympathetic although Protestant allusion to kneeling before statues of the Virgin; and the descent of the 'statue' borrows meaning from a cycle of mediaeval tales, like 'Le Jongleur,' in which images of the Virgin assume life in order to perform acts of mercy. *Hermione*, says, Leontes, *was as tender As Infancy and grace* (26-27). Of her own first *good deed* she herself has said, *O, would her name were Grace!* (I, ii,

99). The idea of resurrection is just as unmistakably obtruded, when Paulina says, *Bequeath to death your numbness, for from him Dear life redeems you* (103-04). The split-second matchmaking between Paulina and Camillo illustrates once more that no single person is safe at the conclusion of a Shakespearean comedy, and this play is filled with his endearing popular touches; nevertheless it is at its heart a poem about death redeemed by life. It is Shakespeare's miracle play.

3

The Tempest

:

I, i

I N S U D D E N tempest a Shipmaster commands his Boatswain to muster the crew to work lest their vessel be driven aground. As the Boatswain shouts his orders, he is harassed by the demands of frightened passengers. Their number includes King Alonso and Prince Ferdinand, as well as the Lords Gonzalo, Sebastian, and Antonio, but in spite of their eminence he orders them bruskly to their cabins. The old counselor Gonzalo remarks, as they obey, that they cannot be drowned since this Boatswain is a rogue born to be hanged. The situation worsens, and Gonzalo, Sebastian, and Antonio return, the latter two belaboring the Boatswain with surly curses. Members of the crew enter drenched and crying that all is lost. As cries of desperation issue from within, the noblemen go to take leave of the King and Prince before all are plunged into the sea.

1-7 Sound effects and shouted orders create an immediate sense of crisis. The orders, here and later, although they may seem only 'atmospheric,' are nautically correct—such as would be given if a sailing ship of ancient rig were driving by a lee shore with little sea-room or time to come about into the weather.   **8-35**   The Boatswain is a stout fellow, deferring to no one where his expertise is concerned. He is called *blasphemous* (38, and V, i, 219) because he addresses an anointed king (immediately identifiable by insignia, perhaps a crown) without use of so much as a 'sir'—*I pray you, keep below* (10)—and persists in this slight of majesty with *What cares these roarers for the name of king?* (15-16). Gonzalo's humorous characterization of *this fellow* (26-31) indicates that the speaker will play a pleasing role, but we need not accept his estimate; the Boatswain's remarks on the limited power of kings are of a kind fairly common in Shakespeare.   **36-47**   Although they appear so fleetingly, the speakers are individualized. King Alonso has adjured the Boatswain only once, and inoffensively, Prince Ferdinand not at all; Gonzalo is the quaint oldster, humorous and loquacious; Sebastian and Antonio are a brace of snarlers. **47 s.d.-63**   The off-stage sounds of the storm, the swiftly shifting orders, and the trooping in and out of passengers have converted the stage into the deck of a ship, without need of so much as a trace of rigging. Now the threat of the elements is rendered visible with *Enter Mariners wet* (47 s.d.). Their *All lost! To prayers, to prayers! All lost!* (47), and the cries of parting and of desperation, *'We split, we split, we split!'* bring this fine opening bustle to a right climax. But we are not too much concerned. The saltiness of the Boatswain and the whimsical garrulity of Gonzalo have taken the terror out of this storm.

I, ii

Miranda sorrows for those aboard the noble vessel and begs her father to allay the tempest he has raised with his magic art. Prospero assures her that no one is harmed, as she will understand better after he tells of things it is now time for her to understand. He is not the mere island hermit she supposes, but is rightful Duke of Milan. Twelve years ago, when she was a child of three, his brother Antonio, to whom he had entrusted his government while he gave himself over to study, betrayed the city to King Alonso of Naples in return for the privilege of usurping the ducal title. Prospero and his child were set adrift in a rotting hulk, and would have perished had not a faithful old counselor Gonzalo placed some provisions aboard, along with Prospero's cherished books. They drifted providentially to this island, where his tutoring has provided Miranda an education better than that of most princes. Now an auspicious star has brought to the vicinity of the island a vessel carrying his enemies. At this point Prospero pauses in his tale, places Miranda in a magic sleep, and summons his sprite Ariel. Ariel reports that he has simulated the storm, made the passengers leap overboard and distribute themselves about the island, and has placed the crew in a trance in the vessel now riding safely in a cove. In return for these services Ariel wants his immediate release. Prospero rebukes him for demanding freedom in advance of the specified time, reminding the sprite of how the witch Sycorax was banished to this island from Argiers, bore the whelp Caliban, and, before she died, penned up Ariel, whom she had enslaved, in a pine-tree where he would still be suffering had not Prospero broken the magic spell. Contritely, the sprite agrees to continue to serve. Prospero awakens Miranda, and, after giving new orders to Ariel, who has assumed the form of a water-nymph invisible to all eyes but his, summons Caliban from his cell. This monster curses Prospero for disturbing his rest, and for supplanting him in possession of the island inherited from his mother Sycorax. Caliban is scolded as a thankless brute who has been nurtured and taught to speak, and whose only return has been an attempt to ravish Miranda. Cowed by threats that he will be racked by cramps, Caliban obeys the order to go gather fuel. Ariel returns invisible, singing 'Come unto these yellow sands.' Enticed by the music, Prince Ferdinand has followed, and as Ariel changes to 'Full fathom five thy father lies,' he stands grieving at this mysterious confirmation of his fear that his father has drowned. His eyes fall upon Miranda. He is amazed that she speaks his language, and so overwhelmed with admiration of her beauty that he seems ready at once to make her his wife and Queen of Naples. She is equally enchanted with him, and Prospero, for whom all is working according to plan, intervenes lest their felicity seem too easily won. He accuses Ferdinand of being an impostor with designs upon the island, and when the youth draws his sword, enchants him into helplessness. He reproves Miranda for pleading on Ferdinand's behalf and leads him off prisoner, pausing only to promise Ariel early freedom after he has carried out further orders.

1-32 As the hubbub of the tempest subsides, we hear at once of Prospero's *art* (1), with which he has raised the blast and now tempers it, with *no harm done* (15). In effect he does what Miranda would do were she a *god of power* (10), then, as she helps divest him of his magician's costume, shifts adroitly into the role of *dearest father* (1). Thus from the beginning he is god-like impressario as well as leading actor, shaping life with his *art* according to the heart's desire. His daughter is compassionate, docile (21-22)—'an excellent thing in woman'—and intuitive; the ship, she says, *had no doubt some noble creature in her* (7)—as, of course, it had (Prince Ferdinand).   **32-188** A twelve-year interval occurs in the story of this father and daughter, as a sixteen-year interval had occurred in the story of Leontes and Perdita, but instead of dramatizing the earlier events as he had done in *The Winter's Tale,* the playwright gives this retrospective view and then dramatizes the denouement. Aware that a hundred and fifty lines of straight narrative might fail to hold the audience, he employs a variety of devices to sustain interest. The story begins with Miranda's own glimpse into the *dark backward and abysm of time* (38-50) and is segmented by her questions, and exclamations of wonder (59-61), sympathy (63-65, 132-35), and moral approval (168-69). The narrator's pedagogical prods—*Dost thou attend me?* (78) . . . *Thou attend'st not?* (87) . . . *Dost thou hear?* (106)—function in a curious way. They serve as stimulus to the audience because so needless in the case of its delegate, who is hanging on every word: *Your tale, sir, would cure deafness* (106). (To have Miranda gazing abstractedly out to sea, or yawning at her prosy father, is one of those cute buds which bloom in literal minds and throw modern productions off-key.) Even before his reverses Prospero was without peer in the *liberal arts* (73), his library *dukedom large enough* (110), and his need for the books he *loved* (166) was as great as his need for the water, food, and raiment supplied with them by *providence divine* working through good Gonzalo. This association of Prospero with learning, of which his magic powers are a benign product, establishes him as a special kind of protagonist. Since no stress is laid upon his error in delegating authority to Antonio, he has no guilty past. Like Leontes he has spent his years of adversity in self-improvement, but, in his case, the process has consisted not in achieving virtue but in perfecting virtue already achieved. He has spent his time also in improving Miranda, whose merits are a product of one aspect of his *art* (173-75) as the tempest was of another. (The virtues of Leontes' daughter Perdita seemed to have been conferred upon her directly by *providence divine*.) Prospero is less the passive beneficiary of Providence than its active agent; and despite the prominence of magic in this play, its focus is really less 'other-worldly' than that of *The Winter's Tale*. Here, divinity 'rough-hews' and humanism 'shapes' our ends. Observe how compact and yet relaxed, how admirably flexible the language, with its rhythms perfectly in tune with mood and idea. The tonal appropriateness of the sounds, observed in the first scene of the first play treated in the present guide, is still conspicuous. Prospero's words as he wills Miranda to sleep have a slow, heavy, soporific quality—*Thou art inclined to sleep. 'Tis a good dullness* . . . (185-86)—as contrasted with the quick, energetic, arousing quality of the summons to Ariel immediately following—*Come away, servant, come! I am ready now. Approach, my Ariel; come!* (187-88)   **189-320**   Lyricism enters with the entrance of Prospero's lyrical sprite, whose description of the mock-shipwreck is as nimble and all-encompassing as his ability *to Fly, To swim, to dive into the fire, to ride On the curled clouds* (190-92). There is marvellous relish in the way he makes the images flame and dance—as reflected in Prospero's responses, *My brave spirit!* (206) . . . *Why, that's my spirit!* (215)—until, with puckish superiority, he imitates Ferdinand, *cooling of the air with sighs, His arms in this sad knot* (222-24). As this delicate Ariel asks for the *liberty* he was created to enjoy, we wish Prospero might be less hectoring—*No more!* (246) . . . *Thou liest, malignant thing!* (257) . . . *Dull thing, I say so* (285)—but the scolding floats a richly colorful account of the triumph of white magic over black as practiced by the *foul witch Sycorax* (258), the *damned witch Sycorax* (263), that sunken-eyed *hag* (269). Prospero's 'worked-up' indignation lets the playwright supply another life-history by indirection so that the tone may be dramatic, not reminiscent, but the price of the ruse is that the magician seems schoolmaster-ish to a degree. No doubt his *art* requires that his sprites be held on a tight rein. Shakespeare's own troop were constantly threatening to escape control, and we are thankful that they were compelled to do their *spriting gently* (298). To militant liberals Prospero may seem like Miranda's Svengali, Ariel's ruthless endenture-owner, and Caliban's slavemaster; but we must remember that we are at a remove from reality, and must not mistake the reality from which we are removed. Ariel and Caliban are symbolized qualities. The first is not, and the second is not quite, human; and although the non-human Ariel is more ingratiating than the sub-human Caliban, neither can be fitted into our institutional patterns. They need be given no 'rights'—and no other author would, as Shakespeare has done, have given them a 'point of view.'

321-74 In the case of Caliban, Prospero's art has succeeded only in effecting containment; the creature is consistently addressed as *slave* and must be held in absolute bondage if he is not to create havoc, as he has already tried to do by attacking Miranda; his nature is purely appetitive, such as will take no *print of goodness* (352). And yet animal instincts, animal appetites, although repugnant when divorced from reason, are real and understandable. There is something pathetic about this elemental Caliban. He is even capable of a kind of loyalty and love, so long as his wants are served and nothing is demanded of him: *Thou strok'st me and made much of me . . . and then I loved thee* (332-36). Caliban is punished by the infliction of internal rather than external pain— by aches, cramps, and stitches. He is the 'natural' flesh and is made to suffer the 'natural' ills that flesh is heir to. Many editors have insisted upon transferring Miranda's rebuke (351-62) to Prospero, on the principle that she is too nice a girl to be so stern; but Shakespeare's nice girls are often stern, and there are a number of reasons for supposing that the ascription in the original edition is correct. Miranda has already called Caliban a *villain* (309), an

even harsher word then than now, and she has just been the subject of his lecherous glee (349-51) so that it would be unnatural
for her to stand silent; and, as his gifted contemporary, she would
be the logical one to teach Caliban his letters. Prospero has had
his say, *I have used thee . . . with humane care* (345) and now it is
her turn, *I pitied thee* (353). We are on more dubious grounds when
we cite the style, but the phrasing, at least at the end of the speech
(358-62), seems to have a more feminine turn than Prospero's.

374-502 The contiguous stage directions, *Exit Caliban ∙ . . Enter Ferdinand,* signal one of Shakespeare's canny juxtapositions.
Ariel's lyrics are like something in nature, as clearly defined as the
plumage of bird and as pure in their melody as its song; they are
unemotional, impersonal, amoral. Out of their context they mean
nothing and suggest everything, and we hesitate to cage them with
interpretation. But *Come unto these yellow sands* (375-87) is an
invitation to *take hands,* curtsy, kiss, and dance, and thus tame
wild nature (*the wild waves whist*) with concord and measured
grace. Although it is not 'about' bringing a groom to his bride, it
is appropriate nonetheless. *Full fathom five thy father lies* (397-
405) in itself is *rich and strange.* It suggests descent into the depths
where everything becomes treasure, perhaps apotheosis in death;
and Ferdinand assumes that it commemorates the death of his
father. Its deceptiveness is in a measure justified by the fact that
Alonso truly is destined to undergo a *sea-change* after his emergence on Prospero's island. The *god of power* (10) in Miranda's
first speech is echoed by *god o' th' island* in Ferdinand's (390).
(Prospero will ultimately repudiate his godhead.) Both Miranda
and Ferdinand see each other as heavenly—a *thing divine* (419)
. . . a *goddess* (422)—and their instantaneously mutual love is a
kind of miracle. It is, however, an arranged, a manipulated miracle,
with Prospero functioning as Providence: *It goes on, I see As my
soul prompts it* (420-21). His word 'prompts' means 'wishes' but
suggests volition of an effectuating kind: Prospero is the prompter
in the wings, his exultant remarks to Ariel expressing joy in his
creation. Ferdinand translates Miranda's name before he hears
it: *O you wonder!* (427) Later he translates again: *Admired Miranda!* (III, i, 37) Her name is as explicitly meaningful as Perdita's.

She is wonderful and full of wonder, admirable and full of admiration. Ideal as the lovers are, they retain their human lineaments. The difficult task of portraying Ferdinand as grieving at the death of his father and, simultaneously, rejoicing at the discovery of Miranda is accomplished by means of verbal tact. He is made to picture his father as observing him from the world beyond: *He does hear me; And that he does I weep* (434-35). He is not unmindful of the royal inheritance into which he thinks he has come—he is *the best* of those who speak his tongue (430)—but he views .this inheritance first of all as something to be offered to Miranda; he can make her *Queen of Naples* (450). In this whole touching colloquy the most delightful speech is Miranda's, when Prospero tells her that Ferdinand is only a Caliban compared with other men: *My affections Are then most humble. I have no ambition To see a goodlier man* (482-84).

II, i

With the attendants Adrian and Francisco occasionally chiming in, old Gonzalo tries to comfort Alonso with thoughts of their miraculous escape, the good qualities of the island, and the chance that Ferdinand still lives. Alonso, who is sure that his son has drowned, is only irritated by these consolations. His brother Sebastian spitefully reminds him that, had he not voyaged to Africa to see his daughter Claribel become the unwilling bride of the King of Tunis, the disaster would not have occurred. Sebastian and Antonio mock Gonzalo wittily as the old counselor persists in his attempt to divert Alonso, especially when he indulges the fancy of himself converting this island into a commonwealth of the golden age. Gonzalo tries to retort their wit, but is no match for these cynical scorners. Ariel enters invisible playing solemn music, and all but Sebastian and Antonio fall asleep. Antonio uses the opportunity to suggest a murderous plot to his easily-persuaded companion. With Ferdinand dead and Claribel in Tunis, only the life of Alonso stands between Sebastian and the throne of Naples. Antonio instances his own success in supplanting his brother Prospero as Duke of Milan, and offers to slay the sleeping Alonso while Sebastian disposes of

Gonzalo. Sebastian agrees to engage in this profitable act of fratricide and the two draw their swords; but while they are engaging in a last-minute conference, Ariel wakens Gonzalo by singing a warning in his ear. The old man starts up and awakens the King. Antonio and Sebastian explain their drawn swords by saying that they have heard a sinister roar, and Gonzalo remarks that he himself was awakened by strange sounds. The group moves off in search of Ferdinand, and Ariel prepares to give Prospero an account of the averted assassination.

1-178 This appears at first to be no more than the long, desultory, time-killing conversation of the marooned, but in its course we are filled in with background information and made abundantly aware of the character of the speakers: King Alonso rendered passive by his grief, non-resistant to designs upon him whether for good or evil; old Gonzalo, kindly, tenaciously optimistic, and even intelligent, but perilously near to being a bore; Adrian and Francisco, the well-schooled courtly attendants, anxious to say whatever the more eminent persons present will consider the more acceptable things; and Antonio and Sebastian, the cleverest and coarsest members of the group, the most 'sensible' and insensitive, betraying through their scornful laughter their habitual ill-humor, truculence, and discontent. The information could have been conveyed, and the characterizations effected, with much more economy, so that the dialogue has something of the quality of a self-contained interlude. We are entertained by the topics of conversation and by the display of coterie methods of self-amusement. We are impelled willy-nilly to 'keep up with,' even to laugh with, the nastier members of the circle, so that our sensations are a little uneasy. This interlude functions as an evocation of worldliness and disenchantment in this unworldly and enchanted island. It puts Naples and Milan on the spot. Even within itself the worldly crowds in upon the unworldly, when Antonio and Sebastian launch their devastating attack upon Gonzalo's dream of *the golden age* (143-64). They, the immoral ones, launch the spears of morality, project evil into Eden, and transform Gonzalo's *innocent people* into *whores and knaves* (160-62). **179-321** Prospero, through his agent

Ariel, first provides opportunity for villainy by placing Alonso and Gonzalo in the power of Sebastian and Antonio, and then, just as arbitrarily, prevents the villainy by removing the opportunity. He does not, however, instigate the villainous ideas; these are self-generated. The evil potential in evil natures is tapped by the unusual circumstances—not the mere sleep of the intended victims, but the isolation on the island and the presumed elimination of intervening claimants to the Neopolitan crown. Assuming that the pair can sooner or later get off the island, Antonio's plan is eminently logical: he will no longer have to render tribute in payment for his usurped dukedom, and Sebastian will be a king. Nothing could better illustrate the influence of artistic context upon our response to fictive actions than the present episode. The cold-blooded fratricide here projected is worse than Macbeth's murder of Duncan which proved almost intolerably appalling in representation. It is such an act as casts its terrible shadow over the whole play of *Hamlet*. The proportion of venality is greater than in *King Lear,* since two of the six persons present are rapacious killers, and two more are assumed to be 'open to reason'—*They'll take suggestion as a cat laps milk* (282). And yet we take this display of evil in our stride, and it little affects the total impression conveyed by the play. Of course the threatened action does not take place— which makes a great difference. But even aside from that fact, we are little shocked by the deadly plan itself. The reason is simply the existence of Prospero and his magic. Providence was not visible in *Hamlet, Macbeth,* and *King Lear*. Here it is so obviously in control that we can look upon the sword-drawing as upon the antics of bad boys, and the reference to *obedient steel (three inches of it)* (277) as so much 'tough talk.'

II, ii

Caliban is indulging himself by cursing Prospero, though he knows that the magician's spirits will hear and punish him. When the court-jester Trinculo enters, safe after a swim ashore, Caliban takes him for a spirit and cowers upon the ground. Trinculo speculates upon the profit he might make by exhibiting this native of the island in

England where the public loves to view monsters. Thunder sounds, and the jester takes refuge under Caliban's gaberdine. Stephano, the court-butler, enters drunk and singing, having ridden ashore on a wine-butt. He takes the pair on the ground to be a four-legged, two-headed monster, and experimentally pours into the Caliban-head some wine from the bottle he has fashioned of bark. When he tries to minister also to the Trinculo-head, the jester greets him with relief and is pulled from under the gaberdine. Caliban is overjoyed to receive successive drafts of celestial liquor instead of the tortures he feared, and he looks upon Stephano worshipfully. As Trinculo makes remarks of envious disdain, Caliban kisses Stephano's foot, hails him as master, and offers to show him all the resources of the island. The butler accepts this tribute as his due, and the three move off to survey the island and refill the bottle, with Caliban singing defiance of Prospero and raising drunken shouts of freedom.

1-153 Caliban has said that his profit in learning language is that he knows *how to curse* (I, ii, 364) and he exercises this talent compulsively. The punishments inflicted upon him are cruel but not unnatural. Since he has been the object of so much romantic solicitude, it might be wholesome to consider whether his pangs are really inflicted by Prospero's sprites; perhaps he is just too stupid to steer clear of bogs and briers, or to pick spots clear of porcupines as he sets down his clumsy feet. True he knows the island (144), but his knowledge is specialized, his affinity with nature apparently confined to its edible parts (156-60, 163-68), including mysterious *scamels*. (These have never been identified, but they certainly sound like something clinging to wet rocks.) Trinculo is designated a *jester* in a list of characters (one of the few of its kind) supplied in the original edition of the play; his name and no doubt his costume would have indicated his profession. He is the only one of Shakespeare's court-jesters whom we see exclusively in his unofficial capacity, and he appears a bit faded offstage, timid and somewhat shrill, dangling on the edges. Stephano, on the other hand, is a *butler,* lordly below stairs and lordly in his new environment. Both these characters have suffered somewhat in literary criticism from being fitted too solemnly into the moral allegory. Essentially they are comics, neither one of whom appears especially vicious; in fact, in this scene at least, Stephano is quite the amiable drunk, and his response to Trinculo's over-zealous greeting strikes a responsive chord in our breasts—*Prithee do not turn me about: my stomach is not constant* (112-13). Although they speak lowly prose whereas Caliban speaks blank verse, we can detect no corresponding distinction in spirituality when we examine the content of the speeches. Trinculo's supercilious envy as the monster pays court to Stephano rather than to himself (140-62) is both funny and the stuff of life. Obviously Shakespeare took delight in these lamentable fellows, as he had in Jack Cade's rebels twenty years before; and his spring of boisterous good humor was bubbling as copiously as ever. Compare Stephano's coarse chantey (45-53) with the delicate songs of Ariel. The higher criticism has tended to draw the curtain here, but the chantey is just as 'Shakespearean' as the songs. The playwright was more resistant than his good King Hal, and the passing years never quite succeeded in 'whipping the offending Adam out of him.'

III, i

As he works at bearing logs, Ferdinand reflects upon the compensation afforded by the presence and sympathy of Miranda. She enters and tries to help him. With Prospero observing them unseen, the two declare their love and exchange betrothal vows. After they have parted, Prospero expresses his satisfaction, then leaves to consult his book. Much remains to be done before evening.

1-96 This scene like the last begins with the entrance of a character bearing logs, and Caliban has again served as Ferdinand's foil. The last scene ended with Caliban's shouting in drunken glee at the prospect of *freedom! freedom, high-day, freedom!* This one ends with Ferdinand's trading of freedom for bondage, *with a heart as willing As bondage e'er of freedom* (86-89). Although not one of Shakespeare's greatest love scenes, this is a fine one, as honest as sweet, a *Fair encounter Of two most rare affections* (74-75). The circumstances teeter on the edge of the laughable—the maid's insistence upon helping her Prince with his unconvincing logs, the father's hovering behind like a complacent duenna—but the scene does not topple over. It is saved by its one-syllable words. The artifice of the setting is canceled by the forthrightness of the sentiments: *Do you love me?* (67) . . . *I . . . do love, prize, honor you* (73) . . . *I am your wife, if you will marry me* (83). The arabesques of rhetoric enhance the simple words they frame. Since a course of true love running absolutely smooth, with no test for the earnestness of the principals, simply would not do, Prospero has provided one as he has provided everything—*lest too light winning Make the prize light* (I, ii, 452-53). We do not object because, subtending this artificial obstacle, there is, or has been, a real one: Ferdinand and Miranda are the children of enemies. This union will help to repair an ancient breach as did that of Florizel and Perdita. Their union just happened. This one is arranged.

III, ii

The bibulous trio continue to ply the bottle, with the jester persisting in his mockery of the monster's devotion to the butler. When Caliban complains, Stephano issues Trinculo a statesmanlike warning. Ariel enters invisible, and earns Trinculo a beating by imitating his voice with insulting interruptions during a proposal being made by Caliban. The proposal is that they murder Prospero in his sleep, so that Stephano may rule the island with Miranda as his queen. To celebrate their general approval of this scheme, the three decide to sing a catch, but have difficulty in recalling the tune. When Ariel supplies it with tabor and pipe, Trinculo and Stephano feel certain qualms, but Caliban assures them that there is nothing to fear; the isle is often filled with strains of melody. They follow the music, postponing for the moment their bloody revolution.

1-149 The 'low' comedy takes up pretty much where it left off, with Trinculo still voicing his disdain, so that the present scene might have appeared as a continuation of II, ii; however the playwright, in his customary fashion, has split the scene so that the comic may alternate with the romantic. Drink has sharpened Trinculo's perceptions, and there is considerable acumen in his remark about the citizenry of this commonwealth—*If th' other two be brained like us, the state totters* (6). Ariel's use of ventriloquism to set the group at loggerheads has become, if it was not so already, an infallible comic routine. It remains difficult to see why so much obloquy has been heaped on Stephano and Trinculo. The underplot is, to be sure, a comic reflection of the conspiracy against Alonso, but Caliban's confederates can scarcely be taken as counterparts of Sebastian and Antonio. As a matter of fact Stephano is gravely aware of his responsibilities as head of state, and Trinculo is something of a social critic. The two enlist in the campaign against Prospero when he is represented as a usurper. Naturally they expect certain benefits to accrue: Stephano and Miranda will be King and Queen, *save our Graces!* (104), and Trinculo a viceroy. Caliban is a different kettle of fish. Our sympathy for him as underdog cannot blind us to the fact that his suggestions about the disposal of Prospero betray a certain lack of graciousness: . . . *with a log Batter his skull, or paunch him with a stake, Or cut his wesand with thy knife* (86-88). Still, though his bestial nature has taken no *print of goodness,* he is dimly, fleetingly, pathetically aware that something other than bestiality exists. His speech on the music of the island (132-40) is truly very beautiful.

III, iii

As Alonso and Gonzalo trudge wearily on in search of the missing Prince, Antonio and Sebastian agree to wait until nightfall before pursuing their plan of assassination. Solemn music sounds, and Prospero observes from aloft while a company of strange spirits enter with a banquet. They dance about it, inviting with gentle gestures the King and his followers to eat. Overcoming their amazement, they are about to comply, when thunder sounds and Ariel enters as a harpy to whisk the food away. Alonso, Sebastian, and Antonio draw their swords but find them too heavy for their strength. Terror assails them as Ariel accuses them of the crime committed of old against Prospero. As punishment, Alonso has lost his son, and all three will suffer lingering perdition unless they repent and amend their lives. Ariel departs to the sound of more thunder, after which soft music resumes, and the spirits reenter to bear off the table with antic gestures of mockery. Prospero commends the performance of Ariel and his spirits before leaving his place of vantage; and Gonzalo observes that the minds of the accused are distracted as guilt begins to gnaw them. He orders Adrian and Francisco to follow them lest they do themselves some harm.

1-109 In this scene and the next Prospero puts on two shows contrasted in type and theme: here, a pantomimic dance and display of magic, frustrating and threatening the beholders; there, a regular betrothal masque, promising joyous fruitfulness. Ariel proclaims that the performers are *ministers of fate* (61); actually they are ministers of the minister. *Fate* continues to bear a striking resemblance to Christian Providence, and, as in *The Winter's Tale*, orthodox penitence and amendment of life is enjoined upon the sinners: *heart's sorrow And a clear life ensuing* (81-82). The three feel mental torment, distraction, *ecstasy* (108), which may either prove purgatorial or lead to despair and damnation. Alonso contemplates suicide, supposing that his son has perished because of his own transgression: he *will seek him deeper than e'er plummet sounded And with him there lie mudded* (101-02). Gonzalo evidently fears that all may destroy themselves (108-09). The play is made up largely of 'token' action, and we must confess that the token-expiation required by its scheme is more suitable to the case of Alonso, whose transgression lies in the faded past, than to those of Sebastian and Antonio. The villainy of the latter two is very much a thing of here and now, and although it adds dramatic interest to the play, it somewhat blurs the issues. Sebastian and Antonio are not being chastened, like Alonso, for sins past, but are being denied access to sins present. Just how 'regenerate' they are remains a dubious item; however, we must not ask too much of Prospero's *art*. The present scene has great appeal simply as spectacle. We can guess at the nature of the *quaint device* (52 s.d.) with which Ariel makes the banquet disappear; we have seen stage-magicians use their cloaks in just the miraculous way in which Ariel uses his harpy-wings. We must hope that the *gentle actions and salutations* (17 s.d.) with which the strange shapes adorned their

dances, as well as the *mocks and mows* (82 s.d.), were as remarkable as the speakers maintain. Prospero fairly chortles over his hit,
and Ariel gets his mead of praise. No back-stage friction now.

IV, i

Prospero ends his pose of hostility, accepts Ferdinand as his
daughter's suitor, and warns the couple to restrain their desires
until they are formally wedded. He bids Ariel to present them with
a betrothal masque. To the strains of soft music, Iris appears and
speaks a prologue, then summons Ceres, who tells of how Venus
and Cupid have been balked in their designs upon the chastity of
this pair of true lovers. Juno appears and joins Ceres in singing a
blessing of fruitfulness upon this union. Ferdinand expresses his
delight, but Prospero warns him to watch silently lest he break the
spell. Juno and Ceres send Iris to bring in a company of Naiades.
These join with Reapers in a graceful dance. Suddenly discords
sound, Prospero becomes perturbed, and the masquers gloomily
disperse. Prospero speaks to Ferdinand of the transience of all
things, and asks him to retire with Miranda into the cell. He now
prepares to cope with Caliban and his co-conspirators, whom Ariel
has led through a bog. Ariel hangs gaudy raiment outside the cell,
and when the three stagger in, Trinculo and Stephano go for it in
spite of Caliban's warnings that they should murder Prospero first.
A noise of hunters is heard, and Prospero and Ariel set upon the
trio a troop of spirits in the shape of hounds. They will be racked
by goblins with cramps and pinches while Prospero is attending to
their betters.

1-59 Ferdinand and Miranda, says Prospero, have *stood the test*
(7). The *test* presumably was his own feigned opposition to the
match, which Miranda properly ignored, and the laborious task
imposed upon the Prince, which failed to cool his ardor. But during
the masque we hear that they have stood another test, by disap-
pointing Venus and Cupid in their wanton plan to make them an-
ticipate the hymeneal *bed-right* (92-101). In fact their strictness in
this matter has made Cupid decide to abandon his mischievous

game of abetting misconduct, and *to be a boy right out* (101). Like Florizel, Ferdinand could obviously be trusted to wait—he equates continence with *quiet days, fair issue, and long life* (24)—but Prospero by no means leaves the matter to the discretion of the lovers. He delivers an emphatic lecture upon pre-marital restraint (14-23), and returns to the subject after they have sat down together to view the masque. We know from the implied stage-direction that the lovers have cuddled up with enthusiasm: *Be more abstemious* (51-54). This byplay lends serio-comic point to the later 'discovery'—*Ferdinand and Miranda playing at chess* (V, i, 171 s.d.). Surely lovers could be no more safely occupied than this. We may say that Prospero's warnings are not really directed to his exemplary daughter and prospective son-in-law but, chorally, to the audience; however his uttering them is in perfect accord with his general role; he is the most 'managing,' the most omnipotent and omniscient character in Shakespeare. He leaves nothing to chance because, in a sense, he *is* chance. **60-138 s.d.** *The Tempest* is sometimes referred to as a 'masque.' As a whole it is not in the least masque-like, but it encorporates the present diversion, which resembles closely the inductions to masques at court after the accession of King James in 1603. There is the opening speech by a mythological dignitary, in this case the messenger-goddess Iris (60-75), a dialogue cued to the social occasion (76-101), a song of dedication (106-17), and a dance of previously-described Nymphs and Reapers. The latter would have been represented at court masques by professional performers, with their *graceful dance* constituting the "anti-masque'—after which would have followed the 'masque' proper, figure- and social-dancing by costumed members of the royalty and nobility. Ariel here functions as 'Master of the Revels,' and the parts of the goddesses, nymphs and reapers are taken by the *rabble* (37), the rank and file of Prospero's sprites. He is himself, of course, the author, referring to the piece as *Some vanity of mine art* (41). It is good example of its type, its pleasing couplets brimming with images of fruitful spring, summer, and autumn—with winter properly excluded (114-15). The Persephone myth of rebirth is alluded to (89-90) as it was in *The Winter's Tale* during the shearing feast, of which this masque is the

functional equivalent. Here Ferdinand and Miranda are the re-
deemers, blessed themselves and blessing the earth with *Long con-
tinuance and increasing* (107). **139-63** Prospero's great lines
Our revels now are ended . . . (148-58), along with several other
speeches in these final scenes of the play, color our whole conception of it. They have the air of a final pronouncement, as if coming
from one who has had a sudden vision of truth. Our lives are not
the final reality, any more than stage representations are our lives.
Rightly or wrongly, we refuse to accept the *foul* (but ridiculous)
conspiracy of Caliban and his crew (139-42) as the sole cause of
the speaker's perturbation. Surely there are other reasons why he
must still his *beating mind* (163), and so a touch of mystery en-
hances the intrinsic power of the words. They express a reconciled
idealism in their view of the wonderful but ephemeral *globe* and
our little life upon it: *We are such stuff As dreams are made on.* If
this is 'philosophy,' it is of the kind which was to be propounded
by Bishop Berkeley and serve as a lasting irritant to philosophers;
there is no such thing as 'matter'—nothing but ideas in the mind of
God.   **164-265** Materialism re-enters with a vengeance in the
persons of Caliban, Stephano, and Trinculo. The *baseless fabric*
of the vision dissolves into an animated description (171-184),
then a farcical display, of the come-uppance of these three. The
filthy mantled pool into which Ariel has led them has so *O'erstunk
their feet* (182-84) that they *smell all horse-piss* (198). At this
point the fastidious may wish that the playwright's wide range were
just a trifle narrower, but the episode is very funny. Trinculo feels
vindicated in his grudge against Caliban; and Stephano remains
loyal to his own special scale of values as he laments the liquor-
bottle sunk in the mantled pool: *There is not only disgrace and dishonor in that, monster, but an infinite loss* (208-09). Caliban is
disillusioned about the company he keeps, and intuitively describes
its most appropriate metamorphosis—into *apes With foreheads
villainous low* (247-48). Notice the stage action. The frustrated
revolutionary is evidently buried in gorgeous fripparies (251-53)
just before Prospero sets on his goblin-hounds.

V, i

Clad in his magic robes, Prospero prepares to finish the work of the day. It is evening, and he repeats to Ariel his promise of early freedom. Ariel describes the grief of Gonzalo, and the distraction of Alonso, Sebastian, and Antonio. Were he capable of human feeling, he would pity their distress. Prospero declares his intention of forgiving the penitents, and sends Ariel to fetch them in. He then invokes the spirits he has commanded, speaks of the wonders he has performed, and resolves to abjure 'rough magic' and burn his book. First he calls for a solemn air, and as the three afflicted men enter, attended by Gonzalo, Adrian, and Francisco, he describes their crimes and present condition, then pronounces his words of pardon. Ariel sings as he obeys the order to array his master in his ducal robes, then speeds off to fetch the Mariners from their enchanted ship. As the senses of Alonso, Sebastian, and Antonio are restored, they realize that they have stood at the mercy of the one whom they have wronged. Alonso accepts Prospero's embrace with true contrition, and Gonzalo his thanks with tears of joy. When Alonso says that his one remaining grief is the loss of his beloved son, Prospero replies that he himself has lost a daughter, and then reveals Ferdinand and Miranda playing at chess. All rejoice at the restoration of father and son to each other, and at the impending union between the houses of Milan and Naples, while Miranda looks with guileless wonder at this brave new world of men. The Captain and the Boatswain are brought in by Ariel, and the nature of 'the tempest' is explained. Caliban, Stephano, and Trinculo are released from their spell by Ariel, and driven in wearing their stolen finery. As they are sent to trim up Prospero's cell for the visit of his guests, the murky mind of Caliban is pierced by a glimmer of light—he has worshiped a drunkard and a fool. Prospero promises that he will tell the whole story before he returns with them to his dukedom in Milan. He entrusts Ariel to provide calm seas and auspicious gales, and then sets the spirit free. In an Epilogue he asks for the auspicious winds of applauding hands, praying that we will forgive all faults as he has done, and as we must pray for forgiveness of our own.

1-318 In order to record a sentiment on what it means to be *human* (19), the playwright makes Prospero renounce a *vengeance* (20-32) he has shown no prior signs of desiring. To enforce penitence and effect reconciliation has obviously been his design from the first. His invocation, *Ye elves of hills, brooks, standing lakes, and groves . . .* (33-57) is one of the great speeches of the play, and one of the reasons why we are impelled to read into it autobiographical significance. We may put it thus—that although Prospero and his *art* were not primarily conceived of as representing Shakespeare and his poetic gift, it would have been scarcely possible for the poet, approaching the end of his career, to remain unconscious of certain analogies. The present speech better expresses what Shakespeare has done with the magic of words than what Prospero has done with robe, staff, and book. Graves have not, at Prospero's command, *waked their sleepers* (49)—indeed that would have been 'necromancy' such as was forbidden a white magician like himself—but graves had waked their sleepers at Shakespeare's command. The first recorded praise of one of his plays, *1 Henry VI,* speaks of his having made English heroes 'live again,' and a long line of English kings and Roman conquerors had been brought back to life by his *so potent art.* The first play treated in the present guide was peopled with *demi-puppets that By moonshine do the green sour ringlets make* (36-37), and it is of *King Lear* rather than *The Tempest* we think when we hear of the *dread rattling thunder* that *rifted Jove's stout oak* (44-45). We should not press the analogy too far. Prospero must *drown his book* (57) because it is presumptuous to play God, and even white magic was practiced at peril of the soul. Shakespeare need have felt no corresponding guilt about the plays he had written, although conceivably he did. And he could have written Ariel's lovely freedom-song (88-94) with its *Merrily, merrily shall I live now, Under the blossom that hangs on the bough* without dreaming of his hawthorne-tree at Stratford. As in *The Winter's Tale* the redemptive principle is thought of as feminine—*her help, of whose soft grace*

For the like loss I have her sovereign aid (142-43). Passive as her role has been, Miranda is the primary symbol of healing and renewing. She it is who has the largest capacity for wonder. In her first speech she spoke of the *brave vessel* (I, ii, 6) on which her eyes rested, and in her last, of this *brave new world* (183). We need read no sarcasm into Prospero's gentle response, *'Tis new to thee* (184). The whole gravamen of the play would suggest that the world will always be new so long as there are new eyes to see it. The good Gonzalo is loyal to his joke about the Boatswain (216-20), and the latter is no more servile on land than he was on sea although he does condescend to say *sir* (229). The mood of Sebastian and Antonio remains ambiguous. Perhaps one thoroughgoing conversion in the play was deemed sufficient. Although it is Sebastian who cries, *A most high miracle!* (177), he and his mate appear to remain pretty much the cold worldlings they have always been, just as Stephano and Trinculo remain the unregenerate clowns. Caliban, however, resolves to *seek for grace* (295)—indeed a *most high miracle*. The Epilogue ought to have been, whether it was so or not, Shakespeare's farewell to his London audience:

> Gentle breath of yours my sails
> Must fill, or else my project fails,
> Which was to please. Now I want
> Spirits to enforce, art to enchant;
> And my ending is despair
> Unless I be relieved by prayer,
> Which pierces so that it assaults
> Mercy itself and frees all faults.
> As you from crimes would pardoned be
> Let your indulgence set me free.

Exit

Index

Index

:

(All the named characters in the fourteen plays treated at length are included in this index, even though a few of the very minor ones are not mentioned in the commentary; the page reference is to the discussion of the entire play, although, of course, all the characters do not appear in all the scenes.)